# The Rock Shall Dance

## PETER SAXTON SCHROEDER

Published by Richter Publishing LLC www.richterpublishing.com

Book Cover Design: Jessie Alarcon

Editor: Haley Morton

Layout Design: Monica San Nicolas

ISBN-13: 978-1-954094-02-4

# Disclaimer

This book is designed to provide information on the life of Mr. Schroeder only. This information is provided and sold with the knowledge that the publisher and author do not offer any legal or medical advice. In the case of a need for any such expertise consult with the appropriate professional. This book does not contain all information available on the subject. This book has not been created to be specific to any individual people or organization's situation or needs. Reasonable efforts have been made to make this book as accurate as possible. However, there may be typographical and or content errors. Therefore, this book should serve only as a general guide. This book contains information that might be dated or erroneous and is intended only to educate and entertain. The author and publisher shall have no liability or responsibility to any person or entity regarding any loss or damage incurred, or alleged to have incurred, directly or indirectly, by the information contained in this book or as a result of anyone acting or failing to act upon the information in this book. You hereby agree never to sue and to hold the author and publisher harmless from any and all claims arising out of the information contained in this book. You hereby agree to be bound by this disclaimer, covenant not to sue and release. You may return this book within the guaranteed time period for a full refund. In the interest of full disclosure, this book may contain affiliate links that might pay the author or publisher a commission upon any purchase from the company. While the author and publisher take no responsibility for any virus or technical issues that could be caused by such links, the business practices of these companies and/or the performance of any product or service, the author or publisher have used the product or service and make a recommendation in good faith based on that experience. All characters appearing in this work have given permission. Any resemblance to other real persons, living or dead, is purely coincidental. The opinions and stories in this book are the views of the authors and not those of the publisher.

# Acknowledgments

I wish to express my deepest gratitude to my editors, Tom Huggler, Marg Stewart, and my wife, Risa Wyatt.

# Dedication

I dedicate this book to my four grown children:
Cyrena, Liane/Rasila, Seton, and Belden.

In reading my recollections, they will discover things they never knew about their father while growing up, despite living together in the same household.

First, many activities I pursued were dangerous, and I didn't want my children to risk trying these same crazy things themselves.

Second, if they tasted the freedom, fun, and joy that comes with these adventures—hopping freight trains, hitchhiking through Europe, living in ashrams, sailing high seas, surfing huge waves—
I feared they might abandon their education.

Third, when they were children, it might have been distressing for them to learn I had, and still have, a disease considered to be fatal.

Read this and learn a little more about your Dad!

# Contents

i

PETER SCHROEDER

# Introduction

Only I can write my life—a journey so filled with twists and turns that no one else could connect the divergent paths. How could anyone other than I link a career working as a nuclear-weapons engineer/physicist with years living in an ashram in India? Or adventures hopping freight trains across America with years of studies at Princeton and Stanford Universities? Then successfully managing five international corporations in four countries but later abandoning the business world to become a freelance adventure travel writer and photographer earning minimum wage.

How could anyone else attempt to explain how I, as a young man, contracted a type of cancer with a fatal prognosis but nevertheless continued to enjoy a full and rich life for decades? Does my rank as an Eagle Boy Scout with four palms—the highest recognition ever attained in the Scouting movement up to that time—correlate with dropping out of the workforce at age 39 with a wife and four children to pursue a life of sailing, scuba diving, downhill skiing, and world travels?

To an onlooker, such an unusual life seems illogical, disjointed, and chaotic. To the man who has actually lived this life, however, every step has been logical, connected, and true to ongoing personal forces.

I write my story for my children and grandchildren who don't know much of what I experienced, mainly because I never told them before now. I didn't want them to emulate the crazy adventures and risks I had undertaken. I have tried to pass on to my offspring the important values of academic excellence, athletic fitness, and strong character. While young, they might have judged that the life I led seemed inconsistent with these goals. Nevertheless, I have adhered to these core standards throughout my life.

My restrictions have been three-fold: (1) never hurt anyone, (2) never endanger myself, and (3) never break the law (not because the law is always correct, but because breaking it can lead to incarceration, incrimination, fines, and entanglement in the legal system). Apart from these prohibitions, everything else in life is fair game.

My life has been about pursuing experiences. Because we are on this earth so briefly, we should use our abilities to explore as much as possible in every dimension. This is what I have done. I have traveled to, and resided in, virtually every part of the world learning several languages along the way. I have lived in solitude, in a family, in communes, in the country, in cities, in a desert, and in the mountains.

I have worked in engineering, science, business, heavy construction, investing, teaching, farming, writing, photography, and given much of my life to volunteerism. For recreation I have hiked, biked, camped, skied, sailed, rowed, fished, hunted, and scuba dived in many of the most beautiful parts of the planet. In short, I have sought to experience as much variety in life as possible.

If there is a Day of Judgment and I meet St. Peter at the Golden Gates, I think he will ask only one question. He won't inquire if I loved my neighbor, if I helped mankind, if I left the world a better place than when I entered it, if I was a good citizen, if I obeyed the laws, or if I worshiped a supreme being.

The question will be something like, "Did you see the wonderful world provided for you to enjoy? Did you hike the mountains, explore the jungles, travel across the great deserts, and sail the seas? Did you see all the beautiful flowers and trees, the animals and birds, the fish and sea creatures? And what about all the wonderful peoples? Did you see how they dress, hear how they speak, appreciate their cultures? Did you embrace and cherish the diversity in bees and whales and crabs, in fauna and flora, in canyons and mountains? And did you journey inside yourself to explore your consciousness, plumb the depths of your mind, and examine how you think, how you reason and figure things out?"

I want to be able to answer, "Yes, yes, and yes. I saw, explored, and experienced as much as I could squeeze into my days, and I loved every moment."

And finally, all I will have to say to whomever or whatever made this possible, is "Thank You!"

# Prologue

*Medical Flight: An End and A Beginning*

FRAGILE! HANDLE WITH CARE! DO NOT DROP! I myself am the air cargo so designated. Suffering from a damaged vertebra in my lower back, I am being transported from Hamburg, West Germany, where I've lived for the past eight years, to Louisville, Kentucky, for surgery. Among the millions of air travelers who pass through the bustling airports of the world, I'm hardly a routine passenger. Airlines are seldom asked to transport stretcher cases, and my case is particularly complex.

The trouble starts on a cold, gray day in early 1980. I'm lying flat in bed at Altona Hospital near my home in Hamburg, and doctors have just advised I need special medical attention not available in Germany. The best option, they insist, would be in the United States. However, they make it clear that traveling must be in a horizontal position—lying flat on a stretcher. Fragments of a shattered vertebra are pressing the spinal column and sitting would risk permanent injury—injury that could lead to paralysis.

As my German wife Barbara and I ponder such a trip, we recognize the logistics will be difficult because she has recently given birth to our twin sons. The infants demand constant attention, and because I am incapacitated, Barbara will have a full-time job keeping the two contented for a 24-hour trip. Nevertheless, we decide that despite potential difficulties, we will make the trip.

After a flurry of phone calls the next morning to Methodist Hospital in Louisville, the intake coordinator makes medical preparations, schedules an orthopedic surgeon to see me upon arrival, and reserves a hospital room. Why Louisville? My 20-year career took me not only to West Germany, but also throughout the U.S. and to Australia, India, and Belgium. Home, however, has always remained Louisville, the city where I grew up, went to school, and where my parents and my sister's family still live. Although one may travel the world, "home" is where one returns in time of need. In the current situation, all I can think of is to get home to Louisville.

We turn the logistics over to a local travel agency, setting in motion international arrangements that will involve ground staff at six airports and three airlines as well as other services on both sides of the Atlantic. The travel agency learns that flights originating only in Atlanta can accommodate a stretcher-bound passenger to Louisville. Next, it contacts Sabena, the national airline of Belgium, to make reservations on its Brussels-Atlanta flight. But the matter is not as simple as booking flights because a non-ambulatory passenger requires special preparations. Sabena personnel in Hamburg and Brussels exchange telexes and phone calls with their New York and Atlanta offices to coordinate ground transportation for a stretcher and ensure that support services prepare for our arrival.

A last-minute complication arises when the scheduled Boeing 727 of the German airline Lufthansa from Hamburg to Brussels is taken out of service for maintenance and replaced with a Boeing 737, which cannot accommodate a stretcher. Sabena has to rewrite our itinerary to connect with its Frankfurt flight to Brussels. Not only does the change add three hours to the journey; it necessitates waking up at 4:00 am to catch a pre-dawn flight from Hamburg.

To comply with airline procedures, we secure a medical release from the physician in Hamburg certifying I can travel without a special medical attendant. Fortunately, as a nurse, Barbara is allowed to carry and administer pain medication. Because these drugs contain narcotics, airline personnel must arrange authorizations for crossing the borders of Germany, Belgium and the United States.

In our haste to complete the formalities, we practically forget travel necessities for our six-month-old sons. Fortunately, cribs, infant food, and baby bottles are standard aboard European and intercontinental flights. The airlines arrange the final travel detail: scheduling ambulance services for connecting between flights at each airport.

Departure day arrives. Traveling from the Hamburg hospital before dawn, we are met at the airport by an airline representative who directs us to the aircraft. Lying on a stretcher beneath the plane's undercarriage waiting for a hoist to lift me to the plane's service door, I have a view never before seen but one to be experienced several more times in the following 24 hours.

The flight to Frankfurt and connection to Brussels go smoothly. During the three-hour layover in Brussels, we enjoy lunch at the airline's medical facility. Afterward, however, there's an unexpected change. The non-stop flight from Brussels to Atlanta is canceled due to mechanical problems. Sabena rebooks Atlanta passengers on its scheduled New York flight, where after a stop at JFK, we'll continue to our destination. To accommodate my situation, the ground crew mounts a stretcher in the New York-bound Boeing 747, delaying the departure. Lying on a stretcher beside this jumbo jet waiting to be loaded, I sense the impatience of 300 passengers already on board, many of whom have a direct view of me below.

Finally, workers install the mounting rack for the stretcher and transport me to a hydraulic lift truck that will raise me the equivalent of five floors up to the service loading door. Halfway up, however, the lifting mechanism jams, and there I am—stuck in mid-air between the tarmac and anxious cabin attendants waiting at the door. Helplessly suspended for several minutes, I'm lowered to the ground and deposited beside an enormous tire while waiting for another lift truck. "Wouldn't it be simpler," I wonder aloud, "to recruit volunteers to carry me up the normal passenger stairs?" I am told, without explanation, this is not possible. Soon a new truck arrives and successfully lifts me to the loading door.

From this point the trip goes as planned. Every detail is attended to—including teething rings for both infants. Following a brief stop in New York, we arrive in Atlanta where Sabena arranges for U.S. Customs and

Immigration authorities to come aboard to grant us clearance. The formalities are completed in a few minutes, sparing us the usual hour-long waiting lines.

Sabena officials then hand us over to the Delta Airlines ground staff who arrange our final connecting flight into Louisville. Now more complications arise. The stretcher can fit only in the first-class section and extends across the top of three seats beside the windows. Barbara, as my nurse, is required to be near me, so we must purchase four first-class tickets. (Although the old rule of two drinks for each first-class passenger would normally entitle us to eight free whiskeys, I don't try to take advantage of this supposed perk.)

Another wrinkle occurs. Delta regulations mandate that Barbara devote herself entirely to me as the patient and not be encumbered by our twins. My father comes to the rescue by flying earlier that day from Louisville to Atlanta to join us. On the return trip, his job is to mind the infants back in the coach section.

Twenty-four hours after our trip began, it ends. At Louisville's Standiford Airport, I'm offloaded to an ambulance and transferred to the pre-arranged bed at Methodist Hospital. Despite the snafus along the way, I'm impressed that despite the airborne challenges of a stretcher case, my journey went almost as smoothly as for the typical passenger. Airline and airport staff on both sides of the Atlantic did an excellent job. Their part of the drama has ended.

Mine is just beginning!

# 1
# How I Began

A mix of English and Irish blood—Protestant Irish, the family would always be quick to point out—flowed in my mother, Natalie Moyra Saxton's, veins. Moyra's father (my grandfather), Alec Ernest Saxton, who towered above his classmates and sported the fashionable moustache of the day, cut a dashing figure at St. John's College at University of Oxford. There he studied Latin, Greek, and the classics in the latter part of the 19th century and served as the backbone of the college's successful rowing team (a pastime that inspired me to take up the sport during my own undergraduate years). As a little boy, I would sit on Grumpy's lap looking up at that same distinguished moustache as he reminisced about his glorious student years in England.

At the peak of the British Empire, the unshakeable conviction that the nation's rule was destined to last forever was instilled into every young citizen. During his days at Oxford, Grumpy surely considered making his career somewhere in the Empire—India, Burma, or even possibly the hoped-for next addition, China. However, he did not make his career in China, in Burma, or even in India. Instead, he ended up in Indianapolis.

When the great "War to End All Wars" broke out in 1914, he enlisted in the infantry. Stationed at the front in Flanders, he recounted in his journals the horrors and tragedy of those years, years he spent mostly in the trenches. To help pass the time, he responded to an advertisement in an English newspaper seeking a pen-pal relationship with Patricia Stopford, a bored-at-home 19-year-old, who wrote from her manor house in Ireland. Months later he earned a leave from the front, enabling the two to meet for the first time in London. Shortly afterward Grumpy and Grummy married. But the war wasn't yet over, so back to the trenches he went.

Following the war, the young couple were no doubt relieved and delighted that a beautiful love grew between them. Although the circumstances surrounding their immigration to America were never clear, the story I like best (which probably isn't true) is that a mixed English-Irish couple would not be accepted in either England or Ireland, so they chose America. What's more likely, however, is that as signs of the Empire's crumbling were becoming evident, Grummy and Grumpy dismissed any idea of taking a civil-service assignment at one of the distant outposts. With the sun setting on such outposts at a rapid rate, only America seemed to offer a future.

So off they went to America, where, after stints in New York, New Jersey, and Pennsylvania, Grumpy ended up with a job at Remington Rand in Indianapolis, bringing his wife and three daughters—the middle among them, my mother—in tow.

The Schroeder side of my family is from German-Danish stock, folk who had left Europe in the late 1700s. They were feet-on-the-ground, nononsense people who worked hard, invested wisely, and made a lot of money—money they lost during the 1929 Depression. My father, George Weaver Schroeder, was born when the family was still wealthy and during his teen years was sent away to Choate Boarding School in Wallingford, Connecticut. Dad was brought up with strict adherence to the values of hard work, guarded speech, restrained emotions, and respect for elders.

The Schroeder family owned two homes: a winter residence in Flushing, New York, and a summer home on the south shore of eastern Long Island in Quogue. Home from school for summers in Quogue, my father practically lived at Shinnecock Yacht Club where he developed into a champion sailor, regularly winning trophies at regattas held throughout the region and later serving as captain of the Sailing Club during his years at Princeton. Sailing remained a passion throughout my father's life, a pastime that I, too, have embraced.

In 1940 Moyra Saxton (my mother went by her middle name) was a wild, 17-year-old redhead attending Kent Place, a fashionable private school in Summit, New Jersey, where her family moved after leaving Indianapolis. At the same time, George was a serious 20-year-old studying electrical engineering at Princeton University 40 miles away. The two met at a tea dance-mixer, an occasion where proper young women and men were introduced. These events were always well chaperoned and highly formal. Their tolerance for only the strictest and most controlled behavior created a repression among hormonally driven teenagers—a repression that can be compared to the buildup of a pendulum's momentum that later swings to the other extreme.

To understand what happened with George and Moyra next, it is necessary to relate a few details about Lake Carnegie located in the woods on the eastern boundary of the Princeton campus. The industrialist, Andrew Carnegie, made a sizeable grant to the university to build a dam across the Mill River, creating a lake so Princeton could build a rowing tradition. Throughout the year the lake also fulfilled other purposes. The Princeton Sailing Club was established and as long as sailors kept out of the way of the oarsmen, there was peace. In winter when the lake froze, students and townies alike enjoyed ice skating and iceboating. *(As an undergraduate at Princeton years later, I would think of my father as I skated the six miles from one end of the lake to the other on a winter weekend.)* The lake was stocked with fish, and in summer, anglers cast lines from its shores. Perhaps the greatest purpose served by Lake Carnegie, however, was a destination where Princeton students took their dates at night after the parties were over. Strict university rules banned alcohol, did not allow women in dormitory rooms after dark, and enforced a formal dress code. Chaperones stood guard at all weekend events when females invaded the campus. So where did one go to be alone with a date? Voila, the shores of Lake Carnegie!

There was only one problem: poison ivy. As if by some device of Nature to thwart lovers (although people joked it was planted by the same people who arranged for the chaperones), poison ivy abounded around the lake. Rashes assumed epidemic proportions at Princeton after every spring party weekend. In fact, bragging about sites on one's anatomy where blisters had broken out often became a point of pride among undergraduates.

The big campus event in late March was the Junior Prom. While seniors were busy trying to meet thesis deadlines and the two lower classes were preoccupied with getting ready for their exams, the juniors took time out to play.

So, in spring of 1940, George Schroeder, a junior at Princeton, invited Moyra Saxton, a Kent Place senior whom he had dated for several months, to Princeton for the Junior Prom. Yes, they did go to the shores of Lake Carnegie after the parties were over. And yes, they did get poison ivy rash all over. And yes, aren't I glad they did! My mother, five months pregnant, married my father on August 27 that summer of 1940. And that's where my story begins.

*(To be fair to my mother, she said I wasn't conceived on the shores of Lake Carnegie, but rather at her home in Summit. But I like my story better.)*

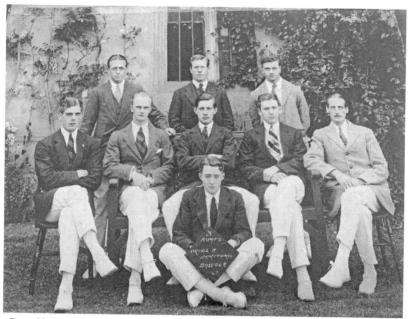

Grandfather Alec Saxton "Grumpy" cut a dashing figure at St John's College, Oxford University - **middle row left**

St. John's College crew, 5th from bow

Thomas Edison's portrait inscription to Grandfather, circa 1915

# 2
# Island Lake

*12/40 - 8/50, Birth to Age 9*

Because my parents were unable to arrange for nine months to pass between their marriage and my birth, neither side of the family could get over the shock. Nobody believed that following their late August marriage, I could have been born four months premature and weighing more than seven pounds. This predicament incurred loss of respectability not only for my parents, but for their families as well. It helped my parents, however, that I arrived on December 27, thus allowing a tax deduction for that year.

As they started life together, Mom and Dad faced a world that seemed to turn against them. Radcliffe College had offered Mom a scholarship starting that autumn; she had to decline. Princeton did not allow undergraduates to be married; therefore, Dad couldn't complete his senior year. Mom and Dad, still basically teenagers, must have felt a heavy burden finding themselves saddled with adjusting to married life, meeting demands of a newborn, facing disapproval from both families, and abandoning now-shattered plans for their future.

Regardless, they went about setting up a home and caring for me at a time when war hysteria was sweeping America. While our small family was settling into a stable life, other young men were leaving families for war fronts in Europe and later in the Pacific. Because of my father's electrical engineering background, Edo Aircraft Corporation in New York hired him to develop radar instrumentation for the war effort; consequently, he received a critical skills deferment and was not subject to military draft, even though at 21 he was prime age for induction. Furthermore, he was doubly assured of deferment because he had dependents at home.

Determined to complete his undergraduate degree, Dad contacted a classmate, Donald "Skid" Skidmore, who was finishing his senior year. While carrying a full course load, Skid also worked as a teaching assistant. Dad jumped on an idea to complete his bachelor's degree: He applied to Princeton's Electrical Engineering Department for the TA position that would be vacated when Skid graduated in May. He was accepted and, as part of the agreement, would be allowed to complete his senior year courses despite being married. *(Years after Skid's wife and my father died, my mother and Skid reconnected at Princeton's 50th Reunion. They began dating and eventually married, living together for 12 years until Mom died in 2006.)*

That autumn of 1941 we moved into a small apartment on Nassau Street in Princeton. While attending classes, Dad conducted research into electronic cooking with high-frequency radio waves. Excited to share his findings, he and Mom invited two junior faculty couples from the Electrical Engineering Department to dinner one evening. While invitees were enjoying cocktails, Mom brought out a raw leg of lamb and announced this would be the main course. Mentally calculating how long the meat would take to cook and anticipating they would be waiting all night for dinner; the guests were aghast. However, half an hour later my mother served a thoroughly cooked leg of lamb that she had prepared in my father's prototype electronic oven. But there was one problem: The lamb looked raw because there was no infrared heat to brown the outside. Although the meat appeared less than appetizing, reportedly the meal tasted delicious!

While in Princeton, my mother knitted a sweater for me in the orange-and-black colors of the Princeton Tiger and regularly pushed me, dressed in my little sweater with class year '62 on the back, around campus

15

in a stroller. She had calculated the year incorrectly because my college graduation would normally have been 1963. *(Years later, however, having advanced one year in elementary school, I was accepted by Princeton at age 17 and, indeed, did graduate with the Class of 1962, exactly 20 years after Dad and with the same degree.)* In May of 1942, Dad, having finished his thesis on electronic cooking, graduated with a Bachelor of Science Degree in Electrical Engineering.

General Electric Company played a significant role in lives of three generations of our family. Henry (Harry) Schroeder, my paternal grandfather, worked at Edison Light Company (which later became General Electric) with Thomas Edison in his West Orange and Menlo Park research laboratories in the late 19th – early 20th centuries. An engineer, Harry later left Edison and started Schroeder Lamp Works in Jersey City, which produced his incandescent light brass bulb socket that was patented October 21, 1919. He authored two books, *The Incandescent Lamp - Its History* in 1923, and *History of the Incandescent Light* in 1927.

Thus, it was somewhat more than coincidental that after graduation Dad took a job with GE where he remained for 17 years. He devoted much of his career to research on electronic cooking for which he received several patents on what became known as the microwave oven. Throughout his career, Dad was often called as an expert witness in legal disputes related to the microwave. *(Perhaps unsurprisingly, my first job— although it lasted only three months through one summer during college— was with GE.)*

In July 1942, our family moved to GE's offices in Schenectady, New York, where Dad worked on the development of radar defense programs, and where, the following year in April, my mother gave birth to Wendy. In February 1944, GE transferred my father to its Hotpoint subsidiary in Chicago.

My first childhood memory is playing on the railroad track near our rented duplex in the Chicago suburb of Brookfield. I recall the day a worker asks to see my home, which I am proud to show him. We walk back to the house where I excitedly present my new friend to Mom. But my joy suddenly disappears when he tells my mother that I shouldn't be playing among the rail cars. I can still picture the alarm on her face as she turns to me and sternly prohibits me from ever going back to this wonderful play area. *(Although I never return, this fascination with trains remains, which may explain my later adventures hopping freight trains.)*

That summer we move to Island Lake, north of Chicago. Our rental home is named by our Swedish landlord "Stugan," meaning "Cottage" in her language. Located halfway up a hill with a view of woods and a lake below, the dark-stained, split-log-sided home conveys a sense of rustic comfort. Wendy and my parents occupy two bedrooms on the ground floor while I'm relegated to a loft accessed by a ladder from the kitchen. I love to retreat to this getaway to be on my own except for one problem. Every night when reaching the top of the ladder, I freeze in fear. The bed and lamp are on the far side of the loft, so I must dash through total darkness to reach the light switch before the boogeyman can catch me. Once light floods the space, I'm safe; but I dread those few seconds running through the pitch-black each night.

In 1948, when I'm seven, Dad purchases an acre of land in a rural area of Island Lake and we build our own home. We pour footings, mount the studs, nail the siding, shingle the roof, sheetrock the interior walls, install electrical and plumbing fixtures, and paint the exterior and interior walls. Scavenging scrap materials, I use my newly acquired construction skills to build a shanty for a secret get-away. Here, entertained by a collection of comic books, I read for hours during summer days and sleep on a makeshift bed at night.

These childhood years revolve around a lake, a farm, a forest, and open countryside. The village of Island Lake surrounds a lake of the same name. Only a couple of miles across and dotted with small islands, this lake is where I learn to sail, a pastime that becomes a lifetime passion. In my 12-foot Penguin catboat I love exploring the shoreline to discover the lake's hidden twists and bends. My whole being rejoices in the freedom of not being land-bound, and the world feels at peace as I ghost along catching silent breezes. Even windless days don't stop me from setting sail in *Yot* (so named because spelled backward it's my "toy"). Something about being a small boy on a small boat on a small lake evokes a sense of

17

exhilaration—one that has stayed with me whenever I find myself near sea and sail.

How well I remember one summer when Dad and I win the Chicago Daily News Regatta on Lake Michigan sailing *Yot*. As a crew whose only job requires shifting weight, I nevertheless feel the trophy is as much mine as my father's when he collects the silver plate for first-place.

When I'm not out sailing, warm summer days often find me joining friends at a favorite fishing pier. Armed with bamboo poles and worm-baited hooks, we while away the hours trying to outwit bullheads, sunfish, perch, and bluegill. With luck, at the end of the day we triumphantly march home, each with a couple of six-inch catches, to present our mothers with the next day's breakfast.

When winter's sub-zero temperatures and blustery winds turn the lake into a frozen sheet, out come the ice skates and iceboats. One Saturday afternoon, while skating with the family, I have the scare of my life. CRACK! A sound like a rifle shot splits the air. I turn toward the source just as Dad falls through the breaking ice. Instinctively I dash to shore while he barely catches himself with armpits at the ice's edge and flails in the water until he can lunge up onto the ice. Then with body spread out to distribute weight, he "swims" across the ice to shore. Never have I been so fearful for, and proud of, my Dad as at that moment.

While summer and winter activities on the lake become the focus of my life, visiting a local farm is another highlight. Although only a 20-minute hike from home, Smith's Farm on a dusty back road feels like a different world. Here I witness the births and deaths of calves, foals, goats, chickens, and cats. Etched in my memory is a sickly three-week-old calf. I assume the job of feeding this weakling by hand. Every morning I tear from the house to the farm to lift the fragile creature outdoors into the sunshine, and in late afternoon carry it back to the barn. One morning I arrive to find the calf standing motionless on its feet. It had died during the night but would not fall over, as though not to disappoint me. Although I remain with it another half day hoping to find some trace of life, my vigil is to no avail.

Early spring—early enough to get at least two grain harvests, but not so early as to risk crops getting nipped by a late frost—is planting time. Every day between planting and harvesting, Tom, one of Mr. Smith's sons, and I inspect the fields of corn, barley, and soybeans. After our thoughtful survey, we give Mr. Smith an update. He chuckles but doesn't seem to care. Nevertheless, we consider these daily inspections essential to ensure a plentiful harvest.

How can a full day at home pass without any significant event happening, while life-and-death dramas unfold on the farm? Watching seasonal changes to the crops and observing the life cycles of animals makes me feel part of something bigger than myself. But what exactly defines this "self" I perceive myself to be at age six or seven? I am aware of two characteristics that influence how people see me and affect everything I do. One is physical, the other temperamental. First, the physical: My head appears as a mass of red freckles topped by a shock of uncombed, bright red curls. The two reds are similar enough that people at a distance need to look twice to know if they are seeing me from the front or from the back. The clue: bright blue eyes peer from under curls separating them from freckles below. This can be confusing when people think I'm looking one direction but actually can't see a single thing they're talking about, or when I observe what's happening when others think I'm going in another direction. For example, I recall a neighbor asking if I wanted to earn some money by washing his car. When I didn't answer, he said something like, "Well, Peter, you must be so rich you don't need any additional cash." Only when I turned and asked what he had said, did he realize he was talking to the back of my head.

Second, the temperamental characteristic: I am quick to anger and ready to jump into a fray with minimal provocation—a characteristic said to be typical of redheads. I often come to a boil when greeted as "Red," or worse, with, "What d'ya say, Red?"—a hint-of-derision question I never know how to answer. Such minor insults lead to many fights, tears, and frustrations. The discipline received at home after a fight teaches me either not to get caught or to curb my temper. Suppressing these emotions builds the determination that makes me headstrong and obstinate, and I learn to face life with a fighting stance. Once my mind is made up, nothing can dissuade me. I grow up as a strong-willed loner who prefers to avoid groups whenever possible. I am happiest alone, when I can let down my guard at the lake or on the farm.

Rebellion peaks at age seven when I'm given a BB gun. Previous contact with creatures has been with a stick or fishing pole, which limited range to only a few feet. But with a BB gun I can interact from a greater distance and change things that don't seem right. When observing frogs pouncing from lily pads to devour insects, I correct this apparent injustice by shooting the predators. After seeing blue jays devour eggs of other birds, I likewise declare war on the blue-jay community. My misguided mission is to protect Nature's smaller, defenseless creatures by eliminating those that would eat them. Targets include water snakes, dragonflies, centipedes, crows, and anything else that preys on something smaller. But all my efforts, whether successful or not, result in frustration. None of these predator-prey relationships ever changes. In the end I give up trying to rearrange the natural world.

Life goes a lot better once I give up interfering and limit myself to just observing. By sitting still and watching without judging, I begin to understand how predator-prey relationships are essential to maintaining a balance among all species. I eventually realize that rather than helping, my self-righteous efforts to set matters right only served to destroy Nature's delicate balance.

*(Upon mature reflection, I realize I had been trying to do what everyone tries to do, namely create a world as we think it should be. A first step is creating division within the unity of life—a unity we're often too blind to see. Such division creates the higher and lower, the valued and valueless, and the superior and inferior, as well as gradations in between. Once divisions are established, preservation of one means destruction of the other. Every nation, every society, every organization, and virtually every person has tried in some manner to preserve the one by destroying the other.)*

At around the same age I received the BB gun I take on a job delivering newspapers by bicycle. Each afternoon after school I fold approximately 50 newspapers to distribute before sundown. Delivering a newspaper involves coordination, control, and forethought to perform four steps almost simultaneously. My strategy to accomplish this: first, keep the bike on course at full speed; second, aim and throw the newspaper to the front door; third, call "Paper" as the daily flies toward the doorstep; and fourth, prepare for the next delivery. But what happens, for example, if the newspaper unfolds while sailing toward someone's doorstep? Or what if I need both hands on the bike while pumping up a hill, but I need to throw a paper? Working out the fine points ensures a perfect delivery. If properly folded and thrown with just the right touch, the paper should immediately flop open upon landing, allowing the customer to read the headlines while bending to pick it up.

For customers who own bicycle-chasing dogs, I must make a quiet approach, then slightly delay before shouting "Paper" while speeding away with a sudden burst of pedaling. A charging dog that nips at my heels might require the sacrifice of the next customer's newspaper to fend off the attacker long enough to escape.

Wind and rain present additional problems. Rain means the paper needs to land under the porch roof. If it misses, I must dismount and deliver it by hand. Thursdays are long days when I collect money and don't return home until dark. As a consolation, customers sometimes offer candy, cakes, and soft drinks...that is, they do if they didn't get too many wet, torn, or mis-thrown papers the prior week.

These are happy years, and I feel secure within a loving family. Because we enjoy sailing, bareboat charter vacations become an ongoing tradition. Dad charters yachts, usually in the 30- to 50-foot range, suited to cruising grounds he selects. I particularly remember our first cruise in 1951 on *Wild Goose* chartered out of Milford, Connecticut, on Long Island Sound. One sunny day, Wendy, age eight, decides to wash the deck using seawater retrieved from a bucket tied to a line. When she throws it into the water, the bucket fills instantly and jerks her overboard. Dad quickly douses the sails and turns the boat while Mom dives in and swims to Wendy who's frantically treading water. Half a dozen nearby cruisers immediately come to offer assistance. Once *Wild Goose* maneuvers alongside Mom and Wendy, the two are brought back on board. Surprisingly, Wendy climbs the swim ladder still holding the line to the bucket, which also is retrieved!

Two years later, we cruise Chesapeake Bay on *Pecusa II*, named by its Episcopal minister owner to stand for *P*rotestant *E*piscopal *C*hurch of the *U*nited *S*tates of *A*merica. Later family cruises include Eagle Rock at Coral Gables in 1958; *Quest* at Galesville, Maryland, in 1959; *Verano IV* at Nyborg, Denmark, in 1974; *Sea Away* at Hatchet Bay, Bahamas, in 1975 and again in 1978; and *Windsong* at Nassau in 1979. These experiences draw us close as a family. *(Following the example set by my father, I continue this wonderful tradition with my own family.)*

But life itself is not all smooth sailing. Those aforementioned red curls along with a fierce determination and fiery temper often give rise to frustration and impatience when I struggle with a difficult task. One day a family friend, Mr. Garland, takes me aside and confides that because as a child he had red hair and freckles along with an indomitable will and short temper, he understands these wild energies. Then, with a slight twinkle in his eye, he shares a secret he had been told as a youth—a secret that he says passes only among redheads.

"Throughout history, many different peoples from different lands have at one time or another thought of themselves as 'chosen people' cut out from others for a higher destiny and purpose," he explains. "These peoples and nations have all come and gone, and nothing remains of any of them." Then lowering his voice, he continues with an impish smile, "Indeed there is a 'chosen group,' namely, the world's redheads."

When I express doubt, he goes on to prove his point. "In the United States, less than two percent of the population have red hair. Including the rest of the world, this figure drops to under one-hundredth of one percent. Now consider famous Americans who were redheads: Thomas Jefferson, George Washington, William Faulkner, Alexander Hamilton, Mark Twain, Andrew Carnegie..." he rattles on through his list. "Throughout world history, the ranks of famous redheads include Julius Caesar, Alexander the Great, Napoleon, Catherine the Great, Genghis Khan, Vincent van Gogh, Winston Churchill, Christopher Columbus, Dostoevsky, Tchaikovsky, and many more. Statistically speaking, if so many people of note come from such a small segment of the population, this stands as evidence of the special role of redheads on the world stage."

This information is heady stuff for an eight-year-old. Suddenly I'm very proud of these red curls and with pride recount this theory of redhead specialness to my brown-, black-, and blond-headed friends. Predictably, they aren't particularly understanding! Nevertheless, with this new-found knowledge I gain new confidence and can now live happily with a short temper, a strong will, and unruly strawberry curls that are no longer a liability. I am content to wait for the day when a transformation will catapult me, too, into the ranks of distinguished redheads.

[April 1942, Princeton University Campus]
A very determined 16-month-old

# 3
# Expectations

*9/50 - 9/52, Ages 9 - 11*

*(During the previous six years in Island Lake, life was not measured by the passage of time, but rather by the flow of one adventure following another. Neither past nor future mattered, only the present. Each day merged into the next, and the days melted into years.)*

But change comes in the summer of 1950.

As though awakening from a dream, I learn our family will be torn from the world of Island Lake because General Electric once again promotes my father—a promotion that means another relocation. Mom and Dad explain we must say goodbye to friends and leave our present life; however, they assure us we will find new friends and discover new places as wonderful as, or perhaps even more wonderful, than those we're leaving behind. Furthermore, they mention, we can come back to visit *(which, of course, we never do).*

*(Some maintain that losing something when it's fresh and wonderful is preferable to retaining it and watching it grow old and stale. I suspect that would apply to saying goodbye to Island Lake, although to a nine-year-old, it's not obvious. Yes, one of the best parts of my life was here;*

24

*nevertheless, in retrospect I know it was good to leave. The simple farm, the small lake, and the little village all retain a magic in my memory. Had we stayed, though, into my adolescent years, I doubt my horizons would have expanded much. Moreover, the glow of childhood adventures would have faded over time, leaving me empty of the richness I still feel when looking back to these years.)*

When Dad transfers from Chicago to GE's offices in Bridgeport, Connecticut, we move to Stevenson, a nearby Island Lake-like community. The prospect of the move created a wishful expectation that I would find new adventures similar to those experienced before. Fortunately, in Stevenson I discover everything found in Island Lake, but on a larger scale. Our new hometown is close to Lake Zoar, a reservoir on the Housatonic River, that is ideally suited for swimming, sailing, and ice skating. Large areas of wooded countryside teem with the same animals and vegetation known in Island Lake. And, yes, there is a farm—a chicken farm said to be the largest in Connecticut. Best of all, we rent a house on the farm property itself! Suddenly the move is not as terrible as it first seemed.

Any lingering doubt is dispelled when prowling through woods one day, I discover every boy's dream—a railroad track. Over the next several days I explore the track in each direction. To the west lies our village, to the east the track twists and undulates with the rolling countryside, then turns sharply into a tunnel. Although I claim the tunnel as my secret hiding place, I soon discover it's known to every nine-year-old boy from miles around. We soon become acquainted and agree this tunnel will be our special place to meet.

Much of my life here revolves around the schedule of the trains. Morning and evening commuters are fast, short, and uninteresting. But the daily westbound freights are loaded with manufactured goods shipped out from Bridgeport and other eastern cities, and the exciting mile-long strings coming from the western states carry livestock and grain to the eastern seaboard. The sharp bend in the track and lengthy upward grade cause these heavily laden eastbound trains to barely creep as they approach the tunnel, and herein lies an opportunity to prove myself to the new friends.

Mustering courage one afternoon, I run alongside an open, flatbed car on a slow-moving eastbound freight train. Just as the tunnel is upon me, I grab the ladder and scamper up. The last thing I remember before being swallowed in blackness is looking back at my friends and seeing panic on their faces. Although I had walked through the tunnel previously, this time it feels much blacker and far, far longer. After an eternity, the train emerges into daylight, and without waiting to judge how much speed it has picked up, I hurl myself into some bushes and tumble down a short ravine. Covered with scratches and cuts, I pick myself up, and, after my shaking subsides and my turned-to-jelly legs will support me, I proceed back through the tunnel. When my friends see I'm all right, they rush up to embrace me. I confess to them, "I won't do that again, but remember, you saw me do it!" I'm now accepted into their group, and no one after that ever dares to hop another train.

My friends and I spend the remaining days of summer by the railroad tracks engaged in less risky adventures such as experimenting with flattening pennies, nickels, and dimes by leaving them on the tracks as a train approaches. The slow-moving heavy-laden freights flatten our coins, but the lighter high-speed passenger trains create hardly any distortions.

As the first summer of the '50s comes to an end, the intense green of the woods gives way first to yellows, then orange-reds, and finally flaming reds as a New England autumn erupts across the land. Along with seasonal change comes another all-too-familiar change in my life. Each day starts with the capture by, and ends with release from, a big yellow caterpillar that lumbers back and forth between our home and Lincoln Elementary School in nearby Monroe.

Being a year ahead of my age group, in fourth grade at age nine, I am, as before, the youngest and shortest kid in class. Although these differences separate me from classmates in athletics, I hold my own in academics. By devoting energies at school toward learning, I almost, but don't quite, make up for what I lack in my athletic and social life. Not surprisingly, I am a loner at school.

After school hours I feed and care for the farm's chickens. Although most people think chickens and eggs belong together, every chicken farmer knows they have little in common as a business—a chicken farm is different from an egg farm. The only eggs we have for sale come from the farmer's wholesale market to assure that tourists who drive out from the city to buy fresh country eggs don't return home disappointed.

The first step in raising chickens is receiving cartons of three-day-old chicks, inoculating them, and sending them scurrying under incubator lamps. After a shipment of these newborns is received, for the next few days, my job is to prevent chicks from killing themselves, which some invariably do by drowning in their half-inch-deep water dishes, running out through a crack in the building into paws of waiting cats, entangling themselves in their food dishes, or fighting to the death with others. I'm surprised how I'm told to deal with sick chicks. Instead of nursing them back to health, I must immediately kill them and bring them to be examined for any one of a half-dozen illnesses. If an illness is identified, the entire clutch must be destroyed. Any humanitarian consideration for a single chick is forfeited for the sake of the others. As the chicks grow, I regulate their liquid intake and change the feed to introduce minerals and nutrients. I learn to adjust the lighting and temperature as well as remove fighters and others that behave abnormally.

After a number of weeks, work doesn't begin until 10:00 at night after the chickens settle for the evening. Another worker and I quietly enter the barns and sit amidst the chickens trying not to disturb them. Reaching out with a hooked metal rod, I snag the leg of a larger one, pull it toward me, and hold it until it stops resisting. Then I hand it to the shadowy figure behind me. "Only seven pounds, try again," I hear the voice as he weighs and then releases it. Thus begins the pursuit to separate all 10-pounders from the flock. These are the fast-growers that have already reached marketable size. Thinning them out early helps the farm's cash flow and creates more space for others to grow. Of 2,000 chickens in each of five barns, over the next several nights we separate out about 200 per barn, confirming the statistical 10 percent that reach maturity fastest.

The following morning these are sent to the killing room where workers slit their throats and drain blood away. The carcasses are flung into hot tubs of water to soften roots of the feathers so they easily come off in the plucking machine. The entire operation, the killing, plucking, cleaning, cutting and packaging, proceeds efficiently. The one time I participate, I become nauseous. After weeks of feeding, watering, and caring for these birds, it seems duplicitous to send them to the packaging room. Thereafter I confine work strictly to feeding and caring. When arriving at work each afternoon, I avert my eyes as I hurry by the killing room.

Our first winter in Connecticut brings with it familiar activities I had known in Illinois: ice skating, sledding, and skiing plus one new activity. Along the front of our house five sugar maple trees offer the possibility of making authentic maple syrup. To get started we drill four holes in each tree (one in each quadrant), insert wooden drain tubes, and hang buckets from notches in the tubes. Throughout the following week, although surprised at the unpleasant odors given off, we continually empty buckets of raw sap into boiling cauldrons. Finally, according to the syrup-making manual, water and impurities boil away leaving pure syrup.

The next morning, with high expectations we sit down to a pancake breakfast and with fanfare pour the homemade concoction onto the pancakes. But on first bite we all grimace. Something must have gone wrong because the taste is more than any of us can tolerate. Staring at each other in disbelief, we wonder: Hadn't we followed instructions to the letter? I dash next door to inform our neighbor, a grandfatherly type who has been making maple syrup since he was a kid, and he hurries over to see what the panic is about. Taking one taste of our brew, he smiles with delight. "You've made it as perfectly as I myself ever have!" he proclaims and invites himself to stay for breakfast. Realizing we had long since become victimized by the food-processing industry and consequently could not stand a taste unless it had been adulterated with preservatives, artificial flavors, colorings, sugars, and other additives, we gladly surrender the entire inventory of our syrup-making endeavor to our delighted neighbor. We, in turn, chalk the experiment up to experience and forget it.

*(Twenty-five years later when a heightened sense of food awareness sweeps across America, I realize the missed opportunity to appreciate the natural flavors Nature affords us. It was an important lesson: Things that often seem to go wrong in our lives can be a reflection of our prejudices,*

*attitudes, and conditioning. If we break out from our so-called understanding, which is often nonsense, we can open to more joy in life. The maple syrup incident was the first of many small, but poignant, jolts indicating that my life was straying from the natural way. However, many years were to elapse before I would comprehend this truth).*

On winter days I bundle up and wander through the snowy woods. Noticing many dead trees, I realize the potential for a new adventure, one providing an opportunity to get exercise and spend more time in the woods. Why not cut firewood for our fireplace? Because we delight in sitting by the open fireside every evening, it's not hard to convince my father to buy a band saw, sledgehammer, and several wedges. In addition, he builds a sawhorse using the spacing of our andirons as a gauge to cut logs to the exact firewood length.

Thus begins a lifelong passion—cutting firewood. In addition to feeding chickens and doing homework, throughout winter I spend as much time as possible chopping down dead trees and sawing and splitting fire logs. In a whimsical moment, the thought crosses my mind that wood fireplaces create the most efficient type of heating because they warm a person five times: first when cutting down the tree; second when sawing the firewood-length logs; third when splitting the logs; fourth when carrying logs to the house; and fifth when burning them.

On weekends I lose myself in the snowy countryside with saws, wedges, saw horse, and sledgehammer. Cutting, splitting, and carrying firewood soon become a meditative pleasure. Time stands still when I'm deep in the woods absorbed in work. The crystal-clear sound of a sledgehammer striking the wedges echoes through the still, cold air. Transfixed in the moment, I feel at one with the surroundings. This intense sense of connectedness seems strangely both fleeting and eternal, yet more real than the life I otherwise know. Returning home in the evening, I feel invigorated. The harder the work and more energy I put into splitting fire logs, the greater the exuberance I feel at the end of the day.

*(For me, a fireplace is the criterion that makes a house a home. Every house I have lived in since this year in Connecticut has had a wood-*

29

*burning fireplace. I have always done homework, read a book, or just quietly relaxed on chilly evenings near a crackling fire. The comfort I feel beside an open hearth perhaps explains the pleasure I derive when cutting firewood—which may actually be more of a compulsion. Long winter evenings in front of a roaring fire are a reminder of those beautiful moments alone in the woods. Moreover, burning firewood gives a reason to replenish the woodpile. It's a wonderful cycle.)*

The quiet white of Connecticut's long winter gives way to an explosion of yellow forsythia blossoms, and soon blues, reds, and pinks spatter every hillside as spring flowers burst into bloom. This riot of color gives way to intense green that is wonderfully refreshing in the early days of a New England summer and then becomes monotonous by its end.

Just as we complete two years in our chicken-farm home, General Electric decides my father should once more be promoted...and once more be relocated. Wondering what to expect next, I retreat into the woods to one of my hiding places to figure out life. I am 11 years old, full of exuberance and full of love for all that life has offered up to this time. Everything about the two places I have lived has felt perfect. However, the prospect of a move means uncertainty; surely I can't expect life to continue to be as perfect as it's been in the past. What if there is no lake by our new house? What if there is no farm nearby? What if there are no woods, no railroad tracks, no friends, and no logs to split? I've been lucky until now because everything has suited me. But I don't want Chance to hold such influence over my life. Suddenly the future is my greatest concern. What can I do to be certain life in the future will be as fulfilling as in the past?

*(As these fears and expectations assume gigantic proportions, I fail to see that childhood innocence is falling away, and a strong ego is rising in its place. I had previously trusted existence without question, and life had felt perfect. Why, now, do I no longer trust, but rather doubt? Doubting means I must take control rather than surrender to surrounding forces. Problems will ensue from this crystallization of ego. For the years that lie ahead, I will follow a long road littered with setbacks. When we stop trusting and start trying to create our own destiny, the ego feels fulfilled; however, we then lose that spontaneous delight of childhood.)*

Faced with the uncertainties of another move and filled with a need to shape a future to meet my expectations, I set out to try to control those things that buffet my life: family, school, General Electric, friends, everything..., an effort that is, of course, to no avail.

# 4

# Competing and Achieving

*10/52 - 8/58, Ages 11 - 17*

In the late 17th century social misfits from the Thirteen Colonies who fled through the Cumberland Gap in the Appalachian Mountains established the first European settlements in Kentucky. Typically, these settlers were criminals, religious deviants, and rebels who contributed more to unsettling than to settling the eastern seaboard colonies. Many who crossed the mountains to Kentucky were escaping punishments that meant prison or even death if captured. Otherwise, who would have been crazy enough to face perils of the unknown beyond the borders of civilization—borders so clearly marked by the Appalachians?

Rebelliousness, distrust of authority, and fear—fear of being caught for past crimes—characterized these early Kentuckians. As America's westward expansion continued in the early 19th century, others clamoring to find better opportunities dashed through Kentucky on their way to fertile lands in Kansas, Missouri, and elsewhere in the Midwest. These pioneers surged through the narrow pass, probably the first expressway in America, on their way to the Ohio River where they loaded possessions onto flatboats and continued west. They traveled the entire length of Kentucky stopping only long enough where Louisville now stands to portage the waterfalls. Because few settled in Kentucky, the state didn't benefit from the entrepreneurial drive or sense of adventure that motivated these pioneers to pull up eastern stakes and move west.

Overshadowed by attractions of fertile richness in the Midwest and mineral riches in the Far West, Kentucky retained the questionable character acquired from its earliest settlers. Consequently, the state, especially the eastern region, maintained a status quo without distinction as either an agricultural region or an industrial center. Because most terrain was rugged and remote, it offered no focal point around which a major commercial complex could develop. Moreover, Kentucky wasn't north and it wasn't south.

It is perhaps ironic that Kentucky's lack of identity should have produced two opposing leaders in the Civil War. Another touch of irony is Jefferson Davis, president of the Confederacy, was born farther north in Kentucky than Abraham Lincoln, president of the Union. During the Civil War, Kentucky continued to be a lost entity. Some in the state favored slavery, while others opposed it. About one-third of the population supported the North, one-third the South, and one-third maintained neutrality. Throughout most of the Civil War, the state remained uncommitted. Only toward the end when victory seemed certain, did Kentucky align with the North.

The groundwork for present-day Kentucky was not laid until the latter part of the 19th century. The state became known for what are facetiously referred to as its four "dirty" businesses: growing tobacco, racing horses, distilling bourbon, and mining coal.

Our family is on the way to Kentucky. What will the new home state be like for an adventure-loving kid like me?

We settle into a large, comfortable house in Louisville's eastern suburb of Indian Hills. Within a week I, at age 11, enroll in sixth grade at Ballard School where classmates immediately test me. First, they straighten out my knowledge of Civil War history. This is when I encounter several anomalies of living in Kentucky. As far as my classmates are concerned (and this reflects attitudes of their parents as well), Kentucky was one of the most important southern states in the Confederacy during the Civil

War. When I protest that Kentucky had initially stayed neutral and then fought with the North, I get a first lesson in bigotry—a lesson that sends me home with a bloody nose. The next day classmates tell me that Jefferson Davis was a true son of Kentucky and a heroic example for all of us. I quickly point out that Abraham Lincoln, having been born in Hodgenville, is likewise a son of Kentucky. But then—bash, bam—once again I return home scratched and bruised. Still intent on setting me straight, they next inform me that Kentucky had supported slavery and had been one of the last states to release its slaves, an action taken only under duress. When, armed with different facts, I counter that Kentucky had very few slaves and had established a major underground railroad for assisting escaped slaves endeavoring to get to the North, I get beat up yet again.

After delving more into Civil War history, I realize I am not wrong. But then why do I keep getting beaten up? My parents are preoccupied with their own problems of settling into a town that hadn't seen many Yankees for almost 100 years. The local population hadn't liked Yankee carpetbaggers then, and it seems this attitude toward northerners hasn't changed. The only advice my parents offer is to avoid the subject of the Civil War, but whenever the subject comes up at school, my temperament won't let ignorant statements go unchallenged. It doesn't help matters that I'm the only kid with red hair, because General Sherman, that much-hated Union army officer who cut a swath through the South and burned Atlanta, was also a redhead. I figure it's best to keep my theories about redheads to myself.

Just as things are settling down, our teacher makes an unfortunate choice for our class's assigned reading. *A Connecticut Yankee in King Arthur's Court*, a classic known to every American sixth grader, stirs everything up again. I represent that Connecticut Yankee and, as in the book, seem to make trouble for an otherwise complacent group of people. Knowing I'm outnumbered and tired of mistreatment, I let my classmates live with their mistaken ideas of the Civil War, their glorified Kentucky Colonels, their Johnny Reb images, and their sense of southern nostalgia. Local society shares these sentiments. *(As shown by busing violence during desegregation of schools in Louisville in the 1960's—violence which made national headlines—these attitudes are slow to die.)*

Another anomaly I find about life in Kentucky relates to the rebellious nature supposedly inherent in the character of every Kentuckian. Stories about early settlers portray them as rebels who had left or been thrown out of conventional societies. The comic-strip characterization of a Kentucky youth, Li'l Abner, verifies this image as does the famed outdoorsman Daniel Boone. Similarly, stories about shoeless, long-haired, unwashed, independent-spirited hillbillies making moonshine and staying out of the reaches of the law fire my imagination. Although I live outside the mainstream of my peers, I'm upholding a Kentucky tradition by sparking my own rebellious spirit.

I am dismayed, however, upon learning that Louisville society, the so-called Bourbon-elite, lives in exact opposition to this tradition. Make whiskey exactly how Grandpa did, don't innovate, don't experiment, and be wary of the unknown. Similar "keep-things-the-way-they-have-always-been" thinking applies to another great Kentucky institution, the Kentucky Derby. Women dress up as antebellum southern belles in outrageous gowns and oversize hats. Before the race, everyone stands to sing "My Old Kentucky Home" composed by Stephen Foster who probably never set foot in Kentucky. *(The song's words, however, have been sanitized in recent times to remove racist inferences.)*

When arrangements were made for our move to Kentucky, I tried to exercise control by determining we would live on a farm near a lake surrounded by open countryside. As it turns out, we settle in a suburban community with no farm, no lake, and no open countryside. So much for being able to control circumstances! Nevertheless, I find happiness in this new world and learn to feel at home in Louisville. Life during these seven years until I go to college offers many fun adventures.

Although America's navigable rivers tend to flow north-south, the Ohio River is one of the few that courses east-west. Because most river cargo travels east to west and west to east, barge traffic on the Ohio is heavy and continuous. The early 1950s witness gradual replacement of sternwheelers, or paddlewheel tugs, by more efficient twin-screw diesels, and by the end of the decade few of these elegant river queens are left.

An easy two-mile bike ride from home, the river offers many adventures on my 12-foot *Yot*. As a pre-teen I bemoan the passing of sternwheelers not for sentimental reasons but for selfish ones when I discover a new sailing experience. Unlike the modern diesel tugs that create minimal wake, as sternwheelers pass they churn up waves five feet high from trough to peak—waves that roll out a quarter mile. When one of these classics approaches, I trim *Yot's* sail to come alongside, then just as it passes, I tack across into turbulent whitewater thrown up by the paddlewheel, sailing as close to the stern as possible. Once in the wake, I turn directly away and for several minutes enjoy pitching violently back and forth as *Yot* surges and plunges. Meanwhile, the tug captain blasts with whistles, horns, and loudspeakers to get me away from his barge, but this only adds to the fun.

Six Mile Island, so named because it's six miles upriver from Louisville, is a wooded, uninhabited island that becomes a second home. On weekends I frequently load *Yot* with camping equipment and, together with other sailing buddies in their own boats, set off to explore this large, undiscovered kingdom. Years earlier a farmer had tried to graze cows there and when the venture failed, left his livestock behind. Today the descendants are wild, threatening, and don't take kindly to visitors. A few close encounters remind us this is their territory, not ours.

A certain beach protected by offshore rocks and tree stumps is a favorite because of the challenge to sail through this maze. Here I set up my campsite amidst raccoons, squirrels, chipmunks, and other wildlife. These critters have been isolated on the island for so long they have no fear of people and are easily tamed with a handful of nuts. Six Mile Island is a young boy's paradise, and I use it as a personal retreat whenever wanting to be alone.

I can't remember when competition first became part of my life, but it seems every activity has always prompted the urge to compete and win. For example, when we lived in Illinois and I crewed for my father during sailboat races, he invariably won. So perhaps it's natural that when I started racing in weekend regattas, winning took on special significance. On the Ohio River I often race with Wendy as crew, and except for those events when our combined weight, less than that of an average adult, can't hold the boat down in strong winds, we are likely to win. In our family, winning is neither praised nor celebrated. It is quietly expected, a highly effective motivator that I accept as the norm. During these years, a typical summer family weekend centers on sailing regattas. Mom and Dad, sailing in a larger-class boat, return home with their trophy, while Wendy and I, sailing in a lower division, return with ours. The next day, trophies already relegated to the back of a closet and forgotten, we make plans for the following week's races.

Tennis presents another family activity that sharpens the urge to compete. Weekends at the Louisville Boat Club's tennis courts find us engaged in doubles tournaments of fathers-daughters, mothers-sons, fathers-sons, etc. The most spirited games occur when four of us team off for family doubles, and it's a proud day when Wendy and I finally defeat our parents.

During these youthful years not only is attendance at the Episcopal Church unimportant; it is a nuisance because it ruins part of a weekend. When compared to playing tennis, sailing, hiking, cutting firewood, or pursuing other adventures, going to church feels like a waste. If Mom and Dad are so motivated on a Sunday morning, off we all go to church; otherwise, we're free to enjoy Sunday morning at leisure.

Sometime in the late '50s Vance Packard's book, *The Status Seekers*, lists, among other rankings, the status of America's religions. Episcopalianism tops the list and immediately membership of our church swells. Mom and Dad, as if to show we had been there long before the influx, begin to attend more regularly.

Dad coordinates a building campaign to accommodate the increase in church membership, and six months later the church building has doubled in size with several architectural features that I find both confusing and disturbing. For example, the cross on the altar is mounted with rollers on a vertical track so that by sliding it down, the cross disappears into a wooden housing. Ash trays are mounted into the church pews along with small pull-out tables for coffee and refreshments. This turns a church for worship into a recreation hall for secular functions.

Worship service ends, down goes the cross into its hiding place, and even before many parishioners finish prayers and rise from their knees, out come the cigarettes and coffee. Talk turns to parties and sporting activities as women flaunt new hats and dresses. My conclusion? Social life at our church is more important than any other aspect.

For years I serve as an acolyte or crucifer at Sunday service. I light the candles, carry the cross in the procession, and try to look pious while attending to the ritual duties I fulfill. Ironically, I'm applauded for exemplary behavior on Sunday and scolded for bad conduct the rest of the week.

Barbara Tucker, the church administrator who becomes a friend, shares a secret one day. As I am looking through the register of church members who died, Mrs. Tucker, looking over my shoulder and pointing as her finger jumps to names on the list, repeats, "Suicide, suicide, suicide...." In this way I learn that church membership doesn't guarantee a harmonious life.

The church presents an enigma. Every activity makes sense and is enjoyable except the part that has to do with worship. Church picnics and outings are fun, as are youth discussions relating to what is going on in our adolescent lives. The parishioners have a good time and are pleasant people, and Reverend Stephen Davenport is a fun-loving guy who relates well to us teenagers. But then why all this somber worship business? Pictures showing a sorrowful Jesus gazing down on us from the cross puts a terrible damper on things. During worship service, people who are normally so pleasant and animated become dour faced as they joylessly parrot from prayer books. The church presents a sad Christ, but if Christ couldn't laugh, then who could? I imagine Jesus must have been an immensely happy guy, enjoying life to its fullest and in constant celebration. He loved to eat, drink, feast, and celebrate with friends. Surely his idea of living life wasn't for folks just to sit around mirthlessly engaging in solemn conversation.

Furthermore, there is this thing about guilt that the church uses to bring us into a relationship with Christ. Surely this judgmental Christ couldn't be the same guy who is also trying to teach us about love. As a young teenager, I can't make sense out of this and when I question our minister or other adults, their answers make even less sense. So I give up questioning and just go along with the game. Worship service, it seems, is the price of admission one pays to participate in the pleasant aspects of church life.

From the onset of cold weather in late fall until the flood waters of the Ohio River subside in spring, there's no possibility of sailing; so, I look for another activity. No farm is at hand to provide endless hours of adventure like those I had known in Illinois and Connecticut. And the relatively mild Louisville winters don't offer cold weather sports activities. Days are drizzly and dreary—the kind of weather that keeps people cooped up. I feel restless until a friend invites me to his weekly Boy Scout meeting. At last I have found what I'm looking for: Scouting offers opportunity for adventures as well as a focus on achievement. The possibility of earning progressively higher ranks as well as a limitless number of merit badges appeals to my instincts to compete and achieve.

At age 13 I enter the Scouting movement and for the next four years this, along with school, becomes the major focus of life. Joining Boy Scout Troop 109 (sponsored by our church), I set objectives of progressing as fast as possible up the Scouting ranks while creating as much fun and mischief as possible. I succeed in both respects, progressing quickly from Tenderfoot to Second Class, then to First Class, and earning merit badges all in the first year. Fearful this will alienate jealous friends who have fallen behind, I redeem myself with constant pranks that become a continual source of amusement, even though the laughter is often at my expense.

My usual punishment is banishment from the troop for two to three weeks. After putting rocks in the knapsack of the slowest, weakest hiker on the Lincoln Trail hike—loading him with a burden he didn't realize he had until he carried it for ten miles—I receive a two-week suspension for not complying with the Scouting spirit. When the scoutmaster finds me swimming alone in the darkened camp swimming pool after midnight at one of the jamborees, I receive a three-week banishment. However, returning to troop meetings after a sentence is served, I'm given a hero's welcome by the other Scouts—a reception that irritates the adult leaders who are further irked because I bring the completed requirements for another merit badge or for the next step up the Scouting ranks.

Most people can identify half a dozen turning points in life. One of mine occurs at age 15 at a Scout meeting after returning from being banished following an alleged misconduct. The leaders reorganize our troop, which had become too large, and create an Explorer Post for those 16 years and older. As names are called out, classmates are assigned to the new unit. I'm not on the list, a reminder I'm a year ahead of myself and thus the youngest in class. With the departure of the older boys, all leadership positions in the remainder of the troop are empty, and now comes the shock. As the scoutmaster calls out names of the new leaders, I sense a mischievous chuckle in his voice and soon learn why: He appoints me as the new Senior Patrol Leader, the troop's highest position of authority! Whaaaaaaat? I am dumbfounded, and it seems as if everyone is looking at me with disbelief—everyone, that is, except the scoutmaster who is smiling mysteriously.

*(It isn't until years later after reading a book on organizational behavior that I understood he was applying the theory that deviant elements of a group will conform when given responsibility. The scoutmaster made a huge bet.)*

The impact of this appointment is overwhelming. Until now I had looked upon leaders as targets for pranks. However, if I am to lead the troop of 50 Scouts, I can no longer be the troublemaker. My sense of achievement, pride, and ego demand that I live up to this position. Determined to succeed in another challenging adventure, this mischievous 15-year-old matures overnight.

My first actions are to meet with my former co-conspirators to tell them this mischief-making must stop. In many cases such directives aren't necessary because several have also been appointed to positions of leadership and are going through the same changes I am. As for others, I know their games and am not about to be fooled the way we tricked the previous leaders.

The first leadership test occurs in a field behind the church one Saturday afternoon when patrols compete to build fires to boil pails of water. One patrol "accidentally" spills its canister of water, so they go back to the church for a refill. On their return I intercept, and putting a finger in the water, confirm suspicions. They have filled their pail with hot water so they could be the first to bring it to a boil. I have caught them in the act.

Another incident involves an old trick often pulled on a newer Scout at jamborees, namely sending him to a neighboring campsite to borrow a "sky hook" purportedly needed to set up an oversize tent. Of course, at the next campsite the Scouts tell him the item was just loaned to the next troop, so the newbie continues the quest visiting a number of other sites until a compassionate scoutmaster tells the frustrated boy it's a ruse. At an assembly of the troop, I explain the hoax to the newcomers and notify the guys that there will be consequences if anyone tries it.

A lot of kids straighten up over the next several weeks, and morale improves as we younger ones fill the shoes of those recently departed from our ranks. In short order the troop coalesces into a spirited, capable group ready to undertake any challenge and adventure. We enter the jamborees in our region and often walk away with victories in the competitions. With the enterprising guidance of a dynamic scoutmaster and the assistance of many fathers, we experience every dimension of Scouting from tracking animals in the wild and canoeing on Kentucky's rivers to learning basic first aid and winter survival skills.

My goal is to rise through all Scouting ranks to the top. With renewed determination I work hard to earn as many merit badges as possible, and in 1956, at age 15, I reach the highest level of Eagle Scout with bronze, gold, and silver palms. Still I continue, earning enough merit badges to qualify for an unprecedented fourth palm. When the scoutmaster inquires of Boy Scouts of America's headquarters about what to do, they tell him this is the highest anyone has ever attained and award me a second silver palm. I also work to earn other Scouting awards: three Lincoln Trail medals (for hiking routes Abraham Lincoln hiked as a youth), the Order of the Arrow (an honorary Scouting society), and the God and Country Award (for service to the church and community). Soon I'm overloaded with sashes, medals, and embroidered patches weighing heavily on my uniform.

All those Boy Scout canoe trips, campouts, and mountain hikes—what better way could there be to build self-reliance than to enjoy the natural world while also learning skills to care for oneself under almost any set of circumstances? (These experiences were instrumental in my choice to become an outdoor travel writer years later.)

I complete elementary education at four public schools in Kentucky: sixth grade at Ballard Elementary, seventh and eighth at Eastern Middle, ninth at Waggoner Junior High, and 10th through 12th at Eastern High. I feel ambivalent about school. Although it takes me away from outdoor adventures and limits a sense of freedom, I nevertheless love learning and relish striving for top grades.

In high school I discover a different aspect of competition. Previously, desire to excel served as incentive to work hard in preparation for an event. Shouldn't one spend hours on a tennis court to become a good player? Or devote many afternoons sailing to master the fine points of racing in regattas? But I discover the attitude of schoolmates is different. If I spend hours preparing for an exam and score high, I won't be considered a winner but merely a "grind." Classmates think that, obviously, anybody who studies is bound to do well. Respect is reserved for those who do well without benefit of studying—success without hitting the books is proof of one's superior intelligence and innate ability.

Having a cavalier attitude about the following day's exam and spending the prior evening engaged in a non-academic activity such as going to a party, can make a great impression. My peers frown upon any evidence of striving. The star athlete tries to give the impression he is naturally talented and doesn't need to put in the hours of practice that less-capable athletes must endure. The school's fastest sprinter, who later wins the state championship, lights up a cigarette after classes and scoffs at any suggestion his natural abilities could be compromised.

How can I make the right tradeoff? On one hand, I feel pressured by classmates not to be labeled a grind. On the other hand, I want to do well academically. Furthermore, I enjoy settling down with books and studies in the evening. Even though I hold offices in several school organizations, write for the school newspaper, and am on the tennis and chess teams, I dare not risk being known as someone who spends spare time cooped up with books. A neat solution unexpectedly presents itself—one that brings me closer to Wendy than anything previously in our brother-sister relationship.

Despite agonizing years of piano lessons, I enjoy listening for hours to the musical geniuses of 17th, 18th, and 19th, century composers. So, I extricate myself from the usual hanging-around-after-school activities by explaining I want to go home to indulge in this pastime. Although my friends find me a little eccentric, they accept this explanation.

Once home with music playing, I delve into my studies. Wendy, three years younger at an age when a sister is subservient to an older brother, willingly accepts the job of turning over the records so I'm not distracted from studying. With a supply of snacks, we seclude ourselves with music and homework. Three symphonies and two concertos later, we emerge to Mom's call for dinner. During those long afternoons with Wendy, although we exchange very few words, we develop a close bond that lasts into our adult lives.

*(From childhood to adolescence, the world of adults never seemed important to me. Adults simply blurred into the background, occasionally coming into focus either to reprimand when I would overstep some boundary or to support when self-sufficiency would fail me. The adult world seemed a static realm in which ideas never changed as years passed. What I didn't realize while changing and maturing through these childhood and adolescent years, is that Mom and Dad, far from being static, were going through changes of their own. Because Wendy and I were five to 10 years older than the children of their contemporaries, they raised us without the advantage of sharing parenting challenges with similar-aged parents. Becoming parents in their teens, Mom and Dad had to pioneer child-raising on their own.)*

Vacation times are bonding times for our family. Passionate about sailing, we often charter yachts to cruise the Bahamas, Chesapeake Bay, British Virgin Islands and Long Island Sound. Cooped up aboard a sailboat for two weeks, we share many rousing adventures as well as peaceful silences. These experiences, which I forever treasure, bind us as a family. Nosing into an anchorage with Dad at the helm, we work in perfect harmony: Dad alerts me when to drop the mainsail, Wendy stands ready to secure the flailing lines, while Mom awaits the cue to release the anchor. Dad and I, both early risers, often sit in silence in the cockpit watching as the soft colors of sunrise light up the sky while the boat swings quietly at anchor.

At 17 I leave home for college. *(Although I return many times over the following years, a phase of life is over. My parents, sister, and I continue to play tennis and sail together on occasion, but the family life I knew growing up is now gone.)* Having yet to experience a sense of openness and sensitivity in relationships, I live life more as a struggle than a flow. Why should I stop striving to control life? Why should I trust? Everything I want comes because I fight for it. I take life on my terms, not on its terms. If the goal I seek is elusive, I increase the effort to bring it within reach.

To experience any real peace and silence, from time to time I retreat from people and group activities. Only when alone in Nature—usually while sailing or hiking—do I experience glimpses of the inner stillness and peace that might help me receive life as a gift instead of fighting to catch it.

Most of the time I feel the need to struggle to get what I want. Competition and achievement are the scaffolding on which I have built my life, and I see no reason to change. As long as I can pick the arena and set the rules for playing the game, I will come out on top. Whenever I find myself sliding into emotion—areas of feeling where control is difficult—I quickly escape into the world of achievement, the world I know. The blinders of competition and achievement have caused me to miss much during my adolescent years. I have missed living from the heart by assuming the essence of life is found in the goals rather than in the journey.

*(Not until many years pass will I learn competing and achieving have little to do with joyous living.)*

[1953, Miami, age 12] Bat Rays

[1953, Louisville, age 12]
(me, upper right), 7th grade, Eastern High

[1957, Louisville, age 16] Boy Scouts and me as Sr Patrol Leader

[1957, Ohio River, age 16] "*Yot*" Leading at the Mark, with Wendy as Crew

[Autumn 1958, Louisville, age 17] Clockwise: Me, Wendy, Dad, Mom

# 5
# Princeton — From Bow to Stern

*9/58 - 5/62, Ages 17 - 21*

I want to study engineering as well as pursue a liberal arts education, a difficult combination because most good engineering universities are weak in liberal arts and vice versa. Furthermore, I'd prefer a campus in the country, not an urban environment. After visiting campuses of five schools, only two fit the criteria: Duke University in North Carolina and Princeton in New Jersey. After receiving acceptances from both, I choose Princeton and enroll as a freshman with the Class of 1962, no doubt influenced by the fact that it was my father's alma mater.

The first week on campus I experience a return to my origins. Strolling down Nassau Street to the apartment where we lived while Dad completed his senior year, I sense I've been here before. Lake Carnegie, which becomes a focal point for the next four years, exerts an even stronger pull. Whether I'm drawn to the lake because it's the alleged site of my conception, or simply because I'm attracted to lakes, I don't know. The former belief is more emotional, the latter more logical. *(Furthermore, when I once asked my mother where I was conceived, she, somewhat embarrassed, assured me it was not on the shores of Lake Carnegie!)*

Moving from familiar Louisville to the unknown of this distant campus stirs up a feeling of insecurity. At home I enjoy a reputation as an honors student, class leader, and Eagle Scout. But at Princeton everyone has claim to impressive honors. Class presidents, football captains, valedictorians, and others with notable accomplishments are no big deal. Several classmates have published books, composed music, or earned national recognition for achievements. Among members of my class, I'm quite average, if even that.

Initially the class divides into two groups: "High School Harrys" and "Peter Preps." Ours is the first class in which the percentage of public school graduates is greater than those from private schools. But even with numbers on our side, the preppies immediately take charge. Because eastern prep schools operate much like Ivy League universities, the preppies adjust with ease to college life. Prestigious boarding schools such as Andover, Exeter, Lawrenceville, and Choate sent 30 or more students each, so many already know each other. Those of us from public schools are initially dazzled by the sophistication of our prep school peers. But then something happens that causes their façade to crumble.

Princeton does not yet admit women, so our only contact with the other sex occurs when they are invited from nearby women's colleges for an evening. As our first mixer gets underway, we drift into the party room in twos and threes, sauntering back and forth while sizing up the guests. Then something strange happens. The so-called unsophisticated High School Harrys are dancing or sitting with their newfound acquaintances and enjoying the party. The shy, uncomfortable Peter Preps are still walking back and forth eyeing the remaining prospects, hesitant to ask for a dance. Because the only women they know are sisters and mothers, they're unaccustomed to first encounters.

By the end of the party, a complete reversal of roles has taken place. While the preppies look on with embarrassment from the sidelines, the rest of us enjoy ourselves on the dance floor and relish their discomfort. Now the preppies get their full share of teasing. Afterward we all relax and drop the game-playing, and our class begins to coalesce into a single unit as we really get to know each other.

The engineering departments at Princeton are separated from the rest of the university by Washington Road, which in many respects represents an impassable gorge. Those on the liberal arts side regard engineers as vocational trainees rather than serious students. The engineers, meanwhile, view their liberal arts classmates as missing an opportunity to prepare for the real world. Washington Road separates these two worlds, and I'm unable to decide which side I want to be on.

At the orientation meeting for engineering students the dean presents statistics that make a guy wonder if pursuing a technical degree is really worthwhile. He tells us to look to our left and to our right and then pauses while we do so. He resumes by saying that of the five of us sitting alongside each other, only four will make it to graduation ceremonies four years later. We have a tough curriculum ahead of us. In addition to carrying a full technical regimen, we must complete the minimum required liberal arts courses. Even if we make it through the program, if statistics are any indication, he says within seven years three-quarters of us will no longer be working in the field. The implication is we will have either dropped out or moved into management. Nonetheless, the doubts the dean casts do not deter me.

I immensely enjoy the academic studies during these four years, and by taking the minimum of engineering courses to meet department requirements, I have opportunities for a variety of liberal arts courses. However, I'm disappointed not to be able to take all the classes I want, because there's not enough time to do all the required work. Then halfway through freshman year I find a way to handle double the normal course load. By auditing courses I receive no credit but can attend the lectures. Relieved of the necessity of homework and exams, I can keep up with minimum reading to audit the same number of liberal arts courses as the engineering classes I take for credit. There is, however, a dilemma—one that gives me nightmares. I sometimes lose track of which are the audit courses, and which are the registered ones. At exam time I must remember to prepare for the courses that count.

I don't intend to spend all the time with my nose buried in books and do intend to pursue a sport: Which one to choose? Tennis and sailing are candidates, but I had enough of those in high school. Soccer, rugby, football, lacrosse, fencing, and hockey are out because they will be dominated by those who played in secondary school.

I ultimately select a sport where chances for success seem doomed from the start. At orientation, I notice outside the office a mark on the wall slightly above the top of my head. Standing nearby are several tall, muscular upperclassmen who every so often address one of us incoming freshmen. A classmate explains the upperclassmen are on the rowing crew, and anyone who exceeds the six-foot mark on the wall is a potential recruit. Standing as tall as possible, I proceed past the mark hoping there will be a tap on my shoulder. When there is none, I pick up course material and promptly forget the matter.

That evening when the same upper-class oarsmen come to our dorm to seek out a tall, lanky freshman down the hall, I listen as they try to convince him to show up for rowing practice the following week. Learning that crew is the only sport for which no previous experience is required, I make a mental note of where and when this practice is to take place.

On the appointed day I stroll down to the boat house at Lake Carnegie. For tryouts, 16 of us sit, eight to a side, in a barge that must have been designed to resemble the ancient Phoenician trading vessels powered by slaves chained to oars. Although there are no chains, there's little other difference. At the stern the coxswain barks out commands and sets the cadence for the stroke. Coach Dutch Schock, a paunchy, heavy-set ex-oarsman who basks in the glory of having been a member of the championship Olympic crew in 1936 at Berlin, parades back and forth along the center walkway staring with apparent disgust at his new prospects. Close on his heels is his black Labrador retriever seemingly alert for the command to attack any oarsman not pulling his weight.

During these trials Coach judges us on size and muscle, both of which I'm sadly lacking. At 175 pounds, I'm too light for heavyweight crew—which averages 190 pounds—and too heavy for lightweight crew—where maximum is 155 pounds. Furthermore, at 5' 11", I'm three inches shorter than the average height of either crew.

These troublesome observations elicit the red-headed determination not to accept physical shortcomings as limitations. Although I don't know how to row, I'm encouraged because neither do many of the others, so in that respect we're all starting on equal footing. In addition, I'm a year younger than my classmates, which means there's a chance to shoot up a few inches and bulk up on muscle. My hips are still wider than my shoulders, but I have hopes of developing further in my chest and shoulders.

When I show up the next day for practice, the coaches appear surprised that I didn't withdraw after tryouts. They shrug and relegate me to the bow section of the barge—the place they assign the weakest oarsmen. They then go about coaching those in the middle and stern seats, leaving those in the bow to pick up what we can.

After a few weeks of daily rowing practice, the more promising oarsmen move into shells, leaving the rest of us to graduate into the center and rear seats, emptying the bow. Although left behind in the barge, I stick with the daily practices, determined to show I merit a position on the crew. Then one glorious day we laggards also move from the barge to a shell. Our promotion, however, is not due to rowing proficiency. An alumnus has donated a new shell, and the other crews move up to better boats, thus freeing the oldest and most deteriorated one into which my fellow would-be oarsmen and I move. It's a great step up, and I resolve it will be the first of many.

Throughout the spring rowing season freshman year, I remain in the lowest boat. Coach assures us that only with our participation does he have the depth to develop good crews that can go on to win. The implication is unfortunately clear: the good crews he intends to develop do not include us. Rather, relegation to our boat is punishment meted out to oarsmen in the upper boats if they don't perform.

We lower oarsmen quickly learn we're in a self-defeating situation. When a demoted oarsman joins us, we aspire to move up to his former seat by making an extra effort to beat one of the boats above us in a racing trial. However, if we win, the coaches attribute victory to the oarsman recently demoted and promptly re-promote him. This practice is so demoralizing that we lose the subsequent trial by a wide margin, which in turn confirms that the former demoted oarsman was responsible.

Although we work as hard as everyone else, we derive none of the benefits. No trips to away-from-home regattas. No meals at the training table. And no racing in the home regattas. Instead we're used merely as handymen to assist in race preparations. It's not surprising that many lower oarsmen drop the sport, but with determination I continue to show up for practice throughout freshman year.

When summer arrives I embark on a body-building campaign by undertaking as much physical work as possible. Securing a farm job in the hills of Kentucky, I engage day after day in strenuous labor. Every night after 12 hours of lifting bales of hay or working in the fields, I collapse into bed, satisfied that I'm gaining both muscle and weight.

By the time I return to college in fall, I have indeed grown, and my shoulders and chest have exploded. Moreover, I have mastered a one-hand chin-up with either hand, an exercise Coach says is the best indicator of arm strength. This feat, which none of the other rowers can perform, elevates me in their eyes as well as in the estimation of the coaches. Because my new body is narrow at the waist and broad in the shoulders, one classmate gives me the nickname "Wedge," which sticks the rest of my college years. (*A roommate later embellishes the name by adding derogatorily, "Wedge—the simplest tool known to man!"*)

Although I have put on enough weight to qualify as a heavyweight oarsman, I still lack the height. Having grown only half an inch to 5' 11½", I'm the shortest on the squad and unlike the taller oarsmen, don't have a long sweep in my stroke. Thus, the start of sophomore year finds me relegated to the lowest boat again. In racing trials our boat consistently comes in last; it looks as though all my effort over the summer is for naught.

Then one day Coach notices that our coxswain consistently turns the rudder slightly to starboard thereby creating turbulence that slows us. He shouts to the coxswain to keep the rudder straight, and we resume rowing. We're all surprised as our shell makes a slow arc toward the port bank. To avoid a collision, the coxswain turns the rudder sharply, which steers the shell back on course but also acts as a brake. Only then is it evident that in spite of my short stroke on the starboard oar, the port oarsmen can't create an adequate offset. Therefore, the coxswain has to compensate with the rudder. Coach immediately pulls me out of the forward section of the shell and puts me nearer the stern where I have less impact on the steering. The next day during racing trials we handily beat the next higher boat because, with everyone motivated, we all pull harder than before.

I'm elated a few days later when Coach moves me to a port seat near the bow of the higher boat. After the initial excitement subsides, I realize I'm in a precarious position. I know my former teammates will make a special effort in the next race to distinguish themselves. If they succeed, it will be to my detriment, and so I alert the starboard oarsmen in my new boat:

"I want to warn you guys that I'm gonna pull you over to the shore, so you better give it everything you can." This fires them up to the extent that we succeed not only in leaving my old boat far behind, but also in beating the shell the next level above us.

I take mischievous delight in creating consternation among the coaches who are baffled that one of the lower boats with less experienced oarsmen could beat the crew of more experienced upperclassmen. Granted the win was a fluke, but again it reinforces the invaluable lesson that fierce determination can win.

Soon I'm moved up another level, but here my progress stops. Strength has brought me this far, but lack of height limits me from going further. The physics of the situation is simple: I'm able to pull water quickly over a shorter distance while the others pull water more slowly over a longer distance. It's an even tradeoff. My shorter stroke offsets the advantage of my extra power.

Princeton crews have never been an outstanding power in collegiate rowing, and several explanations could account for it. The most common theory lays the blame on Lake Carnegie itself. Because the lake is small and well protected by surrounding hills, the calm waters are ideal for developing oarsmen with flawless rowing form for which Princeton's has a long-held reputation. Unfortunately, style alone doesn't win races. Other colleges practice on large rivers or sizable lakes where crews deal with rough water, currents, and shifting winds. Any of these conditions is enough to throw a Princeton crew into turmoil, so regattas held when conditions aren't ideal usually end in defeat.

Regardless, our coaches insist that each oarsman develop a flawless rowing style. Being in one of the higher boats, I must now learn the graceful subtleties of handling an oar, which the coaches had overlooked teaching me. Until now I have capitalized on pure strength, but my rough style can rock the shell and cause problems for teammates. Despite many months of grueling effort, when spring rowing season arrives, I have yet to make it into the varsity or even junior varsity crews.

While analyzing the finer points of rowing, I conclude that it's quite a ridiculous sport. First, all oarsmen face backwards, which in itself is silly. Second, although the sport requires maximum strength and puts a lot of stress on the boat, the hull is paper-thin—a hard push with a finger is enough to make a hole in the fragile bottom, and a misplaced step when boarding can capsize the shell or even sink it. Third, because oarsmen are required to keep eyes on the back of the neck in front, they can't see what's going on. Turning the head can throw off the rhythm of the stroke and start the shell to yawing. Fourth, crew is the only sport with everyone sitting down, in other words, you sit on your ass and work it off at the same time. Fifth, action consists of only four simple motions: catch, pull, release, and recover. That's all there is to it—no hidden tactics or strategies involved, only the mindless repetition of these four movements. Sixth, in a typical season, eight races take place on successive Saturdays beginning in early spring. Each race lasts less than three minutes. Therefore, total time of competition for a season is less than half an hour. Daily training, however, lasts two to three hours and includes dry-land conditioning throughout the school year from September through May, which adds up to more than 500 hours of practice. This regimen yields a ratio of 20 hours of practice for every minute of competition, a practice-to-competition relationship higher than any other sport. The goal, easily forgotten, is to win races, not just develop perfect form.

As the racing season gets underway my sophomore year, I'm still in the third boat and not able to compete. But after our varsity and junior varsity are soundly trounced in the first two races, Coach moves me into the junior varsity shell. Despite intense competition, I retain my promotion.

I now merit a place at the training table with dinners of top-quality meats and fresh vegetables and salads. Oarsmen require the highest caloric intake of any sport, and the chefs feed us 5,000 calories each night. For the remainder of the season, I travel to all the away-from-home regattas. Most importantly, I enjoy the satisfaction that two years of effort have finally paid off.

When the academic year ends, I return home where I need a long rest from sports before returning as a junior in fall. After decompressing for a couple of weeks, I join a summer-abroad program through the University of Louisville and fly to Europe. Beginning with an internship in Paris at the Société Générale Banque, the summer of 1960 proves to be an exciting time. Living at the University of Paris, I commute by Metro each day to work and after sunset explore the nightlife of the City of Lights. But I'm not here just to work at a bank, and after a month I embark on a hitchhiking tour of Europe.

Separating from other students and traveling alone, I have no trouble meeting people at every stopover. Seeing the great European works of art and immersing in the events of history are interesting but not as much fun as meeting and relating to people in the countries I visit. Europe of the present is much more fascinating than artifacts in museums, commemorative monuments, significant landmarks, and statues commemorating victories in battles over 3,000 years of history.

With a student Eurail Pass, I travel at no cost wherever and whenever my whims suggest. Having a limited budget, I find a clever way to avoid hotel expenses. Each evening after dinner I proceed to the local railway station, hop on an overnight train, and sleep without disturbance in a comfortable reclining seat. One night I might travel from Hamburg to Munich. Another night might find me on an overnight from Rome to Amsterdam, and so it goes. Hitchhiking between cities during the day also saves expenses, and my student card buys inexpensive meals at local universities. After hitching from London to Dover and then boarding the ferry to Calais, I befriend a pleasant couple who offer a lift to Paris, the last leg of my travels, in their late model Mercedes Benz—the only luxury travel that summer.

I return home with three things: an attempt at growing a beard, a decision to one day live in Europe, and a case of hepatitis and jaundice that sends me to bed for six weeks. However, I'm well on the way to recovery in time to return to Princeton for junior year, although mindful of doctor's orders to stay in the dorm and rest when classes end each day. Furthermore, the doctor prescribes rigid diet restrictions and bans crew or any other strenuous activities. This last order is toughest of all, but I resign myself to following orders, knowing it's doubtful I could row anyway because the hepatitis has not only weakened me but also slimmed me by 15 pounds.

For three months I follow a quiet, studious life, and my grades and health make significant improvements. Upon returning home at Christmas, I undergo a medical checkup and receive a clean bill of health, which happily means lifting the ban on alcohol. As an eligible bachelor, I am invited to many holiday debutante parties where the young ladies of Louisville are "presented to society." It's a wonderful time full of gala events with dancing, parties, great food, and, yes, Kentucky bourbon. Donning a tuxedo practically every night, I dine and dance with girls I grew up with and knew as friends, but suddenly see as beautiful young women who look ever so stunning in elegant gowns.

Back on campus, I return to a body-building program to put on muscle and weight in hopes of getting back to rowing by early spring. Throughout the rest of winter, I train with the wrestling team, and by the time ice thaws on Lake Carnegie, I'm again able to do one-arm chin-ups. Soon we're back on the water, and I'm as fit and strong as ever although demoted to one of the lower boats for missing fall practice. However, the respite from rowing did a lot of good because in addition to whetting my appetite to get back to the sport, I feel a new rhythm and confidence in handling an oar.

About this time, I enjoy another rare moment of tremendous satisfaction. Due to the resilience and lightness needed, oars are made of pine with a backing of ash, hickory, or other hardwood added for strength. It's the dream of every rower to break an oar, and this is exactly what happens. One afternoon in the middle of taking "power 10" strokes, I'm pulling with all my strength when my oar snaps in two. Suddenly I'm holding one-third of it while the remaining section floats nearby. Dumbfounded, I'm unsure what to do. When Coach barks orders to turn the shell and head for home, there is nothing to do but sit quietly while the others row me, like a pharaoh in his royal craft, back to the boat house. Once we're back on land Coach, who has retrieved the floating section of the oar, presents it to me as a memento.

A few weeks later I snap another oar. This time Coach chastises me for destroying university property, threatens to send a bill for replacement cost, and doesn't let me keep the broken sections. *(Even so, I've kept the pieces of the first oar, which hang prominently wherever I've lived in the years that followed!)* With a twinkle in his eye, Coach Schock then addresses the rest of the crew:

"The only way I can stop Schroeder from breaking all the oars is to give him one of the newest, strongest oars." These oars are reserved for the newest shells, and in this indirect way he promotes me to the varsity boat.

I can hardly contain the mixture of laughter and tears that well up. The varsity boat! The culmination of all I've been striving for, but I'm not prepared for the abruptness with which it's presented. From this point on, my rowing career only gets better. Coach initially seats me near the bow, but before racing season, moves me to the six seat in the middle, the so-called "engine room," reserved for the strongest rowers. *(In an eight-oar shell the bow is the "one seat" and the stern position is the "eight seat" where the "stroke", who sets the cadence, sits.)*

Our first race is against the U.S. Naval Academy at Annapolis. Having represented America at the Olympics in Rome the previous summer, they are the crew to beat. Heading into the race, no one imagines we have a chance—everyone expects us to finish far behind the winner.

However, miracles do happen. In spite of rough waters on the Severn River where the race is held, we prove to be a Cinderella crew by handily beating the Middies. *(Students at the U.S. Naval Academy are called Midshipmen, otherwise known as "Middies.")* Our varsity heavyweight crew claims the first major regatta victory Princeton has won in years.

Rowing tradition dictates that losers give their racing shirts to winners in the corresponding seat. I still chuckle when I recall how the burly, six-plus footer looking down at me while handing over his shirt probably thought, "How in heck did this short, smart-ass Ivy Leaguer beat me?" He should have looked more closely at my arms and chest! Although final results are mixed, other victories make this season Princeton's winningest in many years.

Princeton requires all engineers to work in their field during the summer between junior and senior years, so I get a job in Louisville at General Electric's Appliance Park. I enjoy the daily commute riding with Dad but am less than enamored with developing test equipment to monitor quality-control problems in the Range and Water Heater Department. Although I value my engineering studies at Princeton, this real-life experience of spending all day standing at a workbench designing and building hardware mock-ups to meet test requirements is not for me. I dislike the tediousness and find the career engineers boring.

Off-the-job time this summer is another matter. I spend many happy hours sailing on the Ohio River and playing tennis at the Louisville Boat Club. It's also a bittersweet time, because, although I will always be welcome at home, it's the last summer I'll be living with my family.

Senior year is also bittersweet because it, too, represents the final phase of a happy time in college. I love engineering studies and the audited classes, but now my focus is at the boathouse where I retain a varsity seat despite strong competition from those in the lower boats.

After final exams in spring the crew moves to Syracuse, New York, to begin four hours of daily practice on Lake Onondaga for two weeks leading up to the Intercollegiate Rowing Association Regatta. The regatta coincides with graduation, making it impossible for any of us seniors to attend commencement. The dean's words during freshman year that one of five freshmen would not make it to graduation come to mind. Indeed, I am that one in five, but not for the reason he mentioned!

The crowning point of my rowing career occurs in Syracuse when Coach decides that the stroke—the oarsman sitting furthest in the stern who sets the cadence—does not have the endurance to pace the boat for the three-mile distance (more than double the usual one-and-a quarter mile races). Although late for changes, he moves me to this key position. I'm ecstatic about taking over the stroke seat but sobered by the realization it's now up to me to meld eight of us into a team.

One day when a local newspaper reporter rides with Coach in his launch, I encourage everyone to make an extra effort, and we turn in an outstanding time trial. Thinking he has an exclusive story, the reporter heralds us in his column the next day as the boat to watch for a surprise victory. Expectations are high.

Race day finally arrives. We are up against 18 crews representing all the nation's major rowing colleges and universities. At the gun, our boat gets off to an excellent start and we are among the leaders. However, after passing the second mile, oarsman number seven, sitting directly behind me, and also the former stroke, who had taken my previous six seat, both start to flag and all but collapse. We fall back but finish a respectable fifth.

This race is a fitting climax to my struggle that started four years earlier when relegated to the lowest position in the barge while everyone else moved into racing shells. Over the course of four years I progressed from a scrawny freshman in the bow seat of the lowest boat to a super-fit senior in the top spot in the varsity boat—a success that I attribute to tenacious determination.

*(Twenty years pass before I return to the Princeton boathouse to honor this sport—a sport that I still love—that played a major role during my undergraduate years. At my 20th reunion in April 1982, I donate an eight-person shell in tribute to Grumpy, my maternal grandfather, who rowed on the crew while studying at Oxford's St. John's College.*

*Rather than deeding the shell to the varsity crew, I break with tradition and give it to the freshman heavyweight crew. Thinking of my own experience, as I pour Lake Carnegie water from a champagne bottle on the deck of the shell, I proclaim, "I christen thee 'Alec E. Saxton.' May you win many races and may you provide the opportunity for some scrawny freshmen to move up to a better shell.")*

An ironic sidelight to my four-year-long quest is the change in rowing style that also occurred. Until the early 1960s, world rowing competitions were dominated by tall, slender U.S. competitors who rowed long sweep strokes at a cadence of 32-34 a minute. Then in 1962 a crew from Ratzeburg, Germany, made a tour of major U.S. rowing centers and shocked everyone by winning every regatta they entered and trouncing the best crews in the country. The Germans had none of the physical characteristics of America's image of the perfect rower. Relatively short and barrel-chested with broad shoulders and muscular arms, they were built the way I am.

To compensate for short-sweep strokes, something that remained my constant problem, they adopted two new measures. First, they rowed at the phenomenally high rate of 38-41 strokes per minute—20 percent higher than typical of American crews—and sustained this rapid rate because of their tremendous strength and fitness. Second, they rowed with shovel oars several inches wider and more scoop-shaped than the traditional oar, thereby enabling them to pull more water with each stroke even with a shorter sweep. I've often wondered what my rowing career would have been like if I had been born in Ratzeberg or if our coach had adopted this rowing style. Either way, this German team rewrote the rowing textbooks and set a new style that was followed for many years.

*(Later I would often reflect on opportunities missed by adjusting to a situation, as I did in rowing, rather than modifying a challenge to suit my capabilities. The Ratzeberg crew found success by pioneering a new rowing style that fit the size and stature of the oarsmen.*

*I have come to realize that people are not born to fit into molds created by others. Rather we are here to be ourselves, and if the "fit" of something isn't right, then a person does better to change the situation rather than try to be something one isn't.*

*It would be a mistake to leave the impression that my experience was nothing but an intense struggle to beat out the competition to get from last to first. Although I didn't recognize it at the time, rowing became a deep meditation. Time lost all meaning whenever the shell skimmed across silent waters and nothing could be heard except the swish of oars dipping and lifting. At such times all of existence seemed to pour into me, course through me, dissolve into the sea of my being.*

*As the setting sun cast its last reddish-orange rays, water and land emanated a magical stillness. At twilight as we turned the shells for home, our bodies fatigued, a new energy would flow into us from a source beyond our physical beings. Although no one ever talked about it, every oarsman knows the feeling. Exhausted, we simply allowed ourselves to be enfolded into the intense beauty, the magnificence, of the moment. When we reached the boat house, the first stars beckoned us home. During these blissful moments time stopped, my mind stood still, and a warm relaxation suffused my entire being to produce a state of pure meditative joy.*

*Although I don't often speak of this phenomenon, it's always been a source of pride that I pulled an oar for Princeton...and broke two of them!)*

[Christmas 1959, Louisville, age 18]
Debutante Party with Phoebe

[1961, Lake Carnegie, Princeton Campus, age 20]
Varsity heavyweight crew (me, shorty in back)

[Christmas 1962, Louisville, age 21]
Doing what I love the most

[May 1962, Princeton, age 21]
Stroke position, varsity heavyweight crew

# 6
# Get Ready to Crawl

*1/62 - 5/62, Age 21*

During this final season of crew, my studies at Princeton are in their last months as well. What a top-of-the-world feeling! Life is carefree and beautiful. We seniors are on the downhill coast to the end of our undergraduate years. Until now our class has focused on getting good grades required for graduate school or whatever job we might seek. However, we can't do much to either improve or significantly hurt GPAs, so we relax and allow the following weeks to unfold as they will.

But then a dark shadow falls across our carefree path. A relatively unknown office called the Placement Bureau reminds us that because graduation is only a few months away, we better decide soon what to do with our lives. We need to complete massive amounts of paperwork—applications, resumes, references, interview sheets, and job forms for graduate schools, government agencies, NGOs, institutions, and companies preparing their spring recruitment campaigns.

To ensure we take this seriously, the office adopts a scare tactic. It reminds us that although we are kings of our destiny now, we soon will plummet from our lofty perches to lowly, entry-level positions in real-world institutions. It's up to us to choose what type of "bottom" we want.

This reality check hits as if someone triumphantly marching along receives a sudden kick that staggers him to his knees and reduces him to a slow crawl. This "Get Ready to Crawl" shock shatters our peace.

I have no idea what I want to do. Earlier job experiences have not fired my imagination for any line of work, and the previous summer's experience at General Electric as a development engineer brought disillusionment. What, then, might be of interest?

In view of this disappointment with the business world, I wonder if getting into a corporate training program is the answer. A successful interview with IBM, known for its training programs, results in an invitation to meet the manager of the sales office in nearby Trenton. Despite dislike of IBM's reputed dress requirements—white shirts, conservative suits, and close-cropped hair—I opt to make the visit anyway.

Princeton undergraduates are not generally allowed to own cars or motorcycles. However, I've been granted an exemption allowing me to own a motorcycle, because I signed up with a campus babysitting service and often have local jobs in the community. The motorcycle also provides the much-cherished freedom of getaway weekends. On interview day I pack a suit, tie, and polished shoes into saddle bags; don a leather jacket and motorcycle boots; and set off for Trenton. Arriving at IBM's offices, I park and change into business attire on the street, unaware that anyone is witnessing the performance. Upon announcing the appointment at reception, I meet cold stares. In the manager's sterile-looking, corner office is a large window overlooking the visitors' parking lot. After a cordial greeting, the manager, dressed in corporate code, starts talking about motorcycles, a tipoff he had seen everything. Discomfort sets in when he describes the culture surrounding "IBM family life," and an ill feeling arises as he explains that when shopping at a hardware store on a Saturday morning, he dresses in slacks and a collared shirt that "does credit to IBM." The final straw: "Now we may not hire you in Trenton, but wherever you go, your boss will be wearing the same blue and white outfit I have on today."

The implication is clear—motorcycles, unkempt hair, and behavior that smacks of rebelliousness or non-conformity are not welcome here. It's evident to both of us the interview is over, and I can't get away fast enough. Back in the parking lot I delight in putting on the leather jacket and boots, stuffing business clothes into saddle bags, and roaring away, hoping the manager is watching.

Interviews with General Electric don't go much better. Because of our family's longtime relations with the company through my father and grandfather as well as through my own summer work experience, I'm invited for an interview at the plant in Philadelphia. After traveling there by train, I again return in dismay. The interviewer, thinking he is promoting his organization, outlines a career path for the next 40 years, describing in detail the anticipated progress up the hierarchical structure. He concludes the dismal report with an overview of the company's retirement benefits. I ask if there is any adventure or hope of pioneering into new endeavors within GE's structure, but he doesn't get the point. It's time to write off big corporations.

Would getting military service out of the way be the thing to do? Joining the Marines—not because of their macho fighting image, but because of their sports program—might be a good idea. Recalling the success of the compact oarsmen on the German Ratzeburg crew, I wonder if by adapting that rowing style, I might have a crack at getting to the next Olympic Games in two years in Mexico City. The Corps had supported four Marines from Princeton to train for the 1960 Olympics; maybe they would give me the same consideration.

President Kennedy's new Peace Corps program also offers an interesting possibility—one that appeals to two desires: first, to do something for those in a developing country; and second, to see more of the world. A month after I complete the application forms, the Peace Corps offers me an appointment to an agricultural development project in Hyderabad, India, and schedules me for training at a U.S. Department of Agriculture center in the Midwest. I never imagined those early work experiences on farms in Illinois and Connecticut would qualify me for anything, but my acceptance of this appointment could bring me full circle back to farm life.

Although still unsure about a career, I'm determined to get as far away from the Northeast as possible. The predictably boring lifestyle of classmates from there is unappealing. For most, graduation means going on to the next stage of a life planned since birth. After attending an Eastern prep school and graduating from an Ivy League university, they expect to settle into a Philadelphia insurance company, Wall Street brokerage, or Boston law firm where successive family generations have made careers. Being caught in a web that limits life to the social circles of a few regional cities may suit my friends, but I want to strike out in new directions.

Still undecided, I receive a notice from the Placement Bureau that a representative from Sandia Corporation will be coming to campus. Who, what, or where Sandia Corporation is, I have no idea. The message comes from the head of the office, Gordon Sykes, a man I respect highly. A former coxswain of a championship Princeton crew in the 1930s, Gordon had never missed a major rowing regatta since then, and he takes special interest in helping oarsmen get the best start in their careers. Therefore, I'm keen to follow up on his lead.

A search for literature about Sandia turns up nothing for reasons I will soon learn. Frank Bell, Princeton Class of 1937 who has flown in from Albuquerque headquarters, greets me. The suntanned executive is wearing a buckskin-type suit and a shoestring bow tie, quite a contrast from the corporate types I had met in other interviews! Frank explains the reason for booking a double interview session is because he has much to tell me about the company, including why little is publicly known.

Sandia is a private, non-profit corporation operated by Western Electric, the equipment supply arm of the Bell Telephone system, on behalf of the Atomic Energy Commission. Sandia's charter is to design, develop, and test nuclear weapons for the U.S. government. Research laboratories at Los Alamos, New Mexico and Livermore, California design respectively fission and fusion nuclear "devices." Sandia turns the devices into weapons that have the delivery and performance characteristics required by the Department of Defense. Since its founding in the early 1940s, when the nuclear age was born with the first atomic bomb test at White Sands Missile Range near Alamogordo, New Mexico, Sandia has continued to fulfill its charter while growing into an organization with 5,000 employees. From its Albuquerque base, Sandia has offices throughout the country and at nuclear test sites in Alaska, Hawaii, Nevada, and remote Pacific islands. Security regulations shield the company from the public eye.

The connection with Western Electric is a holdover from the 1940s when Western had what many considered the country's best corporate management structure. The government wanted Western to implement the same practices to operate Sandia, and the fee for taking on this fully reimbursable job was said to be $1.00 per year.

Frank's story is intriguing, but why is Sandia recruiting at Princeton? A Princeton grad himself, he explains the difficulty getting highly qualified engineers to carry out the government's sophisticated weapons-development programs. To meet this need, Sandia recently set up a two-year master's degree program at the University of New Mexico to develop qualified nuclear engineers. The program calls for an initial class of 50 top students selected from the country's leading engineering schools.

My interest and hopes are building, but when Frank mentions "top engineering students," I know all will be lost. Although my grades in liberal arts classes are good, engineering grades aren't much above average. I'm sure I have come to a sudden dead end. As if he can read my fears, Frank asks to see a transcript. Handing it over, I expect his face to drop.

But a miracle happens. He lights up and seems pleased. I lean over to see if somehow there is a mistake, but sure enough the transcript is mine. When I point out a few of the liberal arts courses, he quickly says not to worry because Sandia is interested only in engineering subjects. Stunned, my mind races to figure out what he means. I remain quiet while he confirms that my grades are very good indeed, and, considering the high standards at Princeton, they are exceptional. We conclude the interview on a pleasant note, and I quickly accept his invitation to fly to Albuquerque two weeks later for a final interview.

While walking back to the dorm, it dawns on me what happened. Most colleges and universities have adopted a standard grading system ranging from 4.0, the highest, down to 1.0, the lowest. A grade of 3.0 or 3.5 is considered very good. However, the grading system at Princeton is the opposite: 1.0 is highest and 7.0 is lowest. Those mediocre engineering grades averaging around 3.0-3.5 had therefore impressed Frank. The top grades in the liberal arts he interpreted as being on the verge of failing.

I expect to get word any day that the interview trip is canceled when the mistake about the grades is discovered, but fortune intervenes, and the airline ticket arrives with a letter of confirmation.

It's a cold, blustery day in New Jersey when, bundled in a winter suit and heavy overcoat, I travel to Idlewild (later renamed JFK International Airport). Four hours later I step from the plane into warm, sunny weather in Albuquerque, the country's reputed Sunshine Capital. Enthralled with the mountains, the desert, the blue sky, and the adobe architecture, I can't believe a place so different could exist in America. Another surprise is the friendliness of the people, most of whom are dressed in the same casual style as Frank was. Next day the interviews are a blur but evidently successful, because Sandia makes a job offer conditional upon my being granted the top military security clearance. Then, in no time, I'm back in the dismal New Jersey winter.

Although pondering awhile before deciding, I intuitively knew the moment the plane landed at Albuquerque Sunport I'm destined to move to New Mexico. The options now seem ridiculously far apart. The Peace Corps is an opportunity to help my fellow man. The job waiting at Sandia is to blow him to bits. The Marines might offer the chance to row again, which means clinging to the past. Although the Philadelphia job with GE would lead to the same comfortable, secure life I have known, it lacks fire and adventure.

Accepting the Sandia position has little to do with the job itself or career aspirations. Three considerations are decisive. First, Sandia will take me far from Eastern structured society. Second, New Mexico opens opportunities for exploration and adventure. Third, Sandia will pay a full salary and all expenses for two years at University of New Mexico to earn an M.S.E. Degree in Nuclear Engineering. Best of all, I will work only in the mornings and have the rest of the day to take classes and do whatever I want.

With the decision made, I resume the life of a carefree student. Soon winter snows give way to spring flowers and magnolia blossoms, as traditional to Princeton as its ivy-covered walls, and study and rowing end. Because the job with Sandia won't begin until September, I have four months to "get ready to crawl."

# 7
# Westerly Travels

## 5/62 - 7/62, Age 21

Following the 1962 Intercollegiate Rowing Association Regatta in Syracuse I resolve to visit the World's Fair in Seattle, a prospect that offers possibilities for adventure. Jack Clymer, a fellow oarsman and roommate, is also free for the summer before entering Harvard Law School, so we team up to look for a way to go at minimal cost.

Learning of a car delivery agency in New York City, we hitch rides to Manhattan but learn none of the cars are destined for the Northwest. Our best prospect is to deliver a vehicle to Chicago and ask the office there if any cars are needed farther west.

Two days later Jack and I, ecstatic to have five days and mileage expenses paid, are on our way to Chicago in a new sports sedan. The agency warns, however, that if we exceed the allotted time, it will send out a multi-state police alert listing the car as stolen. *(Although the car delivery arrangement seems to offer as close to free transportation as possible, when returning home two months later I discover an even cheaper way.)*

Leaving behind city noise and congestion, we wend our way through the rolling green hills of central Pennsylvania and that first night discuss which itinerary would be most fun. Jack wants to get to Chicago as fast as possible to tour the city. I agree, but want to make a half-day detour to visit Island Lake, which I haven't seen for years. Reaching Chicago the next evening, I'm excited for morning to break so I can see the village where I spent my early childhood.

But going back turns out to be a mistake—one I realize the moment we arrive. Beautiful memories quickly shatter when I see how the place has changed. The first shock is that within only 20 minutes I see everything I remember. The world of a six-year-old on a bicycle took a lot longer to traverse than it does for an adult in an automobile.

The next cause for dismay is the countryside. Subdivision homes clutter fields I had roamed while seeking wildlife. Even Smith's farm, which I recall as being in the country, is overshadowed by a giant shopping center in the middle of what had been a cornfield. Little streams no longer flow through hilly countryside but are diverted around an industrial park by dikes and channels. The lake itself is still as beautiful as ever, but roads crisscross hidden coves and creeks previously accessible only by boat. Manicured lawns that slope to the water's edge replace reeds and rushes. Although I recognize the two houses where we had lived, they are smaller and not-at-all imposing. "You can't go home again" is a hard lesson.

Disappointment fades as Jack and I take in Chicago's sights. Moreover, upon turning in the car at deadline, we learn there's one waiting to go to Seattle. Although it's five years old and somewhat beaten up, Jack and I are delighted to be so lucky to have eight days to deliver.

Years earlier I had seen the Mississippi River when Dad and I drove to Missouri to pick up a new sailboat, and crossing the river again prompts a fresh sense of adventure. Traversing the plains of America's breadbasket, we roll through the Dakota hills before entering the mostly empty grazing lands of eastern Montana. Avoiding larger towns and eating at cafes in villages saves money; so does sleeping in a tent pitched in farm fields.

Montana is fascinating so we spend half our allotted time exploring it. Every small town has a weekly rodeo during summer, and we take in as many as possible (but never have the courage to enter amateur events!).

Our initial impression that Montanans are provincial proves to be unfounded. Many have traveled widely within the country as well as the world and have come home to Montana, which they say is the best place of all.

Loaded with cowboy memorabilia and the novelty of silver dollars, commonly used in stores and restaurants in this part of the country, Jack and I continue farther west crossing the Rockies, then traversing Idaho's panhandle to reach the rich agricultural land of Palouse in eastern Washington. Then it's up the Cascades through Snoqualmie Pass before we turn down to Seattle to join the steady stream of campers, pickups, station wagons, RVs, and mobile homes packed with families drawn to the World's Fair.

Once we've turned in the car, we head straight to the exhibitions. In the center, the U.S. and Russian pavilions strive to outdo each other with elaborate displays representing scientific achievements and political ideologies. Around the periphery smaller countries feature quiet creativity in their exhibits. France, for example, makes quite an impression by displaying man's depersonalization in a world increasingly dominated by machines. Lights, sounds, and film throw the viewer from the experience of being alone in a pristine, natural setting into the sensation of being among factory workers rushing about an assembly line.

Running low on money, Jack and I need to find jobs. Jack becomes a hawker selling souvenirs, and I get a job as a snack stand salesman promoting a 21st century projection of what frankfurters might look and taste like. The product is nothing more than an ordinary hot dog fried in heavily seasoned oil after being dipped into a coating of spices and bread crumbs. Because it's still a hot dog, no one is afraid to try one, and customers who photograph advertising over the stand will have a story to tell upon returning home. Paying a 15 percent premium for a simple hot dog focuses attention on the advertising, which insists this product is special. We use the cheapest hot dogs available and can't cook them fast enough for crowds that get a taste of the future—one that has to do with price inflation.

Noting the rapid employee turnover, I learn later it isn't only customers our manager is ripping off but also his employees. He hired me at $1.35 an hour for an eight-hour, five-day workweek. My first paycheck includes shocking deductions—federal tax, state tax, local tax, social security contribution, health insurance, union fee—that shrink pay by almost half. Although not happy, I must accept the situation but will need to adjust living habits accordingly.

Two weeks later after paying me for work performed to date, the manager fires me. I protest that I have never been late, performed satisfactorily, and was praised by him on several occasions. But nothing moves him, so out I go. Later I learn most of the so-called payroll deductions were bogus. There were no state and local taxes, union fees, or health insurance program. Furthermore, he never paid the legitimate federal deductions. Upon realizing how the abuse worked and assuming there was no recourse, I rationalize the experience—everyone gets caught in a scam once; it just happened to me at a young age. Regardless, it takes a while before the sting goes away.

Looking for a new job I check out the Argentinian Grill, which offers meats cooked slowly over wood-burning fires. Here I find employment bussing tables, washing dishes, filling water glasses, and doing other menial restaurant work. About this time Jack tires of walking around all day and joins me. Because the proprietors have the franchise for the short duration of the World's Fair and are determined to make money, they cut corners wherever possible. For example, the menu features 12 meat dishes, but the chefs prepare only three. How they slice the meat and arrange the parsley makes the dishes appear to be different. The wine list offers five Argentine wines, and, although they are served in five different bottles, Jack and I learn that managers refill them every night from only two barrels. They tell waiters to get customers in and out as fast as possible while encouraging them to make extra purchases to run up the bill.

Such strategies draw Jack and me in as unsuspecting accomplices. We busboys must fill water glasses immediately when guests sit down. Water flows slowly from two spigots in the dining area, so even though we fill as quickly as possible, thirsty guests see they will have a long wait. Directly above the water taps are shelves of readily available wine, prompting customers to order a bottle. Our instructions, of course, are to serve wine immediately, thereby tempting other guests to follow suit. Moreover, managers tell us to serve water first to guests who have already purchased wine, forcing those with nothing to drink to wait unless they, too, order wine. As a further enticement to the desperately thirsty, we must serve baskets of rolls and Argentine butter, which is heavily salted, as soon as they sit down.

With the meal over, we're to clear a table as fast as possible to prepare for the next guests. This task teaches me the difference between intelligence and cleverness. I approach this job with intelligence, but Jack is more successful because he relies on cleverness. My strategy is to stack dirty dishes in an organized way when offloading from the table. I carefully sort cups, plates, saucers, and utensils into separate sections of the dish trolley and then proceed to the kitchen where it's quick and easy to lift the stacks directly into dishwasher bins. In no time I'm back to clear the next table.

This practice shows the efficiency of an engineering mind, but, surprisingly, my liberal arts classmate gets praise and I don't. When clearing a table, Jack hurriedly piles everything into one big heap on his trolley before going to the kitchen where he takes twice as much time to sort dishes and flatware. I explain how he could save time by adopting my method. Laughing, Jack points out it's he, not I, who gets special tips from waiters and praise from the proprietors under whose watchful eyes we work. Jack then explains that seeing what goes on only in the dining area, they are impressed that he can clear a table and disappear in half the time I can. I copy Jack's strategy and never forget the lesson.

One night at a party I become acquainted with Marilyn Gandy, a student at the University of Washington. She's the daughter of Joe Gandy, owner of the local Ford dealership and, more important, president of the World's Fair organizing committee. Opportunities to join Marilyn in hosting visiting dignitaries soon become routine when her father appoints us as official hosts to younger celebrities whom we take to dinner atop the Space Needle in its rotating restaurant. It's ironic that I bus tables by day and enjoy fine dining on an expense account by night. Marilyn and I also gain access to receptions, parties, and official gatherings where we enjoy a whirlwind of a time.

As rewarding as summer is, it is passing quickly and Jack and I have more to do before fall. So, we quit our jobs and start hitch-hiking down the coast to California. We don't anticipate trouble getting rides, but after two days we haven't gotten very far. Drivers seem hesitant to pick up two big guys with large duffel bags. Deciding to try our luck separately, we agree to meet in San Francisco at the home of a classmate. In a hurry to get there, Jack opts to take the freeway while I choose a scenic coastal route. Before long we catch rides.

The coastlines of Washington and Oregon are as rugged and treacherous as they are beautiful. Few natural harbors exist along this stretch of several hundred miles where the Pacific pounds rocky cliffs that have menaced seamen for centuries. Little towns and villages on natural inlets afford protection for small fleets of fishing boats, and for two weeks I explore these villages as I slowly hitch-hike south.

One day in the middle of Oregon, an enormous logging truck pulls up and driver Mike offers a lift. The cab is so high that getting in is like climbing a ladder. Pulling away, I view the passing landscape as though from a low-flying aircraft. Cars look so tiny that if we run over one, it might feel like nothing more than a small bump. Mike and I strike up a conversation and when he learns I'm interested in his part of the country, his eyes light up, and he says the Pacific Northwest is the most beautiful part of America.

"If you have a few days," Mike offers, "I'll show you around." I enthusiastically accept, and thus begins a fascinating four-day venture that brings me right into the heart and soul of Oregon.

Mike first needs to deliver his load of Douglas firs to the mill, and this offers an insight into Oregon life. In many small towns the economy is dependent on the local mill where even school children are aware of the wood and timber commodity markets. When Mike releases his load, giant logs cascade into a small lake below. Walking across floating logs as easily as though taking a leisurely stroll, loggers prod them with boat hooks toward a conveyor system that whisks them from the lake to the barker where high-pressure, hot-water jets strip the bark. Next giant saws take over. As we watch from an elevated platform, Mike explains how mill operators determine the best cuts and grade the lumber as it is processed. Even pieces of scrap are sorted and sent to a bin where they will be processed into pulp at the paper mill.

After lunch Mike and I set out with his empty rig up the mountain for a half-day drive to the logging camp. As we progress higher on dirt roads, he shows me a favorite pastime of log haulers. Pointing to a fist-size rock ahead near the road edge, he steers the right front tire so that it just clips the rock. This pinching effect sends it shooting out and down the mountainside. After demonstrating this trick a few times, Mike says he will show me some "graduate-level stuff." As we approach a rock, he misses it.

"Too bad for that one, Mike," I say.

"Look in the rear-view mirror," he replies. Just then he swerves and the rear wheel hits the rock with a bang—out it soars into the valley below.

Mike chatters on with variations of this game. The ultimate is when two logging trucks meet each other, and each tries to shoot a rock in the middle of the road at the other. It can be a bit dicey, he concedes, when both drivers aim for the same rock!

The logging camp is jumping with activity when we arrive late that afternoon. Enormous pieces of equipment for dragging, hauling, lifting, trimming, and cutting prepare virgin timber for a trip to the mill. Mike parks his rig to be loaded for the next day's haul. Then, after he greets his friends and gives them local news from the mill, he and I jump into his car and set off toward home. I ask to see the shooting rock trick again, but his shocked look suggests I've said something stupid. Mike then patiently explains a car doesn't have enough weight to launch a rock of any size.

"All that happens is the tire gets a bald spot," he says.

Driving deeper into the mountains over and around many ridges and valleys, we arrive at an open meadow and Mike's home. His wife, Carol, must have been accustomed to her husband's friendly ways with strangers, for she greets me warmly without question or concern. Introducing me to his two pre-teen children, Mike delights in showing the self-sufficient nature of the family's existence. He has enough farm animals to keep them well-supplied with milk, eggs, and home-raised beef. His gardens, orchards, and berry bushes ensure a plentiful supply of fruits, vegetables, and berries. Mike also shows me his hunting guns, contending the family could live all year long on what he can hunt within a mile of home. Then he leads me to a well-supplied tool room with welders, lathes, and grinders needed to maintain equipment. Inside the home are paintings and handicrafts Mike and his wife have made, and I realize I have run across a contemporary Renaissance couple.

These gracious hosts initiate me into the secret beauty of land and life in mountainous Oregon. While making more logging trips, Mike talks about its lure. I'm sorely tempted to send a telegram to Sandia declining their job in favor of signing on as a worker at the logging camp. Whether fortunate or unfortunate that I don't, I'll never know. Head ruling over heart, I default to pursuing a career that complements my engineering education. Following a final run down the mountain, I'm on the road alone, outstretched thumb pointing south.

A day later I cross into California and wind down the Mendocino and Sonoma coasts through magnificent redwood forests until the Golden Gate Bridge comes into view. I'm a passenger in the most elegant car I have ever ridden in, a white Lincoln Continental convertible that had been the pace car at the Indianapolis 500 according to the owner. Driving in open air onto the bridge, we're engulfed in the multi-colored splendor of the evening sun as it sinks beyond the Farallon Islands into the ocean. As if on cue, Tony Bennett's new song, "I Left my Heart in San Francisco," plays on the radio.

Another circumstance seems more providential than circumstantial: My benefactor invites me to dine with him and to crash on his living room couch. Without a cent in my pockets I'm content none the less. Perhaps as we crossed San Francisco Bay, something in the great unknown was telling me that although I will someday experience confusion and turmoil, the San Francisco Bay Area is where chaos will settle into harmony and peace, and I will again know the contentment of that mid-summer moment in 1962.

# 8
# Hitchhiking 101

*7/62 - 8/62, Age 21*

After a peaceful sleep I awaken to a new day, pick up money at a bank, and reconnect with Jack who's been waiting for the past week. He has already toured San Francisco so he's a perfect guide for our final week as tourists. The days fly by as Jack and I eat our fill of fresh-cracked crab at Fisherman's Wharf, tour Sonoma and Napa wine country, ride cable cars, and fall in love with this remarkable city.

Now it's time to get back on the road and Jack and I will be heading in different directions. He intends to set off for southern California while I'm ready to hitchhike home. I have three weeks to get to Kentucky before preparing for Sandia—enough time for side trips to out-of-the-way attractions. Waking early on this last morning together, we recall our fun and adventures, then bid farewell, a hard moment for each. We were great friends in college, shared many joyous as well as heart-breaking moments during our rowing careers, and now are separating after a terrific summer together. The parting is brief. I feel a tightness, an unaccustomed lump in my throat. We both know our paths are unlikely to cross again anytime soon. Within 15 minutes I catch my first ride, and off I go across the Oakland Bay Bridge into the rising sun.

The hitchhikers' world is filled with adventure and fraught with danger. Nothing is certain and keeping to a plan is impossible. An entire day may pass without a single ride. Alternatively, if lucky, one might cover several hundred miles. Waiting hours for someone to pick me up, I've developed an ability to sense the mood and motive of anyone who stops.

Successful hitchhikers know the three distinct phases to be successful in hitchhiking. First comes the "attraction" stage. Ostensibly the hitchhiker simply stands by the roadside and holds out his thumb; however, there is more to it. A driver drawing near has about five seconds to decide whether to stop. If his or her impression is negative or at all questionable, the motorist will pass on by. For this reason, the hitchhiker must quickly convey he will be, first, an interesting travel companion and, second, not a threat.

To suggest I'm a good candidate, I use several techniques. One is holding a sign announcing an outrageous destination. In California, for example, I use a sign saying "New York" or even "France." Coming south from Seattle, I might write "Mexico." Such remote places pique drivers' curiosities, particularly if they have been to the destination and want to talk about it. Another prop is to carry a book, suggesting I'm a student and could share what I'm reading. If these ploys fail to entice, I can always depend upon one of a half-dozen printed t-shirts or sweatshirts. This summer the best one announces "Seattle World's Fair" because everyone wants to hear stories from someone who has been there. Wearing my university sweater with its logo will usually stop a fellow alumnus. Basically, I try to create the impression that I'm an honest, clean-cut student who probably doesn't have much money, which is true.

Wearing light-colored clothes is important; dark clothes can appear both sinister and dirty. An assuring smile helps whereas a pleading or begging expression suggests being down-and-out. To assure I can fit comfortably without the inconvenience of having to make room, I wear snug-fitting clothes and stoop a little to create the impression of not being very big. Hiding the duffel bag cancels any fear about what it contains. Once a car stops, I discreetly retrieve the duffel and approach with it on my back so the driver can't tell how large it is. Getting into the car, I quickly toss it in the back seat.

"Getting acquainted" is the second phase. It's a mistake to ask immediately how far the driver is going, because he may say, "Only to the next town" when he really plans to travel several hundred miles. Once acquainted, though, he may offer a longer ride. Occasionally when a driver is planning to go only a short distance, after we get acquainted, he changes his mind and drives farther to assist me on my way.

It helps to know why the driver picks me up. Does he want to talk, listen, or enjoy a quiet ride? Familiarity can proceed smoothly only if I quickly assess which of the three motives prompted the driver to stop. Following introductions he may have a question or two about the book, the shirt, or the destination. If he holds forth and wants to do the talking, I listen patiently although sometimes it's hard to feign interest in a harebrained topic.

On the other hand, if the driver is a listener and has picked me up as a source of entertainment to break monotony, I find myself in the hitchhiker's toughest role, having to share personal details. What did I think of the World's Fair? What's my background or view of politics? Where am I heading and why? The best riding experiences are with someone who simply wants silent companionship, leaving me in my own space. Often during such quiet periods, I become more tuned-in to my host. Whichever direction it takes, though, this getting-acquainted phase may last from a few minutes to several hours.

Then comes the third and last part: "How far do we go?" If things proceed well, the driver may surprise himself by what he offers. He might treat me to dinner, suggest visiting a local attraction, provide a spare bedroom for the night, and drive farther the next day. The best time to ask how far the benefactor can take me is always after the getting-acquainted step. He knows my story by then and is sympathetic. He knows I have a long way to go and have little money. He also knows my interest in seeing the country before starting a job. Most importantly, he has had time to figure out how to help me. Once a driver announces how far we can travel together, the courtship is over and I can do whatever I want, which is usually to lean against the door and sleep! Reaching the endpoint, we make our goodbyes, and I plant myself back along the roadside with thumb sticking out.

# 9
# Danger Rides the Rails

*8/62, Age 21*

Several days and many weary miles beyond San Francisco I find my spirits sagging. Day after day of sucking in exhaust while car after car whizzes by and sweat trickles down my brow, I sometimes stand for hours waiting for a lift. Hopping in and out of this car and that truck leaves me drained and exhausted by the time evening shadows fall. The journey from Seattle hadn't been so bad because it was relatively short through beautiful countryside. However, the prospect now looming before me—one of endless miles of hot, dusty travels through desert country—strikes me as a different story altogether.

One morning I catch a ride with a farm worker named Dale who says a whole new world could open if I change plans. Listening to his stories, I drift back to that childhood experience in Connecticut when I leapt onto a freight train and rode through a tunnel. Dale explains in detail the western rail systems and how trains are routed depending upon the freight they carry. Over coffee he makes sketches and demonstrates with enthusiasm the art of hopping trains, which he had done for years.

This new friend's excitement fires my imagination with the tantalizing prospect for a new adventure. A journey into the possibly dangerous unknown—one requiring cleverness and physical strength—arouses my competitive instinct. I will need to outwit authorities whose job is to stop people like me from sneaking onto trains. Success will demand every bit of determination I possess.

Nearing Sacramento, Dale offers to show me the rail yards where Union Pacific freights are being made up for the haul east. Farm produce from northern California ships to this central depot where it consolidates for bulk shipment. Trains then climb the Sierra Nevada Mountains, cut through Donner Pass, and cross high alpine country before negotiating the precipitous downgrade on the eastern slopes. Although Sparks, Nevada, the next major railyard, is less than 200 miles away, the overall trek takes most of a day and needs up to five engines to handle the grades.

Just east of the Sacramento yard a wide bend and upgrade limit speed for the first several miles to less than 10 miles per hour. Dale explains I should stand on the inside of this curve to see what types of cars are coming and select the one to board. Thanking him, I step from his car and wave goodbye.

For the next half hour, I wait near the bend to study the situation. Off in the yard I can hear small engines assembling the freight cars for tomorrow's run. The serenity of the enveloping fields and hills offers a striking contrast to this frantic activity down the way. As the late afternoon sky paints itself in ever-changing hues of gold and rose before a sinking great red disk, I hitchhike into town and scout out a cheap motel and small cafe. Over dinner I glean from locals that two freights leave tomorrow. I will try for the first; if I miss, the backup will come along a few hours later. That night I can hardly sleep while rehearsing every step to secure a safe ride.

Dawn tickles the sky when I wake, gobble down a big breakfast, and stuff pockets with pieces of fruit. Returning to the launch site, I realize I must either pitch the duffel aboard or let it hang loose from my shoulder. Having discarded anything unnecessary, my bag is lighter now and tightly packed with meager possessions: sleeping bag, a few clothes, poncho, toiletries, and a canteen. The misty morning is cool. Fields glisten with dew, reflecting the sun's first rays filtered through the Sierras' distant peaks. Trembling with anticipation, I'm poised for this new adventure.

Suddenly the drama begins, one I'll often repeat over the next three weeks, each time more exciting than the last. Five engines struggle to draw the snake-like tail from the yard. The rumble, rumble, rumble grows louder as engines strain, their load coming closer and closer. Scrutinizing the various cars that make up the half-mile-long string, I try to decide which one will be my target. A number of boxcars have doors temptingly ajar, but Dale had insisted that jumping up through a door moving above a snail's pace is difficult and risky. Instead, I watch for a refrigeration car, known in the jargon as a reefer. The closer one nears, the faster my heart beats.

I run alongside, duffel bobbing on my back, to get up to the train's speed. When abreast, I grab the ladder with one hand, then the other, and—with a mighty lunge—pull my legs up to the lowest rung. But the train's momentum slams my body back and around the car's rear! Hanging on with all my strength, I look straight down onto the track directly in front of the next set of wheels. If I fall now, the end won't be pretty. Thankfully, those years of rowing have strengthened my upper body, and I'm securely on the ladder. Scrambling up the rungs, I inch forward along a narrow catwalk atop the car. I've made it! I'm safe! A rush of exultation surges through me.

Next, I arrange a convenient riding position with the unrolled sleeping bag serving as a cushion and the duffel functioning as a backrest. Once I'm comfortably settled and can leisurely survey surroundings, the sheer beauty of the landscape overwhelms me. From my perch atop the reefer, I feel on top of the world, which, in a sense, I am.

The train gathers speed as foothills appear. Gently rolling countryside gives way to rugged terrain that will merge into the cliffs and peaks of America's westernmost range. As long as the land is reasonably flat, power lines and highways parallel the rails; entering the foothills, though, we come to a dividing point. The road and power lines veer right, sweeping away billboards and refuse discarded by the careless. Meanwhile, the train bores straight ahead into pristine loveliness, and, for mile after mile, passing woodlands evoke a sense of peaceful solitude. I feel completely alone and at one with the natural surroundings.

For hours I experience a state of wonder as we climb through ever-evolving zones of vegetation. Feathery grasses give way to plump bushes, which merge to scrubby trees that yield to towering forests of regal oak and sweet-scented pine. Mile piling upon mile, I can feel the train steadily gather speed. Reaching the mountains, it creeps higher and tracks no longer thread around ridges and valleys. Rather, we chug through cuts in the mighty rock—some passages barely wider than the cars themselves.

At several rugged places where rail lines could not snake around rock formations, we encounter trestle bridges and tunnels, all of which set my heart to pounding. Bridges crossing deep valleys are no wider than the tracks, and looking down I see nothing except huge plummeting gorges. My stomach flip-flops, and I cling with white knuckles to the catwalk while gusts of canyon wind roar by.

The slow ascent continues another four or five hours until we reach Donner Pass where I can look back to survey the rugged slope just achieved or turn forward to face a new scene unfolding across alpine meadows. Gradually we slow and then grind to a halt. Ahead I see the train engineers climbing down, presumably to inspect engine couplings and brake hoses. Taking advantage of the interlude, I clamber down the ladder and stretch stiff legs. Careful to remain hidden, I duck into a copse adorned with the oranges, golds, and reds of late summer wildflowers and alive with the joyous chorus of songbirds.

Inspection finished, the men re-board. Starting back toward my car, I have a moment of panic because I can't tell which of the dozen reefers is mine. I scramble up the last one, and once on top, see my belongings about five cars ahead. Scurrying forward and leaping cautiously from one reefer to the next, I return to my perch just as the train starts to move.

The trip down the tortuous eastern slope is faster and wilder than our slow-paced ascent. As the sun drops behind peaks, the mountain air begins to chill my bones, and I'm glad to snuggle into the sleeping bag.

Breaking out the fruit and some sandwiches I had stuffed away, I indulge in a late afternoon snack.

As evening descends the distant lights of Reno's casinos come into view, but the train veers north toward Sparks. Thinking about abandoning my perch of the past eight hours, I recall Dale's warning that every railroad town is patrolled by yard police, so-called "yard dicks," whose job is to keep out rail-riding bums and hobos. Vagrants sometimes invade a town on an arriving freight and vandalize property before leaving on the next day's outbound. Because such itinerants are frequently homeless, shiftless, lawless, and without families, the yard dicks figure they can take justice into their own hands when they catch one. Rumor has it they may shoot first and ask questions later. Their victims, who typically have no identification, are often disposed of with haste to eliminate evidence of foul play. Furthermore, railway supervisors usually hire local rednecks to work as yard dicks. These men have nothing to do all day except wait for an inbound freight with the hope of meting out punishment, sometimes sadistically, to some unfortunate drifter. In any case, I know to be off the train well before it enters any yard.

Approaching Sparks, the train slows, and I scuttle down the ladder and wait on the bottom rung for the right chance to jump. Close to town, I grit my teeth and leap off into a tangle of bushes. "Not such a bad tumble," I think, brushing away twigs and leaves and gasping with relief that I have only minor scratches. Sparks isn't very big these days, and in less than an hour I reach the other side of town. There I find a low-cost motel, eat a decent dinner, and settle my weary bones into bed.

In the morning I set out to learn the east-bound train schedules. Sparks is the junction where huge cargo trains are made up to cross the western deserts to the Rockies, which begin in Utah. The track leads northeasterly to Winnemucca, winds east to Elko and Wells, and terminates at Ogden. Stretching nearly 600 miles across the Great Nevada Basin, this leg takes 12 hours or more, and because of stifling heat, most freights depart in the evening and reach Utah the following morning. As before, the best spot is at a wide bend beyond the yard where the train will be going slow enough to jump aboard.

Light is fading when a deep rumble announces the approach of two slow-moving engines struggling to pull what appears to be a mile-long freight string. Hoping to sleep through the night, I look for an enclosed car. Fortunately, this train has a number of open-door empties going back to the Midwest grain belt.

While jogging alongside, I judge the right time to fling the duffel inside. Running now, fearful I might not join it, I heave on my stomach through the entry and fight to get torso and legs inside. Just then two strong hands grab my arms and drag me to safety. Suddenly I'm staring into the grinning face of another freight-hopper who boarded when the train was going slower. Much older than I, his grizzled face suggests years on the hard-luck side of life. Obviously more skilled at this game, he is amused to meet an amateur.

"Young man, you gonna' get yourself kilt in no time a'tall if you try an' board a train goin' this fast."

I have found a second mentor, Art, who will teach me the finer points of travel on a freight train.

Sitting at the open door, we dangle legs and engage in barroom talk while streaking past miles of fading countryside. At nightfall I'm initiated into a rite of hobo life. Art has brought small pieces of wood and, thanks to remnants of scattered wheat in the car, soon has a small fire burning. Out come a few tins of food, and Art sets to cooking dinner. With my contributions of cold snacks and a bottle of wine I'd bought earlier that day, we share a fine hobo feast.

Trading stories, we pass the hours until reaching Winnemucca where we extinguish the fire and close the door. The train stops for a while, probably to refuel or change crew, and then we're off again racing into the blackness of the Nevada desert. Relighting the fire, my new companion (maybe feeling sorry for me?), repeats how stupid I am.

"You wanna' know somethin'? You're a damn fool! I coulda' pushed you outtta' that door a dozen times since you've been here."

He points out the opportunities he had when I wasn't looking and says some people that I'm likely to meet wouldn't hesitate to do just that in order to steal whatever I had. He warns me never to turn my back on any fellow rider even for an instant, or I might end up knocked over the head and find myself stripped and robbed. He notes the obvious strength of my arms and body would be a deterrent unless an assailant happens to be armed. I take to heart his warning. I'm still an ignoramus.

As we put out the fire and bed down for the night, Art offers one last bit of advice. "When travelin' in twos in the same car, each claims half at opposite ends. In the night if one comes into the other's half, that's a threat, and then anything—and I mean anything—goes. And just so's you know, I got me a knife and a revolver right here a'side o'me."

Not about to argue, I retreat to my side. Because we'll make two more stops during the night, we close the door, unfortunately shutting out the cool night air. I'm awakened during brief stops at Elko and Wells but then sleep soundly until gentle breezes awaken me around six o'clock. Art is already up, basking in the cool morning. Jokingly I ask if he overlooked that I could have easily thrown him out, Art smiles and agrees but adds, in an offhanded way, that no student could allow harm to his teacher, and that's how he sees our relationship. I guess there is honor among hobos.

All too soon morning freshness gives way to unbearable heat when the sun scorches the Bonneville Salt Flats. After breakfasting on last night's leftovers, we sit quietly while crossing Great Salt Lake. Approaching Ogden, Art jumps off and I follow. Here our paths diverge. He's heading north and I'm going east, so we part, knowing we'll never see each other again. I'm sure, however, I'll never forget my 12-hour tutor.

To ease crampy legs, I wander around town until evening when I hitch a ride to the railyard and repeat the evening routine: find a cheap motel, eat a good dinner, and learn tomorrow's freight schedule. The bulk of the Rockies lies east of Ogden, and the next terminal junction is over the mountains at Rock Springs, Wyoming, about 300 miles away. The all-day trip will be cool, so I plan to ride on top again.

Early the next morning I find my way to the tracks. When the cargo train leaves the yard, I'm surprised it's shorter and picks up speed faster than expected. Here I make a dangerous call—one that almost costs my life later that day.

Before the train goes too fast, I grab the ladder of a boxcar near the engines. Mounted atop, I choose the middle of the catwalk, unpack the sleeping bag, and imagine a happy ride through the passes, canyons, and peaks of Wyoming's Rocky Mountains. Thus situated, I lean back, relax, and take in views of the passing countryside. I'm lost in reverie when disaster strikes.

Always on the lookout for tunnels, I see one ahead but don't worry because I've been through a few. I can tell, though, that this one has a lower ceiling than normal. Speeding nearer, I secure my gear and lie back to wait until we come out the other end.

But the instant I enter, I'm overcome with panic. I'm engulfed in a searing hell of hot gases and charred particles that burn my entire body and singe all exposed body hair. Only by squeezing eyes tightly shut can I protect them. I sense I'm burning into a cinder outside and inside. Gulping for air, I feel my lungs are on fire. I hold my breath as long as possible, but the tunnel seems a mile long and I'm wheezing and gasping for air. Finally, just as I'm about to explode, the end of the tunnel appears. Emerging into the fresh, cool air I gulp long and deep to revive myself.

I realize what has happened. Ensconced only a few cars behind the locomotives, there was no way to escape the infernal blast of exhaust gases while passing through the tunnel. What a fool to ride so close to the engines! While passing through tunnels in the Sierras on the longer train, I had been far enough back for the engine exhaust to have cooled by the time they reached me.

Now I must move back, and quickly. But I'm wary about leapfrogging from car to car with my back turned to oncoming danger. Should I race down the ladder and jump off? No. The train is going too fast!

These thoughts are for naught, however, because looming a few hundred yards ahead is the mouth of another tunnel. I dive headfirst into the sleeping bag just as we enter. When cinders burn my exposed legs, I jerk my knees in and curl into a fetal position. There's enough air in the bag to survive—a stroke of luck because this tube seems twice as long as the first. Once through it, I emerge gasping. The sleeping bag is singed so badly it's all but useless and will likely catch fire next time.

No more tunnels threaten for the moment, allowing time to collect my things and move farther back. Carefully descending each ladder, I step onto couplings between cars, swing across, seize the next ladder, and climb to the top. Eventually I'm safely back a half-dozen cars before encountering any more tunnels, which I'm able to survive. The rest of the run to Rock Springs is blessedly uneventful.

Approaching the small community, I leave the train without being noticed and poke around a bit. After a bite to eat, I hike to the east side and sleep in a field.

Armed with local knowledge, I'm back at the tracks early to catch the next train. Soon I have a choice seat atop an empty cattle car. Perched there, I spend the entire day lost in the beauty of the natural world, unspoiled by infrastructure and the clutter of modern society. Seldom have I been as full of peace and joy as during these wind-blown days riding the freights. By evening we've journeyed across the Wyoming Basin to Cheyenne.

It's a new day, and, together with my new-friend-for-the day, Joe and I ride in a boxcar to North Platte, Nebraska. Along the way Joe talks about a common pattern among America's hobos. In spite of appearing to wander aimlessly, they always have a destination in mind. He, for example, a 40-something physically fit ex-military, having heard of a large road-building project in North Dakota, is headed there to find a job. Others will travel great distances for rumored farming or construction work. Although most seek jobs, many are trying to escape something in their past. That something is often a woman, and whether it's because of hate, fear, money, anger, threats, or nagging, there's reason enough to drive a man out. Abandoning family, the so-called provider goes off on an illusory quest to find a job and peace. Rail-hoppers who have had run-ins with the law may be staying ahead of warrants, citations, and even bounty hunters.

North Platte ships freight 400 miles across the Northern Great Plains to Omaha, providing a new riding experience. Because it's hot, dusty country, I hope to travel in enclosed comfort, but the only prospect is an open-top livestock car hauling sheep. I clamber up the ladder and dropping down among them scatter the frightened animals to the corners. The car bed is covered with hay; unrolling the sleeping bag I lie in luxury for hours while gazing up at endlessly passing blue sky. Surely this is the most agreeable way to go anywhere. But, again, I'm naïve about the finer points of being a successful travel bum: Any self-respecting hobo would rather walk tracks for a week than ride with livestock, especially sheep.

By day's end I reek. The expressions on people's faces in restaurants and motels make it clear I'm unwelcome, but somehow, I manage to book a room for the night where I scour myself raw in the shower, wash my hair twice, and scrub clothes as clean as possible.

Next stop, Omaha. Trusting a tip, I'm going to break the usual pattern. Instead of jumping off outside the city, I'll leave when the train stops in the yard. I understand that because the area is in harvest season, yard dicks have been taken off their usual vigilante hunt, and it's now safe to ride into town. The railroads unofficially endorse this policy because their revenue depends upon a successful harvest.

Crossing tracks leading from the yard, I notice a dozen or so other men departing two boxcars near the rear. Rail companies sometimes spot open boxcars there to encourage itinerant workers at harvest time. When picking is over, migrants know the yard dicks will be back, and by then the workers will be gone.

After a night in Omaha, I'm back in the yard looking for a freight train setting up for the 150-mile run along the Missouri River to Kansas City. This time I choose a piggy-back car carrying trailer rigs. Because the car has no sides, I can lie beneath two trailers that will furnish shade and a wind-break while still allowing a view of passing countryside. The trailers carry fresh produce, and I discover that by climbing to the top and then down through a hatch I could travel in air-conditioned comfort. But I prefer the open air. This route goes over the river into Missouri. Replacing expanses of mostly untouched land are miles of wheat fields and small farming villages that seem to compete in cultivating any bare acreage. Hot, humid air here hangs heavy, compared to dry desert heat.

Growing bored with the dull landscape, I feel the urge to hurry home to Louisville. Knowing Omaha trains attract short-term laborers, I figure the yard police in Kansas City won't cause any trouble, so I decide to ride into the yard and save the hassle of hitchhiking one end of the city to the other. I'm pretty sure yard workers themselves won't be a problem; still, I try to be discreet by slipping from sight around the wheel assembly of a trailer. Unaware of any risk, I'm actually setting up another dangerous scenario.

The train begins a series of stop-and-go maneuvers as yard engines break it up and shuttle cars onto different tracks for new trains to go elsewhere. The gentle movements of my car lull me into a reverie, shattered abruptly by someone hollering: "HEY YOU!" "JUMP!" "GODDAMN YOU, MAN, JUMP!" Workers seeing me curled up in the wheelwell are shouting to get off. Stunned, confused, I spring to the ground just as my car lurches, and I realize in horror what almost happened.

Breaking up a train and remaking others within the freight yards is called humping. It involves pushing cars up a slight incline and then releasing them, one at a time, to roll down the other side into the switching yard where they're shunted to different tracks where new trains are assembled. Coming down the grade, they pick up enough speed to pass through flats before crashing into the next car with enough force to trigger the coupling that secures both. I witness the flatbed I just escaped roll down the slope and bang to a stop so hard that the trailer tie-downs shake wildly. Hiding within the wheel assembly, I would have been hurled forward and crushed from the impact of this powerful collision. The near-miss shakes me so badly that one of the yard workers accompanies me to a nearby cafe where I try to calm my nerves over a cup of coffee.

"You're lucky," he exclaims, "*real* lucky we saw you just in time to save your life!" He shares a tale of someone not so lucky, a fellow who chose the front of a low-sided bulk carrier piled high with steel bars. When the humped car violently shuddered to a halt, a cry brought workers running. Impact from the crash shifted the load forward, and ....the storyteller stops and says no more. Yard dicks or no yard dicks, the lesson is clear: Stay away from freight yards.

During the next four days I work my way on a series of shorter trains to St. Louis and across the Mississippi to Evansville, Indiana. From there the ride up the Ohio River through familiar western Kentucky and Indiana is uneventful. Arriving at Louisville, I hop off a boxcar just before arriving at the Bourbon Stock Yards. Home at last! Totally spent, I don't have enough energy to go one more mile on my own. I find a telephone booth and call my parents; within half-an-hour they pick me up. Mom and Dad, however, are rather reserved in their greeting because a lingering stench of sheep remains.

Numb from living on the road, I wander around the house for days trying to regain bearings. In the past I have found solace by writing away other troubles, pouring them from fresh experience onto paper. I do this now. Encouraged by my mother, a columnist for a local newspaper, I take the story to the *Louisville Courier Journal* to offer it for publication.

An editor responds with enthusiasm. Yes, he'd like to run my piece and wants photos to accompany it. Back at the house I retrieve the duffel, charred sleeping bag, and old clothes. Accompanied by a staff photographer to the freight yard, we hunt for railcars like the ones I rode. As I re-enact certain scenes, the photographer clicks away whenever he sees what looks authentic. Sensitive to possible legal implications, he is careful not to include names of the railroad companies in his photos.

A week later *"Danger Rides the Rails"* appears in print and helps ground me to reality again. Now that the adventure is recorded and memories tucked away for safe-keeping, I can get on with preparing for a new experience in Albuquerque. I purchase my first car, a 1962 Ford Crown Victoria, and one week later I'm driving west on Route 66 to the Land of Enchantment.

# 10
# New Mexico

*9/62 - 5/63, Ages 21 - 22*

The four-day drive from Louisville to Albuquerque brings a restful change from frantic weeks of hopping freights back from California. The monotony of dust bowl country in Oklahoma, Texas, and eastern New Mexico provides a gentle transition from the carefree life of a college student and haphazard summer adventurer to the responsible role of a professional engineer.

After crossing into New Mexico, I drive several hundred miles up from the desert to the eastern edge of the Rockies. Three mountain ranges—Sangre de Christo, Sandia, and Manzano—merge in a north-south line in the middle of the state to form a protective shoulder for Albuquerque. I follow U.S. Route 66 as it snakes around bends and arroyos on its way through Tijeras Canyon to Albuquerque and arrive just as a glorious sunset paints the sky. What a sight! Dust stirred up from the desert refracts the sun's last rays to create a symphony of reds and golds that slowly disappears, leaving a dark blue, crystal-clear sky. I couldn't have hoped for a better welcome to my new home.

My arrival coincides when the New Mexico State Fair is in full swing, and it depicts every aspect of life in the Land of Enchantment: handicraft displays, agricultural exhibits, industrial promotions, and events ranging from rodeos to square dances to chili cook-offs. This year's fair celebrates New Mexico's 50th anniversary as the 47th state to join the Union.

Because New Mexico is thinly populated and has no major industrial or commercial base, it's little understood by many Americans. Friends, upon hearing where I intend to work, ask why I would leave the country. I'm about to learn that such comments are no joke to many residents who must constantly correct the mistaken impression that New Mexico is part of Mexico.

The state's residents have roots in three cultures. Native Americans descended from great Pueblo cultures that flourished throughout the Rio Grande Valley for thousands of years make up one-third of the population. Maintaining traditional customs, they live in peace and keep to themselves. Much of their economy is supported by the beautiful pottery and handmade jewelry of coral, turquoise, and silver that they sell to tourists.

Another third of the population originates from descendants of early Spanish and Mexican explorers who were the first non-natives to settle in the Southwest. A thriving trade route, the Chihuahua Trail, once existed between Santa Fe and Chihuahua, Mexico. Up from the south came pioneers seeking opportunities in farming and mining, and they weren't disappointed. New Mexico's Hispanic residents enjoy prosperity and respect and are well integrated into the harmonious lifestyle of this tri-cultural state. Their influence extends to the state legislature with its use of Spanish and English for all official proceedings.

The remaining third and last to arrive were the Anglo engineers and scientists who secretly developed the atomic bomb at Los Alamos Scientific Laboratory and tested it at White Sands near Alamogordo. Since the early 1940s, nuclear programs have increased the number of military and civilian personnel, of which I am one.

The sunny, healthy living environment also attracts people to move here. At one mile above sea level, Albuquerque's clean, dry climate offers relief to sufferers from arthritis and respiratory diseases like asthma and emphysema. One has to be sensitive when inquiring why someone moved to New Mexico because reasons often associate with illness.

I temporarily rent a room while searching for long-term accommodations with New Mexico charm. One day I read a notice on a university bulletin board posted by a professor looking for a house-sitter to care for her dog during a six-month sabbatical. Two days after arranging an interview I meet Professor Lois Law at her ranch-style, adobe home hidden among groves of cottonwood trees nestled in the Rio Grande Valley. Professor Law spent her academic career researching Native Americans of the Southwest, and her home is a treasure-trove of pottery, jewelry, and artifacts from archaeological digs.

Two weeks later I settle into this museum-home with Happy, a crossbreed mutt that makes the rent-free arrangement possible. I can't believe my luck, and all that's required is walking and feeding Happy twice daily. Every evening during weeks that follow, I delve into the professor's collections of artifacts and books to learn about the culture, history, and lifestyle of ancient Pueblo societies.

No sooner have I settled into the new home than it's time to report to work. Showing up with high expectations at Sandia's offices, I'm aware that because of indulging in summer adventures, I'm last to arrive of 50 chosen for the Technical Development Program (TDP). Knowing that except for the likely misinterpretation of my university transcript I might not be here makes me feel insecure. Adding to my uneasiness is that I had taken fewer engineering courses than my peers, many of whom completed five-year undergraduate programs that were focused exclusively on technical curricula. My work is cut out for me to keep up with the others.

The TDP, funded by the Atomic Energy Commission, supports us through a two-year master's degree program in the Graduate Engineering School at University of New Mexico. We're expected to inject a new level of technical knowledge needed to meet America's weapons challenges. The coursework saturates us in fields relevant to nuclear weapons design and development. In the mornings we work on engineering projects as employees; the afternoons are for classes and homework.

The highly touted academic curriculum turns out to be a repeat of several courses I took as an undergraduate, which frees up time to audit more liberal arts courses. Because UNM is reputed to have the country's top anthropology department, I sit in on freshman introductory classes, happy once again to enjoy life as a student.

I spend most of the next two years at the campus's squat, earthen-colored, adobe buildings in the center of Albuquerque. Unburdened at noon each day from the heavy business—business that involves wrapping my mind around how vulnerable America's nuclear arsenal is to the X-ray counter-effects from Russia's advanced defense missiles of nuclear weapons—I change out of business clothes, leave the office, jump on my motorcycle, and head to the university. Afternoons I focus on classes and on getting a weekend date for rock concerts. The contrast between my mornings and afternoons is so unreal I'm unable to take either very seriously.

Weekends afford opportunities for adventures. Elephant Butte Lake, one of the country's largest man-made lakes, offers fun I never expected in a desert: sailing, swimming, water skiing, fishing, and sunning on beaches. Farther south, Ciudad Juarez attracts with bull fights, shopping bargains, cheap liquor, and enticing sins of a Mexican border town. Gasoline is cheap, and savings from liquor purchases offset the fuel costs of the five-hour rum-run from Albuquerque across the border.

North of Albuquerque, the state capital, Santa Fe, is known for art galleries, open-air opera, Native American jewelry stores, and Saint Francis Cathedral (commemorated in Willa Cather's novel, *Death Comes for the Archbishop*). Farther north, in small villages such as Taos, artists seek the peace and quiet conducive to their creativity. Protected as wilderness areas, federal forests, and national parks, the mountains of northern New Mexico provide a cooling contrast to the deserts in the south.

Within two-hour's drive of Albuquerque are more than 30 pueblos, each known for its distinctive pottery, jewelry, and culture. Perched high atop a mesa, Acoma Pueblo, my favorite, is said to be the longest continuously inhabited community in America with a society thriving hundreds of years before Europeans arrived on the continent. Until a road was built, access was only by climbing through cuts in the rock, making it a simple matter to defend and survive through the centuries.

More than 300 years ago Acoma was the scene of a major uprising against the Spanish. A Franciscan padre, who built a church atop the mesa, was tolerated for years, but when he and his works came directly into conflict with ancient tribal deities, the good Father had to go. According to legend, during the Pueblo Revolt of 1680, indigenous people rose up to kill 400 Spaniards including the priest, whom they hurled from the mesa, and drove 2,000 others out of the region. The church still stands; whether the story is true or not, it succeeds in stimulating tourism.

My first winter in New Mexico opens a new pastime that becomes one of the most meaningful activities of my life. In the early 1960s, inventor Howard Head perfected the laminated, plastic snow ski that heralded the popularity of downhill skiing. Although not well known as a skiing destination, New Mexico claims some of the country's best skiing conditions. As Pacific storms cross the Southwest, the Sonoran Desert sucks away moisture. When clouds hit New Mexico's Rockies, they release a snowfall of dry, light powder that makes for superb skiing. The local joke is you can get caught in an avalanche but lick your way out—and still die of thirst!

I enthusiastically take up the sport, and winter weekends find me at one of three main ski areas: Sandia Peak, Santa Fe Ski Basin, or Taos Ski Valley. Sandia Peak appeals to locals because it's only an hour's drive up the mountain's east side. Travel time reduces to 15 minutes the following year when a 2.7-mile tram, longest in the world, is built from the city limits up the west side. I often cut classes in early afternoon to enjoy a half-day on the slopes.

Two hours north, Santa Fe Ski Basin boasts the second-highest base in the country, thus assuring plentiful snow. Taos Ski Valley, another hour farther north, claims distinction as the steepest slope in North America. Called Al's Run, it's named after Al Rosen, a die-hard mountaineer who skied with an oxygen tank on his back, which was his answer to a doctor's warning that his heart could not stand exertion at high altitudes.

High on the ski slopes I rediscover the joy of being at one with Nature, joy that I found as a small boy exploring a small lake in a small sailboat. With much in common, sailing and skiing are individual outdoor sports with only sounds of Nature breaking the silence. The whoosh of a boat's prow cutting through water is similar to the soft crunch of skis carving through freshly fallen snow. These non-exertive sports let one float and flow with natural forces while remaining centered and peaceful in a meditative-like state. Participants move only according to the dictates of wind and sea or snow and terrain. Any attempt to power against these forces breaks a flow of movement. *(From these modest beginnings, throughout my adult years I went on to sail on virtually every major sea across the globe as well as ski at the world's most acclaimed winter resorts.)*

Diversions aside, the purpose here is to train and work as a nuclear engineer along with other young graduates. A condition of employment—one we all meet—is being granted Top Secret or Q Security Clearance, which allows access to dark secrets of America's history in building, testing, and deploying nuclear weapons. A three-day orientation educates us about America's nuclear arsenal. Starting with the first nuclear test at Trinity Test Site at White Sands, presentations cover developments up to the present, which is where our work now, 20 years later, is to begin. I'm surprised that all material is couched in technical and engineering terms with no hint of the destruction and devastation our work can wreak upon humanity. Every aspect of a weapon's deployment is discussed in unemotional, matter-of-fact terms as though we are doing nothing more than designing an automatic can opener.

Discussions focus not on why but how to build nuclear weapons, which present technical challenges unparalleled in the history of science. Imagine trying to build an automobile that will never receive a test drive but will go directly to a garage once it comes off the assembly line. There it may remain for years until one day, with only a few minutes notice, starting it becomes imperative. The key must be put into the ignition, turned one time, and the car must speed off—no second chance possible. Now imagine that an atomic bomb must be built to meet similar requirements. Despite advancements in modern technology, no machine exists that can perform given these conditions. Yet our assignments are to develop such devices. To carry the car analogy further, imagine the garage isn't in a backyard but rather in frigid conditions north of the Arctic Circle; alternatively, it may be in a sweltering equatorial rain forest. It could also be carried aboard a submarine to the ocean's depths or on an aircraft to the limits of the atmosphere. Now comes the crusher: because no one can say how and where it will be deployed, this car must be designed to withstand not one, but all these environments.

Attending meetings to find solutions to these and other technical challenges, I'm awed to be in the same room with Nobel laureates and acclaimed scientists: Edward Teller, Hungarian theoretical physicist known as the Father of the Hydrogen Bomb; Robert Oppenheimer, wartime head of Los Alamos Laboratory; Richard Feynman, Father of Nanotechnology; Isidor Rabi, discoverer of nuclear resonance technology used in magnetic resonance imaging; Norris Bradbury, successor to Oppenheimer and discoverer of electrical properties of gases; Glenn Seaborg, discoverer of plutonium and responsible for production of plutonium-239, a critical element in nuclear weapons; and others. Never once, however, does any one of these luminaries hint at the impact that activation of nuclear weapons will have on our fellow man.

One of these high-level meetings concerns a problem that had arisen in Italy. In the early 1960s the U.S. stored nuclear weapons there—classified information at the time—and suddenly an election put into power a premier with strong leanings towards Eastern-bloc countries. The question is: How does one give a nuclear weapon to a friend and still retain control if he should become an enemy? It's critical that a weapon not fall into wrong hands where it could be used against us. Perhaps more important is to ensure it not be disassembled to reveal the top-secret fusing and firing mechanisms. Any physics textbook explains how a nuclear bomb works, but the real secrets lie in the design of the triggering features.

The most viable solution is a "weapon skin integrity system," namely a small explosive device built to destroy secret circuitry if the weapon's skin is penetrated. Discussions continue: Just how should the explosive be made to kill the perpetrator, i.e., anyone within a few meters? Immediately, everyone focuses on intricate design challenges of creating the precise explosive impact to destroy life within a designated distance while leaving outlying areas undisturbed—a technical problem considered only as a performance specification with no attention given to the morality of destroying human life.

Another example of amoral, calculated thinking is evident during a meeting about developing the neutron bomb *(which fortunately is never built)*. Designed to kill all human life in the target zone, such a weapon would not disturb physical or material facilities. In a combat situation the intent is to capture a city by eliminating its people while preserving communication, transportation, infrastructure, and other facilities, which then could be taken over without resistance. Our engineering minds work with the problem of differentiating human from nonhuman entities with the object of destroying the former without harming the latter. Seen in a purely technical sense, this is a fascinating challenge. *(Unfortunately, it is one that has been solved by both antagonistic superpowers. But I cannot recall anyone at that time raising the slightest protest or expressing disgust about the purpose of devices we're asked to design.)*

It is a far-fetched example, but I could speculate the reaction if one day America's scientists were ordered to build a weapon capable of killing all children under three years but no one else. Design teams would focus on discriminating between three-year-olds and those four or older. Eventually someone would find an answer, perhaps by distinguishing between no teeth, baby teeth, and adult teeth. Most frightening, throughout these discussions no one would ask *Why?*

So, day after day, month after month, and year after year at Sandia, I—along with so many others—am caught up with technical challenges of the work. The unasked question, however, always hovers at the back of my mind. Finally, in fall of 1968 I can no longer live with my conscience. After six years, I leave the company as well as the nuclear weapons industry. But before I do, I'm assigned projects that bring the most wonderful times of my life.

# 11
# Out of Phase

*6/63 - 7/64, Age 22 - 23*

June 1963: As summer approaches and classes come to an end, I dread the thought of being cooped up in an office day after day. Sandia's liberal five-week vacation policy is not enough to satisfy my restless spirit. But when I read on the university's bulletin board about an opportunity with the American Field Service, I see the possibility of exchanging three months of office work for another fun, adventure-filled summer.

A generation earlier a volunteer ambulance driver founded AFS in an effort to mend the broken human fragments of war-torn Europe. Steve Gulatti believed that if youngsters could participate in exchange programs and live in other cultures, they would gain an understanding that could prevent future 20th-century savagery. Every year since it began, AFS has sponsored thousands of foreign teenagers to live with U.S. families while finishing their senior year of high school along with the families' teenage sons or daughters. When school ends, foreign students embark on a four-week bus tour of the country before gathering in the New York metropolitan area for a farewell extravaganza prior to going home.

The posting solicits college students to serve as bus chaperones because they're young enough to relate to the high schoolers, yet mature enough to keep them out of harm. I apply and am selected to serve on a bus departing from Houston in a month. Volunteer service provides justification for an unpaid leave from Sandia, and, combined with normal vacation time, I'm happily free all summer.

Flying to Houston on July 4th, I meet co-chaperone Linda Jane Irwin, a graduate student from Hawaii, and 55 exchange students. A traditional holiday picnic followed by fireworks brings host families and guests together the last time before the tour. Emotions run from sadness to excitement as the students anticipate the forthcoming trip.

Linda and I receive the itinerary but must keep it secret until we are underway. In past years when the schedule was announced early, some host families tagged behind the bus and made final farewells difficult. Holding back tour details will hopefully preclude a repeat. One secret still remains—one that Linda and I are not told. Although we know the final meeting place with other buses arriving from around the country must be somewhere near a New York airport, we can only speculate on the exact location.

On departure day a police cavalcade escorts our Greyhound bus out of Houston. After last choruses of *"The Eyes of Texas are Upon You"* subside and all eyes have dried, I announce the itinerary. The students hastily jot down the schedule and stuff it into stamped, pre-addressed envelopes provided by their host families hoping to make contact along the way.

Our first stop will be Lake Charles, Louisiana. Stopping for lunch, I telephone the AFS chairman in Lake Charles to advise our time of arrival. Approaching the city that afternoon, we notice a commotion ahead with several police motorcycles. The bus is flagged down and stopped, and I get out to see what the problem is. Just then a small band begins to play, and a delegation of city leaders steps forward to welcome us. Taken aback, I graciously meet them, and, after the students disembark, we stand around awkwardly for an official greeting. Flanked by motorcycles flying banners, we then get a police escort into the city.

Here, and at each successive stopover, new host families accommodate and entertain the students by taking them to all manner of attractions. Three days later, tired from nonstop activities but well-feted, we're back on the bus heading to Baton Rouge. First order of business, as per AFS instructions, requires students to write thank-you letters to their host families.

Discussing how to find a way to express appreciation to their hosts, the students decide to organize a variety show to present on the last night at each stopover. The program needs no rehearsal because all 55, who hail from 40 countries, have packed their traditional national dress, and each teen is prepared to present something typical of his or her home culture. Our program, which comes together quickly, includes a New Zealand Maori folk dance with twirling poi balls, Thai candle dance, Dutch folk dance with wooden shoes, Japanese rock song, Turkish stand-up comedy routine, Belgian lace-making demonstration, Japanese sword dance, Philippine folk dance, and a dramatic presentation from *The Diary of Anne Frank* by a German girl who was a finalist in the National Forensic League competition. In addition, because Linda is often mistaken for a foreign student, her presentation at the end of the program reminds everyone that Hawaii became a state four years earlier, and Hawaiians are Americans, too. When asked to prove she really is Hawaiian by doing the hula, she laughingly declines.

At the outskirts of Baton Rouge, a police cavalcade again escorts the bus to a greeting place where the mayor presents each student a key to the city. After a short ceremony and an introduction to host families, we disperse to our newest temporary homes. Over the following three days, families treat us with visits to the State Capitol, Louisiana State University, and nearby historical sites. On the last night in town, our students present the variety show to an appreciative audience surprised at their talents, and next morning we're on our way again.

After visits to a dozen more cities throughout Mississippi, Alabama, Georgia, the Carolinas, and Virginia, we arrive in Washington, DC, highlight of the trip. Our week here includes private tours to inform those unfamiliar with concepts of democracy. I'm fascinated to learn and re-learn things about our government from the perspective of an outsider.

For example, all three branches of government make legal determinations, but only the judicial explains the basis for its decisions. Questions asked and insights shared by the exchange students open my eyes to the wonder and beauty of my homeland and the precious freedoms we Americans enjoy.

After departing the nation's capital, Linda and I learn the final rendezvous point. Several thousand exchange students will converge at Rutgers University in New Jersey. Many original host families have learned the secret and are on hand as the buses arrive. The final four days bring everyone together with a wonderful program of music, food, speeches, and entertainment to provide an altogether memorable send-off. Again, just as in Houston, there are tears and heart-rending good-byes. The difference this time is that I, too, am now a participant and must admit a few tears spring to my own eyes.

With AFS responsibilities over, I travel to my paternal grandparents' home in Quogue on the south shore of Long Island and join family for two weeks of sailing, fishing, tennis, and beach-club pleasures to wrap up a wonderful summer. Now back in the same situation after graduating a year earlier, I plan to go west again, but this time southwest rather than northwest. Another difference: I will not hop freights, deliver cars, or hitchhike. AFS provides a return air ticket from Kennedy Airport *(then Idlewild Airport but renamed six months later for our 35th president)* to Albuquerque.

During the return journey, I begin to notice how people behave in different environments. Passengers waiting in the airport departure lounge in New York seem withdrawn, reserved, and anxious, glancing continually at their hand luggage to reassure themselves it's safe. The gloom of the rainy day is reflected in the mood of people who appear edgy, perhaps a consequence of contending with heavy traffic and crowds. When boarding is announced, passengers leap to their feet, crowd through the gate as quickly as possible, and somberly find seats aboard the aircraft.

Two hours later when the plane crosses the Mississippi River, moods begin to change. As densely populated centers of the East vanish and memories of pollution and traffic grow dim, we begin to see open expanses of plains, deserts, and mountains. People unwind. Several begin wandering the aisles and engage strangers in conversation.

As the plane crosses the 10,000-foot peaks of the Sandia Mountains and begins the descent, I see why Albuquerque is a so-called "strip city." Stretching 12 miles along Route 66 from the Sandia foothills across the plateau and up across the Rio Grande Valley past Three Sisters volcanoes to the west, the city extends only two blocks on each side of the highway before giving way to desert and sagebrush. Amused that the city is essentially a long thin line, I also see possibilities for growth. *(At a later date I purchase land at the edge of the desert by the base of the mountains—a property I hope will be my future home. Those who bought and subsequently developed these large tracts of desert outside the city in the early sixties profited comfortably, as one could see by flying into the area 30 years later. The strip city has filled out in every direction, and the explosive land boom continues unabated into the 21st century.)*

By the time our plane lands at Albuquerque Sunport, everyone aboard seems relaxed. In stark contrast to much jostling and bustling while boarding in New York, we deplane unhurriedly; strolling down the ramp while idly chatting with one another, we emerge into the dry heat of sunny Albuquerque. Although baggage carousels and car rental counters are usually scenes of impatience, here folks are in no apparent hurry. In crowded airports there are never enough of the right types of cars to go around, and similarity of suitcases creates a high risk of mix-up, making travelers alert, quick on their toes, and a bit suspicious. However, in the Sunport's less-crowded area, travelers appear calm and cooperative. I realize these changes in attitude do not reflect differences between New Yorkers and New Mexicans but rather differences between New York and New Mexico—in other words, people's behavior is, to a large extent, a function of the immediate environment. *(In years that follow, I witness similar patterns of behavior. For example, travelers flying east from Albuquerque appear relaxed but grow tense and begin crowding others while rushing for cabs upon arrival in New York City.)*

As cottonwoods and aspens adorn themselves in golden yellow and fiery orange in fall, I begin my final year of the TDP Program. Sam Berry and Bill Steinmetz—two others in the graduate program—and I rent a house in Albuquerque's northeast heights. With a swimming pool and a commanding view of the Sandias, we're well set up to lead happy bachelor lives.

After work I unwind by heading into the desert across plateaus, flatlands, and arroyos on my 250cc motorcycle. The German-made Zundapp is a good dirt bike designed to take spills; so, when inevitable mishaps occur, I simply let go and take a tumble across the desert floor. It's all part of the fun unless, of course, I land on a prickly pear cactus.

The motorcycle offers another advantage: Cars at Sandia and UNM are restricted to designated parking areas, but a motorcycle can pass through most obstructions to park directly in front of the destination.

I also take up riding a unicycle, prompted by an advertisement by Unicycle Corporation of America that capitalizes on the blossoming interest in snow skiing. Its brochures contend that body movement to turn on skis is similar to executing a maneuver on one of these devices; supposedly, mastery of riding one is a perfect off-season way to get in shape for skiing. Bill and I each buy a unicycle and within a few weeks are ready for a job in a circus. Riding the tricky cycle requires strong legs, a sense of balance, and body angulation. Although the practice does little to improve our ability to ski, we have fun fooling around while neighborhood kids gawk at our antics.

That fall Sandia implements a policy that impacts my work. Until now no one in the TDP Program had been given meaningful projects because students couldn't travel or handle full-time responsibilities while in school. But Sandia management worries that when they finish the program, some students will leave for opportunities elsewhere. Therefore, the new policy mandates that everyone be given responsible assignments.

Consequently, I'm promoted to project engineer to oversee a weapons program launched by Bendix Corporation, a prime Atomic Energy Commission contractor in Kansas City. The assignment requires travel to Missouri as well as Pennsylvania, Tennessee, and Florida; so, whenever UNM has a holiday, I pack homework and fly to one of these locations.

During the first visit to Kansas City, I give in to an irresistible urge. Donning old clothes and assuming a disheveled appearance, I head to the railroad yards. Mindful of last year's close calls when the rail car I was riding was humped, I duck into a nearby bar to mingle with railroad workers, hobos, and the usual itinerants. Just for fun, I inquire about next morning's east-bound trains.

I'm intrigued that different appearances determine how people perceive each other. Dressed in a suit as a bright young engineer, I'm acknowledged with respectful seriousness. Dressed more casually as a college student, I easily enter into light-hearted banter, and dressed as a vagrant at the railroad cafe, I sense a coolness and distrust. In later years I experiment with how clothing and behavior evoke different responses. If I'm quiet and timid, people don't pay much attention. If I'm loud and assertive, they back away. When I appear helpless and ask for information, they readily give advice.

For example, one day on a whim I enter a store specializing in religious materials and buy a clerical collar with shirt front. "Nothing illegal about wearing this," assures the salesperson. On the next business trip, I dress in the new garb, wear a conservative dark suit, and set out to explore my new identity. And what an identity it turns out to be! Strangers in airports continually greet me. Older women particularly go out of their way to say, "Good Morning," or "Good Afternoon," often finishing with "Father," and they pause as if expecting a response or a blessing. Caught off guard, I hurry by as though I'm late for my flight while turning back awkwardly to acknowledge the greeting. Soon, I learn the trick every man of the cloth must know: Prepare for these encounters by permanently wearing a pious smile of humility and quickly nodding, thus precluding the need to turn back.

To maintain a composed image in restaurants, I order something simple like soup, milk, and crackers. Service is always quick, attentive, and friendly. Sometimes the manager expresses pleasure at having a man of God as a guest and doesn't charge for the meal. I'm often escorted to the front of a wait line, and, always wearing the same humble grin, go ahead of other customers who, surprisingly, never object. What if someone wants to share a table or chat on an airplane—and that someone is another priest?

Well, I could explain that I'm role-playing for an upcoming movie. What if a situation such as the need to administer last rites or calm a would-be suicide were to arise? I figure I could quickly rip off the clerical collar before anyone noticed. Fortunately, these problems never come up!

Later that autumn I decide to aim for a place on one of the U.S. Olympic teams preparing for competitions next summer in Mexico City. Although a long shot, I still have well-developed muscles in my arms, back, and legs. "In what sport," I ask myself, "can this be an advantage?" Because I'm isolated in New Mexico far from water, rowing is eliminated. After researching, I find a competition that demands immense upper-body strength: Greco-Roman wrestling. This arcane sport doesn't exist in any university program but is retained in the Olympics because it dates from ancient times when the first Games were held. In Greco-Roman wrestling two opponents grapple but touch only above the waist. The object is to lift the opponent and throw him down to pin both shoulders to the mat.

I convert our garage into a small gym and work out daily with weights to further build my upper body. In cool evening hours I jog along trails in the desert, and before long my body returns to the peak of physical fitness last known two years earlier as a varsity oarsman. My life responds favorably to hours spent working in sweaty silence each day: I eat well, sleep well, and feel tremendous energy. But after a few months, realization sets in that I'm not really interested in going to the Olympics, and neither am I anxious to become a Greco-Roman wrestler—certainly not motivated enough to inquire through UNM's Athletics Department about a wrestling coach. I enjoy the pleasure and solitude while working my body, but I must have felt the need for an excuse to do it regularly, which is why I created the dream of competing. Abandoning the idea, I continue to work out with no particular expectation or goal.

When June arrives, I bury myself in books to prepare for two weeks of written and oral exams. I pass with a comfortable margin and am proud to receive the Master of Science Degree in Engineering.

After graduation and completion of the project in Kansas City, I anticipate a new assignment requiring more travel, but, ironically, my next project is management of a construction facility on a desert mesa just south of Sandia's premises in Albuquerque. I ask why I hadn't been given this project while still a student instead of one requiring travel away from classes. No one, of course, has an answer. I also ask why an electrical engineer is given a project in construction, but again no one knows, and the issue is forgotten.

Project Thunderwell will become a test facility to study propagation effects of shock waves emanating from weapon explosions. Elaborate monitoring instrumentation and high-speed photographic units are to be installed in a central command center with three satellite, semi-underground bunker stations. For three months another TDP graduate and I have the satisfaction of watching a barren tract of sage and mesquite transform into a multi-million-dollar project based on designs the two of us develop. Quite an undertaking for a couple of wet-behind-the-ears, 23-year-olds!

This project, however, affords a technique that ensures complete freedom in achieving success. With my two offices, one within Sandia's compound and another a 30-minute drive away at the Thunderwell site, I learn the dual-location strategy: When bosses can't find me at one location, they assume I'm at the other, and presume all is going well. Consequently, I have flexibility in creating a schedule any way I wish. I have no objection to being responsible for completing the project within a deadline and budget, but beyond this I want to be left alone. Completed on schedule, the Thunderwell project is successful. However, the greatest benefit is understanding my need to be independent and free from control. The life of adventure and freedom, which I relish, is inconsistent with being under any form of authority.

*(It is not until 15 years later that I understand the differences between independence, dependence, and interdependence. The first two are merely illusions; the latter is the essence of all existence. Only when I learn this am I able to relax and surrender to the flow of life—authority or no authority—around me. But for now, I relish my new-found sense of independence.)*

While working on the Thunderwell Program I realize I'm unhappy with the direction of my career. I'm not enjoying electrical engineering nor, for that matter, spending time around engineers. Although academic studies are fascinating because they delve into basic truths about the nature of the material world and reveal secrets of universal laws, actual work in engineering fields is another matter. Most projects involve searching through textbooks and literature to find formulas, standards, tables, or equations that are then adapted to the problem at hand. But where, then, is the excitement and challenge of discovery and innovation?

Good engineers, by definition, are specialists who must delve deeper and deeper into their specialty. All this specialization causes many to lose touch with the broader scope of the profession. Furthermore, after specializing for years, engineers tend to become narrow-minded and short-sighted, a tendency evident among many of Sandia's senior employees. Having invested six years of study, this realization is deeply disturbing. While I have no regrets about the years of study, I must acknowledge I have no enthusiasm for the day-to-day work of engineering and feel no affinity with the people engaged in the field.

More disenchantment: although fellow graduates from the Technical Development Program are excited about specializing in new electronic developments such as Integrated Circuits (IC), Large Scale Integration (LSI), and computers-on-a-chip, try as I may, I simply cannot get enthusiastic about sitting all day at a desk in a cubicle as part of a herd of design engineers trying to come up with solutions.

I realize I have an undeniable urge to be, to borrow a technical term, "out of phase." If Sandia's electrical engineers are in big rooms making specialized designs, I want to be in a little room doing anything except that. If the crowd is going left, I want to go right. Whatever activity engages the mass, repels me.

The Thunderwell project, however, offers everything I'm seeking. It requires knowledge not just of electrical engineering but also mechanical, civil, industrial, construction, and nuclear engineering. A typical electrical engineer might spend years developing one of hundreds of instruments used in the Thunderwell facility. I, on the other hand, learn about every system and subsystem being designed, yet retain an overall perspective and responsibility for the project. My hope is to combine all these different fields by working in construction engineering, which will be a big jump. But how to make this jump?

Within Sandia the Field Test Division oversees construction of facilities to test nuclear devices. (Until a nuclear warhead is mounted on a delivery system and becomes a weapon, it is referred to as a "device.") Known for attracting rebellious individuals who won't or can't handle stay-at-home desk work, this division sends these hard-headed specialists to the most remote spots on the globe. Accustomed to flying off at a moment's notice to locations so secret they can't tell their families, field-testers return with intriguing stories both amusing and harrowing—stories that can only be discussed among those of us who have security clearances. They travel regularly to desert locations at Salton Sea (California), Nevada Test Site, Tonopah Test Range, and White Sands Missile Range where they swear that hot, desolate, dusty work brings out the best in a person. In the 1950s these men (sorry, no women in this era) conducted atmospheric tests throughout the South Pacific, and they speak of many little islands as if they were suburbs of Albuquerque. Islands such as Aker, Howland, Kwajalein, Baker, Eniwetok, Bimini, Marshall, Johnston, and others—many of which were obliterated by the nuclear tests—conjure up memories of good old days that will never be surpassed. I'm fascinated by the stories field-testers tell and am intrigued by the prospect of this type of job and the related global travel.

Because President Kennedy signed the Atmospheric Test Ban Treaty with the Soviets a year earlier in 1963, I see an opportunity. As a condition of treaty ratification, Congress extracted a promise from the president that the United States would maintain a readiness capability to resume atmospheric nuclear testing within six months in the event the Russians violate the treaty. This responsibility is passed to the Atomic Energy Commission, which in turn charges Sandia with building up and maintaining the required readiness posture.

While much of this work is to be done in Albuquerque, a skeleton force of field-testers is needed in the Pacific test area, and I'm determined to be part of this group. Completion of the Thunderwell facility on time and within budget should be clear evidence of my ability to manage a large project. Furthermore, the fact that I'm a "TDP golden boy" should give me additional leverage.

When the timing seems right, I approach the manager of the Field Test Department to request a position in the newly formed Readiness Task Force. Recognizing that I'm young, lack extensive experience, and would not be utilizing the two years of studies the company financed, he's ambivalent. However, he acknowledges two things: First, because I'm a bachelor, being away from home on extended travel is not a problem. Second, if I don't get this position, I might leave Sandia. After weighing these considerations, he offers me the job, and I return to my own division, which is responsible for electronic component development, to extricate myself. My manager and mentor, Cliff Selvedge, immediately protests:

"You'll be throwing away your career if you transfer into Field Test!" he objects. "You will fall behind in new developments and soon become obsolete in the field. Electronic engineers don't go into that type of work if they want a successful career."

Countering his arguments, I eventually succeed in being released. Although I don't know where I will be going, what I will be doing, or what responsibilities I will be given, I'm delighted, as happens so often in my life, to be out of phase with my peers.

[July 1963, Houston, age 22] American Field Service bus chaperone with 55 foreign-exchange students

[1964, Albuquerque, age 23] My first car, a Ming-green '62 Ford Victoria

[1964, Albuquerque, age 23]
At home with roommate Bill Steinmetz and Dallas visitors

**[1964, Albuquerque, age 23]**
Desert scramble on Zundapp 250cc motorcycle

# 12
# Quogue

*8/64, Age 23*

My new assignment begins in fall so I return to our family home in the village of Quogue (rhymes with fog) for the last weeks of summer. Quogue is not just a location—Quogue is a timeless experience. I had vacationed in Quogue every summer of my life, and, although my travels later would take me all over the world, seldom has a year passed without returning. Although generations of Quogites have come and gone, the pattern of life has never changed from when I was growing up in the 1940s and 50s. Twenty-five years later my children and the children of the friends I had grown up with would relive these same experiences.

Quogue is a Native American name given to the small village nestled on the shores of Shinnecock Bay three-fourths of the way out from Manhattan on the south coast of Long Island. Across the bay a thin strip of land, barely wide enough to accommodate two-lane Dune Road, edges up against sand dunes, and just beyond lies the Atlantic Ocean. On either side of Quogue—Westhampton to the west and Southampton to the east—developers have been on a building spree that started in the 1950s and has continued unabated ever since. Ticky-tacky houses, cheap condominiums, and sprawling shopping centers have popped up on every vacant property.

Each year growing crowds from the New York metropolitan area swell these neighboring towns almost to the bursting point.

Stately, three-story, turn-of-the-century homes surrounded by immense lawns, manicured gardens, and meticulously trimmed eight-foot hedges testify that Quogue has been spared this surge in development and mushrooming population. My paternal grandparents own one of the old homes in Quogue, and each summer branches of the Schroeder clan—my family included—descend upon them and take over their 13-bedroom, six-bath house.

Community life centers on the village post office where everyone congregates daily after the postmistress sorts letters and magazines into the cubicles, to pick up the day's mail. Even those who have no reason to expect mail show up to share the day's gossip. For us kids this is where we meet our friends and then pedal away to create the day's adventures. Even on Sundays when there is no mail, many show up just for socializing.

As a child I would poke along the shoreline of Shinnecock Bay stirring up marine creatures. Jellyfish, their long downward-streaming tentacles, floated silently waiting to sting an inquisitive hand. Crabs, ranging from enormous, slow-moving horseshoes to tiny scurrying hermits, moved in and out from secret hiding places to escape my intrusion. Digging in the sand was risky; when disturbed, a burrowed crab defends itself by snapping claws around exploring fingers. However, the risk was worth it if I found clams, mussels, and snails that I could open on the spot and pop into my mouth.

Several islands scattered throughout the bay are the exclusive domain of seagulls, sandpipers, and terns. To venture onto one of these spits of land, as I often did, was to invite an attack, particularly during nesting season in early summer. After picking a clam or oyster from the shoreline, birds would soar several hundred feet and drop their prey onto the island below, then swoop down and peck through the broken shells to devour a waiting meal. What a treasure trove for a young boy! Here I would often collect a bounty of broken shells to present that evening to my mother, grandmother, and appreciative aunts.

One could understand the bay only by knowing the tides, weather, and phases of the moon, which determine the rhythms of the sea life. Which fish could be caught, for example, and when? Our seafood diet changed with the moon's cycles. We had the best luck catching snappers in late afternoon on cloudy days during early stages of a new moon. We could always net crabs from dock pilings early in the morning. Knowledge of where and how to find tiny sea creatures was also tied to these diurnal patterns, and those who made a living from the bounty of the sea—the crabbers, anglers, and clammers—adapted to life accordingly.

Granny, my father's mother, first took me sailing at age three and I've been sailing ever since. Through the years on the bay I developed sailing and racing skills in locally designed, 16-foot, center-board wooden boats known as SSs (Shinnecock Sloops). Racing success depends not only upon skill, but also on knowledge of the bay's secrets. Victory goes to those who understand the tides, currents, shoals, and points of land that give winds more draw and strength compared with the prevailing breeze. As I grew older, I regularly beat other boats in weekend races but was never quite able to surpass my father. Everything I knew about racing I learned from him, but I'm not sure he taught me all that he knew.

The bay was a 10-minute bike ride from home and another five-minute pedal over the drawbridge to the ocean beach club. The vast expanse of empty sand dunes and ocean beaches on Long Island's east-west coastline, which stretches as far as the eye can see in either direction, protects the bay's gentle waters from the Atlantic's pounding waves. Ocean waves, which build from their usual height of three or four feet to more than seven feet in rough weather, create an endless succession of rip tides, sea pusses (swirling undertows), and rough surf. Fifty yards offshore five floating barrels anchored to the sea floor serve as a safety measure, offering a hold-on for anyone being pulled out to sea in a rip tide.

My earliest memories of Quogue Beach Club relate to the significance these barrels had for my great-grandfather who had been blind since early adulthood. Although he loved to swim and was not one to let his blindness slow him down, he was, however, unable to be in the surf alone for fear that a breaker would give him a tumble. To ensure his safety, his daughter, my grandmother, would lead him by the hand through the waves and swim with him to the barrels. There she left him and returned to shore. He would swim for another dozen yards out to sea, then turn and—feeling the crests of the slowly forming waves—swim along the coast parallel to shore. After 20 minutes or so he would turn and swim back parallel to the beaches. There was one difficulty, however. He couldn't determine when he was opposite the beach club.

My grandmother solved this problem in a clever way. She kept a large bell on the beach that she would periodically ring to signal his distance from the beach club. A special ring sequence indicated when he was opposite the club. As he neared the barrels, other codes guided him to hold on until my grandmother arrived to escort him back to shore.

In addition to the bay and the ocean, a third center of activity is Quogue Field Club where our family mornings often begin with sets of tennis—a game different from the hotly competitive game we play in Louisville. Whether relaxed by the smell of salt spray or deferring our competitive juices for the afternoon sailing races, I don't know. In either case, tennis in Quogue is light-hearted and playful. Later we pedal to the beach for a swim, followed by lunch on the upper deck of the beach club atop dunes overlooking the sea. Then we're off to the yacht club for sailing, fishing, or crabbing.

*(There was, and still is, a soothing rhythm about life in Quogue. Even after death claimed my great-grandparents, grandparents, and parents, the quality of life remains beautiful, unchanging. Babies arrive and as they mature, the bicycles pass to another generation. Boats receive annual coats of varnish and worn rigging is replaced, thereby assuring all is ready by late spring to offer summer crowds their sought-after sailing adventures. Our arrival each summer never fails to stir a fresh sense of new beginnings combined with a deep sense of timelessness. These summers in Quogue provide one of the only times that, contrary to much of the rest of my life, I don't feel "out of phase.")*

[1964, age 23] Quogue Beach Club with Mom and Dad

[1964, Quogue] Shinnecock Yacht Club

# 13
# Prelude to Hawaii

*9/64 - 10/64, Age 23*

Upon my return from Quogue to Albuquerque, my new boss describes the position in terms so astonishing and marvelous that I'm delightfully stunned. First, the job is a promotion to manager level and comes with a salary increase. Second, rather than being based in Albuquerque, I will be stationed at the Sandia office in Honolulu. Third, I will receive a living and meal allowance that will essentially be another salary increase because I don't maintain home expenses in New Mexico. Fourth, I will be responsible for projects on the four main Hawaiian Islands where I'm expected to fly twice a month, and will also, as needed, visit projects at a half-dozen equatorial Pacific islands and atolls. Fifth, my boss will provide no guidance and expects nothing more than weekly progress reports—in other words, I will be my own boss. I leave his office in a daze. Every hope and dream have come true: I will work on outdoor construction projects, have no supervisor on site, receive a sizable increase in pay, and live in paradise. What more could a guy possibly ask?

For the next month I study classified material about America's nuclear test activities in the Pacific. I delve into atlases to find the tiny islands and atolls—some of which no longer exist—where detonations have taken place and review information collected from each test going back to the early1950s. In addition to this scientific background, I receive a briefing on the political aspects of the Atmospheric Test Ban Treaty signed in August 1963.

The official name, Partial Test Ban Treaty (PTBT), forbids nuclear weapon tests in the atmosphere, outer space, and underwater, but allows for underground tests. President Kennedy assured Congress the U.S. would maintain a six-month, readiness-to-test posture vis-à-vis the Russians. This means that if the Russians detonate a nuclear device in the atmosphere, even if none of our instrumentation or testing equipment is ready at that time, we will follow suit within six months. The U.S. would, for political reasons, conduct a nuclear test for no purpose except to blow a remote Pacific island to smithereens. My job will be to ensure that the instrumentation and test facilities are ready to collect accurate data if the Soviets cheat.

Not knowing when I'll return to New Mexico, I explore once more the beauty of the state. On weekends I join the "Aspencades" driving into the mountains to witness the magnificence of changing aspen leaves. Set against the intense greens of firs and pinon pines, the bright yellows and golds of the luminous aspens weave magical patterns across the mountainsides, making them look as if scattered fires are setting the ridges and valleys alight. Few sights could be more splendid!

I visit numerous ghost towns —sites that bear testimony to many broken dreams. Some of these mountain towns were abandoned following mining busts a century earlier when gold fever ran rampant throughout the West. Others appear as mute testimony to the dashed hopes of those trying to create religious-based societies. And some of these once-thriving towns were destroyed by natural disaster—flood, tornado, pestilence, disease, or drought.

Bidding farewell to friends over wonderful dinners of unique Native American-Mexican foods found only in New Mexico, I question whether it's foolish to leave this place I've grown to know and love. The lifestyle is unique and appealing. I'm acquainted with people from different backgrounds and run into friends everywhere. I've grown accustomed to desert living and feel wonderful in the clear air and blue skies of mile-high Albuquerque. So why leave?

I don't know why; I only know that it's time to move on. The same questions arose when leaving Louisville. There, too, I know the city and the people, enjoy the lifestyle, and always feel at home. It would have been easy to stay there, but then I would have missed New Mexico. True, I can always go back to Kentucky and still enjoy everything it offers. In the same way, I can come back to New Mexico. But now it's time to explore more of the world.

On the evening before departure, I meet friends in the valley at a quiet outside bar surrounded by giant cottonwoods. A Spanish guitar plays mournful tunes in the background, and the sweet aroma of pinon logs burning in the open fire pit fills the air. My heart is in my throat. Forced to choose at this moment, I would elect to stay.

But the decision has ready been made. I have an air ticket to Honolulu and there's no turning back. Furthermore, roommates Bill and Sam are leaving too. Bill is on his way to Harvard Business School. Sam is transferring to Sandia's office in Livermore, California, and then plans to enter the doctorate program at Stanford Business School.

The next morning, after flying to Los Angeles and changing planes, I'm crossing the Pacific. Five hours later I step into liquid sunshine that wraps me in a warm embrace. There's no question whether I made the right decision. This moment is the start of a love affair with Hawaii that lasts not only during this assignment but throughout my life.

# 14
# Working in Hawaii

*10/64 - 1/66, Ages 23 - 25*

A series of volcanic eruptions 28 million years ago along a rift zone in the ocean floor formed the Hawaiian chain. From Midway Island at the north, a sprinkling of atolls, rocks, and islets stretches several hundred miles southeast before the first sizable island, Kauai, appears. Because it is older than its sisters to the south, Kauai's vegetation and terrain reflect the advanced state of lava breakdown into organic soil. The lushness of flowers and variety of plants this rich soil affords creates a profusion of colors and sweet aromas that give Kauai the name "The Garden Island."

A rugged northwest range of 4,000-foot mountains along Kauai's Na Pali coast is inaccessible except by helicopter. Within these jagged peaks is the wettest spot in the country—Mount Waialeale—where rainfall exceeds 450 inches annually, equivalent to 1¼ inches per day. Rainfall drains into the Wailua River, Hawaii's only navigable waterway, which flows across the island to the eastern coast and into the sea. On a boat ride upriver, one passes fern grottos and enters a lush jungle that conjures images of the Garden of Eden. Farther up in its many reaches, one finds the world as it must have been thousands of years ago.

Kauai's main road begins at the northern extent of the mountains and follows the coast clockwise around three-quarters of the island until it dead

126

ends at the western extremity. The northern terminus of Hanalei is arguably the most scenic and tranquil location on all the islands. Sitting with a Mai Tai in hand on the veranda of Hanalei Plantation Hotel (which unfortunately has since been torn down), one could gaze across the bay at water cascading down the face of the opposite mountain; it's easy to get so absorbed in beauty that one loses count of the many waterfalls. Scenes of Bali Hai from *South Pacific* were filmed here. Yet as beautiful as the movie scenes are, they don't compare with the magic of the actual setting. Hanalei is also immortalized in Peter, Paul, and Mary's folk song *Puff, the Magic Dragon*.

At the other end of the road, engineers and technicians at Barking Sands Naval Air Station and Sandia Labs fine-tune America's most sophisticated instruments of nuclear war. The contrast between the road's two ends is chilling—one end a beauty and the other a beast or, maybe more appropriately, one end Heaven and the other Hell.

Sandia built its Barking Sands facility to monitor high-altitude measurements of nuclear test effects. Simultaneous with a nuclear detonation hundreds of miles away on a remote island, researchers at Barking Sands launch multiple rockets a hundred miles into the upper atmosphere. Reaching maximum height, the rockets eject instrumentation packages that parachute back to earth. During descent—before plunging into the ocean where they are lost—they transmit data to telemetry stations connected to Sandia's 40-foot instrumentation trailers.

Technicians outfit these trailers in Albuquerque with sophisticated equipment to receive, process, and analyze these signals. When a nuclear test is imminent, military cargo aircraft transport the trailers to Kauai where they integrate into the command-and-control network. My assignment is to supervise the construction of rocket launchers, telemetry stations, and the trailer park and hook them up with power and communications.

In nearby mountains Sandia stores the rockets in caves secured by gates of thick steel plate across the entrances. Every three or four months, technicians bring a rocket down for a test firing, and my arrival coincides with such an event. Although normally a routine exercise, this time the unexpected happens. During transport the rocket falls off the carrier.

Expecting the rocket to ignite, our group scatters, but when nothing happens, we gather to decide what to do. We can't test fire the rocket because it might be damaged and fly off course. We can't return it to the cave because someone might inadvertently ignite it. We can't simply dispose of it because it would create a hazard.

We finally come up with a solution, one that appeals to the child in each of us. Transporting the rocket to our compound, we use a backhoe to dig a hole 15 feet deep. Carefully lifting the rocket, we place it nose downward in the hole so the exhaust tube and tail fins stick up above ground. Then we wire the rocket for firing and wait until nightfall to begin the countdown.

When Time Zero approaches, we back away and hold our breath in anticipation. Then, *BAAAM!!!* The most terrific burst of sound Kauai has ever known shakes the ground as a column of fire leaps to the heavens. This comic relief eases the tension engendered by the somber nature of our work. Newspapers the next day report an explosion accompanied by a flare of light hundreds of feet high, but for security reasons we make no public report of the incident—until now!

After studying an ancient map of Kauai, I drive a four-wheeler north from the test site along a sugarcane road until arriving at a secluded quarter mile stretch of glimmering sand beach hidden from view by thick vegetation. On the map it's named Queen's Pond and was originally reserved for the Queen of Kauai and her retinue. Fifty yards offshore a coral reef breaks incoming waves assuring calm bathing for the queen. In the weeks ahead whenever I'm back on Kauai, after work I go alone to this beach, strip down, plunge into the calm water. Then I lie in the sand enjoying the day's last minutes as the sun sinks beyond the reef into the sea. In a fantasy, the queen and I play footsies in the sand while her handmaidens loll in the shallows. Alone on this isolated beach, a sense of peace comes over me as I momentarily forget the seriousness of the work that brings me to this paradise.

Comfortable about the week's progress at Kauai, I fly to Oahu, the next island south, where I oversee construction projects at Hickam Air Force Base and Barber's Point Naval Air Station. When the Air Force flies nuclear weapons from the mainland to a Pacific test site, they unload on Oahu where Sandia personnel assemble the final configuration before delivery to the destination. At both bases my job is to construct a weapons-assembly building; at Hickam I'm also building a reinforced pad for parking aircraft carrying multi-ton weapons. It's staggering to think that a freshly minted college grad is allowed to spend millions of dollars on these projects without outside oversight or control. Admittedly, however, the situation suits me just fine!

Most people think of Hawaii as a land of swaying palms, gentle winds, flowering vegetation, and warm swimming waters. But much of the islands have been taken over by the American military and is off limits to the general public. Coastal land from the midpoint of Oahu's south shore at Fort Derussy stretching west is practically all military—Pearl Harbor, Hickam Air Force Base, West Loch Naval Station, and at the southwestern tip Barbers Point Naval Air Station. More military facilities on Oahu include Fort Shafter, Bellows Air Force Base, Wheeler Army Airfield, Schofield Barracks, Tripler Military Hospital, (where Viet Nam wounded were treated), Waiawea Naval Base, Wahiawa Navy Lodge, Kunio Navy Base, Fort Ruger Diamond Head Military Reservation, Marine Corps Base Kaneohe (prime beach area), Honolulu Coast Guard Station, and satellite areas including bombing and gunnery ranges plus extensive military housing developments. Similar military installations have been established on all the other islands as well.

It's perhaps no surprise that when Hawaii was dissolved as a U.S. Territory and given statehood in 1959, a hostile minority of native Hawaiians considered this act a massive land-grab by the U.S. Government. Not only were military installations expanded, but ancestral lands and crown properties of the Hawaiian monarchy were appropriated for national parks, monuments, sanctuaries, and other federal purposes. Many Hawaiians were, and still are, angry. Statehood anniversaries often bring out organized protest demonstrations. However, because Hawaii's economy and most jobs depend upon tourism, visitors to the islands seldom see indications of this discord.

South of Oahu on Maui, 10,000-foot-high Haleakala Mountain blew out its insides eons ago creating the island's main physical feature, Haleakala Crater. On the mountain's western slope, Sandia's small building houses a photo station that films and records data from distant nuclear detonations. Cameras have unobstructed views through unpolluted atmosphere across the ocean to the Pacific test areas. The facility sits atop a mammoth slab of reinforced concrete that prevents cameras and recording equipment from vibrating when seismic waves from the blast arrive. The assignment to upgrade the facility and install a 10-foot, chain-link fence around the building unfortunately brings conflict with the National Park Service.

The mountain is home to the silversword plant, so named because the blossom takes the shape of a silvery sword mounted on a green, cactus-like pedestal. Haleakala National Park Service fences these individual endangered plants, which are endemic to the island of Hawaii, to protect them against hungry deer and other ungulates. The problem is that the fence Sandia needs for security purposes would enclose one of the plants next to the building. The Hawaiian Department of Natural Habitation, maintaining it needs unrestricted access to the plant, objects. In this confrontation between the so-called forces of progress and the vulnerable creations of Nature, I'm happy to say our side loses. I construct the fence as planned but with a convoluted fold to keep the silversword plant outside our enclosure.

In contrast to the profuse vegetation found on the northern islands, vast lava fields cover the island of Hawaii, the Big Island—southernmost and youngest in the chain. Hilo on the southeast coast is a popular tourist center because nearby Kilauea Volcano, the only active volcano in Hawaii, continuously spews fiery ash and lava in patterns that can mesmerize one for hours. Lodges near the edge of the crater provide picture-glass views into the bowels of the caldera. Visiting a century ago, Mark Twain wrote that Kilauea with its belching flames and fiery lava is the closest man will ever come on earth to seeing Hell.

During a recent eruption, hot cinders fell on a nearby forest killing all vegetation and covering the area with several feet of ash. Leaves, bark, and smaller limbs all burned away leaving only ghostlike tree skeletons where a verdant forest once reached skyward. Here along Desolation Walk one feels the starkness of death. The quiet boneyard is all that's left to tell of the disaster that struck with sudden fury—a scene eerily reminiscent of what the world might look like if nuclear Armageddon should occur.

The twin peaks of Mauna Loa and Mauna Kea dominate the island's landscape. Mauna Kea towers above the ocean almost 14,000 feet and plunges 20,000 feet to its base at the bottom of the Pacific Ocean. If measured from this base, it's the tallest mountain in the world, making it almost a mile higher than Mount Everest. Mauna Loa, slightly shorter, is said to be the largest mountain on the planet by volume if measured from its ocean base. High on Mauna Loa's slopes I'm responsible for constructing a telemetry station used for blast simulation. During the test, Sandia's three modified Boeing 707s, still new aircraft in the early 1960s, circle the mountain to monitor airborne data from whatever distance and altitude are required. Mauna Loa's telemetry station generates signals that simulate effects of a nuclear blast, allowing engineers aboard the 707s to calibrate their instrumentation systems. At 12,000 feet the station sits high enough to duplicate an atmospheric nuclear detonation environment, and the deserted mountain assures no signal disturbance.

But the mountains aren't completely deserted. High on the treacherous landscape of Mauna Kea a state penitentiary houses the mountain's only occupants. Minimal security is required because the slope is so gradual that once in the undulations of lava fields, an escapee would find it impossible to determine the way down and would likely wander in circles. Anyone who has walked even 50 feet into a lava field knows shoes are ripped to shreds in no time. The intensity of the sun's rays in thin air, which provides no protection at this altitude, causes temperatures to soar well over 100 degrees Fahrenheit. An individual would soon succumb to heat or die of thirst. Alternatively, he might fall 20 or more feet to his death in a cavern if the thin crust of a lava tube were to break. He would be safe only by following goat trails, but they don't necessarily lead to the bottom. With any luck a runaway convict would find his way to the prison access road and be spotted by guards who would rescue him. If he should miss the road, he would end up as a pile of parched white bones scattered across the black volcanic landscape like the ghost trees on Desolation Walk.

Returning from Mauna Loa at the end of a workday, I often go for a refreshing swim at Kealakekua Bay south of Kailua-Kona on the western coast. This sleepy village, known for great snorkeling with spinner dolphins, is where Captain James Cook, the first European to come upon the Hawaiian Islands, was killed. The Hawaiian Visitors Bureau doesn't advertise the fact that he likely was eaten—the usual fate of enemies of the islanders.

In addition to duties in Hawaii, I'm responsible for projects in more remote areas. One of these involves neighboring uninhabited islands of Baker and Howland—flat palm-tree-studded spits 45 miles apart less than one degree north of the equator. Planning is underway to detonate a nuclear bomb on one island while the control center and instrumentation would be on the other. It's expected the blast would destroy the first island leaving no trace. The thought occurs if someone were to get mixed up and the detonation was on the island designated for monitoring, then the other piece of sand with its few palm trees would, undisturbed by man, continue to enjoy sun and wind as it has for thousands of years.

My responsibilities also include setting up instrumentation facilities on Johnston Island, another staging area for Pacific tests. (It was originally called Johnston Atoll, but military chiefs dignified the place by promoting it to island status.) Rumor has it that poison gases are stored at the western end of Johnston because prevailing easterly trade winds ensure that any leakage would blow harmlessly out to sea. T-bone steaks, astronomically high wages, and Saturday afternoon fights are the main reasons anyone puts up with life on this isolated, scorching rock. These fights must have been the brainchild of a military psychologist who had an insight into life on an isolated tropical island. Five thousand men (and not one single woman!) work under the hot sun all day, and although there is a swimming pool, they are denied a cooling ocean dip because tiger sharks claim these waters as their main breeding ground.

Tempers often flare and angry outbursts are commonplace, but anyone involved in a fight must pay a fine and is removed from the island. Consequently, whenever an altercation breaks out, it's quickly postponed with, "I'll see you Saturday afternoon." When Saturday arrives, those who want to participate—and this means a large majority of the workforce—line up to enter the recreation hall, which is padded with mattresses on the floor and walls. After being searched for weapons—a search that often yields knives, brass knuckles, and improvised weapons—each combatant strips to shorts and enters for battle. Rules are simple: You can fight anyone any way you want. Military police wander throughout to ensure no one is beaten to death: otherwise, no holds are barred.

Each man stalks around searching out someone he had a grudge with during the week, and as pairs go at it, all hell breaks loose. First-aid teams and medical staff stand by, and it isn't long before the first casualties are brought out. Black eyes, bloody noses, and swellings are commonplace. Occasionally someone breaks a bone, but rarely do things go that far because such an injury would deprive a man of his ability to work. At the end of the allotted time the air has been cleared, and everyone goes to the showers and afterward to the bar. I notice the fiercest combatants often sit together over beers as they recount the fun they had smashing each other. They build a friendship that lasts at least into the first part of the following week. The controlled, organized fight every Saturday allows combatants to nurse wounds on Sunday and be ready to work by Monday.

A few months after arriving in Hawaii, I'm assigned an unusual project: to explore the feasibility of hiding nuclear weapons in the ocean as deep as seven miles by harnessing them to buoys tethered to anchors set in the seabed. Activated by a sonar signal, a windlass would pull the weapon down the anchor chain. When the weapon is needed, a ship or submarine transmits sonar signals that would bring it back to the surface where it can be retrieved.

The Navy conducts trials for this program at Andros Island in the Bahamas, and I receive instructions to represent Sandia aboard one of its ships. In short order I am on the way to Nassau. The itinerary from Honolulu calls for a layover in Chicago where I almost freeze in sub-zero weather because I have no warm clothes just for the stopover. Winter's shock makes pleasure that much greater when four hours later I land at sub-tropical Nassau.

I'm delighted to learn the Navy ship conducting trials is on maneuvers and not due back for another week. Taking a much-needed holiday (ha!), I check into the palatial Royal Britannia Hotel and spend the time (on an expense account) sailing, water skiing, skin diving, and lounging in the sun.

When the ship returns, I am off on a 10-day sojourn to anchor simulated nuclear bombs on the ocean floor. Throughout the maneuvers, the ship's captain, more than twice my age, and I engage in a series of altercations, quite serious at the time, but comical in retrospect. Until the design and development of a nuclear weapon is turned over to the Department of Defense, it remains under Sandia's control. The captain naturally is in charge of the ship. Each morning he briefs me on the day's maneuvers. Because I often have different ideas, I respectfully tell him what they are.

He says something like, "Look here, son, we need to...."

In response, I say, "Excuse me, sir, but first we have to...."

Much as he dislikes it, he has to do things my way.

The exercise of anchoring bombs becomes like an Easter-egg, hide-and-seek game. We place anchors and buoy systems throughout deep waters of Tongue of the Ocean, a part of the sea protruding into Great Bahama Bank alongside Andros Island. After each placement we activate the windlass to pull the simulated weapon far below surface. A few days later we cruise back to find these nuclear eggs by transmitting sonar codes that signal them to resurface. Some do. For those that don't, it becomes a real egg hunt, and we call upon the backup system—Navy divers who plunge into shark-infested waters and manually cut the buoy system free from the anchor chain. Once released, the dummy weapon shoots to the surface with such force it's propelled high into the air. I shudder to think what would happen if the package contained real weapons.

The concept of hide-and-recovery of nuclear weapons in the ocean eventually proves feasible, but several years later the government shelves the program. In 1971, more than 20 nations ratify the Seabed Arms Control Treaty banning ocean deployment of nuclear weapons. So, all ends well.

On the way back to Hawaii I stop in Albuquerque, pick up ski gear and clothing, retrieve my car from storage, and drive to Colorado with friends for two weeks of skiing over Christmas holidays. Afterward it's back to the Islands to resume work I left a month earlier. Happy to be back, I understand what Hawaiians mean when they say to truly enjoy the Islands, one has to regularly leave and then return. Otherwise "Island Fever" or "Polynesian Paralysis" can make one numb and oblivious to the unchanging beauty of these remarkable islands. Seen for the first time, evening sunsets, unspoiled beaches, gently swaying palm trees, and fresh, luscious flowers are breathtaking. But when one sees them every day and they never change, one loses sensitivity. Then it's time to leave, but only for awhile.

[March 1965] Getting to know Mary in Aspen and Albuquerque

[July 1965, age 24]
Lounging at Waikiki Beach beside Ginger's pink towel

[December 1965, Honolulu] Living the Dream

[Christmas 1965, age 24, Waikiki] Strolling the beach with Linda

[January 1966, age 25] Sandia Telemetry Station amid lava fields atop Mauna Loa

# 15
# The Big Wave

*10/64 - 1/66, Ages 23 - 25*

My passion for Hawaii, apart from work, focuses on Oahu's northwest coast: Makaha, Waialua, Sunset, Waimea, Pipeline, and Waianae. These beaches, which stir hearts of surfers all over the world, attract top board riders to compete in taking on legendary monster waves that arrive in late fall and winter.

Waves originating on Australia's east coast in September cross the Pacific along the greatest uninterrupted distance on the planet, and during weeks of travel accumulate enormous concentrations of energy. Upon arriving at the Hawaiian chain, they build in shallow water into gigantic curlers often more than 30 feet high. Then they unleash their fury on the exposed coast as if trying to demolish any obstacle that disturbs their journey. From time immemorial these waves held out a challenge to anyone seeking to master them. Early Hawaiians selected their chieftains by their skill with 10- to 16-foot Koa boards in riding these enormous combers.

Not immune to this challenge, I'm soon initiated. Starting at Waikiki where waves seldom exceed five feet, I master the basics but avoid the northwest coast until I feel ready to tackle big ones. I've seen too many videos of giant walls of water crushing down upon surfers as they gasp for air.

The biggest hazard of this dangerous sport is a loose-flying board that can pop into the air and then slice down like a knife. Surf crashes with a deafening roar all around you and, if timing is off—if you misjudge the wave—disaster occurs. In a tense moment you either dive away from the board or try to stay with it at risk of being thrown off dangerously near what could be a treacherous missile. If you jump off, you must swim to the bottom to avoid being crushed by five tons of water and then immediately resurface before the undercurrent that follows a wave drags you across sharp coral and rips you to pieces. It's up for a breath, a quick look for the next wave, and—if one is about to break—another plunge to the bottom. Between dives and gulps for air, you might take a few pathetic strokes to secure the board. Once retrieved, the choice is to go back out and try again or paddle to shore knowing that as you draw closer, breaking surf becomes increasingly violent.

But if you can stay with the wave, the ride is heavenly!

Determined to master at least one medium-size wave, on a Saturday I drive to Makaha. For a half-hour I sit on an isolated section of beach watching how the waves break. Sizing them up from shore is essential, because once in the surf it's impossible to see what's happening. Thrown from your board, you must rely on memory to know where to go for safety. During a quiet interval between breaking curlers, I enter the surf and paddle out to where waves are forming. For the next hour I ride a number of smaller ones. When ready, I make a couple of half-hearted attempts to catch larger ones, but each time lose courage at the critical part of the curl.

Finally, I muster all my energies and commit to a bigger wave. As the board slides down the steep face, I spring to my feet and cut across diagonally. Any attempt to drop straight down the face is dangerous, because with built-up speed I would shoot out in front of the breaking crest, lose momentum, and become engulfed in the crashing turbulence. In spite of cutting broad on the diagonal, I feel as if I'm dropping directly to the bottom of the wave. Although essentially in a free-fall with minimal weight on the board, I manage to keep my feet steady. By now my heart is beating wildly. Only the board's edge makes contact with the wall of water as it slices across. Five feet below is the bottom of the wave, and five feet above the water begins to curl. Leaning sideways and poking an elbow into the curtain of water while engulfed in the pipeline with crashing surf all around, I'm poised in the middle of every surfer's dream. As the wave collapses behind me, a jet of air escaping from within blasts me clear of the foaming frenzy.

How I survive—let alone remain standing—I'll never know. I have no skills in dealing with these waves which to me are monsters but to pro-surfers are considered small. Having succeeded in my quest, I now am ready to quit. Grateful for the experience, I paddle to shore, content from now on to confine myself to gentler waves on the south shore.

*(I have reflected on this one ecstatic ride hundreds of times. The tension of being suspended in a wave and trying to stay upright brought me to a state that mystics talk about—a state of mindless awareness completely in the here-and-now with every sense fully engaged.)*

For a year and a half in Hawaii, I balance job demands with enjoyment of this paradise. On Oahu I rent a room at the Reef Tower Hotel a half-minute walk from Waikiki Beach and keep a surfboard wedged behind the passenger seat of a rented Ford Mustang convertible. When the workday is over, I head to a beach for an hour of swimming and surfing followed by dinner at a shoreline restaurant. Afterward I seek out a bar or nightclub and pass the waning hours sipping a rum while reflecting on the day's events.

Duke's Nightclub—my favorite—is owned by Duke Kahanamoku, the legendary Hawaiian surfer and swimmer who won five gold and silver medals at three Olympic Games. Duke customarily sits in the back of his club while piano player Don Ho, the island's renowned entertainer, performs songs composed by Kui Lee, who also attends regularly. Every night Don sings Kui's songs, holding the audience spellbound for hours with his honey-coated, salty voice accompanied by his inspired piano playing.

At the time Kui was dying of throat cancer but continued to write a steady stream of songs such as "I'll Remember You," "Days of my Youth," and "Ain't No Big Thing." All three became standards for a new generation of Hawaiian music. As death neared, his songs about his beloved islands grew in intensity and strength until one evening his strength gave out and I never saw him again. But I'm awed for having been in the presence of Hawaii's three most famous contemporary celebrities.

One evening while looking for a place to have dinner I discover Chuck's Steak House, a small hole-in-the-wall nestled among towering Waikiki hotels. Decor is not the usual Hawaiian motif of seashells, fishing nets, and surf photos but rather snow-covered mountains, ski scenes, and an alpine mountain village. It dawns on me that when skiing at Aspen last year, I had dined at a similar restaurant also called Chuck's Steak House. Décor there was purely Hawaiian with photos of giant curlers ridden by native surfers. Intrigued, I converse with customers at the bar and learn that proprietor Chuck Rolles is a competitive surfer and downhill skier with trophies in both sports. From this modest beginning, Chuck pioneered a nationwide chain of restaurants featuring steaks and salad bars.

These restaurants have become hangouts for ski and surf bums who live for big snow and giant surf. In these days when no one over 30 years old is to be trusted, Chuck's restaurants are sanctuaries where young people escape from frustration with the Viet Nam War and everything that seems wrong with America. Life for them revolves around autumn surfing in Hawaii followed by winter skiing in the Rockies. These two pastimes coincide with seasonal demands for waiters, bartenders, hotel staff, shop workers, surf instructors, ski coaches, and other jobs to support the influx of vacationing tourists. Itinerant young folks easily find work to pay living expenses so they can spend free time at beaches or on snow.

This wild, rootless existence allows an escape from responsibilities of families and steady jobs. Although I hang out on the fringe of this crowd, I'm not interested in being on-the-go at such a frantic pace. Furthermore, apart from the unpleasant implications of the job, I enjoy my work.

To the west of Waikiki Beach, a jungle of masts and shrouds at Ala Moana Yacht Basin blocks out the sky as completely as Diamond Head dominates the view to the east. Strolling through the marina one evening, I admire the luxury sailing cruisers and multi-million-dollar mega yachts tugging at mooring lines as though to break out to the beckoning ocean. Although made for wind and sea, these magnificent yachts sadly remain tethered all week and even on weekends often remain at the docks to serve as floating bars for owners and their guests.

In a corner of the marina I spot a cluster of older sailing yachts that appear worn and probably have many miles under their keels. I'm surprised to discover young people in their 20s and early 30s living aboard. Intrigued and delighted to have stumbled upon another group that doesn't want to settle into suburban living and daily commuting, I chat with these couples to learn about their lifestyle. The man, usually the skipper, is likely an engineer, architect, or other professional. The woman is typically a nurse, secretary, or teacher. With such readily marketable skills, they can get jobs wherever they go. These adventurers are temporarily in Hawaii as a stopover in their travels to see the world.

Most started in California where they plunked life savings into an old boat on which they lived for months while holding down jobs to cover living expenses and costs to refurbish their vessel. Once well-provisioned, they quit work and cast off for the two-week sail to Hawaii. Here they rent dock space at Ala Moana Yacht Basin for three or four months, find new jobs, and buy an old Volkswagen Beetle or something similar to explore the island.

Eventually they quit the jobs, sell the vehicle, and head south for the three-week sail to Tahiti. Upon arrival they again look for work, buy an old car, likely a Citroen or Renault in this French possession, and enjoy another few months of exploring. Then off again they go, sailing through Polynesia, Micronesia, and other central Pacific Islands until reaching New Zealand or Australia. These new friends explain that their travels typically last a couple of years, after which they're ready to go home. Recapturing their savings by selling the boat at the last port, they return to the mainland and settle into a more traditional life.

Some boats have infants and young children on board. Parents explain it's no problem traveling with young ones as long as they get used to living in life jackets. For kids it's a great experience because they become early swimmers and learn about life at sea before entering school. What a happy, cheerful group I meet that evening. Walking back as darkness descends, I smile to see the beat up VWs in the marina parking lot.

When Sandia's managers come to Hawaii to inspect developments of the Readiness Program, I quickly learn they want to see test facilities in only half the allotted time to justify their expense accounts. For the other half, they want me to show them the tourist attractions. Thus, I brush up on Hawaiian culture and history. By the end of my assignment, I know the islands so well I'm tempted to inquire if the Hawaiian Visitors Bureau needs another tour leader!

For 18 months I live here and relish each moment. Because every three or four weeks I return to Albuquerque for meetings, I experience the joy of returning to this tropical paradise many times. This period is a happy one for me. I appreciate being left alone to do my job and schedule work priorities as I feel best.

Best of all, I love delving into literature, history, music, and culture of the Hawaiians and Pacific Islanders. Like the thrill of standing atop a surfboard riding that big wave, I'm enjoying the best of life. I know the ride can't last forever because every wave has to break. But while the surf is up, I am on a never-to-be-forgotten high, riding the big wave.

# 16
# Down-Hole

*1/66 - 4/66, Age 25*

At the end of 1965, Sandia Corporation reports to the Atomic Energy Commission (AEC) that buildup for the Readiness Program has been completed. A number of dry runs are successful thereby confirming that within six months the United States is prepared to conduct an atmospheric nuclear test. All facilities and equipment are in place, and ongoing work in Hawaii and the Pacific testing area is now strictly maintenance. My job comes to an end, and the big, wonderful wave I've been riding the past year and a half is beginning to break. As every surfer knows, when a wave starts to curl it's time to get out fast and move on.

Soon another wave forms on the horizon. I'm promoted to manager of Sandia's field office in central Nevada at the Nevada Test Site (NTS), later named Nevada National Security Test Site. I'm not keen on moving there, but at age 25 am proud to be the first of 50 engineers in the Technical Development Program to receive this promotion as well as the youngest manager in the 5,000-employee organization. Reporting to me will be 25 employees in Las Vegas who are permanently assigned to support the underground nuclear testing programs.

During the previous two years, feasibility studies of underground testing, otherwise known as Down-Hole testing, had shown advantages over atmospheric testing. Scientists can set up experiments in exact relation to the detonation site and aren't buffeted by storms, winds, or waves. Climate conditions are not a concern, and technical personnel have easy access to the nuclear device and their experiments.

Bidding farewell to Hawaii in January 1966, I return to Albuquerque to complete work in the Readiness Program. I purchase a Mustang convertible similar to the ones I rented in the Islands and, heeding the advice of Nevada coworkers, get one with air conditioning. This choice may seem contradictory, but I'm warned to keep the top up with air conditioning running during daytime when the sun is blazing. Night is the time to lower the top and enjoy balmy, desert air.

After a daylong drive from Albuquerque to Las Vegas, I arrive at my new home, and, just as with my two previous moves, the setting sun paints the sky with vibrant reds and oranges—a welcoming omen for the next phase of my life. For two weeks I rent a hotel room in Las Vegas just off the famous Strip and face an hour-and-a-half commute both to and from work. The southern boundary of the NTS lies 80 miles north of Las Vegas and extends well over 100 miles farther north. Apart from a handful of isolated homesteads and tiny communities, this region is deserted, making it ideal from the standpoints of safety and security.

While learning the job, I realize commuting hours leave no time for anything other than work. Once at the Site, I often must drive another hour or so to visit various work locations. Some days I'm in the car up to six hours. However, a simple solution presents itself. I move into a mobile home at the Test Site, thereby saving three hours driving each day. The trailer is my residence for six months, and apart from weekend sojourns into Las Vegas, I'm near my office 24 hours a day. *(I never imagined this decision would upend my life 15 years later with tragic consequences.)*

Sandia and the two weapons labs, Lawrence Radiation Laboratory and Los Alamos Scientific Laboratory, have devised two methods to conduct underground nuclear tests—one vertical and the other horizontal. A vertical configuration involves drilling a shaft to a depth of a mile or more and inserting a line-of-sight pipe that focuses radiation from Ground Zero at the base of the shaft onto an array of hardware mounted at the surface. An open pipe with a surface diameter of 36 to 48 inches must exactly align with the nuclear device a mile below. Within milliseconds after detonation giant ball valves must swing 90 degrees to close the pipe thereby preventing nuclear effluent from escaping into the atmosphere. Venting would not only endanger those in surrounding areas but would also violate the Nuclear Test Ban Treaty. Because detonations vaporize much of the earth surrounding the explosion, they cause subsidence at the surface resulting in craters hundreds of feet in both diameter and depth.

A horizontal orientation, which requires tunneling a drift into a mountain, offers the advantage that scientists can place experiments at varying distances from the source of the blast rather than just at the surface. It's also more convenient when experimenters can walk the entire length of the drift to inspect stations along the way. A mountainside test requires similar millisecond closure at the opening of the drift to contain radiation.

Engineers and scientists design experiments to monitor and measure the impact of a blast and the radiation emitted at specified distances from Ground Zero. Active experiments connect with cables routed to instrumentation trailers where signals feed into electronic equipment. After the blast, when radiation levels are tolerable, personnel dig out the passive experiments from the nuclear rubble. A main objective of the tests is to measure effects of an enemy's nuclear weapon intercepting one of ours. By exposing our weapon components and systems to countering radiation, scientists can determine their vulnerability and make improvements.

Technical designs and engineering concepts involved in these tests are far beyond the industrial state of the art. One example is a down-hole television camera developed by our Sandia Field Test Office. Sometimes equipment becomes stuck in the pipes and shafts, and with this television system we can lower the camera and lights to record the problem on videotape. Then the trick is to extricate the camera without jamming it. Because the camera often examines a section of pipe following a detonation, the television casing must withstand temperatures of thousands of degrees in a highly radioactive environment. At the time we develop this system, nothing commercially available comes close to the sophistication of our design.

Another of our projects is the design and installation of a three-state seismic system to monitor shock waves from nuclear detonations. The system serves two purposes: (1) to determine whether the blasts reach their full predicted yield and (2) to obtain information about shock damage to structures. Data is used to defend the AEC against construction damage claims allegedly caused by nuclear explosions. Las Vegas casinos and other establishments would sometimes submit claims contending the underground shock waves caused cracking in their foundations. These structures, however, were often built by pouring concrete directly over the desert floor without stabilizing the foundations, thereby not conforming to building codes. The seismic data would prove the blast effects were either non-existent or so weak they could not have contributed to the damage.

Our office provides logistical support for more than 100 Sandia workers who commute weekly from Albuquerque and Livermore to work on the 50 or so projects under way. We provide vehicles, lodging, airline tickets, cash advances, and support for administrative and technical matters. Our machine shop makes special fittings and mounting brackets that must stand up to the desert environment—sandstorms, torrential downpours, 100-mile-per hour winds, snow, and temperatures that swing from sub-freezing to above 100 degrees Fahrenheit.

The job is interesting, but not much fun. There's a soberness surrounding it and little incentive to make a big effort. If budgets overrun or time schedules slip, there's a perfunctory scolding from managers who then accept the new reality. But one thing keeps us on our toes: the danger of radiation exposure. Daily we work with this deadly menace, and, having heard many radiation horror stories (secrets kept well-guarded by the AEC), we know better than to believe public information provided by the government. Radiation dosimetry badges monitor exposures, and each Monday when the weekly computer printout is posted we check how many milliroentgens we picked up the previous week. Anyone exceeding the official limit is required to leave the Site, but long before this limit is reached, those whose readings are close would, on their own accord, make a hasty departure.

According to computer printouts, exposures I receive remain well below allowed limits. Nevertheless, I am worried. I work at the Site for two years, and for the first six months wear a dosimetry badge only during working hours and not during the other 16 hours I'm still on Test Site premises. The actual accumulation remains unknown. *(Since the mid-sixties, various state and federal organizations responsible for establishing acceptable exposures of workplace radiation have reduced the safe levels a number of times. Establishing a direct correlation between radiation exposure in Nevada and what occurs 15 years later is probably impossible. I can only speculate the two are not independent.)*

A nuclear weapon consists of two parts. First is the so-called "device" containing nuclear material with fusing and firing systems that cause the detonation. Second is the more complex weapon delivery system composed of deployment mechanisms, casement, assembly mountings, and missile and bomb configurations. For purposes of conducting underground tests, only the device is needed, assembly of which is the responsibility of the two atomic weapons laboratories—Los Alamos Scientific Laboratory in New Mexico and Lawrence Radiation Laboratory in Livermore, California. Because a nuclear device typically weighs under 100 pounds and can be carried in a suitcase, elaborate security procedures are necessary to ensure its safekeeping.

For an upcoming test, code name Derringer, security teams from Los Alamos transport a fission device to the Test Site where I, as site manager, am to take accountability. On the appointed morning two security guards appear at the office to escort me to the down-hole shaft. This is an awesome moment because I will come into "possession'" of a nuclear bomb. Although assigned to me, the armed guards are to ensure I don't grab the bomb and run!

They ride the elevator with me down the mile-deep shaft to Ground Zero where the device is already in place. In the presence of more armed guards together with representatives from Los Alamos Laboratory, I present identification which is scrutinized and certified by all present. I then sign documents stating I'm taking possession of the device on behalf of Sandia Laboratory. Although I try to look as though I know what I'm doing and that I do this sort of thing on a routine basis, I doubt I fool anybody. Surely, my naivety must be obvious. I look at the little package and endeavor to appear knowledgeable although I have no idea if this is what it's supposed to be. However, I go through the procedures, then ascend back up the shaft leaving behind guards who I hope know what to do because clearly I don't. Later this thought prompts a smile: I am the sixth nuclear power. On this day the United States, Russia, England, France, China, *and Peter* are in possession of nuclear bombs!

Although Sandia takes seriously the work I'm doing, I don't. And the U.S. Army back in Louisville doesn't either. The local draft board has been trying to induct me for two years ever since I lost my student deferment following completion of graduate school. Around this time in the mid-sixties Louisville finds itself in the national spotlight because of her two world-famous sons—both contemporary Americans. One is Colonel Harland Sanders of Kentucky Fried Chicken fame whose photograph is a familiar sight among the chicken-hungry peoples in countries around the world. The other is Muhammad Ali, formerly known as Cassius Clay or the Louisville Lip ("Dance like a Butterfly, Sting like a Bee"), who is beginning to immortalize himself in the history books of the boxing world.

During the 1950s, Cassius and I grew up at opposite ends of Louisville. Upon reaching the age of 18, we both dutifully complied with the law by registering for the military draft at our Local Draft Board #47. For the next six years I was in school and exempt from service. Cassius was called for the pre-induction written examination, took it, and flunked. He was thereby classified as unfit for service and became exempt. However, after a few years when he had earned his first million dollars in the boxing ring and had become the world heavyweight champion, people began questioning if he was really unsuited to serve his country. Or had he simply outfoxed the Army? Made to look ridiculous because of its decision, the Louisville Draft Board felt the sting when people said "Cassius' fame is Louisville's shame."

Consequently, the draft board, hoping to regain the respect and credibility it lost, determines not to allow further exemptions and therefore starts chasing after me. For years the paper battle between the draft board and Sandia rages. First, the board—thinking no one from Kentucky could be smart enough—doesn't believe I am really designing nuclear weapons. When Sandia informs them I am living in Hawaii, the board becomes more suspicious, thinking I might be a surf bum avoiding his patriotic responsibility. Later, when Sandia reports I have moved to Las Vegas, it is too much. The draft board probably has visions of me trading in a surfboard to become a blackjack dealer. It won't exempt me and also refuses to transfer the file to New Mexico as Sandia requests. The board is likewise not impressed with the argument that I have the Top Secret military security clearance and would pose a national risk if captured by the Viet Cong.

Meanwhile I'm becoming increasingly nervous. In the middle of this process I receive a call to come to Louisville to take a pre-induction physical, which I do and I pass. Once again Sandia appeals at the local level, but the board again denies the request. Sandia then takes the appeal to the next level at the state capitol in Frankfort, but the district draft board there also denies the request. Next step is to President Johnson's desk. Here the Presidential Appeal Review Committee establishes that, indeed, I am working within the defense sector and grants me a critical-skills deferment, prompting me to return to work and forget the matter.

But the deferment is valid for only one year; twelve months later the process starts over. Once again, Sandia appeals at the local and district levels to no avail, but the Presidential Appeal Review Committee renews the deferment for yet another year.

*(I'm still unsure which outcome was better. Had the Army drafted me, I would have completed service in two years. As it was, I had to work at Sandia in and around military services for eight years often feeling, as many civilians do, treated as if below the entry-level rank of private.)*

For five months while living at the Nevada Test Site, my private life takes on a pleasant, quiet rhythm. At the end of each workday a two-minute walk from the office has me home where I change clothes and saunter to the Olympic-size swimming pool for an hour of exercise. Back at the trailer, I indulge in a beer or glass of wine and a few hours of reading before strolling to the Site's steakhouse for a quiet dinner alone. Then it's home again to read a few more hours before going to bed. What pleasure it is to follow this routine every weekday and fall out of touch with everything except myself!

On weekends, however, the pattern varies. Saturday mornings I drive to Las Vegas to enjoy the city's entertainment and attractions. Choosing a different luxury hotel each time as a base of operations, I enter, glance at a few rooms to understand the numbering system, and wander outside to the pool where, as though I'm a hotel guest, I register with a room number to use the pool. (Checking rooms beforehand avoids signing in with three digits if the rooms have four.) I spend the day at leisure alternating in and out of the water and enjoying poolside food and drinks.

After changing my clothes, in late afternoon I join happy hour, a Las Vegas tradition to stimulate evening gambling. Options for dinner include one of the two or three hotel restaurants or any of dozens along the Strip. After-dinner shows and entertainment range from raunchy western bands to big-name celebrities such as Frank Sinatra, Dean Martin, Don Rickles, and Sammy Davis, Jr.

The first month I give in to a temptation to gamble, but after finding it impossible, except as a fluke, to win at any games, I discover a method of progressive betting at roulette that, surprisingly, yields $20-$25 each hour. I start by betting one dollar on the black or red. If I lose, I up the bet to recover the loss and still have a net gain. If a losing streak continues, the next bet would equal all the previous losses plus another chip that could get a win. The challenge is to know how much to place on each subsequent bet. Concentrating every moment is essential...and exhausting.

After three or four hours, all the while enjoying free drinks served to everyone at the table, I walk away with enough winnings to pay for dinner and a motel room. Next morning I'm back at a different luxury hotel to enjoy the routine again before returning home Sunday night refreshed and ready to get back to work.

Although happy with life, I consider pursuing a different direction after reading the African exploits of British explorer, adventurer, and businessman Sir Cecil Rhodes. With accumulated wealth, he established the Rhodes Scholarships throughout English-speaking countries (and Germany). These scholarships finance two years of academic studies in England. Rhodes envisioned fostering global peace by giving outstanding young people opportunities to study at one of his country's great universities.

Rhodes' idealism fires my imagination. Furthermore, my maternal grandfather, Alec Saxton, had attended Oxford University and, as a stocky six-foot-three athlete, had been an oarsman on the rowing team of St. John's College. The combination of Rhodes' vision, connection with my grandfather, and love of rowing come together to prompt me to apply for a scholarship. I envision a new adventure stirred by returning to academia and rowing.

After submitting forms along with references and transcripts, I await the invitation to an interview together with other candidates who qualify in the first round. Sure enough, a few weeks later a letter arrives inviting me to appear before the Rhodes State Selection Committee in Albuquerque. At the appointed time I'm called before this august body for several hours of questioning. The interview is to determine how well I can think when thrown unrelated questions ranging from beliefs about God to opinions on foreign affairs. Afterward I don't remember how I answered; I know only that I gave opinions on subjects that had never before occurred to me. I presume the answers were viewed as naive and unfocused. Nevertheless, on paper I present a respectable academic record that surely should serve me well.

At the end of the day the Committee announces two names from our group, and the winners advance to the Regional Selection Committee. As the chairman reads the names...suddenly, cold showers! I am not one of the two. I have been eliminated—a shock that leaves me stunned, but not from missing the opportunity at Oxford. It's the impact of *not winning*. Having never failed to achieve an objective, it hadn't occurred I would fail in this instance. There is no sadness or bitterness, just the shock of rejection. I don't know what to make of it. For hours I wander around Albuquerque in stunned silence trying to grasp what happened. *(Had I been more aware, I could have used this moment to learn something about ego, but I missed the opportunity.)* Later in the evening I fly home to Las Vegas, my self-confidence shaken for the first time.

A few weeks later, upon learning the two candidates selected in Albuquerque were eliminated at the regional level, I have mixed feelings. My reactions are those of a child. On one hand, due to an attitude that anyone who tries to get ahead of me is going to end up in trouble, I'm pleased those two have not won scholarships. On the other hand, if they had won, I could rationalize the very best had beaten me. Therefore, I'm unhappy they did not win. Spirits rise, however, when I learn the winner from our region is indeed the very best. Bill Bradley, a scholar-star athlete, was a classmate a few years behind me at Princeton, and while I was designing bombs at Sandia, he played professional basketball for the New York Knicks. *(Bill went on to become a three-term senator from New Jersey and later a presidential candidate.)*

In time, after stepping back and gaining perspective, I'm amazed and disgusted the experience stirred up such childish feelings and attitudes—things I had no idea existed. A final resolution is to shed these immature feelings and spend the next two years doing something equally or even more adventuresome than whatever I would miss in England. The incident proves to be good for me—a valuable learning experience that knocks me off an ego-built pedestal. Perhaps for the first time, I feel humbled.

The incident behind me, I return to life in Nevada. Having grown tired of casino weekends in Las Vegas, I look for another way to spend time away from the Nevada Test Site. Before long I discover the city's library-museum, a treasure house of information, books, and artifact collections that prompt me to dive into reading about the background and history of Nevada. Thereafter, I spend many weekends digging into everything about Nevada at the library...and it is here that I make one of the most important decisions in my life.

[1966, Yucca Flats, Nevada Test Site, age 25] Instrumentation trailers monitor experiments at Derringer Test Site

[1966, Rainier Mesa, Nevada Test Site] Drift tunnel of Midi-Mist Test Site

# 17
# Knowing Myself

*4/66, Age 25*

What I have achieved by age 25 is clear, but what about who I am? Although I haven't been very tuned in to my inner self, it hasn't mattered because my energies are directed outward. The focus of life is on doing, not being. Still, there are glimpses of my inner self—a few insights into what make me, *me*. Here's what I observe:

**SEPARATENESS.** The dominant feeling is separateness. Although I relate to and connect with different types of people, my background, work, education, interests, and activities are different from others, and I don't identify with any groups. I have always tended to avoid crowd-think. Whichever way a group is going, I take another direction. Being on my own has always been satisfying. For example, in group projects in college I would offer to do all the work myself, knowing I could work better alone than with others. I am not a team player. Likewise, I've never been interested in group events. Spectator sports, concerts, rallies, and other large gatherings have no appeal.

Separateness gives rise to alternating feelings of aloneness and loneliness. The dictionary says they mean the same, but I experience aloneness and loneliness as opposites. Celebrating inner wholeness in aloneness, I know moments of bliss and joy. Resistance, tension, and worries disappear. When I don't need to relate to anyone, defenses fade and social expectations—considered prerequisites when in the company of others—are dropped. In aloneness I relax into a feeling of trust and surrender to whatever comes.

But on occasion, the sense of separateness brings not the joy, the bliss, of aloneness, but rather the sadness of loneliness. Instead of feeling the inner wholeness of aloneness, I feel the absence of the other. I yearn for companionship—but no one is there. Emptiness surrounds me. Waves of loneliness engulf me; I feel fragmented. Why am I not part of a group with others all around? In such states of loneliness, I sometimes enter the darkness of deep valleys—valleys made dark in contrast to sunny peaks felt in aloneness.

*(If I had been more aware at these times, I might have seen beauty in sadness and accepted it for what it is, the complement of joy. For without these dark valleys, sunny peaks can't exist.)*

**GOAL ORIENTATION.** My energies are directed toward accomplishments, particularly at work. In Hawaii I took pride in overseeing the building of aircraft runways, telemetry stations, warehouses, testing facilities, roads, storage bunkers, antenna fields, and other such constructions; in Nevada, personal satisfaction derives from carrying to completion underground nuclear tests.

This drive to achieve pays off on the job and earns top marks with management. Unfortunately, it doesn't pay off in private life. For example, I look upon surfing as something to be mastered—a skill to be perfected rather than simply enjoyed. The compulsion to succeed prevents laughter each time I fall off. I miss the fun of the sport because after every spill I become angry at my "failure." When I eventually do succeed, the accomplishment doesn't give pleasure for its own sake; I merely add one more achievement to the list of accomplishments. In focusing only on the end result—in other words, by making the destination the goal—I miss the journey.

*(Later in life a therapist explains the connection between goal achievement and separateness. He will point out I am an "outstanding" person but am unable to grasp what outstanding means. On the surface it means one who accomplishes and thereby distinguishes himself; however,*

*on another level it means "standing out" or apart, and in my case means separating from everything and everyone. In striving for achievement, I stand apart from the crowd, thereby creating a distance. Focusing solely on achievement of a goal, I miss the experience of the moment. I dash into something, master it, and then dash off without being touched by it. By standing out and being separate—by focusing on future success—I pay a price. I not only deny the joy that comes from simply being involved but also miss the human connection, the camaraderie that others enjoy.)*

**PRAGMATISM.** I'm attracted to the philosophy of Will James, Father of Pragmatism. He doesn't go to the ruthless extremes of Machiavelli ("The end justifies the means"), but James suggests morally right deeds can justify morally wrong actions. For example, he would willingly lie if doing so would result in an outcome that benefits everyone. Regarding issues of honesty and dishonesty, he explains how the former is not necessarily preferable to the latter. Sometimes honesty can hurt, while dishonesty can bring relief. For instance, when talking with a person who is dying, it may be preferable not to be completely truthful.

As another example, when asked if he drank a cup of coffee in the morning, James weighs consequences of answering "Yes" compared with "No." If they're equal, he answers truthfully. However, if consequences of a "No" answer are significantly positive (for example, receiving a million dollars), and if "No" doesn't bring an extremely negative result (such as going to prison), he would take the practical approach at the expense of truth. Buddha states this more succinctly, although in a different context, when he says, "If it works, then it is good."

Applying pragmatism at work, I willingly stretch the truth if necessary to get a job done. For example, when I want a building constructed in a certain way on a time schedule and the contractor resists, rather than argue I try to find a way around his resistance. Altering facts, I might say the structure is needed as a matter of national security or is required because of safety issues, neither of which is necessarily true. However, this pragmatic approach brings results.

Knowing the pragmatic way—truthful or not—is effective, I often manipulate situations. Yes, positive results occur, but people also see me as less than candid. Bosses appreciate that I get projects completed on schedule and aren't concerned how I do it, but this approach doesn't endear me to co-workers who are unsure where they stand and how much they can trust me. The job is to meet deadlines; however, if that means compromising worker relations, then pragmatism dictates!

**LEARNING.** I love learning anything new, not to accumulate or display knowledge, but simply for its own sake. When I moved to New Mexico, I read everything about the Southwest and the pueblo nations. In Hawaii, I absorbed books about volcanology, oceanography, geology, Polynesia, astronomy, and tidal waves that relate to the islands. In Nevada, I spent weekends in the Las Vegas Public Library learning the state's history that grew out of mining booms of the mid-nineteenth century. I read only non-fiction books to learn something I don't know as opposed to reading fiction which, although interesting, is limited to the author's imagination. Over the years I have read extensively about oceanography, astronomy, psychology, alternative medicine, geology and many fields of natural sciences. When approaching a new subject, I'm thrown back into a wonderful state of innocent ignorance that opens me to whatever is forthcoming.

**ADVENTURE.** Related to thirst for learning is desire for adventure. I organize business trips to begin Fridays and end Sundays so I can explore wherever I am over the weekend. *(Travels throughout my life have taken me to more than a hundred countries to ski, sail, scuba dive, hike, bicycle, or simply explore. Likewise, although I enjoy living in Las Vegas, I will one day welcome moving from Nevada to wherever and whatever comes next.)*

**RELATIONSHIPS.** With men, on the job I maintain professional cordiality that includes sociability and teamwork, but after hours I seek no further contact. Although most co-workers respect me, I am seen as a loner and keep distant to the point of being considered cold. I have the fortune or misfortune of being a graduate of the Technical Development Program and am earmarked as a rising young star within Sandia. This stature and my work ethic both attract and repel co-workers, but no matter—the priority is getting jobs completed, not relating to people.

In private life I'm close to only a handful of men, mainly undergraduate and graduate student roommates. Otherwise, I never seek close male companionship and even go out of my way to avoid it. Spending an evening at a bar in all-male discussions doesn't appeal to me, because companionship for its own sake is unimportant. I have no difficulty relating to men when engaging in recreational activities such as skiing or sailing, but afterward those relationships fade.

Relations with women are different and more complicated. Unlike with men, I find it awkward to meet and get acquainted with women. Sports, business, finance, travel, politics, and mutual friends are common interests among men. However, with women I become disarmed and at a loss because these subjects seem irrelevant. Once acquainted, though, I immensely enjoy a woman's company and feel relaxed and open. Even if there is no significant relationship and we simply sit in silence, I prefer to have a woman near me.

With a woman, I can be vulnerable, not competitive and on guard. I never feel threatened by women, which makes it easy to drop defenses and show emotions. Until now, though, I have not met the "right woman," and a deep yearning to truly open up with her—whoever she is—remains unfulfilled.

These, then, are the traits I recognize in myself as I come to the mid-point of the third decade of my life.

[August 19, 1966, age 25] Dancing with Granny at my wedding

[1967, Jemez, New Mexico, age 26] Building hot-springs pool

# 18
# Mary

*4/66 - 4/68, Age 25 - 27*

One Saturday morning in April 1966, while reading at the Las Vegas Public Library, I pause, suddenly struck with the idea of marrying Mary. Where does this come from? I don't know, but it's a powerful feeling that leaves me dazed for some time. Content with my peaceful life, I enjoy a solitary existence shuttling between the Nevada Test Site and Las Vegas. Not comprehending what love means, why would I want to make a life change? For some reason, it simply occurs to me that now, at age 25, it would be a good idea to get married.

Who *is* Mary?

Mary Overton is one of many women I meet during travels between New Mexico and Hawaii, but she doesn't disappear as many others do. I first met her at a 1964 New Year's Eve party in Albuquerque shortly before returning to the Islands. It may sound trite, but the meeting is a scene from "Cinderella"—well, not exactly the same, but here's how it happened.

Mismatched with a blind date, I turn attention to a blond, blue-eyed stranger wearing golden high heels. Carrying an open bottle of champagne, I approach and ask permission to drink champagne from one of her slippers to toast the arrival of 1965. She replies that anyone stupid enough to do this should certainly go ahead, and she presents one of her shoes into my waiting hand. Already semi-inebriated, I fill it as best as possible and proceed to drink, although the floor receives the greater portion.

Immediately the golden yellow fades to a darker hue as alcohol saturates the fabric. Seeing this, Mary offers the other shoe, saying I may as well drink from it as well and ruin both. Then, if I can get them cleaned, she would like them back. She presents her phone number to arrange returning the soggy items, and that's the last I see of her that evening. Next morning on the phone, I speak to her irate mother who doesn't consider the incident a romantic gesture but rather a financial waste.

Although I return to the Islands shortly thereafter, during trips back to Albuquerque I see quite a bit of Mary over the following months. Late in the spring she travels to Europe for five months; upon her return we meet in New York and together visit my family home in Quogue for a week of sailing, tennis, and bodysurfing. It's wonderful to see how Mary enjoys these sports. Afterward we fly to Louisville where Mary charms my parents. By the time we return to Albuquerque, I have stars in my eyes.

After I return to Hawaii, torrid letters fly back and forth, and shortly before Christmas I invite Mary to join me for a week. Mindful not to compromise other female relationships, the moment she arrives I whisk her to the inter-island terminal and fly to the Big Island for a week. Our relationship continues to grow. Back on the mainland in January, we drive to Aspen for a week of skiing and—thanks to a snowstorm that closes all roads—stay for two weeks.

The relation isn't only romantic—it's also financially advantageous. Mary purchases my car, which has been in storage, and saves me the monthly expenses. She also helps find property for sale at the foot of the Sandia Mountains, where one day I hope to build a home.

The Overton residence becomes a second home whenever I'm in Albuquerque, and I'm included in the family's social events. Mary's mother Helen is a patron of the arts and a gracious hostess who supports charitable causes by organizing benefits. Dr. Lewis Overton, a prominent orthopedic surgeon, was instrumental in founding Lovelace Clinic in Albuquerque and Bernalillo County Indian Hospital in Santa Fe. On weekends I often accompany the family to their cabin in the Jemez Wilderness where Mary's father proudly explains how he constructed, plumbed, and electrified the cabin himself.

But what about Mary? What attracts me? In addition to sharing the joys of sailing, bodysurfing, and skiing, we explore the attractions of Hawaii as well as pueblos and historical sites throughout New Mexico. Mary is attractive and vibrant with a zest for life—all the traits I seek in a woman.

I never propose, so Mary doesn't respond. But one day in spring, I announce that August 27th falls on a Saturday, which is my parents' wedding anniversary, and on that day, I want her to become my wife. It isn't a question, and Mary doesn't answer, only reflects a moment before we have our first disagreement. She points out that a week earlier on August 19th would be more convenient for her. So, the 19th it is.

The following weeks are a whirlwind of planning and preparations. Weekends I return to Albuquerque to a steady flow of parties and festivities leading up to one of the biggest weddings the city has ever seen. And so it comes to pass that on August 19, 1966, Mary and I are married.

I have been accused in jest by friends of marrying Mary to get my old car back, but I reply if that had been the motive, I could have gotten it back for a cheaper price; nevertheless, it's good to have it once again. Because we have each been owners, we name our car "MOPS," which combines the first letters of each of our names, Mary Overton and Peter Schroeder.

After the wedding reception we load MOPS with four sacks of cement for a construction project and drive to the Overton family cabin. Water for the cabin comes from a natural hot spring that Mary's father had diverted to supply the kitchen and bathroom. Perhaps unique in the world, the toilet flushes with hot water! The honeymoon project is to cement rocks together to form a swimming pool filled by the hot spring. After a week of work the pool is finished, and Mary and I soak for hours while sharing dreams of how we want our life to flourish.

The honeymoon over, we drive to our new apartment in North Las Vegas where life quickly falls into an easy rhythm. The hour-and-a-half commute each way to the Test Site is pleasant while riding in air-conditioned comfort on modern buses. Because the dangerous, curvy road, nicknamed the "widow-maker," is now a four-lane expressway with hardly a curve, commuting is no different than sitting in a comfortable chair at home. This enables me to devote three hours of enforced leisure to daily reading.

Meanwhile, Mary, who received an undergraduate degree from Northwestern University, pursues graduate courses in elementary education at the University of Southern Nevada. In addition, she substitute teaches in the local school district.

On weekends when people around the country fly into Las Vegas to play, Mary and I leave the city to explore the surrounding area, which abounds with forgotten ghost towns vacated when mining prospects dried up in the late 18th and early 19th centuries. As amateur archaeologists, we seek out Native American ruins and enjoy digging in rubble to retrieve shards and collectibles. With our Sunfish sailboat, a wedding gift from my parents, secured atop MOPS, we make frequent trips to nearby Lake Mead and cruise among the coves of its twisted shoreline. We also travel farther afield to sail on Lake Tahoe, Lake Powell, and the coastal Pacific waters of southern California.

Months earlier my family had planned a Thanksgiving reunion to celebrate the 50th wedding anniversary of my maternal grandparents, Pat and Alec Saxton—otherwise known as Grummy and Grumpy—at their home in Monroe, Connecticut. Paying for the cross-country trip would create a financial bind because every cent is tied up in furnishings for our apartment. Then I have an idea how to arrange free transportation. I send a dozen resumes to major firms on the Eastern seaboard and within two weeks receive several positive responses. A company in New Jersey and another in Delaware invite me to visit for job interviews. By accepting both, we secure two round-trip air tickets from Las Vegas to New York.

The job interviews go well, but prospects of moving back east are unappealing, and I mention this in the interviews. At the firm in Cherry

Hill, New Jersey, the interviewer doesn't quite get the picture when I explain I prefer to live in the West. He assures me this would be no problem and points out that many employees live in the western part of New Jersey and commute daily to the east side. Seeing that he doesn't understand, I drop the matter.

A joyous affair, my grandparents' anniversary celebration brings together more than a dozen friends and family members from three branches of the Saxton lineage. Also on this occasion I learn an invaluable lesson from my father. At the conclusion of the Thanksgiving dinner served at Hawley Manor Inn in nearby Newtown, I notice that he, unobserved by anyone except me, quietly asks for the bill. Surprised, I say something like, "Dad, that's way too expensive for you to pay alone."

"Peter," he replies, "there are times when things like this need to be done for the family. When you have a family, you will know when it's time for you to do likewise." *(I've never forgotten his words. At every family gathering I pick up the tab thinking of, and thanking, my Dad. I hope this gesture passes to my sons as well.)*

Back in Nevada, Mary and I suffer through December dust storms and escape over Christmas holidays to Sun Valley in southern Idaho for a week of skiing. As we enter 1967, we're living the happy life of newlyweds. In January, Mary completes the semester of graduate work and accepts a full-time teaching assignment.

Like all visitors to Las Vegas, we have become so mesmerized with the glitter that we can hardly believe our eyes when we discover a blighted area that the city leaders keep well out of public view. It is here at an all-Black school in the city's poorer section that Mary begins teaching. Although she often reports to the administration that students come to school in tattered clothes and are underfed, she finds little support to address these problems.

In spring I attend a three-week geology seminar in Albuquerque conducted by University of New Mexico professors to study phenomena of underground nuclear blasts. During a visit to a uranium mine in western New Mexico where we learn how uranium ores are extracted, a seemingly unimportant incident occurs. *(Thirteen years later, however, consequences of this incident drastically change my life.)*

As preparation for descent into the mine, participants are equipped with hard hats mounted with miners' lights connected to battery packs strapped on the right side of our belts. Exiting the elevator, we board an electric train for a half-mile ride along a drift to a location where mining is in progress. Riding three abreast in open seats, I'm squeezed with the battery pack tightly wedged against the right side of the car as we jostle along for a few minutes before arriving at the face of the drift where we observe miners extracting the different ores. Stooping to move around and in some places crawling on hands and knees, I feel both admiration and sympathy for the miners who put up with this daily work.

Returning to the elevator shaft, the battery pack again abrades my right hip. At the surface, grimy and dusty from head to toe, after removing the battery pack I discover my shirt and pants soaked with blood. Closer examination shows a deep cut with flecks of ore dust covering the wound. After local medics flush it with water and apply disinfectant and a bandage, I forget about it.

A month later a scar has formed, but Sandia's doctor in Albuquerque explains abrasion-type wounds often leave scars; so, it's nothing to be concerned about. Thus assured, I pay the wound no further attention.

*(I don't think about it again until seven years later in 1974 when a chest X-ray taken during a routine physical exam shows distortions in the ninth rib on the right side exactly beside the scar. The rib is doubled in thickness and full of lesions, making the bone porous and brittle. At that time, however, there are no physical symptoms, so I see no need for further concern. It isn't until February 1980, after six more years have passed, that I am confronted with grim pathological findings from a biopsy of that rib.)*

One day while commuting, I realize how little of my six years of university courses in electronic engineering and physics applies to my job. Having worked three years in construction engineering and management, I am no longer up to date in the fields I studied, and there is scant future for non-technical managers in Sandia. I'm bored with the Nevada Test Site, which is where my technical future lies if I remain at Sandia, and I'm tired of the monotonous landscape: brown desert, brown mountains, brown dust storms.

Two conclusions come to mind. First, I need a change of scenery. Because I have worked at three Sandia facilities—Albuquerque, Nevada, Hawaii—the remaining site is Livermore, California. I recall pleasant experiences five years earlier in 1962 when I hitchhiked to San Francisco from Seattle. Something told me then I would be coming back, and now is the time.

The second conclusion is that I need to find work in electronics. I want to try a conventional career path again even though—contrary to my earlier vow—this means working with a crowd. I need to determine once and for all whether a career in engineering/physics is personally fulfilling.

Making inquiries, I soon land a seemingly ideal position in Livermore as project engineer designing advanced electronic instrumentation equipment for monitoring nuclear tests. The job starts with the parent group in Albuquerque for three months and then transfers to the subsection in California. Although the job entails regular trips to the Nevada Test Site, the responsibilities are different.

After Mary's courses are finished in late spring of 1967, we pack a small cargo trailer and move back to Albuquerque where we rent a quiet poolside apartment. While enjoying a lovely summer interlude before moving to California, Mary applies and is accepted for the fall semester in a one-year program leading to a master's degree at San Jose State's Graduate School of Education. Keeping in mind we will one day settle in Albuquerque, we often drive to the property in the Sandia foothills where we plan our dream house. However, I somehow feel this will never come to pass. I recall that Ernie Pyle, a famous war correspondent from Albuquerque who spent WW II in the front-line trenches, planned to return. But Ernie's life ended tragically, and he never made it home.

Standing on our land and gazing at the magnificent views, I try not to think about Ernie. To the west and southwest sprawls the growing metropolis that had brought me out here. At night the temperature differential a thousand feet above the city creates a magical twinkling when looking down upon the panoramic splendor of Albuquerque. Farther west brilliant sunsets paint the skies behind dormant volcanos and distant mesas. Up the Rio Grande Valley to the northwest, a line of cottonwood trees marks the erratic meanderings of the namesake river. To the north stands the majestic Sangre de Cristo (Blood of Christ) range that merges into the Sandias to the northeast. Eastward, their sheer slopes rise another mile to 10,000 feet, and southward, they descend into the gentler Manzano range. The scenery is unique in every direction, and the land perches on a ridge with unobstructed views of these breath-taking surroundings.

In early summer I yearn to go back to Quogue for a few weeks of vacation, but again the bank account is empty. Recalling how interview trips financed our easterly travels at Thanksgiving, I decide to try again. And who is to say? If the right job is offered, I would be open. Once more, out go a dozen resumes and back come invitations to visit firms in Vermont, Connecticut, and New Hampshire. Although it's interesting to see job opportunities offering higher salaries at large firms, the prospect of moving east leaves much to be desired. Regardless, these trips serve to finance air tickets for a visit to our family's summer home.

Then, after enjoying the last weeks of summer back in New Mexico, we ship belongings ahead and set out on a leisurely two-week drive to our new home. Traveling south from Albuquerque, once at the Mexican border we continue west across Arizona and California. Along the way we slip into border towns—Juarez, Algodones, Nogales, Tijuana—for shopping and entertainment, including a bull fight. Upon reaching the ocean, we welcome the invigorating sea air, which cleanses our lungs of the Southwest's desert dust. Like thousands of other newcomers migrating west in the mid-1960s, we're excited about starting life in California. Bubbling with enthusiasm and expectations, up the Pacific Coast Highway toward San Francisco we go.

Where do we want to live in the Bay Area? The decision is easy: Fremont, on the east side of the bay, is the midpoint between Sandia's

Livermore offices and San Jose State University. Here, in a penthouse apartment with a garden, we make our new home.

California—not so much a place as a way of life—is a separate kind of Americana. It's a fun lifestyle with people constantly on the go trying to get into whatever new thing comes along. Although Mary and I think we're an adventuresome couple, we're sophomoric by California standards. Within a couple of months, though, we too become caught up in this fast-paced lifestyle. Each Monday at work—or in Mary's case at school—people devote much of the morning and most of the lunch hour to catching up on what everyone did over the weekend. Disbelieving stares greet anyone among our 20-something set who claims to have merely stayed at home and relaxed. You can bet that the following weekend that person will get out and do something just to maintain credibility in the group.

Some of our new friends are into rock climbing, meaning not just hiking, but scaling sheer faces with ropes and pitons. Others are taking up hang gliding. A few build cabins in the wilderness; others renovate Victorian homes in San Francisco. Several build boats to cruise around the world; some, intent upon exploring for sunken treasure in Mexico, take scuba diving courses. Many grow organic vegetables while others experiment with drugs. Whatever the activity, it's intense and all-consuming. California is going crazy. Flower children blossom in San Francisco's Haight-Ashbury district. Yippies are trying to coalesce into a movement as Hippies did five years earlier. Free speech movements flourish at Berkeley, and protests against the Viet Nam War are happening everywhere.

Issues that aren't even thought about elsewhere in the country are hot subjects in California. Abortion is being legalized and citizen groups push for legalization of marijuana. The Sexual Freedom League is gaining credibility and gay movements deal openly with a long-held taboo. Whatever is new, different, controversial, and contrary to conventional ideas of society has a following.

But interests wax and wane. If someone building a sailboat is asked six months later how it's coming along, the answer might be it has been abandoned in favor of, say, drag racing or marijuana farming. In fact, if someone is into the same thing for more than half a year, suspicion grows. Why hasn't that person gone on to something new? Everyone is having great fun experimenting with life in all its facets. Who cares if efforts don't meet expectations? It is all about an expenditure of energy outdoors in wonderful year-round weather.

In our free time Mary and I explore the Bay Area and northern California. We take a course in skin diving, make wine-tasting trips to Napa and Sonoma, and go camping along the Mendocino Coast. Otherwise, we devote ourselves to studies and professional activities.

While trying to get excited about electronics again, I develop sophisticated instrumentation equipment for a forthcoming underground nuclear test. In early autumn the work moves to the Nevada Test Site, necessitating four months of weekly travel: Monday mornings, I fly from San Francisco to Las Vegas; Friday evenings, home I come. Working with dozens of engineers and technicians, I am, contrary to my solitary nature, one of the galloping herd.

My former employees at the Test Site can't believe I gave up a management job to join the ranks of instrumentation engineers. I have my own doubts but redouble efforts to go thoroughly into the engineering experience. In addition to the publication of several technical papers, my research into engineering measurement techniques leads to a patent (for Sandia, not for me).

During the two-week shutdown over Christmas holidays, Mary and I take off for ski slopes in the Sierras surrounding Lake Tahoe. Then it's back to commuting to and from the Test Site a few more weeks. When the underground test is conducted in early 1968, my instrumentation works to perfection. After we analyze the data and publish the findings, security officers immediately whisk away the reports and stamp them Top Secret. Although this work isn't as rewarding as I had hoped, management commends me for making significant contributions and promotes me to lead project engineer on another underground test scheduled for fall.

This assignment brings on a deep sense of depression. After immersing myself in the field and proving to be good at this work, I find electronics and engineering boring. Life is passing me by. Engineers, with their narrow focus of life, seem more like machines than people, and I don't enjoy their company. As a manager/senior engineer, I have advanced high enough in the Sandia hierarchy to see what is going on in this macabre world of nuclear weaponry, and what I see makes me sick: neutron bombs, weapons in space, multi-megaton warheads, shower bombs, chemical bombs, munitions anchored to the ocean's floor, and more. This career choice has brought no satisfaction. I don't like the work. I don't like the people. I don't like the weapons business. The paradox is that my success has wrought the highest evaluation appraisals along with significant salary increases. This poses a contradiction: How can successful achievement be so unfulfilling?

Two years earlier I was riding high on the crest of the wave. I felt everything in life was going my way. Now I'm at the bottom of a hole with a bomb about to go off—a bomb that will destroy me if I don't get out.

I have to get out—but how?

And where will I go?

I have no idea what to do.

Thus begin five months of deep, dark despair.

# 19

# Abyss

### 4/68 - 8/68, Age 27

As spring rains turn the hills of the Bay Area from winter brown to bright green, I wish I too could undergo some sort of rebirth. But the beauty of the natural surroundings only heightens the anguish and depression I'm experiencing. It's spring of 1968, and I'm 27 years old. On paper it looks as though I'm on top of the world. With two college degrees, a responsible, high-salary job and a career path envious to many, what more could I want in my working life? Others may think I'm on top, but I feel as if I'm on the bottom, burdened by the weight of a world I created for myself. In a word, I'm miserable.

I arrive late to work each day, wander alone outdoors during lunch hour, and return home early to withdraw. Unable to sleep at night, I drag myself half-awake through the next day. Stomach pains grip with increasing frequency, but I don't see a doctor because I know they are a symptom of stress and anxiety, something no doctor can fix. The problem is mine and I need to work it out. But how? Although I'm trained to solve problems, this one won't submit to any techniques I know. What exactly is the problem anyway? I eventually come to five realizations:

First, in spite of studying engineering at two excellent universities, I have to admit I don't like this field. I've certainly demonstrated competence, but if I'm so good at engineering, why don't I enjoy it? Maybe I'm not that good; maybe I've created a false impression. True, I succeed at completing jobs on time, but that doesn't make me a fulfilled engineer. This lack of satisfaction prompts me to consider a different career.

Second, I don't enjoy associating with engineers. Although invariably intelligent and clear thinking, they're, nevertheless, boring. Engineers contribute technical solutions. Non-engineers offer a sense of humanity when the subject is non-analytical. I work with engineers out of necessity, but my friends are from other walks of life. Thus, I need to remove myself from the daily company of somber, analytical engineers.

Third, I must acknowledge a deeper truth: I can never be at peace while helping develop nuclear weapons. Such utterly and indiscriminately destructive weapons are immoral—a crime against mankind. Although I can accept their necessity as checks to threats, others will do the work with enthusiasm. I am neither enthusiastic nor essential and, for the sake of my sanity, can no longer participate.

Fourth, I'm not a team player and don't function well with groups. For six months I've played the role as "one of the boys" but now need to be on my own.

Fifth and final, I want to get back to a life of adventure—one that will lead again into the unknown, away from this boringly predictable career. I long for novelty, the excitement of hopping a freight train, moving to a new city, or learning a different subject.

These realizations have slowly evolved, and now I face a new question: how can I make a career change? I'm at a loss; my depression, fueled by fear, grows deeper. Leaving one career to start another will be like walking a tightrope over an abyss. I want to leave the known side, but the passage across holds unknown dangers. Seeking inspiration, I recall having fun with the surf, ski, and tennis bums in Hawaii, but that life seems superficial. Trouble is, I just can't think of anything that does appeal. I need to talk to someone, but who?

Remembering that my father went through a major career change, I decide to consult him. As a manager with General Electric for two decades, several times he accepted promotions that required our family to pull up roots and move from one city after another. In 1960, the company offered him a top management position running one of its larger divisions. The advancement meant relocating to Iowa, but until we could move, Dad worked in Iowa during the week and returned home to Louisville on weekends.

At the time Mom had recently left a successful career after many years as director of the Louisville Children's Theater to become an editor at the local newspaper. Wendy was happy and well-adjusted in a private girls' school and was active in music, dance, sports, and church activities. Our family was comfortably settled in a town we loved, and the prospect of yet another move was not a happy one.

After pondering the matter, Dad decided he was no longer interested in being a corporate loyalist at the expense of disrupting family life, and he mustered courage to quit. He left a high-paying, promising job to become a stock-broker trainee earning one-fifth his former salary. I respected him for making a decision that was practically unheard of in the early 1960s. At that time people would occasionally change jobs but typically stayed in the same industry. Dad, however, didn't just trade one job for another—he changed careers!

Although the switch in professions was a struggle, my father was happier than he had ever been. In no time he proved his value by bringing an engineering approach to quantitatively evaluate stocks. Few people in the financial sector were trained in analytical thinking; when Dad pulled out his slide rule to calculate financial ratios, not many understood what he was doing.

Within a few years he was hired to head the trust department of First National Bank of Louisville, the largest of its kind in the South. Once he got his new bearings after a tough transition, his career seemed to go up and up. In less than five years he had moved into a position of greater responsibility with a higher salary than if he had remained with GE.

Although Dad's story is encouraging, it's his story, not mine, and doesn't give me much heart. However, he understands I don't want to be around engineers and assures me I'll find more interesting people in the world of finance. I follow his advice to talk with investment colleagues he knows in San Francisco.

He is right about the people. Finding them to be stimulating and knowledgeable about a wide range of subjects, I become excited about the prospect of joining the world of finance and investments. One meeting leads to another, and a firm offers a position as a financial analyst trainee. Even though the pay will be miserable, my enthusiasm grows with this new career direction. Mary and I begin to socialize with people from this new world to learn more about careers in finance.

But the shine tarnishes as I perceive many negative aspects of the financial realm. The money obsession, the wheeling and dealing, the dependence upon good contacts for success, the need to be a team player—all turn me off. Before long I'm back to not knowing what to do or where to go. I'm certain, however, that it won't be the financial world.

After finishing graduate studies at University of New Mexico four years earlier, I enrolled in a correspondence program offered by Duke University (coincidentally, the second school to offer me undergraduate admission back in 1958). Oceanography had caught my interest, and I had taken half-a-dozen related courses. I gobbled up everything I could read about ocean exploration and followed activities of companies investing in commercial ocean research. This background, together with my life-long interest in the sea, inspires a new idea: Why not pursue a career in this field?

Letters to a number of select companies elicit positive responses because of their interest in my engineering background. The prospect of becoming a pioneer opening up a last frontier excites me. But in spite of my hopefulness, it is clear in interview after interview that these firms are focused on making money, and I'm interested in making new discoveries regardless of commercial implications. Furthermore, their policy and procedures manuals make me anxious that I would become a corporate minion, which would prevent me from being an ocean pioneer.

Doubly disappointed, I stay with Sandia while becoming more and more distraught. Stomach pains increase in severity, and I'm being eaten alive from the inside. Seeking escape, one weekend Mary and I drive to northern California's Mendocino Coast with friends. After setting up camp, we go skin diving for abalone; in the evening, with a bottle of local wine, we feast on our hand-gathered sea delicacies. The campsite on the rugged bluffs overlooking the sea is lovely and deserted, the company is fun, and the diving superb. This should be a slice of heaven on earth. But not for me. Not now. Even here I'm consumed with career worries. Consequently, I'm nothing more than a robot going through mechanical motions. At one point the thought occurs just to dive down and not bother coming up. I'm in agony—trapped in a hell of my own making—and I have no idea how to free myself.

Back home I continue to brood. Constantly rehashing and re-examining unappealing options like a hamster running round and round on a spinning wheel, I'm driving myself bonkers.

Because my love for the sea is all-consuming, I can't completely relinquish the thought of the ocean as the environment in which to work. Knowing now that I don't want to be an employee of a large corporation, I eventually light on the idea of looking for alternative companies but can find no small ones focused on ocean exploration. Various branches of the government are engaged in research programs, but I don't want to work within what I perceive to be a stifling bureaucracy.

Finally, I hit upon another idea. Two research institutes—one on the East Coast, the other on the West Coast—are in the vanguard of ocean research. Woods Hole Oceanographic Research Center, working closely with Massachusetts Institute of Technology, is located on Cape Cod. Because I'm absorbed in West Coast living, I focus on Scripps Institute in La Jolla just north of San Diego, an affiliate of University of California (UCSD). Through correspondence and follow-up phone inquiries, I learn that, yes, Scripps does have several doctoral programs related to the ocean sciences, and fellowship money is available to graduate students.

Following a trip to San Diego for interviews and completion of application forms for admittance to UCSD, within two weeks I am accepted into an engineering department conducting research in the field of Ocean Optics, whatever that is. But it doesn't matter. At last I've found what I'm looking for. I'll be back in an academic environment enjoying student life again and will be near the sea. And maybe engineers involved in this work won't be similar to the ones at Sandia. I'm invigorated by these possibilities and feel a burden has been lifted. The crash experienced each time I pursued other career ideas does not materialize this time.

With a new direction I set about arranging logistics of moving while still employed at Sandia. Mary will receive a master's degree and California State Teaching Credential at the end of the semester at San Jose State University and is looking for a teaching job. Over Easter vacation in April, we make a second trip to San Diego where Mary interviews with six different school districts and receives job offers from each. After selecting an area where we'd like to live, we return to Fremont to wait out those remaining months before I quit my job and head south. Everything seems settled, and we adjust to the prospect of a new life.

But just as Mary adjusts to the prospects of our new life, I realize something is wrong. In spite of my initial enthusiasm, nagging doubts gnaw away at my conviction about this new path. A career in the ocean sciences should be an open door to opportunities in the future, shouldn't it? I'm excited to get back into the university environment as a Ph.D. candidate, am I not? I'm delighted to take up a career that brings me close to the sea, am I not? The questions continue, and I have to answer "No. I am not excited. I am not delighted." Having studied six years in two universities, the thought of another four or five years doesn't appeal. To be honest, I don't really want to derive a livelihood from the sea. It indeed is my lifeblood, but that's quite different from one's livelihood. Apart from the logical arguments for and against this new direction, my heart is clearly not at peace about this move, and once again I plunge into an inner agony. The problem now is worse than before, because Mary has committed to her new job in San Diego. I can't just say we aren't going, because I have no alternative. I keep my doubts bottled up, hidden from Mary, but also from my colleagues at Sandia.

I mentally race back through all the alternatives: Going into the investment and financial fields still feels unattractive. Returning to Sandia's main office in Albuquerque would be a step backwards. Trying to get my previous job in Hawaii isn't an option. Going to India in the Peace Corps—an opportunity that was offered six years earlier—would still be possible but makes no sense now. Nothing makes any sense, and time isn't stopping to wait for me to make a decision. Mary graduates in June, and, before I know it, July—the month I plan to quit my job at Sandia to make the move—is here.

Suddenly I'm given a gift from the beyond—a gift that allows me to pull my life back together. My friend Sam is the agent who delivers the life-saving gift. Sam Berry, a University of Kentucky graduate, and I joined Sandia's Technical Development Program in Albuquerque in the fall of 1962 and were roommates the second year of the program. After Albuquerque, Sam worked briefly at Sandia's Livermore facility but then left to accept a fellowship in the Sloan Program at Stanford's Graduate School of Business. Following that, he entered the doctoral program and continued a carefree life as a perpetual student. When I moved to Fremont, Sam, who lives across the bay in Palo Alto, and I renewed our friendship and we get together frequently.

One Saturday afternoon Sam and I meet to play one of our regular games of tennis. Usually we're an even match, but on this occasion I'm dead on my feet and my arms might as well be spaghetti. I can hardly hold the racquet. Sam proceeds to win one game after another, until he finally sets his racquet down and joins me on my side of the court. Unburdening myself to him, I explain the turmoil and confess the sense that I'm plummeting into an abyss.

Sam, in his quiet self-assured way, typically expresses understanding but seldom makes any suggestions. This time is different though. Picking up on the image I used, Sam shares some insights about me.

"Look," he says. "You feel you're falling into an abyss, and you're trying frantically to catch onto something to get out. But you're grabbing wildly because you don't know what you want to catch onto. Your real problem, Peter, is your fear of falling. You can't worry about trying to find something to get you out of the abyss until you find a way to stop falling. And the way to stop the fall is to quit your job at Sandia.

"Pulling out of the abyss is another problem altogether. Right now, you don't know what else you want to do. The thing is, Peter, you don't have to figure out everything all at once. What you need to do *first* is to stop your fall. *Then* you can take time to decide what to do next.

"Accept this fact, and then instead of falling, you'll be floating. You can just enjoy the sensation of floating for a while and take as much time as you need to sort out your career path. Give yourself some space to breathe, Peter."

Sam's words ring true. His insights are accurate. Nevertheless, my chest tightens. I feel a new sense of panic because I'm afraid to quit my job at Sandia. I don't want to let go of the known until the next step is clear. But Sam points out it is a three-step process: First, extricate yourself from the known. Then welcome the unknown of just floating. Finally, trust that eventually something will come up.

The irony dawns on me. In the past I always welcomed venturing into the unknown, forging a new path through uncharted territory. I always felt I could find my way. This time I'd lost confidence. But as Sam says, my problem is I've been unwilling to accept uncertainty.

In a flash of awareness—miracle of all miracles—I'm suddenly able to accept not knowing. Relaxation floods through my body. Granted, I still have no answer to the question of what to do, but that no longer feels insurmountable. The point is, I can now accept a situation I have tried to avoid. Whereas in recent months I've been tormenting myself because knowing what I want to do and where I want to go seemed essential. Finally, I've gained enough perspective to see there is nothing wrong with not knowing what I want to do or where to go.

"Okay Sam," I sigh with relief. "I'm ready to float. Now what?"

Sam is ready for my question. "Stop looking for something to do and just get into an environment where you can be exposed to a variety of opportunities." Sam even has a suggestion: The Graduate School of Business at Stanford University five miles away across the bay.

I'm struck dumb. I immediately understand not only in my head, but in the depths of my heart. We resume our game, but to no avail. Sam's insight and suggestion have turned my emotions upside down. I've gone from the depths of depression to the height of elation and can't concentrate on hitting a tennis ball. Again, we are compelled to give up our game. But I assure Sam I will see him Monday morning on the Stanford campus where I intend to talk with the director of admissions.

I spend the next several hours alone mulling over implications of what Sam has said. Even if I don't get accepted into the business school, I at least have an understanding of how to accept the turmoil in my life. And if I *am* accepted, I'll have two years to float in my abyss—two years during which I won't seek anything but will remain open and receptive instead of aggressive and assertive—two years that should prepare me for a variety of careers not just in the profit-oriented sector, but, if I so desire, in the non-profit and public sectors as well.

I awaken Sunday morning with a vitality and freshness I haven't known for months. This is the right direction, and it's time to tell Mary. Sitting with her in the afternoon, I share my thoughts, feelings, and plans: We won't be going to southern California, and I won't be entering the Scripps Institute graduate program. We're going across the bay to Stanford; and if that doesn't work out, we'll find something else. But there is no urgency and no crisis.

Quiet tears roll down Mary's cheeks, and she withdraws to our bedroom for an hour of solitude. She's been like a yo-yo spinning up and down with all my changing ideas that start with excitement and end up like wads of paper thrown one after another into the scrap basket. Mary thought we'd finally found what we were both looking for in southern California and had committed to a new job that was to start in just over a month. Once again, her hopes and expectations are dashed. But when she, eyes still bloodshot but tears dried, emerges from the bedroom, she carries herself with a fresh sense of renewal. Deep down she had known the answers we are seeking do not lie in southern California, but she'd kept those feelings to herself, just as I had.

With a new sense of clarity, we make plans to move in this new direction. Theoretically, we're starting too late to do everything we want to do: The deadline for submitting applications to the Stanford Business School has passed, and teaching positions in Palo Alto for the coming autumn were filled months earlier. But in spite of not being able to see exactly how, Mary and I trust things will work out.

Monday morning I drive to the Stanford campus and walk into the Office of Admissions at the Business School where I'm warmly greeted by Dean Hanneman. I'm surprised to hear he expects me, but Sam had stopped by earlier to explain my situation. After glancing at my student transcripts, the dean informs me I am well-qualified to be admitted, but I need to take the Graduate Record Examination in Business before the application can be considered by the Admissions Committee. Then I'll need to have an interview, and, if things go well, perhaps an exception could be made because the admissions deadline is already long past.

I frown, "Isn't there some way I could cut a few corners since I've already worked in a management-level job and done well at Sandia?" I explain that I feel the need for professional training as well as time to refocus upon my career direction.

With a sly expression, Dean Hanneman discloses that our present discussion qualifies for the interview and that he himself is the Admissions Committee. Because he knows I have to hurry to make private arrangements, he agrees then and there to admit me upon one condition: I must get a respectable grade on the Business Graduate Record Exam. I depart his office with wings on my heels, my feet barely touching the ground.

Two weeks later I take the exam and pass. A week later I receive the letter of acceptance into the MBA Class of 1970 at Stanford University's Graduate School of Business.

Mary gracefully breaks her teaching contract in southern California and applies to school districts surrounding Palo Alto for an elementary teaching job. In no time she lands exactly the job she is looking for as a fifth-grade teacher working with disadvantaged children in an all-Black school in East Palo Alto.

Life begins to be beautiful again. Although I still have no answers about future directions, I am extricated from what was tearing me apart. I'm grateful to Sandia for offering wonderful opportunities and exciting experiences early in my engineering career and have no regrets for the six years I worked with the company. The job provided possibilities to see much of the world as well as opportunities to confront and challenge myself in different ways. But I've known the depths of the dark hole and am ready to let go of this phase of my life.

On the final business trip for Sandia, I drive with Mary rather than fly from Livermore to Albuquerque. Along the way we meet with Bill Steinmetz, my former Sandia roommate, and his wife Carolyn, for a two-day climb up Mt. Whitney, the highest peak in the lower 48. I suppose this has significance, but I'm not sure just now what it is—maybe scaling a grand height out of a personal abyss.

The great news is this: I am no longer falling but floating with a new understanding about myself. I once again bid farewell to people and places I have known.

A month later, Mary and I move across the Bay to Palo Alto.

[1968, Fremont] Living in Penthouse #6, 37950 Fremont Boulevard while working at Livermore Labs

[1968, San Jose State] Mary's Master's Degree

[1968, Foster City, age 27] Sailing on San Francisco Bay

[1968, Monterey Peninsula] Skin diving for abalone

# 20
# Stanford Year I — A Student Again

*9/68 – 5/69, Age 27 – 28*

It's a relief to feel positive about life again. The career dilemma that lasted for months had caused me to wither for lack of focus. Now my direction is clear and there's much organizing to do in a short time.

The main problem is managing financially for two years on one salary. Our meager savings, Mary's teaching salary, and a financial grant from Stanford look to be adequate. Moreover, rather than terminating me, Sandia grants me a leave of absence, which offers three unexpected benefits. First, all academic expenses are tax-deductible because they provide skills necessary for my job. Second, I retain the company's health insurance policy. Third, Sandia agrees to pay for our next move, which covers expenses for having belongings professionally packed. Renting a U-Haul trailer for three days, which Sandia allows for our relocation, Mary and I make half-a-dozen trips across the bay on Dumbarton Bridge to move to our new home. Because we'll be living on a shoestring budget, we economize by driving west around the bay's south end through San Jose to avoid bridge tolls and return across the bridge on the toll-free, east-bound lanes.

In Palo Alto we rent a rambling, two-story farmhouse built in the early 1900s. It offers spacious rooms and the luxury of much unused

186

space—wide hallways, hidden alcoves, walk-in closets, and large storage cabinets. In the 1950s, developers built modern, single-story houses in the surrounding fields leaving our house an anachronism waiting to be torn down and replaced with something contemporary. Although in constant need of repairs, the house exudes a welcoming warmth that makes us feel at home. We buy a washing machine and two bicycles as a last splurge before resigning ourselves to the modest life of struggling students.

What a joy to stroll on a warm autumn day across the campus that Leland Stanford built on his farm near the bottom of the bay peninsula! Registration at the Graduate School of Business (GSB) takes place outside under towering palm trees. After signing up for courses, I wander among booths displaying extracurricular activities and realize how out of touch I have been. Around me is a microcosm of what's going on in the world. Dozens of groups are seeking new members to join their causes: gay rights, environmental protections, women's equality, population control, revolutionary movements, Black Panthers, recycling, Save the Whales, Preserve the Redwoods, Safeguard the Wilderness, Protect the Elephants, and save whatever else you can think of. Representing every political movement are conservatives, liberals, socialists, radicals, libertarians, and Viet Nam War protesters.

Many movements want to either ban or legalize something: DDT, marijuana, abortion, prostitution, contraceptives, nuclear reactors, and so on. Among these groups is a table with a sign "Ban the Bomb." Curious, I stroll over and am immediately inundated with literature describing the horrors of nuclear weapons and radiation. Students at this booth, unlike rowdy crowds who demonstrated at the Nevada Test Site entrance gates, are articulate, informed, and passionately committed. They talk about radiation-induced cancer, aquifer pollution (from underground tests), environmental degradation, food-cycle contamination, ozone layer destruction, nuclear waste, atmospheric deterioration, and radiation damage to all life. I find nothing to say in response, particularly because research conducted by government agencies supports many of their points. Realizing how asleep I have been, I come to a slow boil. Never had I seen or heard such information during years working in nuclear weaponry. I feel as though a giant rock has just crashed down on my six years at

Sandia. And yet, I understand the paradox: my experience with Sandia couldn't have been more challenging, exciting, and fulfilling.

At age 27 I thought I'd be among the oldest of almost 300 entering GBS students, but seeing balding heads and graying hairs at the orientation session I judge otherwise. Class statistics indicate I'm the average age, which ranges from 22 years for recent college graduates to 42 for military retirees starting a second career. Most classmates have similar backgrounds to mine involving four or five years of work experience. We passed our mid-20s and faced career crises, prompting us to enter the GSB to gain skills to further or redirect our careers.

Another newcomer joins the business school in autumn of 1968. Ernest Arbuckle, previous dean who is leaving to be chairman of the board of Wells Fargo Bank, is replaced by Arjay Miller, former president of Ford Motor Company. Frustrated by civic unrest while with Ford in Detroit in the early 1960s, Arjay realizes that corporate interests need to balance with social responsibility. It's a credit to Arjay that he starts Stanford's Public Management Program, the first of its kind in the country, designed to educate managers for public organizations.

*(For a number of years, Stanford had trailed Harvard as the number two business school in the country. Then, in the early- and mid- '70s, polls showed Stanford had ousted Harvard from the top spot. It's likely that Arjay's initiation in his first years by the Class of 1970 brought Stanford to the top, or so we like to think!)*

Readjusting to student life is a tough but stimulating experience. Days start with breakfast at 7:00 am followed by a 20-minute bike ride to campus. Classes begin at 8:30 and continue until noon. Lunchtime finds us outdoors in sunshine eating brown-bag lunches while rehashing morning lectures. Afternoons bring more classes, computer labs, library reading, and study groups that run into evening sessions if necessary. Pedaling home, I welcome evening breezes that clear away mental stresses of the day's studies. After a refreshing shower, puttering around the house breaks the tiresomeness of sitting all day. Once dinner is over and the dining table cleared, out come the books, except on occasion when I head out for a night discussion group.

With hundreds of pages of case material, textbook information, and reference readings to absorb every day, there's hardly time to grasp each new concept before moving to the next topic. Weekends are a welcome respite—a breathing space of 48 uninterrupted hours to catch up on what we missed during the week. In spite of the rapid-reading course I took years earlier, I seldom finish studying before midnight. Although the pace is grueling, the excitement of learning at such breakneck speed is exhilarating.

In the first weeks we learn that every organization—every company, government agency, charitable organization, foundation, church, or other enterprise—requires five disciplines to operate effectively: Operations, Accounting, Finance, Marketing, and Human Resources. For example, hospitals, police departments, universities, and foundations all have marketing challenges, and principles we learn apply to every organization. Traditional thinking that management is exclusive to business is clearly wrong. Management is essential to any group that forms to fulfill a purpose, and the focus of the GSB is on management, not business. *(In later years this thinking becomes obvious, but at the time the experts thought that non-business organizations simply needed to be administered, not managed.)*

Through real-life case studies we tackle issues faced by municipalities, fire departments, mental institutions, foundations, and farms. Zeroing in on problems and stripping away superficial layers, we discover techniques and strategies to resolve problems related to capital budgeting, resource allocation, cost accounting, and more. For two years I put in long, happy hours in this exciting environment.

While keeping up with normal studies, I also renew a long-term interest in writing. I had written for my high school newspaper and later had published articles about hopping onto freight trains and other adventures. I now become an editor for the business school bi-monthly newspaper, *The Reporter*, for which I submit a regular column called "Alumni Sketch." For each issue, I interview and write about GSB alumni and their careers.

Twice each month, after searching alumni records for someone in San Francisco working in a field of interest to me, I schedule a personal interview. Afterward back on campus I transcribe my notes and hammer out a 500-word article to accompany the photo I take. Much as I enjoy the assignments, the primary focus is on envisioning whether someone's area of work is of interest to me. Would I like to pursue a similar career path? Typically, the answer is "No."

The stories the interviewees tell and experiences they share are fascinating. George Ballou, '39, a Vice President of Standard Oil of California, explains that because of having a rough childhood and growing up poor, he was looking for security in a well-capitalized, stable organization when he chose a career in oil. Another alum was so angry after being fired from a large electronics firm that he formed his own company that today has more than $100 million dollars in sales. When I interview Claude Rosenberg, '52, in his dingy office in a small, nondescript financial firm, he speaks of a company he plans to start one day. *(Sure enough, years later Rosenberg Capital Management became one of the country's largest financial services firms, and Claude became a billionaire.)* I meet John Young, '58, a top executive at Hewlett-Packard, coincidentally on the day he is promoted to president of HP and scoop the *New York Times* with the announcement. In an era when few women attend the GSB, I interview Ellen Uhrbrock, '56, who works for an advertising firm. She's a breath of fresh air because, unlike the men, she talks about unleashing her creativity in serving clients who can't quite grasp how to convey messages to their audience.

I meet both corporate and non-corporate men and women. Some are so-called winners, others, so-called losers. Some are successful at work but failures in their home life, while others have failed on the job but enjoy a rewarding home and personal life. Because I keep looking for the thread that "winners" find and "losers" miss, I can't say who are winners and who are losers. Nobody really has it all together, but each is somehow managing. None—not even a single one of the entrepreneurs—has been able to control his or her career direction. All have been buffeted by fate and changes beyond their control; all ended up where they chanced to land rather than where they thought they were going at the start of their careers.

I realize that if a formula for success involves knowing what one wants to do from the beginning, I should be concerned. What a relief to know there is no pat formula! The key seems to be that one should stay open to whatever opportunities come along and not be afraid to jump when they arrive.

Once a week I read announcements on the GSB bulletin board—low-cost flights to Europe, items to be bought or sold, visiting lecturers, and dozens of happenings are posted each week. One posting about a Washington, DC-based organization with the cumbersome name "Institute for the Study of Health and Society," catches my eye. The Institute is hosting a three-day conference on the world's population crisis and invites students from all fields of study to attend. Thinking of courses in Arjay's new Public Management Program, I see an opportunity to test how management theories can apply in a non-business setting. Population issues are a hot subject, because Stanford Professor Paul Ehrlich had recently published *The Population Bomb*, warning that trends in population growth would lead to mass famine in the following decades. In addition, the conference offers an expense-paid venture to the nation's capital. I apply and two weeks later receive a letter of acceptance along with a prepaid airline ticket from San Francisco to Washington.

Airlie House, a plush lodge in the Virginia hills two hours outside Washington, hosts the event, which brings together 200 students, most from the East Coast. As the lone attendee from engineering and business, I play a triple role. First, as the sole Californian and the only one who is familiar with Ehrlich's lectures, I bring a first-hand, West Coast point of view. Second, I'm expected to bring an engineer's perspective on the technical feasibility of feeding a world about to outstrip earth's carrying capacity. Third, I'm called upon to describe management methods for projects such as encouraging 100 million fertile women of India to practice birth control.

Discussions swirl around avoidance of population crashes, advocation of two-child families, distribution of free contraceptive devices, promotion of family planning, and control of the world's rapidly increasing birth rate. However, no one can figure out how to implement the appropriate programs. When I suggest the private sector would perhaps afford the most qualified and efficient means, I'm confronted with howls of protest that big business would turn any effort into a profit-making opportunity. Even if profits result, I argue, private undertakings would still be more efficient and less expensive than typical government-run programs. Although I'm dismayed to hear such negative views of business, the conference is, nevertheless, fun and stimulating.

As Christmas approaches, Mary and I plan to venture into Mexico. Strapping the Sunfish atop MOPS, we drive south through San Diego, knowing that except for a last-minute twist of events, we would be living there. After crossing the border at Nogales, Arizona and continuing through the desert to the east coast of the Sea of Cortes, we overnight at Guaymas. The next day we drive along the coast to Mazatlán. I assume this is far enough south that big waves could roll in without obstruction from the Baja Peninsula and I can relive my surfing days in Hawaii; however, instead of big rollers, the waves are disappointingly small. But the sea and winds are ideal for sailing, so every day we explore by boat the small islands just off the coast.

Each evening when fishermen lay their catch on the beach for everyone to admire, we stroll over to see what the sea yields. A frightening collection of sharks up to 15 feet in length—that's longer than the Sunfish!—convinces us to be cautious when swimming from our little boat.

A week after our arrival, Mom and Dad fly down from Louisville to join us for a sun, sand, surf, and sail vacation. I feel particularly close to Dad as we share our love of the sea and sailing. At a small nightclub where we are the only English speakers, the four of us welcome the arrival of 1969. Conversing late into the night about our past family events over the years, I feel some of the closest moments I've ever known with Mom and Dad.

Realizing after my first semester that I'm not about to flunk out, I create time to enjoy other benefits of California living. Mary and I often drive to Half Moon Bay to free-dive for abalone, which saves our pocketbook by providing food for the following week. An hour away in the other direction, we hike and camp at Yosemite National Park. Everywhere around the bay we discover marinas from which we can launch the Sunfish for a day's sail. During winter we enjoy ski weekends at Tahoe. Although partial to Squaw Valley and Heavenly, to economize we often frequent smaller, less-expensive resorts at Homewood, Incline Village, Alpine Meadows, and Sierra-at-Tahoe.

Other weekends we drive north across the Golden Gate Bridge to explore picturesque communities in Tiburon, Sausalito, and Belvedere, and then visit the giant redwoods at Muir Woods. A favorite outing is wine country where, provisioned with San Francisco's famous sourdough bread and fresh-cracked crab, we check out winery tasting rooms in Mendocino, Sonoma, and Napa. Back home, thanks to year-round sunny weather, Mary and I often play tennis before dinner at one of the courts on Stanford's campus. With so many nearby attractions, Palo Alto is indeed a great place to live.

In spring of 1969, the war in Viet Nam is tearing the country apart. Protest groups spring up daily, and hardly a week passes without newspaper headlines reporting anti-war demonstrations frequently with violent confrontations. College campuses are hotbeds of protest activity, and Stanford is no exception. Many Americans contend the war isn't fought for the oppressed people of Viet Nam, but rather for the benefit of America's military-industrial complex. The military receives unlimited funding, and Fortune 500 defense contractors report unprecedented profits. Massive military spending and exorbitant corporate profits, together with the weekly body counts, incense every sector of American society with student protests at the forefront.

Demonstrations continue on Stanford's campus and it isn't long before protesters single out the GSB as a target. After all, it is thought that we are being trained to take over the reins of big businesses and would presumably continue to support Viet Nam War policies in the interest of making profits. When the first wave of protests occurs, we cancel classes and meet the demonstrators to engage in constructive dialog. It's a pleasant surprise to both sides to find we share similar views. It's a dumb, senseless, immoral war, and America has no business being involved. Even veterans in our class who don't share this view eagerly meet with the protesters.

On one occasion the radical group Students for a Democratic Society (SDS) stages a protest at the GSB, and again we cancel classes to meet them. They have another objective in mind, however, to occupy the building. Amused at this prospect, we gladly show them around so they can develop a strategy. The protesters are taken aback when they learn the building has about 25 entry doors and an indoor-outdoor architectural style making it impossible to block all entrances. They are also surprised to learn that several business school students are themselves members of the SDS. Suddenly the GSB is no longer a target.

When US troops invade Cambodia in spring, student strikers close down the Stanford campus. We, too, in the business school vote to boycott classes. It's a meaningless gesture but the only action to express outrage about the expansion of the war. One class I boycott is an accounting course. The final exam at the end of the quarter includes a question covered in lecture that day—a question I initially feel is unfair. Upon reflection, however, I realize that it is a fair question because missing class is no excuse for not learning the material. *(I have long forgotten my exam grade; however, this incident has always stayed with me.)*

[1968, Palo Alto] Old farmhouse at 672 Colorado Avenue
was home for two years

[Christmas 1968, Mazatlán, age 27] Mom and Dad

[1968, Mazatlán] A favorite memory of Dad, who was 49 at the time

# 21
# Europe — Summer of '69

*5/69 - 9/69, Age 28*

As the first year at Stanford ends, I give little thought to the three-month summer break ahead. Enjoying each day as it comes, it seems unimportant to plan for a job...that is, until the Placement Office calls to ask if I'm interested in a summer assignment in Europe. Sometime earlier I had mentioned I'd like to work abroad but then thought nothing more about it, so this call is a pleasant surprise.

Robert S. First, Inc., a small consulting company conducting market research in the medical field, seeks an MBA student with an engineering background to conduct a survey in Western Europe. I jump at this opportunity and write the firm at its New York headquarters to express interest. A week later I receive a reply inviting me to meet at the earliest opportunity.

The following week I fly to New York and meet Bob First who explains he has sold a market research proposal to several large U.S. corporations. One aspect is to study applications of computers used for medical purposes. Because Europe is ahead in this field thanks to heavily funded national healthcare programs, the American clients are interested in developing similar applications in the States. To complete this 100-page study, Bob is looking for someone with a background in engineering, familiarity with computers, and writing skills. My resume looks good, and the selling point is my experience as an editor on the GSB newspaper— which presumably means I can write. Letting me name a salary, he hires me.

I'm ecstatic! The job is a big one, and, because there's not much time before the September deadline, on the last day of the spring semester I return to New York to begin preliminary research. I visit all the computer companies to learn their European locations and gather names to contact. A week later Mary finishes teaching, closes up the house, and joins me in New York. The following week during after-work hours, we enjoy taking in museums, art galleries, Broadway shows, and great dining.

Then, hardly believing how fortunate we are to have such an exciting summer before us, we're on our way to London. A hotel near Piccadilly becomes our home for a week while I work days and Mary and I see London at night. During visits to companies involved with the new technology, I learn terms like Medical Diagnostic Algorithms, Hospital Information Systems, Automated Patient Monitoring, Medical Data Banks, and Computerized Clinical Laboratory Data Processors. In addition to making copious notes on all this new-to-me-jargon, I also learn who's who in this small but fascinating fraternity. Once I complete this background work, Mary and I board a train to the south coast and cross the English Channel to Ostend where we take another train to Brussels, location of the European offices of Robert S. First, Inc.

We find a lovely furnished apartment on Avenue Louise in one of Brussels' plushest neighborhoods. Settling into Belgian life, we adopt a routine—shopping daily at small open-air markets, enjoying an evening aperitif at local sidewalk cafes, and indulging in gourmet cuisine offered by neighborhood restaurants. While I learn to be a market researcher, Mary explores museums and the city's art treasures.

In the late1960s, Brussels is evolving into a modern golden era. The city's skyline represents three periods: First, spires and church towers recall earlier centuries. Second, office buildings that house international banks and firms date from the mid-1950s after the Common Market was established. Third, construction cranes are erecting modern steel, glass, and aluminum skyscrapers to house hundreds of organizations near the headquarters of the North Atlantic Treaty Organization (NATO), World Health Organization (WHO), International Labor Organization (ILO), World Bank, and dozens of United Nations departments. Because international organizations and corporations avoid favoring the larger countries—France, England, and Germany have a recent history of wars with each other—Brussels has the advantage of being in a small, neutral country. A few years earlier Switzerland, which is also neutral but not in the Common Market, clamped down on issuing foreign work permits, prompting Geneva and Zurich to quickly fall out of favor.

Robert First's headquarters as well as offices where I conduct meetings during the first week, are in modern skyscrapers in Brussel's new business sector. But when it comes time for lunch, dinner, or business entertaining, everyone heads to old parts of the city. Within a few hundred feet of the Renaissance and Baroque buildings surrounding Grand Place, center of "old" Brussels, one can find charming restaurants, bars, and cabarets. At first it appears these 100-year-old structures are being demolished to make way for the new, but on second glance it's evident the old section is holding its own with its unique attractions as a drawing card for the business community.

I learn that an American executive's ability to function in Europe is tied to the current state of world events. When the U.S. invades Cambodia, curries favor with Russia, or enacts legislation contrary to European interests, the continental community tacitly adopts an anti-American attitude that spills over into business meetings and can lead to uncomfortable discussions. However, by late June of the historic summer of 1969 when man lands on the moon, American prestige abroad is at an all-time high. Consequently, it's quite easy for me to make appointments wherever I go, and meetings often dwell more on questions about America's space programs than on medical applications with computers. But even with current sentiment in my favor, a tremendous logistics challenge lies ahead.

Fifty workdays are precious little time to complete the project. Allowing 10 days in the office to finalize call reports, handle correspondence, arrange appointments, and write the concluding report, only 40 days remain in which to gather information. During these eight weeks I intend to visit four types of organizations: First, the central government agency responsible for healthcare activities being computerized; Second, computer companies involved with medical services; Third, several dozen hospitals and medical institutions using computers; Fourth, computer consultants and software specialists. This plan calculates to 15 visits spread between four or five large cities located in 16 countries for an impossible total of more than 200 appointments. Even traveling on weekends, I still would have to average more than five calls daily, a prospect that fills me with panic. The supposed vacation in Europe is turning into a frantic rush to make all these visits. Reworking the numbers, I decide to telephone less-important contacts in order to save time. In smaller countries it will suffice to visit only the main government agency and the central IBM office. With this plan in mind, I turn over arrangement of logistics for an eight-week travel plan to the office secretary, who will try to return me to Brussels every weekend.

The first week I travel to the Netherlands, the second week to France. After a few days back in Brussels, I fly to Sweden to the Karolinska University Hospital in Stockholm and then north to Uppsala's University Center. Sweden's national Medical Information System is the most advanced in Europe. Every newborn is assigned a number that serves as a lifelong identification for all government dealings, and satellites transmit personal medical data to every city and town in the country. If someone from Stockholm falls unconscious in Malmo, the patient's health information is instantly available. A second application is a computerized network of hospital information systems that includes doctors' instructions, pharmacy information, and billing records. A third application automates data handling in clinical and hospital laboratories.

I usually depart Brussels on Sunday afternoons to ensure time at the new destination to exchange money and secure a hotel room where I peruse phone books and city maps to locate places I need to visit. Returning to Brussels Friday afternoons, I drop off dictated call reports, pick up the week's mail, and review earlier reports typed while I was away.

Throughout the summer I learn many new medical applications for computers. For example, Switzerland developed a computerized blood bank in Lausanne that tracks citizens with rare blood types who can be called upon in emergencies to donate blood. The computer keeps records of those who donate blood and reminds staff to send postcards when more blood is needed.

During another week I cover the remaining Scandinavian countries followed by Austria and Italy, and late in August, during the hottest week of summer, I suffer while visiting Portugal and Spain. The remaining days are spent working in Belgium or retracing earlier travels to meet key people previously missed.

By the end of summer, having visited 25 or so hospitals as well as dozens of clinical laboratories and medical centers, I never want to see another medical facility again. Also, having gone to every major European office of IBM, Digital Equipment Corporation, Burroughs International, Olivetti, and other companies, I am also fed up with computers. The last frantic week before leaving Europe, I review the data, make calls to resolve conflicting information, assemble visit reports, and write a basic outline of the study. Then Mary and I close our apartment and fly to New York.

We manage to squeeze in a week at Quogue. Each day after sailing, swimming, and playing tennis, I continue assembling data and writing the report, which is basically a book. Finally, it's finished, and I send Bob First *Computers in Medicine in Western Europe*, the first comprehensive analysis of its kind. Despite the frenetic travel and long work hours, summer has been delightful and the report is well received by the clients.

But now it's back to California to resume the life we know. Mary has a contract to teach again and is happy to be back at the same school to work with disadvantaged students. The second year at Stanford is relaxed and carefree. The pressure and tension I felt a year earlier is gone. I'm not going to flunk out, and I have no urge to knock myself out for top grades. At this point I'm just interested in learning what I can and having time to pursue whatever other opportunities catch my eye.

[Summer 1969, age 28] Exhausting European travels

[Summer 1969, Amsterdam]

# 22
## Stanford Year II – Abreast of Things

*9/69 - 5/70, Age 28 - 29*

Soon after school resumes the class selects 20 classmates, including me, to attend a seminar with five business and labor leaders to discuss the country's major social issues. Retreating to a resort in the hills above Carmel, by the end of a three-day weekend we conclude that problems are of such consequence that America's corporations need to assist in finding solutions. The old attitudes that "the business of Business is business," isn't true anymore. Companies must start addressing pollution threats, minority rights, individual privacy, equal work opportunities, civil unrest, and other social issues. As future MBAs from the nation's top business school (according to the most recent survey by *U.S. News and World Report*), our class can use its credibility with the business community as a prod.

At the conclusion of the seminar we create the Committee for Corporate Responsibility (CCR), which has two purposes: (1) to measure the degree to which America's largest corporations are working on such problems within their local communities, and (2) to encourage corporations to make more resources available to focus on them.

Back on campus, we form committees to implement the CCR objectives. I'm elected to lead a group that will send letters to the CEOs of

203

the Fortune 500 companies with the goal of learning how they view their responsibilities to society. Within a week we mail letters asking 10 questions about policies and activities. Questions are tight and specific, leaving little possibility for glossed-over responses. The letters carry endorsement by Stanford's 1970 MBA Class. Because the firms recruit from the GSB, it's not surprising that all 500 respond within a couple of weeks.

After reviewing the responses, we establish benchmarks, grade the firms, and contact *Business Week* magazine. Excited about this research, the editors send a reporter to write an article about the CCR. When the story is published, it lights a fire across the country. Within months similar CCR-type organizations spring up at other business schools whose leaders inundate us with requests for information. Several Stanford graduate students receive grants to investigate in greater depth how corporate involvement is helping to solve America's social problems, and one doctoral candidate uses these findings for his dissertation. *(Returning for our 10th Class Reunion, I was pleased to find the CCR is still flourishing.)*

My recent research on computer use for medicine holds potential for further development in America, and I'm confident someone here in Silicon Valley is working on it. I soon meet a medical doctor (whose name I forget), also degreed in electrical engineering, who is starting a company called Spectra Medical Systems (SMS). Following several meetings, he hires me as vice president of marketing to work part-time while in school and full-time thereafter. This job becomes the research project for a course called Entrepreneurship and Management of the Small Business Enterprise. With full-time engineering, administrative, and software development managers already on board, Spectra's first priority is selecting the computer upon which to build the software package. After reviewing available models and meeting with company representatives, we settle on a Honeywell product.

Things go smoothly for a while, and I invite the SMS founder to class to explain his vision. Before long, however, he and I realize our perspectives on running the company differ significantly. Whereas I want to build the information system slowly and work with the client medical center through each phase, the founder wants to build the entire system at once. He doesn't have adequate financing and not a single customer but thinks that after the software is ready, he can then find clients. Furthermore, whenever I visit the office after classes, I find him playing chess or practicing basketball shots with paper wads. When I suggest we write a business plan and approach local venture capitalists to secure the first and second round of financing, he disagrees. This conflict leads to a falling out, and he terminates me. Although the dismissal is a shock, I don't regret it. Not having decided what to do after graduation, I can't imagine staying longer in California and working in this interesting but narrow field.

Several consolations come from this experience. First, I learn the problems and headaches, as well as the thrills, of starting a new business. Second, I earn much-needed income. Third, the professor gives an A on my research paper. Fourth, I receive a refund of the $4,000 I invested in the company *(which later goes out of business)*. Finally, I have now experienced a familiar truth: "Every good executive has been fired at least once!"

One day Bob First, my employer the previous summer, calls to ask if I would make field calls to West Coast computer manufacturers to assess their involvement in medical computing. Glad to stay in touch with this field, I make several trips to Southern California and learn that virtually nothing is going on compared to what I had seen in Europe. The reason: None of Bob's potential customers has funds to invest in these projects.

This finding illustrates a classic example that every business school student learns: "Don't confuse a need with a market." Although business executives agree on the need to introduce computer power into the health-care sector, unlike in Europe where programs are financed by governments, in the U.S. no market exists. When I report these findings to Bob, I meet the same fate as a messenger carrying bad news in the time of ancient Greece...well, not exactly the same fate—I lose the job, not my head.

At the end of fall term the class holds an election to select the class secretary whose lifetime responsibility after graduation is to maintain connections among classmates, write quarterly news columns for the

*Stanford GSB* magazine, and represent the class at school functions. Because the position appeals to me, I decide to run along with five others. Considering the theme developed by the Committee for Corporate Responsibility, I campaign to move the school's program away from its focus on business to a more active role in non-business areas. Mary paints a colorful campaign poster showing the GSB floating in the ocean with the caption, "Let's get off our Island." Around the island are references to population control, pollution reduction, corporate responsibility and, yes, nuclear arms limitation. Unfortunately, the campaign doesn't resonate. Many classmates say they like our island and have no wish to get into the turmoil of the world's problems.

Applying ABCs from marketing courses, I realize the criterion for selecting class secretary has nothing to do with campaign platforms but rather how much fun the class will have if I'm elected. Seeking a more creative approach, one evening, along with a classmate photographer, we venture to a topless bar on El Camino Real, the main street in Palo Alto, and offer the proprietor publicity if his girls will pose with me. He agrees, and we set up the scene. Wearing a business suit, I sit at a desk and pose as if writing a business letter. On one knee sits Judy, on the other, sits Marilyn, both topless, looking intently at the missive I'm writing. The next day on classroom walls, I plaster dozens of photos with the caption, "Always Abreast of Things." Everyone has a lot of laughs, and I win the election by a landslide!

Dean Arjay Miller (we all call him Arjay) holds small meetings throughout the year with students to keep in touch with our problems and concerns. Often, he tells stories about his career as one of the Whiz Kids who transformed Ford's management practices to bring the company into the modern era. The following two anecdotes stick in my memory:

--One day during the height of the Viet Nam War protests that embroiled the Business School, Arjay exclaimed, "Hell, anyone can be president of Ford; it takes something extra to be dean of this business school."

-- At a White House gathering while drinking whiskey with Tex Thornton, Robert McNamara, and other Whiz Kids, President Johnson turns to Arjay, then president of Ford, and says something like, "I don't know what kind of cars you make at Ford, but the one you gave me sure gives us a lot of trouble."

"Mr. President," Arjay replied, "the car we sent you was perfectly fine. It was when you cut it in half and expanded it three feet into a limousine and then added extra weight with bullet-proof tires and windows that the troubles occurred."

Over Christmas break Mary and I return to the Sierras for what will presumably be our last winter of California skiing. When classes resume in January, I'm heading down the backstretch to the finish line. Having fulfilled all requirements to graduate, I choose elective courses in international business and new enterprise development.

While coasting through these remaining months, I learn of another extra-curricular project. McKinsey and Company, the international consulting firm, is working on a problem for a client in the paper and pulp business and hopes the solution will be a learning experience for their own new hires. The company's San Francisco office offers to bring in a few students to work on this project. Although it's never mentioned, McKinsey uses this opportunity to look over potential new hires before the GSB allows formal recruitment to begin. I apply, am accepted, and for the rest of the semester spend two days each month in San Francisco.

McKinsey has another motive, namely, to benefit from our critiques and suggestions that include newer business theories. The client's problem is deciding which mills should produce which grades of paper and pulp. Finding a solution requires iterative linear-programming analyses ideally suited to computer simulations. Stanford's new computer lab offers courses to address such problems, and finding the optimal solution is straightforward. (*McKinsey, no doubt, presented our solution to its client along with a fat bill for service.*)

For our part, we students enjoy the opportunity to work in San Francisco and gain experience from this project along with a free lunch. Most important, this adventure confirms I want nothing to do with consulting. Consultants give clients an analysis of problems, suggest alternative solutions, make recommendations, and then leave when it's time to implement the plan. But implementation is the part I enjoy the most. Pleased to learn something new about myself, I'm grateful for this experience. When a McKinsey recruiter visits the campus later in the spring and offers me a job, I politely decline.

In the meantime, Mary and I acquire Glee, a six-month-old dachshund. Glee spends all day enclosed in our yard waiting to welcome us home each evening, and she travels everywhere we go. This foot-long bundle of fur with wagging tail is a source of great joy. *(Less than a year later, however, Glee's death plunges me into the deepest sorrow I had ever known.)*

Because our time in California is ending soon, every weekend Mary and I seek new adventures. We ski until the snow melts. Then we hike in the mountain wilderness, sail in the bay, and make excursions along the coast. Now, after two memorable years at Stanford, I begin to think again about the future and probable trips for job interviews.

I also reflect that "Always Abreast of Things" is more than a publicity gimmick. While at Sandia I felt out of touch with the world at large and especially with myself. Now, with so many new ideas and projects to consider, I feel a boundless sense of enthusiasm.

Moreover, having grown during this time, I have caught up and, indeed, am abreast of life itself. What a difference these Stanford years have made!

[1969, age 28] Stanford Graduate School of Business, 2<sup>nd</sup> year, campaigning for class secretary

# 23
# Finding A Job

*5/70 - 6/70, Age 29*

Emotional distress having faded into a remote memory, I'm no longer a tightly coiled spring. The constant need to strive and compete has melted away and my creative juices are flowing. I'm stimulated by my business studies as one day dissolves into the next. Relaxed, I sense an openness, a receptivity not felt for years. Is there a plan for tomorrow? No, but I trust that whatever happens will be perfect. As spring arrives, gone is any anxiety about finding a job. Something will come my way; no need to force anything; simply remain open to whatever happens.

A few ideas have crystallized about what I want. First, I want to work in the world of business, not in a non-profit or other type of non-business organization. Second, I want to run a business myself. For two years we studied the role of corporate presidents: with this background, why not run one from the start? Third, I want to live in an international environment.

The idea to run my own enterprise grew from a whimsical blueprint made while an undergraduate: (1) Be a manager by age 25, (2) Advance to CEO by 30, (3) Oversee an international group of businesses by 35, and (4) Become financially independent by 40. The first goal occurred at

Sandia at age 24, a year early. Now 29 years old, I'm looking to fulfill Goal 2. Numbers 3 and 4 are too far off to be of immediate concern.

The plan grows real during the final semester in Professor Shallenberger's course on small business. He sharpens my vision by saying in lecture something to this effect: "If you don't trust yourself, if you have no self-confidence, if you are mainly interested in job security, then take a job at IBM, Boeing, General Electric or one of the big consulting companies such as McKinsey or Boston Consulting Group. You will rise to vice president or senior partner and have a very comfortable, secure life."

He goes on to say, "Only the mediocre guy will choose this career path. However, if you have enough confidence in your abilities to take a risk, you should start your own company or join a small, growing organization. Stanford MBAs do not typically work for giant corporations where they will likely become absorbed anonymously into an inflexible organization."

Shallenberger repeatedly challenges us to take the chance of making it all or losing it all in an entrepreneurial venture where the stakes are high. His examples demonstrate how big companies don't develop new ideas but rather get them by purchasing dynamic, smaller companies. He convinces me to rise to a big challenge by running something small!

The desire to live overseas is also growing stronger. Life in America is familiar and predictable whether in the Midwest, Northeast, Southwest, Far West, or Hawaii—all great places, but I've already lived in each and am eager to see more of the world. In addition, I anticipate future career opportunities will be outstanding for those with international backgrounds. Twenty years earlier an assignment to a factory, say, in Brazil probably meant an executive was being put out to pasture. However, because foreign earnings now account for up to 50 percent of corporate profits for some large U.S. corporations, management positions abroad are losing their tarnished image and growing more appealing.

In the 1950s, companies drew senior executives from the ranks of production supervisors because manufacturing problems were the big ones to be solved. By the '60s, the focus shifted to marketing, prompting companies to move sales managers to the corner offices. Now, in the '70s, the trend favors financial leaders who arrange creative funding to expand into overseas markets. It's my guess that as corporations seek global markets and as modern communications and transportation continue to shrink the world, the end of the century will be the day the international executive shines. Leaders of the future will need experience to offer insights into the outlook, culture, and perspective of peoples in the rest of the world. Therefore, I decide to embark upon an international career.

I ponder these two seemingly incompatible, impossible-to-attain, objectives. Finding small companies in the U.S. looking for a young manager with enthusiasm and creative ideas isn't difficult. Finding an offshore position with mid-level responsibilities in a large American multinational corporation is also straightforward. But finding a U.S. firm with foreign operations, one willing to let a 29-year-old manage even one of its smallest divisions? Probably impossible. So, it seems I have to make a choice: Go overseas and enjoy living in another culture but pay the price by getting swallowed in some mammoth corporation or remain in the United States living a predictable lifestyle but having the freedom to run my own company. Worrying about winning the lottery won't help to win it. Besides, recalling the profiles written for the "Alumni Sketch" column, there is little anyone can do to force a career to one's liking. Rather, one must be patient, wait for the right opportunity, and then use it to every possible advantage.

Graduating MBA students have two cop-out or deferral strategies if they can't find the ideal job. One is to enter the Ph.D. program and stay a few more years in the academic environment. The other, sometimes referred to as the "third year" of the MBA Program, is to join a consulting firm where opportunities often arise to find the perfect job with a company client. I dismiss both possibilities as being too abstract. I'm eager to get out in the world now and follow my dream.

When I learn that American Standard Corporation is looking for MBAs to work in its European headquarters in Brussels, I arrange for an interview. Because the interviewer likes my work experience in Europe the previous summer, he arranges an interview trip. Soon I'm on the way from

San Francisco to Brussels for a long weekend. I'm excited and can hardly believe I'm on an expense-paid trip to Europe for only a one-day interview. Naturally I expect the Brussels office will have scheduled a full program of activities, and I'm prepared to stay an extra day if necessary.

Once there, though, I'm taken aback that no one expects me or even knows who I am. After waiting quite some time, I decide to see the general manager whose name the interviewer had supplied. When I arrive at his office, he greets me with confusion. He's busy, but as my introduction from New York headquarters is sufficiently weighty, he can't ignore me. He mumbles something about the American parent company being so out of touch about doing business in Europe, they don't even communicate, myself being a case in point. The rest of the day is spent hastily being shuttled to busy, impatient executives pressed into giving me half an hour. Seeing no point in staying around, I quietly leave. The whole experience is a prime example of the inflexibility of large corporations. But I'm free to return to favorite spots in Brussels and enjoy the rest of the weekend in the city.

Returning home, I decide to consider large corporations only if there's an autonomous department free from the stifling bureaucracy and regimentation that characterize how such organizations are run. Next, I register for an interview with Monsanto Corporation, the St. Louis-based chemical and fertilizer firm. After wallowing for years in stagnating commodity markets, Monsanto is looking to develop new directions and has created a New Enterprise Division with vice presidential status. The goal is to staff the division with so-called bright entrepreneurial types who will be free to operate unencumbered by the usual company dictates. Following a strong campus interview, I'm off to St. Louis.

There I meet the new division head who strikes me as a semi-eccentric, flamboyant character who thinks he can shake up this lethargic organization. His many ideas are those of a consultant's theoretical background rather than a practitioner's understanding. During the visit I request, and am granted, interviews with other vice presidents and division managers. When I ask their thoughts about this new plan, without reservation they laugh. Explaining that Monsanto's focus is on chemicals and fertilizers—and nothing more—they give the new division six months to a year before it will fold and hint they won't be sorry to see it dissolve. When they attempt to interest me in the bread-and-butter business, such as the market for sulfuric acid or prospects for bulk phosphates, I stand up and politely end the interview with, "That's not the type of job that interests me."

Again, the hope of finding what I want seems dashed.

Before giving up entirely, though, I schedule an interview with another company. General Mills has had some success in the toy market and is seeking to expand. Because this venture is under vice-presidential direction, it presumably has a high priority. This time the invitation to visit company headquarters includes Mary, an impressive gesture that could be an influence if I don't find cracks in their edifice.

On a Thursday evening, Mary and I check into a Minneapolis motel. Next morning the company makes its first mistake by letting me talk to a former classmate from Stanford. He starts with what a great place it is but then quietly confides he is leaving, because he feels stifled in the big-company environment. Later I discern from other top managers that, as at Monsanto, they are set to torpedo this new endeavor when the chance comes. Furthermore, I'm told the division's vice president will be leaving.

The crowning blow comes when a company guide takes Mary and me on a tour of Minneapolis to show us communities where we should or should not live. Carefully pointing out neighborhoods where up-and-coming executives have homes, he assumes we would want to live there too. None of these experiences appeal. To find some sanity that evening, we drive across the river to the University of Minnesota campus in St. Paul where we relax with a mix of students whose delightful conversations convey a greater sense of humanity.

Considering the time consumed and work involved, the campus interview game might as well be another course on the business student's schedule. Most interviewers are faceless executives who assume their company's name is all that's needed to prop them up and attract prospective candidates. Coming from an earlier generation, they are more or less clueless about what we younger recruits are seeking. Whereas they talk about pension plans, insurance packages, and benefit programs, we are interested in job responsibility, independence, and new ventures. Seldom is there much real communication, but that matters little to the screeners who will decide who gets invited to headquarters for real interviews. Knowing it's all a game, we students become skilled in gamesmanship. If the interviewer is conservative, it's wise to respond likewise. If he expresses strong opinions against student demonstrations, again it's good to agree.

Of course, we don't always play for the sake of the interview. If a special event is taking place somewhere, a positive interview can lead to a visit to a nearby firm, which will pay travel costs. If, for example, someone's girlfriend (there were only six females in our class) in another part of the country has a birthday, why not show up for the party and then return to California the next day after the "interview?"

With the Kentucky Derby approaching, I'm determined to get home for the event. Checking the interview schedule, I notice a Cincinnati drug company representative will be on campus. Because Cincinnati is only a two-hour drive from Louisville, I study up on the drug business so I can score a trip. Discussions go well, and I'm invited to fly to Cincinnati. However, when I suggest the early part of May, the interviewer apologetically says that key people won't be in the office that week. Then I apologize that the mid-May date he suggests is inconvenient, and the whole thing falls through. Because the interviewer probably read on my resume that I'm from Louisville and knew the Kentucky Derby is that weekend, he likely suspected my ulterior motive when I walked into the room.

Another firm I interview is Palo Alto-based Hewlett Packard, a leader in electronic products including medical computing. When I inquire about a position in their Switzerland location, they're interested. Further discussions result in a flight to Geneva for a day of interviews. This fits conveniently with family plans. My paternal grandmother has invited us on a cruise from New York to Bermuda the week before Easter, and the interview trip helps finance Mary's and my airfare east to join family. The timing is ideal because the trip coincides with Easter holidays when Stanford closes for spring break, allowing time to enjoy both Bermuda and

Switzerland. After a week in Bermuda, Mary flies home and I catch a flight to Switzerland.

At Hewlett Packard's Geneva offices, the interviewers are interested in my book on medical computing, and I'm excited about continuing in this field. However, the Swiss government has recently cut back on foreign work permits, and HP already has more than its fair share. Once again writing off another prospect, I nevertheless have a wonderful, long weekend. Driving a rented car the length of Lake Geneva to the ski resort at Gstaad in the Swiss Alps, I enjoy a skiing holiday before flying back to California for Monday morning classes.

Before leaving the resort, I mail a picture postcard to myself. A week later when it arrives and I'm into the daily routine of classes, the words I wrote are amusing: "Hey you dumb guy, why aren't you over here skiing instead of in school grinding away?"

Another interesting sojourn takes Mary and me to the Seattle-Tacoma area, bringing back fond memories of the Seattle World's Fair eight years earlier. Weyerhaeuser Corporation, the giant timber company, is looking for MBAs, and we decide to see if the Pacific Northwest appeals. It does. After the Friday interview we enjoy a wonderful weekend exploring the waterways and mountains that make this region so attractive for outdoor enthusiasts. Nevertheless, it's even clearer that I do not want to work for a large organization.

In deference to my father and his new financial career, I look into international banking, mindful that I declined a Singapore job with First National City Bank the previous summer. Now the company invites me to New York City headquarters to talk again. The opportunities within the international division certainly appeal, but career success would mean a promotion back to Manhattan, a dismal prospect.

Although the Bay area holds no interest, I look into local engineering jobs anyway. But after more interviews with technical firms in Silicon Valley, I conclude that abandoning this field was the right move. Yes, I loved studying engineering but still have no interest in returning to the profession. Throughout this winnowing process I stay calm, feeling no panic or urgency, and know that by simply trusting, something wonderful will come along.

And sure enough, something wonderful does. The Placement Office staff has continued to look for a small business needing an overseas manager, most likely an impossible find. But one day they send a notice to come by and check out a new opportunity.

The position is in the fields of West Flanders in Belgium managing a small, specialty textile factory, a subsidiary of The Schlegel Corporation of Rochester, New York. The job description fascinates me because of the obvious lack of polish and attention to drafting the announcement. I'm bored by slick brochures and their elaborate descriptions about some wonderful assignment. Those first-class, four-color brochures, produced by a public relations department, are sterile and artificial. The Schlegel information has obviously been put together on short notice and no one took the trouble to do a thorough job or even wordsmith the text. I had worked enough around small businesses to know this lack of attention indicates a fast-moving, dynamic organization that has neither the time nor interest in creating a polished facade. Rather, the lack of concern about minor details indicates an organization interested in simply getting on with business.

I submit my application to Rochester and wait anxiously for a reply. Within a few days a telegram arrives offering a weekend trip to upstate New York. Upon arrival I meet the personnel manager, Jim Bullock, who presents a company overview and some business literature. Everything is so beautifully unsophisticated that I lose my heart to the firm without knowing much about it. Whatever it is doing, the company is down to earth with an honest, direct approach.

Meeting the chairman of the board confirms everything I'm feeling so far. Although Dick Turner is not very relaxed, he makes every effort to make me feel comfortable. When he describes Schlegel's nuts and bolts operations, his eyes light up. Rather than confusing me with numbers or making a sales pitch, he shares a vision and treats me as if I'm a partner. Rambling along for an hour (and despite the fact that he has a law degree from my college rival, Yale), Dick mesmerizes with his country charm.

Although I don't learn much about Schlegel Corporation or the position in Belgium, I find my mind humming in tune with this fascinating man and his company.

Further interviews support the image I have that Schlegel's markets are dynamic, and the company is growing rapidly. No one seems to know the direction it is going, but everyone is committed to seeing it succeed. Each person exudes a vibrancy and dynamism that confirms this is the job I've been searching for and the company I want to join.

Catching a flight home the next morning, for the first time in a long while I feel anxious, wondering if I'll be offered the job. Did I convey my enthusiasm during the interviews? Did the management of this tiny company see I have something to contribute to its overseas operation? Did I show enough interest and ask the right questions? What else can I do?

The answer: there is nothing else I can do because nothing else is necessary. After a long week of waiting, a phone call from Jim Bullock, who initially interviewed me, announces I am the successful candidate. Soon after comes the formal offer to be managing director of the Belgian company, N.V. Schlegel S.A., located in the small farming town of Gistel an hour's drive north of Brussels and 15 minutes from the North Sea. Of the seven job offers tendered during these final Stanford days, this one promises the lowest salary and has the least-defined expectations. But those things don't matter. I will have my own company and live overseas. The miracle has happened; my twin objectives are, after all, attainable. I respond with an immediate and unequivocal "Yes" to Schlegel, and for the remainder of the school year can barely contain my excitement.

# 24
# Washington, DC

*5/70 - 9/70, Age 29*

Because Mary and I have already made plans for the summer, I postpone the start of the new job until autumn. At the conference I attended a year earlier sponsored by the Institute for the Study of Health and Society, I learned that the Institute had received a grant to develop a curriculum for elementary schools to teach students about ecology and the environment. Mary had applied and been accepted to attend this summer workshop in Washington, DC.

With the MBA Degree now a reality, we prepare to depart California. Because Schlegel is shipping our belongings to Belgium, we can travel unencumbered. Like so many other occasions, I'm choked up at the prospect of saying goodbye to friends and leaving a happy place. On our last day in California, we sell the convertible Mustang and, with the Sunfish lashed atop MOPS, Mary and I pull away from our Palo Alto farmhouse to start a new life.

Driving southeast into the Sierras, we wind through back roads to the eastern slopes. Mount Whitney casts its shadow as we emerge from the high country of crystal-clear streams and wildflower meadows onto the scorching heat of Death Valley. There must be some significance in choosing a route that includes America's highest and lowest places. Maybe it's related to having experienced the low and high points of my life at Sandia and then Stanford in such a short time.

Over the course of a week we stop often along the way to Albuquerque. Knowing we won't return west for some time, we take advantage of this opportunity to visit both familiar and also new places we haven't seen before. In Las Vegas we reconnect with friends and former colleagues before diverting to Zion and Bryce National Parks in Utah after which we head to Lake Powell and launch the Sunfish for a few days of sailing. Next is a jog south to the Grand Canyon and then to the Painted Desert in Arizona. When we reach Albuquerque, Mary's family hosts several parties for us with old friends, and we fill two short days with a series of "hellos" and "goodbyes."

Because Mary must arrive soon in Washington for her research fellowship, she flies from Albuquerque while Glee and I drive east with the Sunfish and suitcases. Before joining Mary I stop in Louisville to see family and drop off the boat with my father who looks forward to sailing it on the Ohio River at the Louisville Sailing Club, where he is a founding member.

Our temporary home in D.C. is a fashionable girls' school in Georgetown where we live with 50 other scholarship recipients. Mary joins the group of elementary school teachers to collect information for each grade level, a fertile area for research, and by summer's end they have pulled together materials to be published as a teacher's handbook.

That development is not all that's fertile this summer. Mary is too, and we're ecstatic over the joyous news. In spite of constant morning sickness, Mary blossoms with the wonder that lies before us.

Having nothing structured to do over the summer, I decide to learn whatever language is spoken in Belgium. Simply identifying the lingo is more difficult than one might think. Virtually every crisis faced by the Belgian government dates to the French-Flemish conflict, a strange history that keeps the country eternally divided. Because Gistel is located in the north, Flemish is the local language. Although it's a dialect of Dutch,

Belgians won't appreciate if I learn Dutch. The Flemish-speaking Belgians seem to have as much animosity toward their Dutch neighbors to the north as toward their countrymen to the south; so best to stick with Flemish instead of Dutch or French.

Mevrouw (Madam) Hefner, a Jewish Holocaust survivor who grew up in the Netherlands assures me she speaks Flemish, and we begin a series of evening Flemish lessons. The choking, guttural sounds are practically impossible to remember, and Mary and I find it difficult to believe we're actually learning a spoken language. But our instructress assures us we're doing fine, and by the end of summer we can carry on a semi-respectable conversation in the language of our new home.

My other interest is to see firsthand the inner workings of the federal government. Hearings are underway at the Department of Commerce questioning activities of American multinational corporations, and I become a regular attendee at these sessions. Every day top managers from U.S. corporations appear before the congressional committee to testify about the behavior, or misbehavior, of their global enterprises. The government is concerned these firms circumvent both U.S. law and the laws of countries where they have a presence. Shifting assets and resources around the world, some companies don't consider the implications for any particular country. The committee tries to assess how great an impact such corporations have on national economies, particularly in small countries like Belgium. I collect reams of material published from these proceedings. When the hearings conclude, nothing much changes the way American corporations operate. The entire process is highly bureaucratic: lots of paper, lots of discussion, lots of proposals, lots of press coverage, and no action, thanks to the efforts of the lobbyists.

To understand how special-interest groups operate in Washington, I call upon different organizations—Pew Foundation, National Rifle Association, AARP, AAA, and others—and introduce myself simply as a guy who's interested in a particular theme dear to them. I schedule a meeting, follow up with a visit, and soon find myself involved in a variety of initiatives they hope to pass into legislation. When I check on my favorite subject of computer applications in medicine, the Department of Health, Education, and Welfare takes an interest in my background and shares plans to get the country moving in this area. I also check with several environmental organizations—Sierra Club, Wild Turkey Federation, and American Hunters and Anglers—to learn their agenda. Then I visit the Bureau of Indian Affairs to see how they are cooling tensions that heated up over recent land disputes on a Southwest reservation.

I enjoy playing the role of Mr. Private Citizen concerned about current issues. Having no responsibilities or affiliation to represent, I just wander around investigating this and that. When bored, I visit museums, art galleries, and tourist sites. I wouldn't mind staying another six months but summer is drawing to a close, and although I've enjoyed this final, short-lived fling of freedom, now it's time to launch my new career.

Mary and I pack up, bid farewell to Washington, and drive to Rochester.

# 25
# Rochester

*9/70 - 10/70, Age 29*

Rochester sprang up near the Canadian border on the Genesee River which flows north into Lake Ontario. In the days before steam power, energy of the Genesee was harnessed to operate mills clustered along its shores. Each fall farmers in upstate New York shipped their wheat harvest to these mills, earning Rochester the name "Flour City" in the 1800s. When the steam engine replaced hydroelectric power late in the century, the mills moved to the farming regions. Although this move dealt a crippling blow to Rochester, the city nevertheless recovered and endured into the 20th century. Were it not for men such as George Eastman and Hiram Sibley, Rochester might have met the fate that awaited many other upstate cities that couldn't keep up with the times. When Eastman set up Eastman Kodak Corporation and Sibley established Western Union Telegraph Company, the city's continued growth was assured. Later in the mid-20th century, Xerox Corporation added to it.

C. P. Schlegel was born when the flour mills were still active, and he lived in Rochester a few years beyond his 100th birthday. He witnessed the rise and fall of the economy many times and from these observations put into practice lessons learned about changes that buffet a company. When he founded The Schlegel Manufacturing Company in the late

1800s, the main product was the cloth fringe on the canopy of horse-drawn carriages, the same fringe referred to in "The Surrey with the Fringe on Top" from the musical *Oklahoma!*

But his small specialty textile firm ran into problems when cars began replacing horse-drawn carriages. Initially cars were produced with fringed tops, but as speeds increased, the fringe became a hindrance and was discarded. A normal but never successful reaction to a classic problem faced by leading firms in a dying market is to make a better product or reduce the price in hopes it will sell again.

Knowing this approach wouldn't work, C.P. looked closely at the machine responsible for his company's pain to see what he could learn. What would future automobiles need that could be woven on his looms? C.P. found a range of possible products: door seals, glazing mountings, trunk liners, anti-rattle fabrics to place between metals, and numerous padding pieces. By converting his company into an automotive specialty textile business, he saved it.

During WW II, C.P. adapted his expertise to produce webbing for machine gun belts, gun slings, and parachute cords and harnesses. Although demand later disappeared, the experience helped the company expand into new markets. After the war, C.P. eyed the fast-growing construction industry and entered the woven weatherseal business. During the 1950s his company supplied both woven and plastic seals for windows and doors in both the automotive and building products industries.

Now C.P. had to solve a problem that plagues every successful entrepreneur as he ages. Who will take over the enterprise? Because his sons were incompetent in business matters, he looked to nephews and grandsons, but they, too, had no sense for the business. Searching outside the family, he turned to his personal attorney, a bright, young, Yale-educated Dick Turner, to whom he handed over the reins. C.P. set up a legal structure that left ownership of the firm with his family but gave tight control to Turner to avoid family squabbling. When C.P. died, he must have felt satisfied: He had built a successful company, left a small fortune for his family, and most importantly, assured The Schlegel Manufacturing Company would be left in good hands.

In the following years Turner expanded the company into overseas markets through acquisitions and licensing agreements in Australia, England, Canada, Germany, and Japan. When I join the company, Schlegel's annual sales are only $10 million, remarkably small for a firm with a global reach.

Turner charges me with bringing a newly constructed plant in Belgium, built to produce textile seals for the construction markets of Europe, to full operation. In order to get acquainted with headquarters executives and learn the firm's products and businesses, I am to spend six weeks at Rochester. Realizing this time period is too short to rent a place and too long to stay in a motel, I place advertisements in Rochester's newspapers during the summer for a house-sitting opportunity.

Mary, Glee, and I spend two days driving from Washington, DC and arrive in Rochester on a cool September afternoon. After checking into a motel for what we hope will be a short stay, I head to Schlegel's offices eager to read the dozen replies to my ads. Unfortunately, most are from lonely or infirm persons looking for companionship.

But one response has the prospect of an ideal arrangement and mentions something about keeping up an indoor pool. I telephone for an appointment, and the next evening Mary and I drive to a large, craftsman-style home on a wooded plot in one of Rochester's exclusive communities. As we pull into the driveway, Herman, a small dachshund that could have been Glee's brother, trots out to greet us, a positive omen.

The owner's wife interviews us in the comfortable living room. Seeing how friendly we are with Herman, she's no doubt convinced we're the right ones to take over the house; however, she continues to question us to assure herself that we're responsible people. She then explains that she and her husband are separating; she is moving out, and he will be around only at night to sleep in a private basement bedroom. We will have total run of the house but must agree to maintain the pool and feed Herman. This arrangement suits us fine, and the next day we move into this exceptional home.

A couple of days later, however, we are caught up in a real-life melodrama when I receive a late-night call from the police. The owner has been in an automobile accident, and they're trying to locate his wife. Sensing this is going to disrupt our lives, I give them her phone number. In the morning I hear on the radio about the accident; it had been a messy one, and our landlord is in critical condition at a local hospital. His wife suddenly becomes the attentive, caring spouse who apparently loves her husband more than anything in the world.

Because the wife was not involved in running the household and her husband is incapacitated, she turns to me. Suddenly I'm paying the couple's bills, making home repairs, cutting the grass, cleaning the pool, and attending to other maintenance chores. On top of this development, the wife asks for help with medical insurance paperwork and legal matters. She comes to the house every other evening to unburden herself and ask advice. When we offer to move out, she insists we're doing a favor while she attends to her husband, so we stay put and, despite the unfortunate circumstances, enjoy our living situation.

On the first day of work at the administrative offices I receive a warm welcome from the people I had met months earlier. That afternoon at the manufacturing plant I start learning the production processes. The clamor of 50 looms churning out woven-pile weather stripping makes it easy to find the weave shed. Ironically, my education has given me a firm grasp of advanced technologies including solid-state electronics, integrated circuits, and computer programming; but when it comes to weaving, one of the world's oldest, most basic labors, I'm clueless.

Jerry Jarawala, a shift supervisor from India, teaches me everything about weaving. He begins by going over basic terminology—warp and weft yarns, bobbins, trays, reeds, shuttles, breast beams, drop boxes, treadles, and more. Then he shows how to set up a loom with proper emplacement of bobbins and cones to meet the required dimensions of pile height and backing width. Next step is coating the pile with polypropylene as a backing stiffener. Finally, we get hands dirty as we adjust the speeds and performance of the moving mechanisms and do routine maintenance to replace worn parts on the looms. By the end, Jerry acknowledges I have learned everything known to a 17th century weaver, little of which has changed in the intervening 350 years.

The end of our house-sitting time approaching, Mary and I try to see and do everything we can to learn about life in upstate New York. The landscape explodes into a splendor of yellows, reds, and oranges bringing two glorious weeks of Indian Summer with warm days and chilly nights. On weekends we explore the surrounding countryside, particularly the Finger Lakes region where Riesling vineyards are ready for harvest. Produce stands selling fresh corn, tomatoes, apples, and vegetables pop up along country roads, and cider mills are busy. Knowing this will be our last taste of "Americana" for some time, most evenings we attend a concert, lecture, ballet, art opening, or other community event.

Perhaps our most important activity is taking a course in natural childbirth in hopes the Belgian medical system will allow us to be together for the delivery. Normally classes begin in the mother's seventh month but although Mary is only in her fourth, we sign up. We also buy every book we can find on prepared and natural childbirth.

The house-sitting drama takes a tragic turn. Our injured benefactor dies. For a moment I consider delaying our departure, but this affair is not ours. I do what I can while adhering to the original plan.

By mid-October it's time to say goodbye and make our seventh move in less than six months. I've enjoyed the freedom of being an investigating ombudsman while delving into every aspect of Schlegel's operations and gathering documents that range from maintenance procedures for looms to tax regulations for international corporations. Although I may not need to look at the documents again, I'm glad to have them and send reams of paper ahead to Belgium. Having established good relations with key employees in different departments, I can count on them to clear up problems I may encounter.

Mary and I are weary with impromptu-style living. Packing MOPS for the last time, we drive to the home of my maternal grandparents, Grummy and Grumpy, in Monroe, Connecticut, where we stay a few days before flying to Europe. MOPS, still in good condition after eight years, has little resale value. Even if she had more value, we probably wouldn't sell because she's part of our family. She took me to my first job in New Mexico before passing to Mary and then coming back to me when we married. She took us to our first home in Las Vegas and then to both

Fremont and Stanford in California. She carried our sailboat everywhere throughout the West and into Mexico and appears in photographs taken from the snowy peaks of the Sierras to the shores of Mazatlán.

But now it's time to say goodbye to this old friend. With a simple ceremony, I hand the keys to Grumpy who promises he and Grummy will keep her for us until we return. We give MOPS away with reverence, and my grandparents receive her with gratitude while Mary captures the event on film. But MOPS must have suffered a broken heart that day, because over the next several months everything goes wrong. Finally, with no point in making further repairs, my grandparents mercifully sell her to a junk dealer.

That bright, sunny autumn day before we fly to Belgium is the last time I will see MOPS or my grandfather.

[1970, Monroe, Connecticut, age 29]
Grummy and Grumpy accept keys to MOPS

# 26
# Bruges, Balmoral, and Bridges

*10/70 - 10/71, Age 29 - 30*

The next day after saying good-bye to my grandparents in Connecticut, Mary, Glee and I depart Kennedy Airport on Sabena's all-night flight to Brussels where we touch down and deplane with exhilaration—a sense that we have come home.

In Brussels I meet my predecessor, Steve Hamlin. After a year setting up the bare bones of the company, Steve eagerly awaits my arrival so he can return to Rochester. After he transfers the company's directorship to me, we embark on a two-day whirlwind tour to meet bankers, lawyers, accountants, and consultants with whom I will be working. I feel welcomed back in the familiar setting where one year earlier I had worked as a consultant with Robert S. First Company.

Business introductions over, Mary and I, traveling in a new company car, head toward Ostend where we plan to make our new home. Driving past scattered villages and flat farmlands, we feel life is showering the best of everything upon us. The trip takes us through three cities that will impact our lives during the next two years: Ghent, capital of East Flanders province; Bruges, capital of West Flanders province; and the popular seacoast resort of Ostend.

Mary and I laughingly recall our previous visit to Ostend a year and a half earlier when we arrived by ferry from Dover on the way to Brussels. Having little idea where we were, I asked a local what language they speak in Ostend. Grinning, he said in accented English, "A little bit of everything." We never dreamed that one day this town might be our home, and now, here we are.

At the pre-booked hotel, we receive a bouquet of flowers, a basket of fruit, and a cordial note from my new Schlegel employees making us feel welcome. For several days we explore this charming locale as we hunt for a place to live.

Within a week, however, we are thrown into the deepest sadness either of us has ever known. With no warning, Glee, the joy of our life, starts acting strangely. She has no appetite, becomes listless, and loses weight. We've been feeding her locally canned dog food, and when she refuses to eat it, we try alternate brands, but nothing works. A veterinarian prescribes medication, but Glee only gets worse. Next day the vet x-rays her and discovers her entire intestinal tract is destroyed.

He asks what we have been feeding her. "Local canned dog food," we respond as before.

This time the questioning goes deeper. When he hears we are staying in a hotel, he asks if we keep the dog food chilled. We reply that this has never been necessary in the States and we hadn't thought about it in Belgium.

But unlike in the States, dog food in Belgium doesn't contain preservatives. Glee's un-chilled, Belgian food has turned toxic.

Mary and I unwittingly poisoned our beloved Glee.

When she dies the next morning, a part of us breaks down as well. Tears roll down our cheeks as Mary and I walk along the cold, windswept beach. Acting in ignorance, we had killed our pet.

Wanting to get away from Ostend as soon as possible, we check out of the hotel, cancel appointments with real estate agents, and drive south to Bruges.

And that's how it happens that our new home is in Bruges.

Bruges is like a museum. From the 14th to 16th century, Bruges was one of Europe's largest, most prosperous cities. Connected to the sea by a canal big enough to accommodate merchant ships, the city built a reputation as a major trading center with the East. Silks from India and spices from Indonesia passed through the city's warehouses. This commerce created a wealthy burgher class that attracted the greatest artists such as Jan van Eyck, Hans Memling, and other prominent Flemish Masters, and the greatest architects of Europe. As a major western outpost of the Hanseatic League, Bruges rivaled Hamburg, Antwerp, Novgorod, Venice, and other major trade centers of the time.

But then the canal—the lifeblood of the city linking it to the sea—gradually began silting. Oddly, the merchants didn't recognize this threat to their livelihoods and ignored it. As the canal shallowed, larger ships were offloaded at sea and smaller vessels brought goods into town. However, soon the water passage was not deep enough even for shallow-draft vessels. Because the citizens of Bruges didn't dredge their waterway, it was only a matter of time before the city became lost in the pages of history.

Had the Bruges burgermeister foreseen the consequence of neglect, he surely would have brought in engineers from every corner of the continent to find a solution. However, he coped with, rather than solved, the problem and thus ended up with municipal bankruptcy. *(This history is reminiscent of many parallels with business school cases I studied in which management becomes preoccupied with operational details and fails to see a looming threat.)*

The lack of foresight was suicidal. Silting occurred so rapidly that Bruges simply died as it was. No renovations kept the city current with the times. The result is that with streets and buildings preserved in their original styles, Bruges today looks the same as it did 500 years ago.

Because many early Christian relics are housed within some 40 churches of Romanesque, Gothic, Renaissance, and Baroque designs, Bruges is Belgium's most popular tourist attraction. Most famous is a small vial said to contain Christ's blood, stored in the Romanesque Basilica of the Holy Blood *(Heilig-Bloedbasiliek)*. Once each year during the "Procession of the Holy Blood," the venerated vial is paraded through the streets amidst much fanfare.

Sometimes referred to as "Venice of the North," Bruges is surrounded by a moat and is laced with canals. Although this makes for a romantic, picturesque setting, it isn't practical for living. Small houses that preserve the historical quality of the city are not allowed to be destroyed, forcing residents to live in cramped quarters with limited electrical capacity and out-of-date plumbing. As Mary and I look for a home, we become increasingly discouraged by the primitive living conditions behind Bruges' charming facade. Following real-estate agents through one house after another, we find nothing suitable.

Resigned, I start looking beyond the city's outer circular canal. One evening after work I come across a rental notice for a palatial home referred to as a "petite chateau." The listing agent discourages me, saying the structure is old, cold, and haunted. Regardless, I press for a tour and he reluctantly agrees.

The next day Mary and I are shocked to discover an enormous estate enclosed behind a high brick wall. On a gigantic wrought-iron gate, a large plaque announces "Balmoral," perhaps influenced by the name of the English Royals' summer castle in Scotland.

Balmoral is the most enormous house we've ever seen. To call it a mansion would be to belittle it! For the next hour we explore the many rooms of this three-story estate villa. The grand front hall is furnished with a 17th-century Italian church pew originally carved for a noble family. In time the pew will end up in a museum but meanwhile will stay with the house and whoever rents it.

Left and right off the hallway two elaborate sitting rooms with 13-foot-high ceilings are filled with antique furniture. Another room, presumably the music salon, is dominated by a large piano. An ornately carved wooden staircase ascends to four large bedrooms each with its own bathroom. Smaller bedrooms, bathrooms, and sitting rooms on the third floor are staff quarters. Tall windows ensure plenty of daylight throughout the house, and massive chandeliers light up every room. Best of all, the house is fully renovated with central heating, updated plumbing, and modern bathroom and kitchen fixtures. Returning to the ground floor we wander into an enormous kitchen. A cluster of smaller rooms in back serves as pantries, vegetable cellars, mudrooms, and utility storage.

The rent is inexpensive because the owner is desperate to have the place occupied. Obviously a white elephant on the rental market, the estate has remained vacant since the owner moved to Brussels some time ago.

Two evenings later we return to meet the owner. Madame de Porcq is a gracious Belgian lady who speaks perfect English and whose father bought the estate after World War I. We learn why we had been put off by the real estate agent; because he could make a sizable commission if he sold the house rather than renting it, he had not been showing it to prospective tenants. We can detect guilt as he retreats to a corner while we talk with Madame de Porcq.

Mary and I are fascinated as she recounts the sordid history of Balmoral. In the late nineteenth century it was built by a wealthy German burgher who became the governing official when Germans occupied Bruges during World War I. After the armistice, the Belgian government took possession of the estate and sold it to Madame de Porcq's father. He had made a fortune importing trucks needed to rebuild the country and invested much of his wealth in this estate.

When Germany invaded Belgium again in World War II, the owner and his family fled the country. Because Balmoral was the largest home in West Flanders, it became headquarters for the German High Command. The occupiers built an ammunition dump behind the house and brought in free-running guard dogs to ensure security. Large sections of new brick in the old compound walls showed where portions had been removed for dogs to patrol adjoining fields. During the occupation, locals feared and hated Balmoral because of the tyranny emanating from behind its high walls.

When the Allies swept across Europe, the invaders abandoned Bruges, but not before setting fire to Balmoral's front hall and fusing the ammunition dump to explode once they were gone. A few hours later when Canadian troops liberated the city, Balmoral's owner was right behind.

"My father arrived in time to see that the ammunition dump had only partially detonated, but the blast set Balmoral afire," Madame de Porcq explained. Her father mustered neighbors to fight the flames, and, with the same good luck that prevented the ammunition depot from completely exploding, he saved Balmoral.

Yet another stroke of good fortune was that the invaders had not found the secret hiding places that contained valuables and other treasures hastily stashed away before they arrived. Because Belgium has historically been the fighting ground for the major powers of Europe, Belgians build their houses with numerous false panels, hidden chambers, and secret cupboards to hide valuables during times of strife.

Despite this grim history, Mary and I feel we have found our new home and within days move in. Still living out of suitcases while awaiting our household goods, we learn of another glitch—one that at first seems bad news but turns out to be fortuitous. The moving company shipping our belongings from Palo Alto to Belgium reports that someone had ransacked our possessions while temporarily stored in New York. After eight moves during four years of marriage, our belongings show considerable wear and tear. Therefore, we aren't at all disappointed when insurance very generously covers the loss.

Neighbors vividly recount atrocities committed during the German occupation. Although we try not to dwell on these stories, we often hear sounds at night that make us think of SS Troopers in their hobnail boots stomping around downstairs. We remind ourselves that wind whistling down the seven chimneys can make eerie sounds; even so, visions of our predecessors persist. Other frightening disturbances—soundings like rifle shots downstairs—might occur at 3:00 am on freezing winter nights when a piano string lets go or parquet floors crackle as they adjust to temperature swings. These sounds combined with those made by squirrels in the rafters, magpies in the eaves, a grandfather clock that chimes at odd hours, and the boom of the furnace when it comes on, create a calamitous symphony.

The grounds of the three-acre estate are as magnificent as the house itself. The wife of the original owner, a horticulturalist who traveled the world, collected trees and shrubs to plant throughout the gardens. Apple trees provide ripe fruit from June through November. Other trees and bushes produce enough pears, cherries, peaches, plums, currants, and berries to supply not just us but also our neighbors. A small pine forest planted at the west end of the estate serves as a natural air-conditioning system by allowing prevailing winds to waft fresh fragrances toward the house. What a surprise to find a New Mexico Century plant and a Hawaiian silversword tucked in on the grounds.

Winding pebble pathways on the north side connect several small rose gardens, creating serene, romantic settings. Love seats hidden behind trellises supporting climbing roses invite one to sit in meditative silence. In the midst of one garden, a pond with a small fountain is filled with goldfish. Pink, blue, and purple flowers adorning garden paths provide color and fragrance throughout the seasons.

An ornate, formal Italian garden on the south side of Balmoral creates a feeling more of grandiosity than relaxation. Short, manicured hedges border symmetrical pathways crisscrossing a grotto framed by statues of life-sized mythological figures. The garden ends at an ivy-covered, 10-foot wall that surrounds the estate. Two nearby ponds, one saltwater and the other freshwater, previously held two species of eels, a mainstay of the Belgian diet.

As if in answer to the question about who maintains these gardens, one day from an upstairs window I catch sight of an old man on hands and knees working in the rose gardens. Well into his 80s, Peer is as much a legend as the house itself. A tall, sturdy, regal-looking gentleman, he has a shock of snow-white hair that constantly falls across his brow. With a characteristic gesture, he tosses his head to throw the tangled mane back where it obediently stays until the next time he bends forward.

After struggling to converse with Peer in my newly learned Flemish, I realize it's impossible because Peer speaks an old regional dialect, *(one that likely dies when he dies five years later)*. Since words seem to be more of a barrier than a help, we give up trying to speak. Instead, with simple gestures we get along fine.

Over the course of two years I learn many things from Peer—how to fix a leaky faucet with waxed string, how to set up transformers to adapt U.S. appliances to Europe's electrical system, and how to turn stubborn hens into good layers. For two generations Peer has been the gardener and handyman for the estate, even during the German occupation. Needing no direction, he simply comes and goes on his own schedule doing whatever is necessary to keep up the grounds. He's such a permanent fixture that Madame de Porcq had neglected to tell me about him.

Without Peer we couldn't survive in Balmoral. Although he had never attended school and couldn't read or write, he knows how to fix almost anything. When the furnace breaks down or the power fails, he makes things right. As fruits ripen, he knows exactly when to pick and how to preserve them in the fruit cellar. Even when things are going right, Peer has a knack for knowing when something is about to go wrong and attends to preventive maintenance without delay.

Peer is a lifesaver in taking care of our American appliances. We had heard that large home appliances were hard to find in Belgium, so we shipped from the States a refrigerator, washer, dryer, and dishwasher that all work fine once Peer installs the transformers. But when an appliance breaks, no one in Bruges can repair it, so we call Peer. He discards the instruction manual and wiring schematic (which he probably would do even if he could read) and sets about troubleshooting. Once he finds the problem, he recruits a friend in a metal shop to construct the replacement part that can't be purchased. In a short while, everything works. When Mary gets closer to her due date, I joke that we should let Peer handle the delivery since he seems fully qualified to manage anything.

I didn't move to Belgium just to live on an estate and stroll in its garden. I have come here to work. N.V. Schlegel S.A. is located 10 kilometers from Bruges in the village of Gistel on land that a year earlier had been a beet field. When Rochester decided to build a plant here, a government development program offered incentives: worker training, reduced taxes, and cheap land in agricultural West Flanders. My predecessor Steve Hamlin had been sent from Rochester to construct the building, install five looms, and hire office and factory workers. My job is to bring the plant into full operation.

The first task is to learn to pronounce the name of the company, which under Belgian law must be in both Flemish and French languages. The simple form is "NV Schlegel SA" where NV and SA stand for "Incorporated" in Flemish and French respectively. The tongue-twister is that NV abbreviates for *"Naamlose Vennootschap"* ("nameless partnership" in Flemish) and SA for *"Société Anonyme"* ("anonymous company" in French).

Twenty employees, all recent hires from surrounding villages, greet me the first day. In their eyes I sense a mix of fear and excitement: fear because we American businessmen are rumored to have a ruthless "hire and fire" approach to running businesses; excitement, because most are farmers enticed by prospects of learning a trade and earning more money in an industrial job.

Uwe Marwedel, a German who has lived in Flanders for many years, escorts me into the marketing and sales area he manages. In addition to his native language, Uwe speaks Flemish, French, and English, and I'm surprised to learn his two assistants, who have never traveled outside of Flanders, also speak these languages plus Italian and Spanish. Their fluency makes me, an American struggling to learn one new language, feel linguistically inadequate.

Rene LeFevre, the comptroller who understands both Flemish and American accounting systems, goes over sales figures and expenses. I see it will be a challenge to bring operations out of the red.

The production manager is Mike Henno, a burly, chain-smoking Fleming from Ostend who speaks rapid-fire English. He leads me into the production area where I see five looms and other machines identical to those I had trained on in Rochester. To show I know something about their operation, I walk up to the looms and comment about the yarns and mounting of the bobbins.

The production process consists of three steps: weaving weather-stripping lace, stiffening the backing with a polypropylene coating, and slitting the lace into widths to fit into aluminum extrusions of windows and doors made by our customers. Observing that three-quarters of the building is empty, I realize my job is to build enough business to add more looms. Knowing that aluminum frame windows and doors are rapidly replacing wooden constructions throughout Europe and that our company is the only producer of weatherseals on the continent, I feel confident we can capitalize upon this growth.

The final member of the administration is my secretary, who amazes me with her proficiency not just in speaking, but also in writing English as well as the other major European languages. Although Steve's tenure had been short, he had done an excellent job in getting the building constructed and, with assistance from local personnel recruiters, putting in place an outstanding staff.

At the onset I need to create an organization that can work as a team. Because we are the only industry in an agrarian region, the employees had been farmers accustomed to working on their own schedule. But the plant can't run efficiently on this basis; the looms, for example, can start only when everyone is here. To get everybody accustomed to showing up punctually at 8:00 am, I put in place minor penalties for those who are late. Everyone quickly adjusts to this stricter environment, and within no time our workers can perform as well as or better than their counterparts in Rochester.

Soon we find ourselves trying to keep up with increasing customer demand. Five industry trends work in our favor. First, shopkeepers throughout Europe want larger front-display windows that are possible only with the strength of aluminum frames that, in turn, require weatherseals. Second, timber shortages in Europe boost demand for aluminum fenestration products, and we are a necessary part of this business. Third, as the only firm in Europe's Common Market producing woven weathersealing products, we are less expensive and faster with deliveries than competitors who must import. Fourth, as a nascent business in the Common Market, we are protected with tariffs imposed on imports. Fifth, the trend worldwide is to replace old wooden windows and doors with the modern look of aluminum.

During the next two years we triple the number of looms, increase the factory workforce to 50 employees, and expand from one shift to three shifts. Even with this nine-fold increase in capacity, we still have difficulty meeting demand. In no time we are shipping products to more than 50 countries in Western and Eastern Europe, the Middle East, Far East, and Africa. How ironic that from a remote outpost in the hinterlands of Belgium, we are serving countries on three continents. And most importantly, we're having fun! We enjoy pioneering rapidly and extensively into new markets and company morale is high. As operations grow through evolving stages, I utilize nearly every business school concept I learned. This new career allows me to be creative, entrepreneurial, and independent, and I love it.

The arrival of 1971 brings many new developments. At Christmas I give Mary a small dachshund puppy we name Sativa, and once again we are three. Mary delves into the art and history of Belgium while I'm engrossed in building the company. The snow blanketing Flanders melts sooner than usual, and we're presented with an early spring. Twice a week Mary pedals her bicycle to Bruges' train station and travels to Brussels for painting lessons or gatherings with other American expatriate wives. Other days she sets off to explore Bruges' museums and churches. She becomes so familiar with the city that she begins giving informal tours for those women who come to Bruges for the day. Mary finds this not only fulfilling but a welcome connection from our isolated outpost to the happenings in Brussels' stimulating international community.

As Mary's delivery date approaches, we review the books about natural childbirth. Every evening I serve as coach while she practices breathing and relaxing exercises, and soon we've relearned everything taught five months earlier. Having found a good doctor at University Hospital in Ghent a convenient half-hour train ride away, Mary often stops for regular examinations on her way to Brussels.

The day—which starts as a typical one but changes our lives forever—arrives. In the morning Mary pedals to the station to catch the train to Ghent for one of her checkups. That evening after dinner the contractions begin, most likely induced by earlier bike rides along pebbled roads, and she telephones her doctor. "Come right away," the doctor says.

Although we've witnessed this scene many times in movies and read about it in books, now that it's our turn it's totally new and exciting. In no time we're packed and driving to Ghent. After Mary checks into the hospital, the doctor examines her and reports everything is coming along fine.

As contractions grow more frequent, Mary moves through successive stages of breathing. With a watch in one hand and a training manual in the other, I coach and encourage her, much to the interest and amusement of the doctor and nurses standing by. When the contractions become more intense, Mary is given a spinal block to take the edge off the pain. After an anxious night, just before dawn on March 24th, Cyrena is born. Our joy is beyond measure, and we are indeed proud parents.

Before leaving the hospital, Mary and I discuss a design for Cyrena's birth announcement. Wanting something whimsical that shows a connection to Bruges, we create the perfect card. On the front is a sketch of the 400-year-old Bruges Bell Tower that dominates the town's central market and is visible from miles away. Below the Bell Tower we write the caption: "The American population of Bruges has just increased 50 percent ..." On the next page the caption continues, "...and females outnumber males two to one." Then we announce the arrival of Cyrena Elizabeth Schroeder—giving statistics not in inches and pounds, but, in deference to our host country, in centimeters and kilograms.

Spring is blooming, and we again expand our family. After cleaning up an old chicken coop, one Saturday at the local market I buy six hens guaranteed to be good layers. Peer sneers at the extorted price, but in four weeks when we start getting a more-than-adequate supply of eggs, I feel triumphant.

Next, I set out to plant a vegetable garden. Over a long weekend, I dig up a large section of the backyard. I return to the marketplace for seeds, but this time I'm stymied. Familiar garden vegetables from the States don't seem to exist in Belgium, and those for sale are unfamiliar. Determined not to leave empty-handed, I return home with a collection of strange seeds, and with trust and hope, plant them in the garden.

Shortly thereafter I notice Peer at work on a construction project in the garden. When I ask what he's doing, he mumbles a word I've never heard before. Consulting a Flemish dictionary, I learn the word "*konijn*" (pronounced ko-NAY) means "rabbit." Peer first trenches six inches deep around the perimeter of my vegetable patch and then stakes a four-foot-high wire-mesh fence that's buried below ground level to discourage burrowing. Thinking this high fence is overkill, I read further that the Flemish Giant Rabbit breed, often called the Great Danes of the rabbit world, is the largest of its species. Perhaps four feet high is not such an exaggeration.

No sooner does Peer finish, than the spring crop of rabbits comes to life all over the grounds of Balmoral. They eat every tasty green bud and shoot they can find, but thanks to Peer, the vegetable garden is saved. Over the following months we're continually surprised to see what comes up. To the delight of neighbors, much of the crop is unpalatable to our American tastes, and we give away sizable amounts of the harvest. But the remainder keeps us well stocked with fresh produce throughout summer. Mary harvests, cans, and stores fruits and in-season produce. For evening desserts, we enjoy her rhubarb, apple, peach, and plum pies.

Life at home revolves around the gardens of Balmoral, the charms of Bruges, and Cyrena. On cool summer evenings we stroll Cyrena in her pram along the winding canals inhabited by white swans that are as much a hallmark of Bruges as the city's lace designs. On rainy weekend afternoons we seclude ourselves in one of the out-of-the-way churches where we make rubbings of 13th century monumental and religious brasses. *(Our timing is fortunate because a year later most Belgian churches prohibit brass rubbing due to the damage it can cause.)*

Delightful restaurants lie hidden in every corner of the city. Belgian brewing is legendary, and we adopt Stella Artois as the beer of choice. With due respect to the French who claim naming rights, the French-fried potato was invented in Belgium. It complements the country's main gourmet dish—eel— served in dozens of tasty preparations. Pea soup comes with every dinner—restaurants often deliver bowls of it to your table even before you order the main course. On one occasion when Mary and I invite Flemish neighbors for a typical American dinner, "Where is the pea soup?" they ask when seated.

Bruges was named for the hundreds of bridges over its many canals. Mary and I reflect that "bridges" indicates where we are in our lives as well. No longer a student or teacher, Mary is moving into new roles as mother and overseer of Balmoral. She continues to explore local churches and museums and soon becomes a sought-after English-speaking guide to the treasures of this remarkable city.

Career-wise, I am bridging from engineer to manager. Psychologically, I shift from feeling uncertain and confused about life to being self-confident and focused. Leaving behind the carefree attitude of a student, I am transitioning to a sense of being grounded and directed while settling into a new life and job. After becoming a father, I'm not just responsible for taking care of myself. I need to watch over a family.

*(Life in Bruges bridges the gap to a far-beyond shore where everything is exciting and unknown challenges await. This new life fulfills all the hopes and expectations I could ever have dreamed.)*

[1970, Bruges, Belgium] Balmoral estate

[February 1971, age 30] Schlegel Belgium management team

[March 1971, Bruges] Welcoming newborn Cyrena home to Balmoral

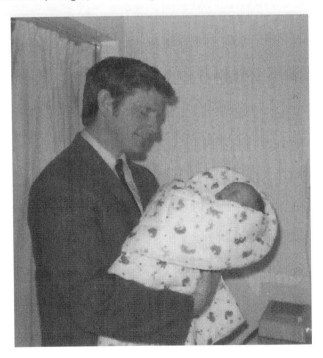

# 27
# Enroute to Australia

*11/71 - 12/71, Age 30*

November 1971, exactly one year after arriving in Bruges, our family is packing suitcases to leave on a most extraordinary trip. We will be away from home six months and visit more than 25 countries while encircling the globe.

This trip was put into motion the previous spring when Schlegel's board chairman, Dick Turner, asked if I would temporarily take over as managing director of the company subsidiary in Sydney. The firm is trying to acquire two other Australian companies, and Dick thinks my background can be useful. Because the remoteness of the plant leaves it out of touch with North American and European divisions, he wants me to introduce ideas and practices that have proven successful at the Belgian subsidiary. Furthermore, the Australian managing director is of an older generation and has been operating with, as Dick put it, "a small business-trader mentality that needs to change." A six-month exchange would provide opportunity for my counterpart to learn management ideas established in my company.

I readily accept the offer, and during the following weeks Chairman Turner, Australian managing director Sigurd Sjoquist, and I work out details. We managers agree to trade companies, houses, and cars from November to May. To avoid a lame duck problem, each will be legally vested to hire, fire, expend funds, and make legal commitments on behalf of the other company. We plan to overlap in Sydney to brief each other on our respective operations, but the transition should go smoothly because the products, technology, and markets are similar.

Several business journals write about this unique exchange as an innovation in management style. However, it is not innovation, but practicality that prompts the idea. A larger firm would have no problem sending corporate staff on a regular basis to Australia, but as a small organization operating on a global scale, Schlegel can't afford to send many people halfway around the world. Therefore, exchanging chief executives provides a cheap alternative.

If we were to fly straight through, the family could travel to Sydney in one day. Instead Mary and I have opted to take time to tour along the way. But how long can the company in Belgium perform without a managing director? We ultimately decide to stretch the outbound and return journeys to three weeks each. During the summer we study the *World Atlas* and pore over travel brochures to establish an itinerary with the best tradeoff between scenic and historical places versus metropolitan areas that will have baby care supplies like bottled water, disposable diapers, standard brands of baby food, and access to modern medical care if needed for six-month-old Cyrena. The around-the-world tickets we purchase include scheduled stopovers at what we consider the most desirable cities in unfamiliar southern hemisphere countries where weather will be warm.

Throughout a beautiful summer and early autumn Balmoral's gardens and fruit trees yield a steady stream of flowers, vegetables, pears, apples, plums, and berries. Then blustery days in late fall signal it's time to depart. As autumn in the northern hemisphere yields to spring south of the Equator, we look forward to enjoying three consecutive summers and, more important, missing a gloomy northern Europe winter.

After dropping off our dachshund, Sativa, with friends, we continue to Brussels airport where we catch an evening flight to Geneva that

247

connects with a Swiss Air midnight flight to South America. We awaken briefly when the plane lands to refuel at Dakar, Senegal, and notch our first visit (if one can call it that) to the African continent.

Arriving on a warm spring morning at Rio de Janeiro, we check into a hotel and then stroll down to Ipanema Beach. After a refreshing swim in the ocean and lunch at a seaside café, we set off to see the sites. The view from Sugarloaf Mountain is as breathtaking as travel brochures proclaim, but wandering amid lush jungle vegetation in botanical gardens abloom with spring is even more delightful.

In the evening we meet Rick and Virginia Lima, friends from Stanford Business School, for dinner. We had known them as quiet, gentle-almost-to-the-point-of-being-timid individuals, but that night we observe two totally different people. When they pick us up at the hotel, they angrily demand service from the concierge. Later in the restaurant, they loudly berate the waiter for forgetting napkins and order him about sharply. After this behavior goes on for some time, I mention to Rick how amazed I am to see his petite wife and him behaving like tyrants. With a laugh, Rick whispers they will explain later when we're alone. Meanwhile the loud, bossy behavior continues.

Back at the hotel for a nightcap, Rick and Virginia explain about life in Brazil. They are among two percent of the population that controls the rest of their countrymen, so it's necessary to constantly remind the majority who is in charge. At every opportunity members of this privileged class criticize, scold, and threaten retribution for the slightest insubordination or impertinence. Although it's a sad commentary on Brazilian society, the practice is how the ruling group maintains control. As Rick explains, Mary and I recall how most other restaurant guests, obviously also part of the controlling elite, had behaved in similar manner.

Rick explains, "Our two years at Stanford were relaxing because we didn't need to stay on guard with people waiting on us. We could be our real selves in California, but we can't here in Brazil. It's a tremendous strain constantly to play this commanding role."

On this note we end our evening with ambivalent feelings about these dear friends. We're glad they have a comfortable life, but sorry they're caught in this system. It must be as much of a psychological strain on the privileged class to keep lower classes in their places as it is for the lower classes to be mistreated in such a way.

Following another pleasant day sightseeing in Rio, we fly to Buenos Aires. After visiting the attractions of Argentina's capital, we return to our hotel where the manager approaches and in a hushed voice advises us to avoid certain areas of the city and to refrain from going out at night. I reply there's no need for concern because I can take care of my family. He interrupts that his warning is for my sake, not the family's. At check-in he noted I registered as an American manager and cautions that this makes me a potential kidnapping target for any of the city's dozen terrorist groups. Gulp! I now recall a pattern of American businessmen being kidnapped in Argentina. For the rest of our visit we confine ourselves to the vicinity of the hotel.

Although relieved to get safely out of Argentina, we face another tense situation in Chile. Our arrival in Santiago coincides with the day Cuban dictator Fidel Castro makes a state visit to confer with President Allende on their dreams for swinging all of South America to the left. On the taxi ride from the airport to our hotel, we weave through crowds thronging the streets as they wait for Castro. Signs of welcome for Castro abound while anti-American slogans are plastered on every wall. We breathe a sigh of relief upon reaching the hotel and readily heed the manager's advice to be cautious. After a hasty tour of the city with a private guide service, we watch from the security of our room the fanfare welcoming the Cuban dictator in the square below.

Each stopover of our trip through South America has aroused increased anxiety. In Brazil we experienced a mild sense of discomfort with Rick and Virginia because of how they treated waiters. In Argentina we became anxious because of possibly being kidnapped. Now here in Chile, we admit we're scared. But after Castro departs the next day we relax, and the following morning sees us on the Air France flight for Tahiti. With the South American capitals behind us, our journey begins to measure up to expectations.

Because the flight across the Pacific is long, the plane lands to refuel at Easter Island where we're greeted by what seems to be the entire population eager to show their incredible statues. Carved from tuff (compressed volcanic ash) and basalt, these ancient giant heads and torsos still remain a mystery even though they have been researched over hundreds of years. Who created these monoliths and why? How did they carve stones with such precision and transport them, some weighing up to 100 tons and measuring more than 30 feet high, across the island and hoist them into an upright position? What is the significance of their precise placement in relation to each other and to the stars? Mary and I, dumbstruck, ponder these questions as we wander among the statues that are even more enormous than pictures suggest. After several absorbing hours, we're jerked back to reality as the refueled Boeing 747 awaits to continue to Tahiti.

It is night when we land at Papeete where we look forward to three days to swim, sun, and relax. When planning this stop, I had selected a quiet, isolated hotel apart from the usual tourist listings. We're left behind while fellow passengers are whisked away in modern hotel buses to luxury hotels, but I take pleasure knowing we're going to see the "real" Tahiti away from the flow of tourists. Finally, thinking the shuttle has been delayed, I hail a taxi.

Twenty minutes later the driver announces we've arrived, but I see nothing resembling a hotel—no lights and no paved entrance—only a gravel path leading into the bushes. After the driver again insists this is the place, I get out and follow a path leading to a cluster of old, thatched-roofed huts with a sign giving the name of the hotel. Entering what looks like a reception office, I ring several times before a sleepy desk clerk appears. He answers my questions:

"Yes, you are expected."

"No, the Belgian travel agent was wrong that you would be met at the airport.

"Sorry, the restaurant is closed."

"Yes, you can have a room with a sea view because there are no other guests tonight."

"No, there is no porter to carry the bags."

After registering, I return to the taxi to break the news to Mary. She's a good sport as we make several trips carrying luggage to the room, which, of course, is farthest from the road. The hotel's brochure had looked so attractive, but I'm disheartened to see litter and garbage all around the property. Needless to say, the next morning we check out and join our fellow travelers at a modern resort hotel that offers everything we're looking for—skin-diving tours, sailboats, surfboards, restaurants, and a warm Tahitian welcome.

Next stop is Fiji where we expect to continue the beach life enjoyed in Tahiti, but we're in for an unpleasant surprise. The beaches look lovely, but the water turns out to be less than inviting. The coral reef extends a quarter mile out from the beach making it impossible to go into the sea without shoes. Because the water is less than knee-deep for several hundred yards, it's impossible to swim. In addition, deadly stonefish, said to be the most venomous fish in the world, camouflage as rocks in the coral and are nearly invisible. Poisonous, ray-finned dorsal needles can puncture a shoe sole and kill a person within hours if an antidote is not quickly administered. The hotel provides tennis shoes with aluminum plates as insoles. Tourist brochures conveniently overlook these facts and encourage visitors to sun themselves on the beach but refresh themselves in the hotel pool.

All is not lost, however. Here in Fiji we see one of the most amazing sights of the trip, the island's famed fire walkers. Fires burn all night heating large stones scattered in their midst. In the morning fire walkers arrive to perform purification rituals in an ancient religious ceremony while dancing around glowing embers. Suddenly they spring from dance formation onto the fire-heated stones and walk around for minutes with no hesitation or apparent discomfort.

Afterward I head toward the stones still lying in the smoldering ashes, but the heat is so intense I can't get closer than a few feet. Veering to where the men are sitting with outstretched legs on the grass, I check out their soles expecting to see burn blisters, but their feet are surprisingly unaffected. I can't believe what I'm seeing. After overcoming skepticism, I ask one of the Fijians, an onlooker who obviously is also astounded, for an explanation. He reveals that the ritual is an expression of the faith these men have in their gods—an explanation that leaves me even more perplexed.

We've been traveling more than two weeks with five stopovers, and now it's time to move on to Australia and the world of work. We fly from Fiji to Sydney and taxi to the north peninsula suburbs where we check into a hotel. The next morning I don a summer suit, and my Australian counterpart, Sigurd Sjoquist, whom I had met a few months earlier in Rochester, picks me up to begin the orientation to his company, shortly to be mine.

| 4 NOVEMBER | : | BRUSSELS/GENEVA | SR 779 | 21.10/22.15 | OK |
| | | GENEVA/RIO DE JANEIRO | SR 200 | 23.45/08.25 | OK |
| 8 NOVEMBER | : | RIO DE JANEIRO/BUENOS AIRES | SC 403 | 09.00/12.25 | OK |
| 10 NOVEMBER | : | BUENOS AIRES/SANTIAGO | AF 095 | 09.00/10.55 | OK |
| 11 NOVEMBER | : | SANTIAGO/PAPEETE | LA 131 | 12.30/20.00 | OK |
| 14 NOVEMBER | : | PAPEETE/PAGO PAGO | PA 838 | 12.30/14.35 | OK |
| 16 NOVEMBER | : | PAGO PAGO/NADI | TE 529 | 06.15/07.20 | OK |
| 21 NOVEMBER | : | NADI/SYDNEY | QF 575 | 17.00/20.20 | OK |

[1971] It took eight flights and a leisurely three weeks to reach Australia

# 28
# Three Summers

*11/71 - 5/72, Age 30 - 31*

On the plant tour Sig introduces me to his 50 or so employees who immediately make me feel at ease. Unlike Flemish-speaking Belgium, here I can communicate in English and immediately take a liking to the friendly Australians. The company itself needs no explanation because it's a twin to mine so briefings proceed quickly. Lunch at a nearby restaurant where I meet members of the board, bankers, lawyers, and auditors, completes orientation.

The next day after driving Sig and his wife to the airport to catch a flight to Belgium, Mary and I check out of the hotel and settle into their home. The house, a rambling, four-bedroom designed around an outdoor swimming pool, is a delight. What a joy to start and end each day with a swim! A profusion of flowers and semi-tropical vegetation surrounds the house, and the back of the property looks onto a park. I become addicted to eating on the rear terrace on sunny mornings and warm evenings. And we have the latest model Mercedes Benz—the car Sig had purchased a few months earlier—at our disposal. The house, the neighbors, the gardens, the pool, and the Australian lifestyle couldn't be more pleasant. How could we not enjoy every minute of our six-month stay?

At work, based upon manufacturing experience from Belgium, I identify many areas that I can improve. After sharing suggestions with plant manager Gordon Smith, who quickly agrees, we shut down the main production line and replace it with an updated process. We tinker with the looms and extruders, thereby making a 50 percent increase in productivity and a corresponding reduction in costs. By replacing resin backing on the weatherseal lace with polypropylene, we produce a better product at lower cost. This spirit of shaking things up becomes contagious, and soon all workers are experimenting with different ways of doing their jobs.

Working with accounting manager Bob Mutch, I discover his department uses a simplified bookkeeping method with no cost controls, no cash-flow projections, and no inventory management. In short order we set up new accounting systems to include this information and initiate weekly performance reports for every department in the company. Together with Gordon, we establish time and material production standards and provide variance reports to assess the efficiency of every process. When the new management accounting system reveals that a side business of industrial fasteners and hardware is unprofitable, we close this operation.

Analyzing the pricing structure with the marketing manager Tom Currie and his sales manager Brian Tye, we calculate profit margins on each product, leading us to focus on better cost controls and to increase prices on low-margin items. In addition, Tom and I acquire a company specializing in automatic door openers and earn the contract to install doors at the Sydney Opera House, which is currently under construction. To complement the weatherseal business we complete a licensing agreement with a Japanese company to market their high-quality window and door hardware.

Once matters in the office are operating smoothly I move to my fondest passion in management: marketing. Although Australia is geographically the size of the United States, most business occurs in Sydney, Melbourne, Adelaide, Perth, and Brisbane, and in less than two weeks I visit major customers in all five cities. Armed with feedback, I spend the following week in the office clearing up problems with deliveries, quality, accounts receivables, advertising, and performance specifications.

Next, I take two aggressive actions that do little for the American image in Australia but significantly increase Schlegel's profitability. First, I raise prices on every product, something that hadn't been done for a number of years. In Australia's inflationary economy of the early 1970s, the doomed firm is the one that doesn't put through regular price increases to maintain or increase profit margins. Our customers manufacture windows and doors, collectively called fenestration products, which need weatherseals. Air infiltration, which is determined by the quality of the weatherseal around a window or door, is a key performance consideration. Because our product represents only one or two percent of the overall production cost, we point out that a customer should not be overly concerned with the weatherseal price.

Second, I fire all the outside sales agents. It's a myth that local representation can best serve local markets. Because air travel is cheap, company salesmen can serve the national markets from the home base in Sydney and save on paying agent commissions. Typical is the comment from the biggest customer in Perth on the opposite side of the country, who said they don't want to deal with a local agent. Rather than communicating through a middleman, they prefer to see someone from the home office who can provide authoritative answers directly.

After visiting our own customers, I travel to companies supplied by competitors. I want to know why they don't buy from us, the sole manufacturer in Australia. Our competitors in Japan and America incur stiff duties and import costs on products sold in Australia, but even so, their prices are lower than ours. These customers say they would like to buy from us but we're too expensive, and now that I have recently raised prices, they say we don't have a chance. I ask how they handle shipping delays or product quality problems. Their explanation is to order a temporary supply from us until the normal supplier straightens things out.

I anticipate this answer but want to hear it directly before making a counter argument beginning with economies of scale. Explaining that naturally we are more expensive because we lack the volume of their offshore suppliers, I admit that buying from our high-volume parent company in New York is cheaper than buying from us in Australia. Then I pull out two trumps.

First, I explain we are converting the entire Australian market to a new and improved weatherseal with a polypropylene backing, a noticeable improvement over the old resin-backed product they buy from overseas. Because our price is the same as our older product, all our customers are changing over to the better product at no additional expense. I don't mention that the polypropylene-backed weatherseal is cheaper for us to produce, but I point out that the high protective duty on polypropylene would make it prohibitively expensive for them to import.

My second trump is advising we are accepting only one-year supply contracts. Therefore, henceforth they can't count on us when they have supply problems. I leave them with the thought that by continuing to import instead of contracting with us, they would be buying a lower quality weatherseal as well as risking running out of supplies with no backup from Schlegel. Although I should feel like a sleaze, I don't! The strategy is simply good business, and it works. Within weeks, all these wayward firms come to us and sign one-year contracts—all, that is, but one. And that firm is a special story.

The third largest weatherseal user chooses to stay with the competitor, and, after making a second visit to force the issue, I understand why. For a number of years, the purchasing manager and his wife have enjoyed an annual two-week vacation in Fiji with expenses paid by our competitor. He concedes that if Schlegel will match this arrangement, he will give us his business. Having never been approached with a proposition like this, I leave to ponder the implications. He is talking about a cost under $2,000 to get business worth $35,000, only six percent of sales value. The expense is easy to justify from a purely business point of view and would then give us 100% of the market. But finding bribes offensive, I can't agree. How can I get around this barrier?

I decide to call the firm's managing director to let him know what his purchasing manager is doing. Nervously, I explain to him I don't understand this way of doing business. I expect the director to be horrified, but his answer comes as a surprise.

"You better learn about doing business like this, because we Australians learned it from you Americans," (my accent is a dead give-away), he explains, and then refers me back to his purchasing manager. So, we don't get the business.

*(Months later in Rochester I discuss this incident with Dick Turner and ask what he would have done. At that time there was no law against this practice and no "new morality" that would condemn it. Dick paused a moment and then said he would have picked up the vacation tab. But six years later when the Foreign Corrupt Business Practices Act made this arrangement illegal, I felt a moral justification for my decision. And I had the satisfaction of learning a few years after my experience that both the purchasing manager and managing director were replaced, and the company became Schlegel's customer.)*

Further research shows that the weatherseal market in Australia is insignificant compared with potential markets to the north. We serve Australia, which has fewer than 15 million inhabitants, but overlooks markets in Southeast Asia with a population 15 times larger. To lower our production costs by increasing volume, I convince headquarters in Rochester to allow Australia rather than the U.S. to supply this market.

A two-week trip takes me to Hong Kong, Taiwan, Guam, and the Philippines. Guam is mostly a whimsy allowing me to spend the weekend at America's western outpost where business is exceedingly small but expanding rapidly. Because this trip is my first contact with Asia, I am hampered by unfamiliarity with different cultural and business practices here.

An episode in the Philippines is an example. I spend two days visiting every potential customer, giving the same presentation to each. When finished, I feel pleased to have put in so much leg work to track down every contact. There is one last obligation to fulfill before leaving. I have accepted a client's invitation for a farewell dinner. He picks me up at my hotel, and when we arrive at the restaurant, I'm surprised we're escorted through the main dining area to a private room in back. Upon entering I stop in my tracks, dumbfounded. Inside are all the businessmen I had just visited. But the biggest shock is that they're surprised that I am surprised, thinking I must have expected this. I quickly learn that in the Philippines everyone in a related business knows each other and works together, which is contrary to our antitrust laws. In accordance with their business culture, they give this dinner together to show appreciation for my visit. In the future I'll save time here by making a group presentation.

One more thing. At this dinner I unknowingly violate a rule of etiquette by casually reaching for my beer to take a sip. Immediately the host grabs his beer, and everyone else reaches for theirs. Apparently, custom dictates that no one drinks until the host lifts his glass—only then does everyone join in.

Tom Currie, who now has responsibility for the international market, has been on a trip of his own to Singapore, Thailand, Indonesia, and Malaysia. Upon returning to Australia and comparing notes, we conclude that this enormous market warrants more than simply shipping products from Australia. We create a marketing plan to establish an office in Singapore, and—following approval by headquarters—Tom eventually becomes its managing director.

Because my parents as well as Mary's use our assignment in Australia as an excuse to combine world travels with family visits, we spend much of our free time showing them the attractions of the area. When my parents arrive in February, we plan a pleasure-business trip to the neighboring country to the southeast—one known for having three million people and 60 million sheep, except in lambing season when the figure balloons to 90 million! We find New Zealand a delightful surprise of contrasting landscape—particularly the South Island where snow-capped mountains plunge straight into the sea creating magnificent fjords along saw-toothed coastlines. We enjoy wine tastings, sheep-shearing contests, farm stays, and the local cuisine of lamb cutlets paired with grassy Sauvignon Blanc.

The summer sojourn in the southern hemisphere is coming to an end, and by early April the heat has passed and autumn is upon us. Following a week of farewell events, Mary and I pack bags for the continuation of travels around the world. As a parting gift from my company, I receive a treasured gesture of gratitude—a three-foot wooden paddle engraved "To the World's Biggest Shit Stirrer!"

When we made our itinerary the previous fall in Belgium, we anticipated needing a vacation after six months in Australia and booked the first stop at Bali. On the morning of our departure I feel guilty for going on vacation because the pleasant time in Australia has seemed like one long holiday. Nevertheless, we stick to the plan.

Late in the afternoon, we land at Denpasar Airport in Bali. What a delight to visit this magical paradise! In contrast to the orthodox Islamic culture that dominates the rest of Indonesia, Bali embraces a variation of Hinduism. Temple depictions of deities are light-hearted and appear to laugh and dance as if enchanted by the magic of the island. With luscious gardens, jungle forests, and colorful birds wherever one turns, the simplicity and beauty of life on Bali evoke a deeply spiritual sense of attunement with Nature. For several days we lose ourselves in wonder as we meander among small villages and temples dotting the island. These days are a relief from the hustle of the business world—a respite that allows a chance to recharge and get ready for the transition back to European life.

Our next stops are Singapore and then Bangkok where we spend a full week exploring both the hubbub of these dynamic cities as well as the outlying countryside. By now our suitcases are practically exploding with wonderful treasures and artifacts we purchase along the way.

Next is Delhi where we hire a car for a three-day tour to Amber and Jaipur before going to Agra where we experience one of the most breathtaking sights in our lives. After the day's drive we check into a hotel and relax over a pleasant dinner before our guide picks us up late in the evening. Ten minutes later we get out of the car and walk a short distance following the guide through the clear, moonlit night. As we turn a corner my heart suddenly jumps. Before us in all its glory and splendor rises the Taj Mahal, the dazzling 17th century mausoleum built by Muslim emperor Shah Jahan for his favorite wife, Muntaz Mahal. Recent monsoon showers have cleansed the majestic white marble domes and columns of this wondrous work of love and devotion that now glows before us in the light of the full moon. Ever-changing clouds cast mirage-like patterns on the ornate façade as spellbound, we sit in silent awe.

Our journey takes us next to Iran for two days—days that happen to coincide with a visit by President Nixon to Tehran. Because of heightened security at the airport and throughout the city, we encounter hassles that remind us of Santiago when our visit overlapped with that of Fidel Castro. This time, however, we experience no anxious moments because there is no eruption of anti-American sentiment.

We had planned to go next to Israel, but the day before our scheduled departure three terrorists recruited by the Palestinians from the Japanese Red Army execute a bloody massacre at Tel Aviv's Lod Airport (*later renamed Ben Gurion International Airport*). We quickly cancel plans and bypass Israel in favor of Turkey. The change in itinerary is not motivated by fear of more violence, but rather by expectation that tight security measures in Israel would create hours of delay. Istanbul is the final stop, and after exploring this famous city on the Bosporus, we head home to Belgium.

Early May is the perfect time to be back at Balmoral. Spring flowers are in full color everywhere in Bruges, and the fruit and chestnut trees have come into full bloom. Our dachshund Sativa is pregnant, as arranged before our departure, and within a month we look forward to having a house full of puppies.

Mary and I have just been through two consecutive summers and anticipate enjoying a third. We are happy, young, and excited. Life feels full to the point of overflowing. Nothing else, it seems, could make our lives more adventuresome and stimulating.

But a week later in Rochester, I learn how wrong I am.

[November 1971, Sydney, age 30] Schlegel Australia management team

[November 1971, Sydney] Our home for six months in the Pymble suburb

[November 1971] Sailing in Sydney Harbour

# 29
# Hamburg

*6/72 - 1/73, Age 31 - 32*

It's June 1972. We returned to Belgium from our world tour a week ago and have comfortably resettled. The company survived with no changes in my absence, and now I'm at Schlegel's Rochester headquarters to undergo a briefing.

While in Australia I had received a late evening telephone call from halfway around the world with wonderful news. Dick Turner's call from Rochester heralded two of the most important changes in my life. First, as a participant in a management compensation plan providing bonuses in company stock, I now have the opportunity to purchase additional stock. Living overseas precluded my buying a home, but now I have a wonderful outlet for my savings. Because I believe in my contributions to the company's growth, I invest all surplus funds into Schlegel stock. Second, Dick surprised me when he asked that, upon returning from Australia, I accept the position of managing director of Schlegel's subsidiary in Hamburg, Germany.

Here in Rochester, I join Sig and Dick to review the previous six months. My report summarizes five contributions to Australian operations: (1) reduction of costs and initiation of technical improvements in the production department; (2) introduction of new accounting methods, administrative reports, and marketing analyses; (3) completion of two outside acquisitions and two product licensing agreements; (4) increase of weatherseal market share in Australia and New Zealand from 50% to almost 100%; and (5) recommendation to establish a sales office in Singapore. *(The office was established the following year.)*

I feel satisfied with these results, and Dick is pleased the exchange of managing directors worked so well. Although Sig made no changes in the operations of my firm, he says he learned a lot, so everyone is happy.

After Sig returns home, Dick and I discuss my taking over the German subsidiary. This company, although acquired 10 years earlier, never has fully integrated into the group nor has it been profitable. The challenge to turn the firm around is exciting, and, although sorry to leave Bruges, I need to accept this offer to advance my career. Dick agrees to defer the assignment until the following winter, allowing us one more summer and fall at Balmoral.

Back in Belgium we settle into another pleasant summer. Our home is idyllic, and we will never again find such a beautiful place; however, we're isolated in Bruges and it's time to return to the main current of life. With heightened awareness of the impending move, we savor each remaining day of our final days here. Balmoral's gardens again bless with an abundance of vegetables and berries, and the five chickens produce a steady supply of fresh-as-can-be eggs. One morning Sativa gives birth to a litter of eight pups and easily settles into a regular nursing rhythm. When fall approaches, Balmoral's orchards inundate us with fruit. What we don't eat, we can. To keep up with the bounteous harvest, I buy a juicer and store enough pear, plum, apple, and currant juice for several months' supply. When rows of rhubarb ripen all at once, we make pies and jams but, even so, are overwhelmed. Knowing we will leave in winter, Peer, our beloved gardener/handyman, is overly attentive to the flower gardens to assure they are in their finest glory. Keeping the paths and hedges immaculate is his way of communicating his love for our small family.

As we come to the end of our stay in Belgium, I reflect with pride on the growth of the company. Within two years, annual sales have grown several fold to more than $3 million with dominant market shares throughout Western Europe. In addition, we developed business in Eastern Europe, North Africa, and the Middle East. With amazing efforts from the enthusiastic Belgian managers who selflessly put in many hours of overtime, our subsidiary has become Schlegel's most profitable overseas division.

In October 1972, the second anniversary of our arrival in Bruges, Mary and I prepare for another move, the eighth in six years of marriage. Knowing that whatever home we find in Hamburg can never match the size and uniqueness of Balmoral, we part with the oversize furnishings we had purchased to fill the many rooms of our petite chateau.

After two weekend house hunting trips to Hamburg, I find an ideal home. Located in the western part of the city along the Elbe River, the house is one-fifth the size of Balmoral, but the rent, which reflects the difference between living in a rural, museum town that died 500 years earlier and a bustling modern European city, is four times higher.

Having struggled in Belgium to communicate in fractured Flemish, I'm determined not to repeat the mistake and therefore intend to learn German. This decision becomes a point of conflict with Chairman Turner who contends that because Schlegel is an American company, everyone should speak English at all subsidiaries. He goes even further by encouraging me not to learn German, but instead to pressure the managers to learn English. I counter that this is a neo-colonial attitude many American international firms have fostered—an attitude that has given rise to the Ugly American image abroad. I contend it's necessary not only to learn the language but to become familiar with German culture so as to be sensitive to attitudes and customs. Although my boss never supports this point of view, he agrees to pay for language training.

Because Schlegel's policy for overseas Americans allows home-leave every two years, Mary and I plan to return to the States for the year-end holidays. In late November after movers pack the household belongings and ship them to Hamburg, Mary flies with Cyrena to visit her family in Albuquerque while I travel to Kochel-am-See, a charming Bavarian village nestled in a setting of pines and firs in the foothills of the Alps. Here at the

Goethe Institute Language School, I enroll in a four week immersion program. Within days after my arrival, the first snowfall turns the village into a winter wonderland.

Our class consists mostly of immigrant workers who have come from Italy, Turkey and Yugoslavia to seek jobs. Although at first I feel out of place, within days we mix with ease. Because we speak different languages, we communicate in the language we're trying to learn. As we sit together at restaurants in the evenings, locals overhearing our attempts to speak can hardly contain their laughter. Ironically, even though the villagers have no idea what we're saying, we communicate with one another in our version of German with no problem. But there isn't really much to say anyway, so we simply enjoy each other's company.

Each weekend I rent skis and head to Garmisch-Partenkirchen, the twin ski resorts favored by day-trippers from Munich. Although tempted to cut classes and stay on for a week or more, after two days on the slopes I'm ready to settle down for Monday's classes. In addition to language, the program concentrates on the country's literature, history, music, and other aspects of German culture—exactly the topics I want to explore. These four weeks are intense but invaluable in helping me settle into the land of my namesake forbears.

At the conclusion of the program, I fly from Munich to Paris and then to Chicago where a snowstorm cancels the connecting flight to New Mexico. Stranded in the crush of holiday travelers, I envision spending Christmas Eve at O'Hare Airport. But what luck! The storm subsides and flights resume. Although I miss dinner, late Christmas Eve I join Mary in Albuquerque.

During the holiday week we visit friends and take trips to our favorite ski resorts in northern New Mexico: Taos, Angel Fire, and Santa Fe Ski Basin. The following week we fly to Louisville where my sister Wendy and her husband Art have made me an uncle—twice over—with the recent birth of twin sons. This is a memorable Christmas, particularly for my parents who relish being together with their growing family. The joyous holiday season passes quickly, and soon it's time to move to the new home in Hamburg.

Hamburg has few claims to fame, which is surprising because it is the largest city in the Federal Republic of Germany. (Although Berlin is larger, it is not, at this time, part of the Federal Republic.) Apart from two renowned composers, Felix Mendelssohn and Johannes Brahms, no notable Germans claim Hamburg as their place of origin. Hamburg's harbor, third largest in Europe, makes the city nothing more than a big, conservative, commercial center with few attractions for artists, musicians, and other creative people. Even at the time of Hamburg's founding in 800 by the Holy Roman Emperor Charlemagne (Karl der Grosse), it was known purely for its commercial importance. From the 14th to the 17th century, the city was a member in the medieval Hanseatic League, and its stature as an international trading capital continues today. As export-import businesses have flourished in the years since the Second World War, Hamburgians are proud to say, "We have our backs toward Germany and faces toward the world."

Affirming their sense of isolation from the rest of Germany, inhabitants say Hitler never came to Hamburg because he knew he would not be welcomed. *(This isn't far from the truth. A list of Hitler's dozens of speeches indicates he was only once in Hamburg where he harangued crowds at the city's main train station from the balcony of the Hotel Reichshof.)*

Our Hamburg house sits in an affluent neighborhood in the charming western suburb of Blankenese located at the end of fashionable, tree-lined Elbchaussee on the northern bank of the Elbe River. This village, known to modern travelers as the Sausalito of Germany because of its similarity to the famous town north of San Francisco, clings to steep slopes that drop down to the river's edge. Originally, Blankenese was home to wealthy sea captains who would be months away at sea carrying cargo to cities around the world. When they sailed 75 miles up the Elbe from the North Sea on a flood tide to return home, they would disembark at Blankenese where harbor pilots took command of their ships for the last miles into the harbor. For outbound ships, harbor pilots would navigate the vessels to Blankenese where the captains would be rowed out to resume command.

On January 1, 1973, we move into our new home, an attractive, two-story, timber-framed house surrounded by gardens and trees located across from *Hirschpark*, a large park with wild deer. The home is a fairytale dwelling deep in the woods. Yet a mere three-minute walk takes us down to the shores of the Elbe, and farmers' markets, restaurants, and shops are only a short distance away. An unexpected benefit of our new home is the caretaker for the previous owner until he died, Frau Pless, lives in an attached apartment and becomes a readily available babysitter anytime Mary and I go out for the evening. *(Remaining in Hamburg for seven years—longer than any place I have thus far lived—suggests a period of relative peace and calm. However, no other period of my life would be as turbulent.)*

Within weeks after settling into the home, we integrate into the international community. As if to compensate for two years of isolation as the only non-Belgians living in Bruges, Mary now joins the German-American Women's Club, a painting class, a book club, and other groups. Relieved that she involves herself with the local community, I concentrate on problems of the company.

And the problems loom large.

Schlegel GmbH (*Gessellschaft mit beschraenkter Haftung*, meaning company with limited liability) had been founded 50 years earlier when partners Erich Weill and Hans Reineke set up a trading firm dealing in textile and plastic products. After the Second World War the founders imported products from Schlegel in the U.S. for resale to the German automotive industry and in the late 1950s were licensed to produce parts for this growing industry. In the early 1960s, Schlegel, intending to establish a subsidiary in Germany to serve the growing automotive and building markets, endeavored to acquire a different company engaged in these industries. When discussions broke down, Schlegel bought its old licensee instead. Knowing they were second choice, the firm's managers were always resentful. In years that followed, relations didn't improve because the company failed to turn a profit. Management argued it couldn't become profitable until given capital to build a new plant, but Schlegel's chairman responded they would get a new building only when they made a profit.

The stalemate persisted for years until Turner agreed to pay for a new facility—but stipulated one condition: He wanted an American, namely me, to become managing director. The incumbent director, who had been in this position for 40 years, was to retire in two years; so, for this interim period two of us would be co-managing directors.

From the day of this decision, the German company begins to go from bad to worse. Its main product, the black PVC running board mat on the Volkswagen Beetle—a product that for 20 years represented one-third of sales—suddenly becomes obsolete because production of the model ceases. The replacements—the Rabbit, Polo, and Golf—are designed with no running board and therefore need no mat. Because the managers are manufacturing people focused on making this mat more efficiently, and, characteristic of German thinking, with better quality, the company lacks the marketing mindset to deal with this crisis.

A second problem occurs when the bottom falls out of the market for the company's second-best-selling product, a high-quality, plastic weatherseal that had dominated the top end of the building weatherseal market for years. Because the industry is shifting to seals made of EPDM rubber, a synthetic elastomer, the plastic business is dying.

Disgruntled with American influence over the company, the marketing manager and the top salesman both quit. Finally, the German economy, particularly the automotive and construction sectors where the firm's business is concentrated, is now heading into the most severe recession since the end of World War II.

When I enter the company in early 1973, the company is in chaos, and there is no assurance I will be welcome.

[Spring 1972, Blankenese-Hamburg, age 31] Cyrena, age 1, with Dad in backyard

[1973 Hamburg]
Corporate Photo
Doesn't seem like me

[1973 Hamburg]
This is more like me

# 30
# Turnaround

*1/73 - 1/76, Age 32 - 35*

The first months in Hamburg I focus on learning about the business while also learning about Germans. The dismal profit situation requires radical changes, but how can I motivate the managers to make them?

First step is to understand what makes Germans tick. Reading about the country's history and culture as well as visiting art galleries, museums, theaters, and the opera helps me understand something about Germany's turbulent history and the character of the people. Germans typically exhibit a sense of national superiority and a lack of gentleness and compassion. They tend to respect hierarchy, defer to authority, disdain foreign workers, adhere to procedure, emphasize punctuality, take pride in their large corporations, and love to travel. Furthermore, I find them to be quick to take offense, thorough in performance of any task, and sticklers about following rules. Armed with these observations, I now have insight about how to work with my colleagues.

When I speak German, even though the accent is terrible, the gesture earns respect. I trade in my long, California-style haircut worn with an American baseball cap for a no-nonsense, short German crop minus the cap. I drop the American practice of calling co-workers by their first names—a practice they tolerate with curious amusement when we speak English with visitors from headquarters. At those times we refer to each other as Peter, Uwe, Ingo and Ulrich; afterward, we revert to Herr Schroeder, Herr Mantz, and Herr So-and-So. Because bright ties and shirts are not worn in this land where business is regarded as strictly serious, I banish these articles from my wardrobe. I lengthen pant cuffs to the tops of my shoes after hearing Germans snicker "*Hochwasserhosen*" (high water pants) when they catch sight of Americans with their short, ankle-length cuffs.

The style of handshake is another example of cultural differences. With no thought of protocol, Americans typically saunter up, offer a hand, speak first and last name, and express a greeting while looking the other person in the eye. But Germans first straighten their backs and bring heels together as if coming to attention. When taking each other's hand, they make stiff little bows without smiling, and their eyes never meet. If introducing themselves to someone for the first time, they murmur tersely and almost incomprehensibly only their last names. If already acquainted, they make one of a limited number of standard greetings. To an American such exchanges seem cold and impersonal; therefore, I practice with the managers, much to their amusement, how to greet Americans by smiling, looking them straight in the eye, and never clicking heels or bowing.

My German surname helps break the subtle distrust toward me as an American, as do my efforts to follow the many little rules expected in civil society. Bow graciously when meeting a neighbor on the street. Never jaywalk. Don't cut the grass on Sunday, otherwise known as "*Ruhetag*" (Quiet Day). Always walk on the right side of the sidewalk, and on and on. Germans are quick to point out, even to strangers, whenever customary standards are not upheld. Following rules is their main preoccupation. For example, if I absentmindedly start to cross a street against a red light, I'll hear several voices shouting, "*Entschuldigen Sie, mein Herr*" (Excuse me, sir). Although I follow most of the societal customs, my behavior at times teeters on the edge of unacceptability. But at least I'm trying, and this alone endears me to neighbors and colleagues.

Having had success in the Belgian and Australian companies, I intend to apply the same formula in Germany by referring to business school

272

textbooks for examples of problems that I encounter. Adapting textbook answers to real life situations is usually straightforward, but in Germany, when applied to the field of organizational behavior, this approach fails terribly. Industrial psychologists tout advantages of participative management, job enrichment, Theory Y versus Theory X, delegation of authority, management by objectives, and other buzz words. But when put into practice here, everything goes wrong.

For example, in one of the first meetings with department managers I present a problem and invite suggestions. Because no one responds, I throw out an idea to stimulate discussion. But still no discussion, so the issue is left pending while the meeting continues to other matters. Imagine my surprise the next day to find my idea has been implemented! Astounded, I ask a confidante, "What happened?" He explains that an open discussion such as the one attempted the previous day, is unthinkable. If three ideas are presented, only one can be accepted, which leaves two people feeling humiliated. The thinking is that any problem has only one solution, and the only person who can make the right decision is the highest ranking manager. Therefore, any idea he suggests will be implemented. Others are present only for instructions to carry out the decision; consequently, there's no point in having discussion. I also learn that if a solution doesn't work, blame falls on those responsible for carrying it out, not on the one who proposed it.

Constructive conflict and brainstorming, apparently, have no place in the German business world. This thinking reflects the notion that the boss and those in authority cannot be wrong. I now understand that our company, as is typical of many German firms, operates like a military organization with ideas coming from the top down rather than from the bottom up, as is advocated in most theories of modern management.

While wandering through the plant, even weeks after arriving, I sense a coolness toward me from employees. What can be done to remedy this problem? I hatch a plan. With Easter a week away, I direct the purchasing manager to buy decorated chocolate rabbits to hand to employees leaving for the holiday weekend. But when word gets out, union representatives (*Betriebsrat*) storm into my office to announce I can't proceed because employee compensation is carefully regulated and negotiated by the union. With a wink, I respond, "Well then, let's negotiate." With that, they laughingly agree the treat would be an appreciated gesture. After this successful "negotiation" for which they claim a share of the credit, 325 employees go home with chocolate bunnies for their kids. Even the 200 Turkish workers, all Muslims, appreciate receiving the Christian holiday gift!

Not all is work. In March I attend a one week management meeting with Schlegel's European directors in Malaga, Spain. Learning that the hotel has a selection of boats to rent, in the evening I enjoy sailing in the Mediterranean. Sailing adventures continue three months later when Mary and I join friends at the Yacht Basin of St. Malo on France's north coast for a one week cruise among the English Channel Islands. How strange to hear people in this archipelago just a few miles off the coast of France speak British English—a throwback to the time the English Crown ruled the Duchy of Normandy.

When spring arrives, the company moves into a new 70,000 square-foot building. Unfortunately, due to loss of the longtime automotive and building products markets, this transition doesn't improve the company's profitability. With a full workforce still in place and sales reduced by half, the firm is running deep in the red.

Now is the time to introduce my turnaround plan—a three part strategy. Step one: Negotiate with automakers. I arrange to meet with upper management at Volkswagen in Wolfsburg where I'm greeted warmly and immediately engulfed in a rapid fire discussion that outpaces my German language skills. Everyone laughs good-naturedly after I explain that despite the German name, my fluency in German is limited because my forebears immigrated to America in the 1700s.

Supposing my purpose is to plead for a running board on forthcoming models, my hosts start by saying that is not possible. I protest that is not the intent and then explain that as they phase out the Beetle, our company is doomed unless we pick up business on its replacements. Citing goodwill from Schlegel's 20-year relationship, I ask if they will ship the chassis of the new models to Hamburg and let us develop door seals, trunk seals, edge protectors, belt line profiles, hood strips, draught excluders, and other extruded plastic parts. If we do a good job on the prototypes, we hope to be awarded production contracts. To this proposal, the hosts agree.

Following this example, our engineering sales team approaches Ford of Germany, Opel (General Motors of Germany), Audi, Daimler Benz, and BMW. These endeavors also prove fruitful. We receive enough contracts for prototype development to, if successful, assure production orders for years to come. But before reaching that point, we need to survive long enough to complete engineering designs and fulfill these development orders. Unprofitable in themselves, our efforts will prove worthwhile only if they lead to business.

Step 2: Find new markets for plastic weatherseals. Although plastic protection for windows and doors is being replaced by rubber seals in Germany, the market for plastic products thrives elsewhere in Europe. To tap this potential, salespeople begin making calls in France, Benelux, and Scandinavia. Meanwhile, in Germany we develop new applications for plastic products outside these traditional markets.

Step 3: Implement cost reductions. I charge the plant manager to make radical internal changes by overhauling the entire production operation. He is to cut out inefficiencies and make changes that yield a minimum of 20 percent cost reduction. Furthermore, I direct the purchasing manager to review all suppliers and press for minimum 10 percent price reductions, or alternatively, find replacement suppliers willing to charge less.

Finally, I instruct every manager to formulate an action plan to implement his (sorry, no female managers in Germany in this era) portion of the overall three part plan. If enacted successfully, I am confident these three programs will bring the company back on its feet within a year. But much hard work lies ahead.

While settling in for this long haul, I'm attacked from the home front. Dick Turner and several corporate officers in Rochester raise questions about what I intend to do and why. Due to language difficulties, they had previously been unable to make much sense of what was happening in

Germany, but now they expect me, although here less than a year, to explain reasons for years of past poor performance. Soon I'm making trips to Rochester every six to eight weeks to keep headquarters posted. Explaining that results should not be expected until a year from now in the summer of 1974, I'm continually challenged until they reluctantly accept the turnaround strategy.

During these months of shuttling, doubts arise in my own mind about how I'm managing the company. I accept that headquarters wants quick results, major cost cuts, and labor force reductions. But I also understand the German point of view regarding what is culturally and legally acceptable and find it difficult to answer questions posed by Americans who are ignorant of foreign business environments. Similarly, I understand the confusion and misunderstandings Germans have about corporate staff. Within this context I am neither American nor German. I understand both points of view but am unable to provide satisfactory explanations for either one to the other.

For example, an American looks at a map of Europe and asks why it's not possible to supply the raw materials our plant needs, from England, where production costs are cheaper since the distance between the countries is comparable to that between Ohio and Pennsylvania. When I explain problems with quality differences, shipping challenges, servicing issues, design tastes, and performance standards—to say nothing about currency exchange, import duties, and language barriers—Americans are incredulous. When they suggest simply laying off dozens of workers on short notice, I try to explain legal tangles, termination costs, and protests from the powerful *Betriebsrat.* Again, my American colleagues think I'm crazy.

Likewise, I'm at a loss to explain to Germans why Americans typically have only two weeks of vacation compared to five or six weeks in most European countries, and why the U.S. has only one-third the number of holidays Germany has. Furthermore, Germans don't understand the low-quality standards in the U.S. or why Americans build cars and household items to last two years instead of 10 or more. And what about the American employment philosophy of "hire and fire," which is unthinkable in Germany?

Turner finds it unbelievable that when we shut the Hamburg plant for summer vacation, we are legally required to double all salaries for the month. German logic is that rent, utilities, and home expenses still have to be paid, and, of course, everyone needs extra money to have a vacation in Italy or Spain. Germans, for their part, cannot understand why Americans don't get double salaries on their vacations. On flights across the Atlantic my stomach ties up in knots as I anticipate encounters in which I must attempt to reconcile a German with an American point of view. I trust my strategies will be successful if supported. My biggest fear is that before the year is out I will be recalled to Rochester and fired, or that someone from headquarters will come to Hamburg to shut down the factory. The situation is frustrating, but finally the chairman reluctantly agrees to wait until mid-year 1974. It goes without saying my job is at stake if there's no improvement.

Pressure from both sides of the Atlantic pushes me to stay on top of the tiniest details to ensure the strategy unfolds as planned. Even when the plant shuts in August, I continue to work without another break until Christmas.

Frustrations aside, however, during the summer we celebrate the joyous news that Mary is pregnant again. Our family will expand in the spring, and Cyrena, now two, can look forward to a sibling.

During winter holidays Mary and I vacation at a German-speaking ski resort to work on pronunciation and grammar while enjoying time on the slopes. After a day's drive to Kitzbuehel in Austria, we delight in tackling the steep terrain and legendary racecourses of this famed ski area. But as far as improving our language abilities, we're out of luck. Going to Austria to learn German is like trying to learn English in Alabama. Although one can pick up vocabulary, the accent is of another world.

Entering 1974, our second year in Hamburg, we prepare for the baby's delivery by again reviewing the natural childbirth books. We're overjoyed with the prospect of another child, and although work is demanding, I cut back on hours in the office to make family a priority.

After a busy mid-March weekend, one Sunday evening Mary and I ask Frau Pless, who is living upstairs, to babysit for Cyrena while we dine out. Our favorite fish restaurant perches on a steep bank overlooking the Elbe River. From here we gaze down on a steady flow of commercial vessels—red port lights enter the harbor with goods from around the world, while green starboard lights move downstream laden with high-tech equipment, autos, and machinery destined for distant ports. Along the shoreline of the far bank, flickering white lights mark a world of small farming villages.

But our enjoyment of the view and dinner is suddenly interrupted—Mary's contractions are beginning. Abandoning our meal, we rush home to grab the suitcase Mary had packed earlier and speed to *Altona Frauenklinik*, a hospital for women, minutes away. As we did for Cyrena's birth, we bring the childbirth books to guide us. Settling into the labor room, we time contraction intervals according to the manual, and Mary adjusts her breathing in accord with their intensity and duration. We're confident things are going well.

Unfortunately, we have forgotten we are in Germany. Into the room storms the head nurse who promptly informs us we're doing things all wrong. She proceeds to show how breathing should be done and implies that if we continue as we were, we should expect no help from the medical staff. After a moment of panic, a quick appeal to the doctor on duty elicits a sympathetic response, and the troublesome nurse is discreetly moved into the background.

Early in the morning of March 18, a typical rainy day in Hamburg, Liane Christine enters the world without difficulty. I'm now the happy father of two daughters. The rest of the day I photograph city scenes and collect newspaper headlines to make a scrapbook commemorating Liane's birth.

As the balmy days of spring give way to summer, we're delighted to have a baby in the house again. During this second summer in Hamburg, my parents visit to see their new grandchild and to explore a new sailing venue. An hour's drive north plus a ferry ride to Denmark at Nyborg on the island of Funen—home of Denmark's 19th century author Hans

Christian Andersen—we bareboat charter a 35-foot sloop for a week to explore the waters of the South Funen Archipelago with its 300 islands. Charts are up to date, buoys guide us through narrow channels, and obstructions are well marked. Each day a dependable wind and open water ensure brisk sailing before we seek shelter in one of many small harbors. Little islands such as Langeland, Aero, and Tassinge offer quiet anchorages adjoining charming villages. Sailing with a three-month old is no problem, because, aided by rocking of the boat, Liane sleeps almost continuously. Fresh salt air and the boat's gentle swaying make three-year-old Cyrena drowsy as well, and for much of the trip she curls up below deck with her new sister.

This cruise begins our love affair with Denmark, and in years that follow Mary and I sail these waters many weekends throughout summer and fall. Even after visiting the Baltic numerous times, I still find new hidden anchorages. Often after a hectic week at work, escape with family into this sailing paradise provides a welcome relief. My ancestry traces to this region of Denmark, and I feel that heritage of the sea flowing in my veins.

In summer expected results begin to materialize. Success with automotive development brings in production contracts for door seals, belt line sections, and edge protectors for VW's new vehicles as well as models at BMW, Audi, and Daimler Benz. Efforts in the non-German automotive markets pay off with purchase orders from Daf (Netherlands), Renault, Volvo, and Saab. Several European bus manufacturers begin purchasing our plastic glazing profiles, which prove strong enough to retain large front windows when subjected to crash tests.

After months of working with potential French and Scandinavian window manufacturers, we receive orders for plastic weatherseals specialized for double- and triple-pane application. A surprising new market for extruded plastic profiles opens up nearby. Airbus, the product of the 1970 consolidation of the European aerospace industry, is designing the A300 fuselage, the world's first twin-aisle, two-engine aircraft, right here in Hamburg. Our marketing team is eagerly received by their engineers who immediately issue contracts for dozens of plastic strips, profiles, edge protectors, and trim strips to cover gaps throughout the aircraft's interior.

Efforts within the plant have been successful as well. Factory managers have eliminated inefficiencies and freed up excess production capacity; consequently, as new sales orders arrive, managers take on the added business with enthusiasm.

By standing firm with the strategy instead of acceding to suggestions from Rochester, I'd been judged to be a maverick, not a team player. However, I didn't know what else to do to achieve turnaround. Fortunately, the strategy has now proved successful. In the end I am vindicated.

*(The company became profitable in mid-1974 and went on to become successful for years afterward. Four years after my joining, annual sales had increased five times to $20 million while the employment figure of 300 remained below the level when I entered. Schlegel expanded its base of new products and continued to develop markets in various sectors throughout Europe. I felt a deep personal satisfaction with the turnaround and, although often frustrated, enjoyed the personal and professional challenges.)*

Taking a three-week, late-summer Austrian vacation in Mayrhofen, a mountain village in the Zillertal Valley, Mary and I book a program offering mountain climbing in the mornings and study of the culture of German-speaking people in the afternoons. Because we both enjoy mountain hiking as well as in-depth learning, Mayrhofen provides a fun-filled break.

At year's end we again take a biennial leave returning first to Mary's family in Albuquerque where we see old friends and once again ski in northern New Mexico. Afterward, we join my family in Louisville for a few days and then, together with Mom and Dad, fly to the Bahamas where we charter a 42-foot ketch at Eleuthera for a two-week cruise in the Exuma Cays. With three generations on board, we celebrate as a family while enjoying carefree days of swimming, sailing, and exploring islands scattered throughout these turquoise waters. But good times come to an end, and the transition from boarding a flight in warm, sunny Nassau to disembarking in cold, snowy Hamburg is difficult.

During these visits with family and friends, Mary and I observe that little has changed back in the States. By comparison, life in Europe is full of adventures, and we're thankful to have adopted a different lifestyle. We don't have anything against living in America, but life there seems predictable compared with the novelty and variety of European foods, wines, museums, architecture, politics, opera, literature, music, and cultures that we enjoy abroad.

The next year, 1975, unfolds comfortably. Because the company is running smoothly and profitably, I join a hiking club in the Austrian Alps and learn basics of mountaineering with ice axes, crampons, ropes, and pitons. Later Mary and I, with another couple from Hamburg, charter a bareboat 37-foot sloop out of Trieste, Italy, and sail along Yugoslavia's Adriatic Coast. How fortunate we feel to be among the first to discover the joys of chartering in this beautiful area.

We do, however, experience one disturbing episode. A Yugoslav gun boat accosts us, and, after demanding we drop all sails, crew members check our yacht's papers and passports. We're informed that we are sailing too close to the summer estate of President Tito and are directed to cruise in the opposite direction. We think we can guess the real reasons they intercepted us: First, they had nothing better to do, and second, they spied through binoculars the two women sunbathing topless! The rest of the cruise is uneventful as we discover one charming island after another. Peacefully sailing and swimming in clear, warm water while gazing at majestic, snow-capped mountains rising straight up from water's edge— what other experience can measure up to such serene joy? Sailing is becoming more and more a meditation and ultimate relaxation, and this Adriatic cruise will always count as one of my most beautiful experiences.

We end our third year in Germany with Christmas holidays at St. Anton in Austria. It's here that Cyrena, now four, skis for the first time and quickly masters the beginner slopes.

By now we're familiar with Europe's major cities and are comfortable with the European lifestyle and languages. We've traveled extensively and done things we had hoped to do upon arriving in Europe five years earlier. Those dark, career crisis days at Sandia in 1968 are well behind me, and

281

now I'm enjoying everything I had been looking for back then. The company's turnaround is complete—an appropriate parallel for my personal life which has turned around as well. I feel thankful for all the opportunities I've had. I've toured the world, managed three companies, lived abroad, twice become a father, and creatively faced career challenges. Thinking back to those years in Hawaii, I feel as if I'm riding the crest of the big wave again.

As we enter 1976, this idyllic state of affairs continues. Mary is teaching at the International School in Hamburg. I receive an outstanding bonus for the company's success and am developing new directions for the firm. What lies ahead is unclear, but we're not worried. We're happy!

These halcyon days, however, are merely the calm before the turbulence that will hit in summer. Unforeseen life-changing events will prove both frightening and thrilling, and I make no attempt to resist what is about to overwhelm me.

[March 1974, Hamburg] Mary and I welcome Liane home to Blankenese

# 31
# Herr Heiner Zee Hammer

*2/76 - 4/76, Age 35*

It's early 1976. Changes are in the air. Some I bring about myself; others come unbidden. Although appearing content and even happy outwardly, I feel a restlessness gnawing within. It's time for new directions.

The initial inclination is to fault the job. I have orchestrated a successful turnaround with the German subsidiary, and the business is now running smoothly. As long as we follow existing action plans and strategies, the company's profitability is ensured. I could, of course, remain in the driver's seat to enjoy the success except one problem interferes—the thrill of the challenge is gone, and I have no interest in being a maintenance manager. Herein lies a quandary: Hamburg is the largest overseas Schlegel subsidiary; there's nowhere else to go. Opportunities exist to manage smaller subsidiaries in Spain or England, but that would be a step backward. I send résumés out inquiring about managing director positions with other firms abroad that garnish responses, but despite a number of interesting interviews, nothing feels right.

While still in Belgium I had casually mentioned to Turner I'd be interested in running the German company, and he later gave me this opportunity. Now it's time to decide what to do next, yet nothing obvious comes to mind. Then, realizing it's not just a bigger company I am seeking, but rather a fresh challenge, I look for the biggest problem Schlegel is facing.

The search turns out to be a short one. An opportunity pops up here in Hamburg. A second Schlegel subsidiary, Schlegel Engineering GmbH, has recently run up enormous losses and absorbed excessive capital. Except for the chairman's stubborn resistance, this fledgling firm that's draining the company's worldwide profits, would have long since been disbanded.

Its origins go back four years to the time when an obese, arrogant German inventor named Heiner Hammer walked in off the street. Heiner was brilliant, articulate, enthusiastic, and persuasive. Never mind that he had just been through two bankruptcies; his enthusiasm remained undaunted. Responsibilities for the past disasters were, according to Heiner, the fault of others. Meeting with Chairman Turner in Rochester, Heiner presented his concept, which he said was patentable, to produce a huge 33-foot-wide plastic sheet that could be manufactured in varying thicknesses up to three millimeters and rolled up as long as anyone wanted.

This concept alone had, in the absence of an understanding of the possible applications, failed to generate much excitement. But in the early 1970s, disposal of solid waste was becoming a worldwide concern. Previously it had been a simple matter to dump waste into a hole in the ground and forget about it. But these landfills turned out to be ticking time bombs. Toxic materials filtering from the waste into the water tables were contaminating aquifers.

Existing solutions to air pollution included smokestack scrubbers, automotive catalytic converters, and emission-removal equipment; and solutions to liquid pollution included settling ponds, precipitation basins, evaporation lakes, ion exchange devices, and reverse-osmosis techniques. Solutions to deal with municipal and industrial solid waste, however, were non-existent.

Until new recycling technology could be developed, governments around the world mandated that solid waste be isolated in containment basins. But traditional lining materials such as clay, concrete, asphalt, and thin films used for reservoirs offered no resistance to the corrosive chemicals in industrial waste. Plastic sheets were the only material capable of providing adequate resistance, but they required enormous amounts of seaming to build a basin liner, and these seams were unreliable. Heiner proposed a solution: a thick, giant sheet of High Density Polyethylene (HDPE) that he claimed he could manufacture. Furthermore, he had developed a patentable technique for making weld seams with his sheet— seams as strong and reliable as the sheet itself.

Turner, intrigued with Heiner's concept, envisioned it fitting in with Schlegel's existing businesses. The company has a worldwide reputation as the leading producer of weatherseals and other perimeter designs with applications in many industries. Schlegel can make just about any spaghetti-type product from textiles, rubber, and plastics. Already expert at edge sealing, why couldn't Schlegel become proficient in sealing surfaces as well? Because the concept seemed both timely and straightforward, Turner created Schlegel Engineering GmbH in Hamburg to back Heiner and develop the technology.

An attorney with no technical background, Turner made this decision without understanding the complexity of the technology or the nature of the business. He conducted no market research and engaged no consultants for advice. He failed to recognize that Schlegel's existing business was strictly as a supplier of products, whereas the area-sealing business would involve installation of a previously unknown product at major construction sites by company field crews who would travel all over the world. Furthermore, Turner did not recognize that failure of the sheet could have damaging consequences, including bankruptcy.

For the first year, development went well, and worldwide patents were issued to Schlegel protecting both the manufacturing of the plastic sheet, now called Schlegel Sheet, and the weld-sealing processes. Heiner hired a superb team of about 25 mechanical and construction engineers and engaged a professor from University of Aachen, one of Germany's top technical universities, to consult on waste disposal technologies. Taking a calculated risk that fortunately paid off, instead of first building a prototype, Heiner skipped the development phase and went straight to constructing the production equipment. In less than two years he built a machine, just as he said he would, that could produce a 10-meter-wide plastic sheet of HDPE that could vary in thickness from 1.5 to 3.0 millimeters and coil into giant rolls 150 meters or more in length. Throughout the Schlegel organization enthusiasm ran high, and every report of an ecological disaster anywhere in the world caused by industrial pollutants seemed to affirm HDPE's potential.

But once the technology was in place and time came to build a business, problems began. When a number of early installations failed, constant repairs rapidly drained the company's resources. Paying no heed to these initial failures, Heiner entered into a contract with a major international construction company to line a basin at the world's largest copper mine at Sar Chesmeh, Iran. When the liner failed, Heiner incurred immense expense to air-ship, rather than send by boat, additional HDPE rolls and to deploy additional field crews to make repairs. Before long the company became bogged down as all effort and expense went into salvaging the contracts on hand rather than building new business.

These setbacks were classic problems resulting from failure to recognize three distinct phases of building a new enterprise. The first, the innovation or inventive phase, requires a visionary with decisive and authoritative leadership to establish priorities needed to build the technology. This phase went well because Heiner, with his blustery, ego-driven style, proved ideal to oversee the implementation of his ideas.

The second phase, the entrepreneurial stage, requires leadership to build a team of capable people comfortable working in an unstructured, pioneering environment. Decision making must be delegated and information should flow fast and unrestricted within the group. In this, Heiner proved disastrous. Refusing to delegate authority, he micro-managed every detail, a style that had worked in the development phase but now impeded the company's ability to develop a marketing and sales program. Whenever anyone criticized or tried to correct him, a red faced Heiner would angrily erupt, "I am not zee anvil; I am zee Hammer, so I vil do zee pounding!"

Once a startup gets through the initial steps, it enters the third phase when professional management needs to introduce policies, procedures, controls, and backup systems to ensure smooth day-to-day functioning. Having just brought my previous company into the third stage, further pursuit of this type of management holds no interest for me. However, the challenge of bringing area-sealing technology into the entrepreneurial stage intrigues me, particularly because Heiner is clearly in over his head. Knowing this is where my talents could best be utilized, I visit Rochester in the spring to ask Turner if I can have a crack at trying to pull Schlegel Engineering out of the current mess. The chairman, who has backed Heiner all along but is under increasing pressure by the board of directors to stop the bloodletting, is surprised at my request and agrees to consider it.

A month later Dick calls me to Rochester to offer the job. He asks, however, that I serve as managing director of both German firms until he hires a replacement for my former company. I readily agree. Shortly afterward Dick indirectly fires Heiner from Schlegel Engineering by asking him to move to Rochester to take on corporate R and D assignments. Heiner apprehends what is happening and, to no one's surprise, promptly quits. He immediately forms a competitive company that can, without infringing upon what are now Schlegel's patents, produce similar giant rolls of plastic liner and weld-sealing techniques. Obviously, he had not disclosed to Chairman Turner everything about his technology.

The leisurely days of spring 1976 when I was running a single, well-organized company suddenly become frantic as I take on a troubled second firm that, in addition to its own problems, now has a formidable competitor.

[1976, age 35] Schlegel Hamburg offices and plant

[1976, Blankenese] Family on front steps of Pepers Diek 8

# 32
# Bhagwan Rajneesh

*4/76 – 7/76, Age 35*

I feel confident in my ability to meet the challenge as the new managing director of Schlegel Engineering. Only one question remains: How long will the turnaround take? Whether it's three or five years matters little, because I now realize that afterward I would look for a bigger company, and after that, another, even bigger still. On and on it will go. But what is the point?

I've been receiving compensation in the six-digit range for several years *(quite high for the mid-1970s)* and am not interested in accruing more wealth or raising my status in the business community. I'm doing exactly the things I originally set out to do. Although the new job is an exciting prospect, I am disturbed by a vague feeling I should be doing something different. I readily acknowledge that my life is comfortable and even rewarding and my family is wonderful. Nevertheless, I am not at peace within. I yearn for something of higher value, but whatever it is, is not to be found in the material plane.

In the West this quandary is known as a mid-life crisis—a time when men change jobs and sometimes wives, thinking this will bring a new perspective and add adventure to their lives. But in the East such uneasiness is understood to signal the start of a spiritual quest. I am 35 years old, which in Eastern religions has special significance, as does every age divisible by seven. In the average lifespan of 70 years, a person goes through 10 seven-year cycles. At 35, the mid-point, things important in the past start to drop away, and the quest for deeper meaning begins. I seem to fit this pattern.

One evening in April, as Mary and I dine with Jane, who teaches at the International School, and her architect husband Steve, we hear the name Bhagwan Rajneesh for the first time. Our friends share that this Poona-based Indian mystic has taught them to meditate and, as a result, are experiencing a transformation in their lives. My first reaction: Here's one more typical guru story to add to the list. Having read about people like Maharishi, Babaji, Reverend Moon, and about the Hare Krishna movement, I had categorically rejected the lot. These "supermarket gurus" fly around the West pedaling their brands of Eastern mysticism, which basically are commercial ventures designed to take advantage of people's gullibility. The devotees themselves appear to be fanatical dogmatists who adamantly revere their so-called masters and aren't open to anything else that life offers. Furthermore, the followers never appear to be especially happy.

However, as dinner continues I'm intrigued by what Jane and Steve share. Bhagwan Rajneesh seems to be different from other so-called gurus because he neither solicits money nor imposes rules or restrictions on those around him.

The following weekend Mary and I join Jane and Steve to participate in our first experience with meditation. The methods created by Bhagwan are unlike classical "sit-silently-and-contemplate-your-navel" exercises. His Dynamic Meditation (which, at first, seems a contradiction in terms) incorporates dancing, shaking, jumping, and other movements. He explains that people today are unable to sit silently because their lives are filled to overflowing with activities. If one just sits with closed eyes, suddenly a hundred ideas, problems, plans, memories, and disjointed thoughts spring to mind, so rather than becoming peaceful and quiet, one feels fragmented. Strenuous activity, however, tires the body and quiets the tumult in the head. Following this active phase, one stands, sits, or reclines in silence. The surprise is that serenity envelops one in blissful emptiness.

Bhagwan teaches that in the apparent opposites of life—which he says are actually complements—lie many keys to understanding meditation. As a clock pendulum swings to the left, it's gathering energy to go to the right. If one wants a good sleep, lying down and trying to force sleep to come does not help; rather, one must go to the other pole, the complement, by engaging in energetic activity. Then, in the evening, sleep will come of its own accord. Likewise, if one wants to inhale deeply, one must first exhale deeply. Herein lies the key to meditation. Bhagwan (later known as Osho) has created dozens of meditations—walking meditation, martial arts meditation, smoking meditation, breathing meditation, dancing meditation, swimming meditation, couples meditation, and more. He further explains that the three main religions of the West—Judaism, Christianity, and Islam—approach God through prayer; and the three of the East—Hinduism, Buddhism, and Zen—approach the divine through meditation. Each practice is missing something very beautiful, but if one learns both meditation and prayer, many new dimensions of beauty can open.

All this is heady stuff for Mary and me, and we decide to continue these meditations for a few weeks. After only a few days we experience feelings never before imagined. As though an unseen hand is plucking chords within, or petals of a bud are beginning to unfold, a world of blissfulness starts to open. As we listen to tapes of Bhagwan's daily 90-minute discourses and read his books, we're overwhelmed. His extemporaneous outpourings cover such diverse subjects as nuclear physics, capitalism, psychology, sex, world religions, and more. He speaks about Hegel, Heidegger, Nehru, Buddha, Marx, Jesus, Mahavira, Gandhi, Nixon, Sartre, Bodhidharma.... The list is endless. He explains how ego and lack of awareness drive people to act in destructive ways. Bhagwan's words are simple, direct, poignant, and often infused with humor and playfulness. Most important, while shining a light on much of the hypocrisy in the teachings of modern society, his words have a clear ring of truth. A continual theme is that the West needs to learn to meditate, the only way to gain true insight.

Mary and I are fascinated by Steve's experiences during his recent visit with Bhagwan at his ashram, a meditation commune in Poona. The more Steve tells stories of the hundreds of people from all over the world he met there and the more he speaks of the daily living and meditation practices, the more enthralled we become. That unknown something within myself I had begun to notice earlier is now churning. Although sensing I have caught hold of something of significance (or should I say something of significance has caught hold of me?), when I attempt to examine whatever it is, my mind clouds up. The more Steve describes his experiences in Poona, the crazier the whole thing seems. Yet he is a professional architect with international acclaim; so how can I just shrug my shoulders and say he and Jane are naïve and have been duped? On the other hand, if I accept Steve's explanations about what Bhagwan teaches, clearly this is one of the most incredible phenomena in the world today. Finally, I come to the only conclusion possible: I must travel to Poona to discover the truth for myself.

Back on the home front, in addition to raising our two daughters, Mary is teaching fifth grade at Hamburg's International School and pursuing her interest in painting. She has exhibited at several art shows in Hamburg, and as celebrations for the 200th anniversary of our nation's birth take shape, she's invited to exhibit at the Amerika-Haus. Afterward Mary and the girls return to the States to stay with my parents in Louisville where, in order to maintain her American teaching credentials, she takes summer classes at the University of Louisville.

Meanwhile I make plans to assume responsibilities as managing director of both Schlegel companies in Hamburg.

Then comes that auspicious day I meet Barbara.

# 33
# Barbara

*7/76 - 8/76, Age 35*

July 14th, Bastille Day, when the French celebrate the beginning of their revolution, is just another workday here in Germany. Hoping to clear the residual boredom of a long business day, I stop on the way home after dinner for a drink and entertainment. Kaffee Keese nightclub in the Reeperbahn district features a live band and a policy whereby most dances are women's choice.

I sit at a table, watch the fun, and accept a few invitations to dance. To ensure a woman's pride is not hurt, if a man refuses a dance, he's asked to leave the club. I speak in German with my first partners—an administrative assistant in an insurance company and a trading company receptionist—before lapsing into silence with a couple of others. Then a particularly attractive woman strolls over and issues an invitation. As we thread across the room toward the band, just for a change I address her in English, expecting a response in faltering English before reverting to German. What a surprise when she replies in heavily accented but almost flawless English! Conversation flows easily, and I learn that Barbara (pronounced the German way with three syllables, BAR-ba-ra) has worked as a nurse first in her native Germany, then in France and England. She lived in the States as an au pair caring for the children of the director for the Philadelphia Museum of Art. When briefly telling Barbara about myself, I conveniently forget to mention being married with children. We enjoy a pleasant dance, and because the next one is on the hour and is men's choice, I invite her.

Our second dance is also delightful, and after the music stops, we linger, feeling a magical connection. When the music begins again, she asks for a third dance. Afterward, she has to leave, saying she works the early nurse's shift at a clinic.

My heart is beating like that of a 16-year-old on a first date, and I don't want the night to end. Although she is 32 and I'm 35, we stand together stammering like a couple of shy kids half our ages. Then she suggests that perhaps we can meet sometime and have a steak. Yes, she says "steak!" As she starts the sentence, I anticipate she will suggest having a cup of coffee, but what is this about a steak?

*(Much later Barbara recalls she was so nervous she couldn't think what to say about a future date, so one of her companions suggested steak because Germans know how fond Americans are of it.)*

I immediately respond this is a wonderful idea. Again, we stare at each other in silence. When I ask if I can call her, she rummages through her purse but can't find a pencil or paper, so I try to memorize her phone number. This gives something to talk about for a moment, but when memory proves hopeless, we lapse once more into silence. Although not professing to be an accomplished Romeo, this isn't the first time I had met a woman in the evening, and there had never before been difficulty knowing what to do. This time, however, I can't break free from the trance. Finally, since we both live in the same direction, I suggest that perhaps I could follow her home to get a pencil to write the phone number. After another silence, we agree. Once in our cars, I follow her blue Volkswagen Beetle, my heart throbbing all the way.

When we arrive at her apartment, both still feeling the fresh innocence and awkwardness experienced at the club, Barbara fumbles for her key, drops it, and I retrieve it. Finally, she opens the door, and in we go. While she searches for pencil and paper, I survey books in her wall-to-wall bookcase. Then, having at last written down her number, she thrusts the paper into my hand.

The shock of her touch breaks the spell that has paralyzed me. I immediately enfold her in my arms, and the moment I bend to meet her upturned face, we lose ourselves in a kiss. Time stops. I melt into a pool of flowing energy yearning to merge into the energy meeting it. No longer two, we are one.

After what must have been several minutes we pull apart, and as we gaze into one another's eyes, we each see a mirror image of our own feelings. Without speaking we drift from bookcase to sofa and from sofa to bed. Allowing ourselves to move with our energies, we explode into passion, ecstasy, gentleness, love. Savoring every beautiful feeling that arises, for hours we float in a heavenly realm reserved for beloveds.

At dawn we're awakened by a chorus of birds outside the window and waves of joy wash over us as we realize the magic of the night wasn't just a dream. No words are possible; we simply commune with our eyes and bodies to assure ourselves this is all real.

Then Barbara rises noiselessly and slips into her nurse's uniform. A moment later she kisses my eyelashes and disappears out the door. I lie in bed another half hour, not trying to figure out anything but basking in the warmth and wonder that still enrapture me. Who is she? Where did she come from? What does she do? What do I know about her? I know nothing and, at the moment, don't care. More importantly, I know *her*, and if anything, that "about" is almost a block between us. Knowing *about* someone is a result of communication, but we had tasted communion. Barbara and I touched something deep within each other and experienced the bliss of perfect harmony. Everything else is peripheral to this innermost experience.

Climbing out of bed and scanning the surroundings, I begin to learn something "about" this woman. The furnishings are sparse and simple: a couch, a table, two straight-back chairs, and a couple of old easy chairs. There is no bedstead, just a mattress on the floor, and instead of side tables, old orange crates support simple lamps and half a dozen partially read books. Along one side of this single-room apartment is the enormous bookcase where last night's drama began. Books in French, German, and English—three languages in which she is fluent—crowd the shelves. The room's other walls are covered with her artistic creations—sketches and paintings as eclectic as her reading tastes: seagulls soaring over the ocean, prehistoric buffaloes, Indonesian market scenes, still lifes, and landscapes. Without drawing conclusions, I simply allow the scene to enter my senses before pulling myself together to leave for work.

Once there, I avoid involvement in business activities for fear that doing so will chase away the sensations still churning within. In the afternoon I call Barbara and, trying to sound as natural as possible, invite her for a steak dinner.

Upon arriving at Barbara's apartment, I hesitate. The thought occurs she could be a beautiful, charming prostitute adept at captivating men during the night. Am I about to come face to face with Cinderella who has changed into one of the ugly sisters? Before knocking, I fight off a wave of fear. But the moment Barbara answers, doubts disappear, and we are instantly back on the same wavelength discovered hours earlier. Later over our first steak dinner, we begin to get acquainted, although we both know this to be an unimportant formality. Again, we spend the night together and give ourselves over to the rapture of the night before.

Every night for three weeks we're together—each time as beautiful, yet different from the others. Some evenings we grill steaks on her patio and go to bed tipsy from a bottle or two of wine. Sometimes we go to restaurants, movies, or live performances and other times sit in her apartment talking late into the evening. Several weekends we rent sailboats on a small lake in Hamburg. After she proves to be a capable crew in dinghies, I introduce her to sailing on a large yacht in the Baltic Sea.

During moments alone I ponder the implications of having Barbara in my life. Things have so far been uncomplicated, but at summer's end when Mary and the girls return from the States, what will happen? Life with Mary has been comfortable. She is supportive and has been an asset in furthering my career. She is a wonderful mother, a superb hostess and entertainer, and at company dinner parties always the perfect charmer.

Although I love living in Europe, Mary, however, prefers to seek friends in the American community and seldom connects with the lifestyle here. She enjoys reading about the history and culture but has difficulty learning languages and relating to local people beyond interactions when she shops. I sense she would be happy to return to the States, one of several differences that have arisen between us.

The balance sheet on Mary leads to no obvious conclusion. On the asset side, she is everything society expects in a wife, mother, and partner to a successful manager. On the liability side, I no longer feel vitality, joy, or deep connection with her. Our life is comfortable, secure, and predictable; yet we share little real happiness. In recent years Mary and I have been almost like objects to each other rather than flesh-and-blood, heart-and-soul people. Whereas Barbara and I laugh, talk, and are playful, Mary seems to regard such things as nuisances that take time away from the girls, domestic life, and her teaching. But discussions I have with other men about their wives indicate this to be the norm. Fire diminishes over time, and, in our case, there was very little fire in the first place. Finally, I conclude that disrupting the status quo would have grave consequences not only for Mary and me, but also for the girls. So, I decide to accept the situation with Mary and get on with life as it is. This apparently is the way life is meant to be.

At least that's what I thought until Barbara von Herff appeared.

These past three weeks have given me a glimpse of a different life. As a result of her exhaustive reading and extensive travels throughout Europe and the U.S., Barbara has a wide range of interests. She is independent and comfortable on her own, not needing others around for companionship. Euro-savvy, she is self-confident but without superficial mannerisms. Her minimal makeup and modest, yet tasteful, clothes reveal her natural beauty. She speaks in a soft, warm, expressive voice that complements the graceful way she moves. Probably what I love most is how she relates to me from her heart.

One day I tell Barbara about Mary and the girls. She, of course, knew the situation (as any woman in similar circumstances would), yet wasn't about to create a problem by bringing up the subject. Afterward, however, we become totally open with each other. I tell her about my childhood as a red-headed, freckle-faced, under-sized kid who found solace on a farm or alone in the woods. She describes her experience as an East German refugee. Near the end of the war, when she was three and her brother five, her mother wheeled them in a baby carriage for more than a week to escape from Rostock, which was ceded to the Russians, into the safety of the U.S. zone. When her father, a prisoner of war in Denmark, was released, the family reunited and was given accommodations in a barn on a West German farm where she spent her childhood.

We listen to each other with open hearts and each furnishes details as the other requests. Barbara knows how to listen and when to respond. She makes me feel like a musical instrument played by a skilled musician who elicits heretofore unheard songs from deep within. We dance, we love, we play, and we rejoice in the life we open to each other.

Three weeks later, in early August, it's time to depart for Poona to meet Bhagwan. Where am I now? Three major changes have occurred in only a few months: I am the new managing director of two companies; I'm about to go off to the ashram of an Indian guru; and Barbara has turned my personal life upside-down. These changes disturb my entire being—mind, soul, and heart. The added responsibility of managing a second company will challenge my mind; Bhagwan has awakened my soul with the first steps in a spiritual quest; and Barbara has touched my heart.

I mull over the difference between "meaning" and "significance". Why have Barbara and Bhagwan entered my life? When looking for meaning, I find none. But there is tremendous significance—the significance of a flower releasing fragrance to the dancing winds. I am stirring out of a stupor. A new vitality is arising within!

The new job, on the other hand, is a different matter. It has tremendous meaning, but no significance. There will be new challenges, activities, tasks, and problems—all amounting to nothing more than a modified repetition of the past. It is clear the new job will not be a life-giving undertaking.

But the stirrings of heart and spirit I'm beginning to discover now at age 35—these have the fragrance of Life. And I'm eager to move on to see where these stirrings will lead.

# 34
# Coming to Bhagwan

*8/76, Age 35*

The eight-hour nonstop flight from London to Bombay (Mumbai) is the first opportunity in months to be alone. Caught between demands of work and the intense relationship with Barbara, I'm now about to explore a newfound dimension represented by Bhagwan.

What do I know about this man I am traveling so far to see? Bhagwan Shree Rajneesh was born December 11, 1931, in India and experienced enlightenment March 21, 1953. He was a student and later professor at University of Jabalpur. After teaching philosophy for nine years, he traveled about India trying to communicate what had happened to him. Then he settled with his closest disciples in Bombay to conduct meditation camps. Twenty-one years after his enlightenment, on March 21, 1974, he established the ashram in Poona.

Prior to embarking on this journey I had listened to hours of recorded discourses. Yet the vastness of the man and his message make it impossible to say anything definitive about Bhagwan. The first difficulty is his words. Almost 20 million of his words have been published in more than 350 books; all these, together with publication of 25 additional books each year, make him the most prolific author on the planet. Due to the range of subjects, any summary of his teachings is impossible.

The second problem is that everything Bhagwan says somewhere, he contradicts elsewhere. But what can he do, he laments, because he simply speaks about life, and life itself is so contradictory.

The third problem is that his real message is not in his words, which, he says, are just a technique to attract the attention of the mind and keep it distracted. The real message is in the silence of intervals between words; only by listening to his silence can we understand what he's trying to convey. Communication is not taking place between minds; rather a communion is felt between open hearts. On other occasions, however, Bhagwan maintains even the heart can create a barrier. The message is like a prayer that's beyond feeling and is experienced only when one is in absolute emptiness.

Finally, confusion peaks when Bhagwan says he has no message to share through his teaching—instead, he is simply sharing a vision. Bhagwan asks nothing of us—no money, no rituals—and gives no commandments. The only request he makes is that we dress in the colors of the morning sunrise—shades of orange, ochre, and red as a constant reminder that we are to live every moment in festivity and joy. Ochre is a reminder of meditation, the first color one sees when meditating.

Bhagwan takes us beyond mind, beyond words, beyond logic, and into other realms—realms of bliss and beauty. He speaks of love and freedom and how these are the highest reflections of human consciousness. He describes restrictions and limitations societies have imposed throughout history—shares how we have allowed ourselves to become distorted and diverted from our natural state of bliss and ecstasy. Life should be a celebration and a dance, he insists, but it gets turned into a duty and a burden. Over 3,000 years man has fought 5,000 wars, making our history one of constant bloodshed. Mind has become master and created the false entity of the ego, which remains constantly unfulfilled in its quest for enhancement and recognition.

Bhagwan's words touch chords within me. He maintains there are many paths to enlightenment and discusses them in detail. Zen spiritual masters, Islamic Sufi dervishes, Jewish Hasidic mystics, and Hindu Baal swamis—he embraces them all. He speaks of Buddha, Kabir, Lao Tze, Jesus, and others with equal love and understanding for each of their paths. His words and meditation techniques serve as devices to wake us out of our slumber and stimulate a glimmer of awareness.

Arriving at Bombay's airport in the pre-dawn, I step out into heavy, steamy air that settles like a weight on my body. After hassles with customs inspection, baggage claim, and passport control, I drag luggage to the domestic terminal to await an early morning flight to Poona. Sprawled across the suitcases so anyone trying to steal one would disturb me, I fall asleep.

*Beep! Beep! Beep!* Awakened a few hours later by my wrist watch alarm, I can't quite remember where I am and why. Oh yes, I'm on a "spiritual quest." Suddenly everything seems absurd as people all around scurry this way and that to do something important. Such intense busyness is the *modus operandi* I know, so what am I getting into now with this sudden desire to venture off in a completely different direction? Shaking the tangle of cobwebs from my mind, I trudge off to the check-in line for the Poona flight. Twenty minutes later I make a mad dash across the tarmac through a drizzly, monsoon rain to board the waiting DC-3 for the 40-minute flight 120 miles southeast to the 2,000-foot elevation Deccan Plateau.

Three hundred years ago Poona was the capital of the Marathi Empire that controlled most of the peninsula of the Indian subcontinent while Moguls dominated the northern regions up to the Himalayas. When the British established a foothold in India, power of the Marathis was diminished, causing Poona to lose its political importance. However, with its ideal, semi-arid climate, and refreshing tropical vegetation, Poona remains one of the most pleasant places to live or visit in India. A modern, progressive center, the city claims more than one million inhabitants (of little note in this heavily populated country).

As the plane approaches the modest airfield east of the city, I'm struck by the lush beauty and undulating landscape contoured by the Mula and Murtha rivers that meander through the countryside until joining as the Mula-Murtha River at the center of this metropolitan area. Men washing water buffaloes, women laundering clothes, and sadhus performing morning rituals dot the riverbanks. The rising sun casts a pale yellow haze causing the verdant land to sparkle as if the landscape itself is alive. By the time I load bags into an auto rickshaw and head toward the ashram, the whole city has begun to stir. Children play while women sweep the road in front of their homes and burn dried cow dung to brew morning tea.

The rickshaw pulls up to the ashram's "Gateless Gate" around 7:30 am. Perfect. After traveling more than 24 hours, I have arrived with just enough time to attend the 8:00 am discourse. Upon entering the ashram, I'm immediately embraced by the luxuriant foliage and sweet fragrance of gardens and small subtropical forests—frangipani, plumeria, bird-of-paradise, monkey puzzle, and flamboyant abound.

After storing belongings, I am directed past the gate of Lao Tzu House where Bhagwan lives, before following a narrow path along the edge of a garden to a marble tiled veranda. I sit down among about 500 others and for 15 minutes wait in stillness broken only by the chatter of birds and hum of insects.

Suddenly noticing others placing their palms together and raising hands in the traditional Namaste gesture, I follow their example and look toward the porch door where Bhagwan is about to enter. What happens next is unclear because I lapse into a brief, trance-like state. A graceful apparition in white robe and sandals enters, glides to the center of the auditorium, slowly turns, and returns our Namaste greeting before sitting down to begin the discourse. Bhagwan's movements, although simple and ordinary, appear as effortless and quiet as if there is activity without an actor—doing without a doer.

When Bhagwan starts to speak, a shock snaps me out of this trance-like spell. His words are in Hindi, not English. Then I remember: The English series starts on August 11th, and today is the 10th, the last day of the Hindi series. For 90 minutes I sit uncomprehending without missing a single sound or gesture. Bhagwan's hands and fingers create a dance that accentuates his words—words I cannot understand. But it matters not, because I'm transfixed by the gracefulness of his gestures. In what seems like no time, he ends the discourse, stands, raises his hands in a parting Namaste that we all return, and retreats into his house. Minutes pass before anyone moves; then slowly others rise to depart. I follow, and once outside go off by myself to recover from this incredible experience of being in the presence of an enlightened one.

Once I feel grounded, I leave the ashram to find a hotel. For $12 a day nearby Blue Diamond Hotel offers a clean room, private bath, and swimming pool—the pool practically a necessity for surviving 100-degree, humid, monsoon temperatures.

After settling, I return to investigate this ashram that attracted me from halfway around the globe. My impression is that these six acres of land aren't India, but rather a microcosm of the world. About 2,000 people have come to be near Bhagwan with more arriving every day. Many with dark faces are from India, but the majority with Caucasian faces hail from East and West Europe, North America, New Zealand, and Australia. Chinese, Japanese and other Asians make up a significant number of the ashram's population, and to complete the picture, Africans and swarthy-complexioned Mediterraneans are also much in evidence.

During the following days I learn more about the others who have been enticed to come to Bhagwan. They come from middle- and upper-class lifestyles and show no signs of addiction, criminality, homelessness, or mental health issues. Although most are under 35 years, many with gray hair appear to be in their 60s, 70s, or 80s. No one can express exactly what prompted him or her to give up a promising career, stable home life, academic studies, or comfortable lifestyle. Yet all felt a powerful sense of seeking—seeking that led to the most important change in their lives—a change inspired by attraction to and love for Bhagwan.

Logic cannot explain such decisions because they arise out of a feeling—the feeling one experiences in the presence of an enlightened or awakened person—the same feeling that attracted followers to Jesus,

Mohammed, Buddha, Mahavira, Nanak, Moses, and other prophets. Because Westerners aren't familiar with the concept of an enlightened person, we have difficulty making sense of this phenomenon. The closest example we know is Jesus, but the Christian Church has so deified Jesus that it is impossible to appreciate his humanness. Meanwhile, many enlightened persons in the East, living in blissful ordinariness, have remained hidden from the world. Such people are never encountered on superhighways of life but rather on quiet back roads. Seldom are they known by words or actions, but rather through their silent state of bliss.

Limited by the blinders of a Western mind, I see and understand only simple, obvious facts about Bhagwan. Although something is stirring within—something I can't understand—I stay primarily in the realm of my mind, not recognizing the limitations of this approach.

Ashram life has a well-defined structure, and I throw myself into its rhythm. Days begin at 6:00 am with Dynamic Meditation followed by a cup of tea at Vrindavan, the ashram canteen, before discourse at 8:00 am. On the first day of the English series, I join twice as many people as were present when Bhagwan was finishing the Hindi series. Lost again in a mesmerized state when Bhagwan appears, I sit enthralled for two hours as he gives a perspective on Jesus never presented in the Episcopal church of my childhood. Speaking lovingly about Jesus, he maintains the Christian Church has misrepresented him. One will never see a picture of Jesus laughing, he says, because the Church uses him to remind us of man's guilt and of how Jesus carries the burden of sins of all mankind. Bhagwan claims this is totally wrong; Jesus loved to laugh, dance, and celebrate with those around him. If Jesus didn't laugh, then who can? Jesus was one of the most joyous people who ever existed. How unfortunate that churches have created a sorrowful portrayal of such an ecstatic individual. This insight into Jesus fills me with joy and opens new wonder about who he is. When Bhagwan concludes, once again teary-eyed from the beauty and joy he conveys in both words and presence, I leave to be alone.

Morning discourse is followed by a wonderful hour spent in the canteen garden enjoying a quiet breakfast while getting acquainted (Bhagwan jokingly said gossip is preferred to gospel) with others. Next, I attend a Sufi dance session followed by a dancing meditation before lunch.

Afterward I migrate to the meditation hall to listen to a taped discourse from one of Bhagwan's earlier series. Three additional hour-long meditations—Kundalini, Nataraj, and Nadabrahma—follow throughout the afternoon and into the evening with activities concluding at 7:00 pm. The day's five meditations, several of which involve intense exercise, prove exhausting. Following a quiet dinner with new acquaintances, I go early to bed, reading myself to sleep with one of Bhagwan's books.

In addition to this program for short-term visitors, there are other activities for permanent residents. Bhagwan has said that God is Creativity; thus, to grow close to the divine, one should become creative. Therefore, creativity designed to allow as much unstructured flow as possible is the basis for all ashram activities including artistry, woodwork, pottery, dance, music, theater, and more. Everything—walking, eating, talking—is to be a creative act conducted in meditation. A stay at the ashram is an immersion in such totality.

Now, after several days of participating in life at the ashram, the day to meet Bhagwan face-to-face is at hand.

[1976, Poona] Bhagwan Shree Rajneesh, aka Osho

# 35

# The Rock Shall Dance

*8/76, Age 35*

Three days ago I plunged into the routine of the ashram. Meditations go deep, and I feel a softening, a relaxing. No question about whether to become one of Bhagwan's people. I want to be near this man. Am I ready to take sannyas? An ancient term in Eastern spirituality, *taking sannyas* means surrendering the superficial part of oneself while retaining the pure freedom of living life with joyful, meditative awareness. Ego, desires, ambitions, expectations—these are to be surrendered if one desires to approach life with authenticity and openness. To seekers of truth, taking sannyas simply means abandoning much of the outer to explore the inner.

I am ready, and the day arrives for my *darshan*. Darshan refers to coming into the presence of a spiritual, revered, or enlightened person. It is Friday evening, August 13, 1976. I and 20 others, mostly Westerners ranging in age from mid-20s to mid-60s, will have a private audience with Bhagwan. This evening is to become the end of so many old things and the beginning of a new life—in a sense, a second birth.

Because Bhagwan has always been in delicate health and has a particular sensitivity to odors, before coming into his presence we must pass a "sniff" test. We have been instructed to shower with scentless soap, brush our teeth, and wear freshly laundered clothes. Several women, selected because of their keen sense of smell, hover as we file in and often pull someone aside with instructions to book another session.

In the early evening light those of us who have passed the sniff test gather on the marble porch behind Bhagwan's house and wait in silence for him to appear. One moment there is nothing; next moment he's smiling warmly and giving a Namaste greeting.

After he sits, my name is first to be called. Trembling, I kneel in front of his chair and meet his gaze. He quietly instructs me to close my eyes and feel his energy. I should allow anything to happen that develops. Within a few moments I become overpowered by a tightness that engulfs my entire body. I recall falling to the right and lying a few moments just whimpering softly. Then Bhagwan's warm voice calls me back. He has felt my energy and seen I'm tense and tied in knots. He bestows a new sannyas name indicative of the direction to find my path, then continues to speak for several minutes, but, transfixed by his presence, I don't comprehend his words. *(It isn't until two years later when the book with this darshan is published that I understand what he said.)* However, the moment he gives the new name, *Deva Nartan,* something resonates. *Divine Dance.* I was and am Nartan. I've always been Nartan. Bhagwan is reminding me of something long ago forgotten and there's no need for him to elaborate.

The transcription of the darshan, as published in the book, *Dance your Way to God, A Darshan Diary,* is as follows:

*\*Friday, August 13, 1976*

*Bhagwan (to Peter, a large, blond-headed American visitor): Your new name: Swami Deva Nartan.*

*It means divine dance. Deva means divine, Nartan means dance. And that has to be your approach towards god. No need to be serious about it. All seriousness is illness. Laugh and dance your way.*

*To be joyful is the only prayer. And to learn how to dance so deeply that the dancer disappears in the dance, is the only worship.*

*To remember it, your name will be a constant reminder. Just be joyful. Religion is a way of celebrating life. It has nothing to do with that church-type seriousness; something has gone morbid. Otherwise there is nothing to be serious about.*

*God is not serious, otherwise he cannot create such a beautiful world with so much delight in it, with so much love in it. He must be more of a dancer, a singer, painter, or poet. It is difficult to conceive of him as a theologian or a priest or a Catholic monk. It would not be just to imagine god that way. Hindus are more colorful about it.*

*Just see... (indicating the luxuriant green foliage of the trees and shrubs around the auditorium) all around, it is so green. This world cannot fit with a theological god. It can fit with a poet, a painter.*

*So let this be your constant reminder—that you have to dance your way to god, to laugh your way to god.*

*Anything you would like to say?*

*Nartan: Bhagwan, this is so far away from what I am now.*

*Bhagwan: I will bring you closer to it. I am so far—far out! (much laughter) You will come closer, don't worry.*

\* Copyright 1978 by Rajneesh Foundation; first published by Ma Yoga Laxmi, Rajneesh Foundation, Shree Rajneesh Ashram, 17 Koregaon Park, Poona 411-001, India, pp 229-230.

-----------

Bhagwan homes in on seriousness as a blockage in my life and gives me guidance how to remove it and come away dancing. After I return to my place, now a sannyasin, others go forward. To another sannyasin he emphasizes comments made to me:

\* *Bhagwan: ...and sing more—that's all we can do. We can dance, we can sing. There is nothing else for man to do. Nothing else is possible. We can pray, we can be full of wonder...and we can allow the mystery to mystify us.*

*And look at life more like an artist—aesthetically. That is the only religious way to look at life—in an aesthetic way. When your eyes are full of beauty and you start looking through beauty all around, you have heard the song; the first presence has been felt. Beauty is the first entry of the divine into human consciousness. So sing, dance, feel beauty more and more...relax.*

\* Ibid, 230 - 231.

----------

Later Bhagwan speaks to a sannyasin whose critically ill wife is hospitalized in Germany. (*Only years later when my prognosis becomes known, do I attach significance to these words.*)

*\*Bhagwan: ...don't be worried.... She is in a good state. If she stays a little longer, good. If she goes, that too is good. But she has surrendered and is not fighting. If she dies, she is dying in a good state. Just don't be worried.*

*And this will be good for you also. If you can just remain silently in deep acceptance of whatsoever happens, this may prove your greatest moment in growth. There may not be another opportunity again....*

*So use it...use even death. Everything has to be turned into a skillful situation. Buddhists call it 'upaya.' Everything, even when death happens, let it become an 'upaya,' a situation to grow. It is happening whether you use it or not, so why not use it? Just accept it, and by your acceptance, she will also be helped.*

\*Ibid, pp 240 - 242.

----------------

When Bhagwan finishes speaking with the last sannyasin, musicians of the Ashram Music Group move to the center of the auditorium. The dark green lushness of the surrounding garden creates a delicate contrast to the twinkling lights illuminating the spacious area. Seated in a close circle, the musicians begin to play and slowly, with flutes, tablas, and sitars they build the tempo. We sannyasins draw in closer, leaving Bhagwan to look on the scene we spontaneously create. At first we simply lift our arms and sway while still seated, but as the music gathers strength we stand and allow our bodies to be absorbed in movement. Weaving in and around one another, we flow into a joyful dance of light and movement.

At first, I am the dancer, but beginning to soar, I melt into dance, my new name coming to me. Although still in a physical body, I'm more a presence than a physical self. As if I've become one with Love Itself—love for the existence cradling me—I float in a dreamlike space of bliss. Together we sannyasins dance for joy, for life, and for death.

The commentary on the dance following darshan that evening concludes with the reference to the dying wife of the one sannyasin.

*It seemed a beautiful and appropriate farewell for a sannyasin, and a demonstration of the acceptance of death as part of life—as not something somber and sobering, but as an event to be heralded and celebrated as festively, as joyfully, as life itself.*

* Ibid, pp 245.

---------

My given name—Peter—which has both Greek and Hebrew origins meaning "rock" or "hard place," describes the way I have been living—resistant, unyielding, firm, solid, and, yes, serious. *(Years later another Indian mystic observed "Peter" had been a destructive name, but Nartan introduces a sense of flow, movement, and dance.)* Bhagwan is helping the rock learn to dance. This new direction is natural and clear, familiar in a vague and distant way, a reminder of something long ago forgotten. In darshan I felt far away from this new path, and yet I long to pursue it.

A few days later in discourse, Bhagwan again speaks about seriousness, clearly distinguishing it from sincerity, a distinction that reinforces his message to me. I had always thought of sincerity and seriousness as synonymous, but he says they are opposites. Seriousness, he explains, is pathological, an illness of the mind, and the greatest disease or dis-ease. Jesus was always sincere but never serious. Although we link these two attitudes in the modern world, they cannot go together. A serious person can never be sincere because sincerity comes from the heart, while seriousness comes from the mind. A person can be one or the other, but not both.

Previously I had equated honesty, authenticity, and sincerity in a person with being serious, while judging one who is not serious to be lacking sincerity. But Bhagwan contradicts this thinking, contending it is backwards. Have I—Peter the oh-so-serious, Peter the Rock—been living my life backwards?

People experience many coincidences around Bhagwan and tend to seek meanings. Such a coincidence—one referring back to my darshan—occurs a few weeks later. Although I depart Poona August 24, my photograph appears in *The Passion for the Impossible, A Darshan Diary,* for darshan on Friday evening, September 3, 1976. Upon discovering this apparent mix-up, I read the transcription and learn Bhagwan was again talking to the same sannyasin whose wife had been critically ill the evening of my darshan. A few days later (the night before this entry), she died.

*(The irony of appearing in this darshan only became apparent when learning of my illness, said to be terminal, three and a half years later.)*

Following are Bhagwan's words:

*\* Bhagwan: Mm, so (she) has left? Very good. She left in a good state. She was not fighting at all. She accepted and surrendered—and the greatest surrender is the surrender to death....*

*But one thing—meditate, because this moment will be of significance for you. Whenever somebody dies, somebody you have been intimately related to, someone with whom you have been very intimate, somebody with whom you have been happy and unhappy, sad and angry, somebody with whom you have known all the seasons of life and somebody who has somehow become a part of you and you have become a part of him or her—when somebody like that dies, it is not only a death that occurs outside, it is a death that occurs inside also. (She) was holding a part of your being, so when she dies, that part of your being also dies. She was fulfilling something in you. She disappears and wounds are left.*

*We have many holes in our being. Because of those holes we seek the company of the other, the love of the other. By the other's presence we somehow manage to fill those holes. When the other disappears, those holes are again there—yawning abysses opening. You may have forgotten about them, but you will feel them and the pain. So use these moments for a deep meditation because sooner or later those holes will be filled again. These holes will disappear. Before it happens, it is good to enter those holes, to enter that emptiness that (she) will leave behind her.*

*So use these moments. Sit silently, close your eyes, go inside. And just see what has happened. Don't think about the future, don't think about the past. Don't think about the memories because that is futile. Just go in. What has happened to you? (She) is dead—now what has happened to you? What is happening to you? Just go into that process. That will reveal many things in you. You will be completely transformed if you can penetrate those holes. You will not try to fill them again, but still you can love.*

*One can love without in any way taking the other inside and fulfilling some deep need there. One can love as a luxury—because one has to share, and one wants to share. Then love is no more a need. You're not hiding your wounds behind it.*

*So go into these wounds, go into this emptiness, go into this absence, and watch—that's one thing. The second thing: remember that life is really fleeting, slipping by...so momentary. We live in a magic world. We go on deluding ourselves. Again and again the delusion drops. Again and again the reality erupts. Again and again when somebody dies you are reminded that life is not reliable, that one should not depend too much on life. One moment it is there, another moment it is gone. It is a soap bubble—just a small prick and it is gone. In fact, the more you understand life, the more full of wonder you are about how it exists. Then death is not the problem; life becomes the problem. Death seems natural.*

*It is a miracle that life exists—such a temporary thing, such a momentary thing. And not only does it exist—people trust it. People depend on it, people rely on it. They put their whole being at its feet—and it is just an illusion, a dream. Any moment it is gone and one is left crying.*

*With it is gone the whole effort, the whole sacrifice that you made for it. Suddenly everything disappears. So watch this...this momentary dream-like illusory life.*

*And death is coming to everybody. We are all standing in the queue, and the queue is continuously coming closer to death. (She) disappears; the queue is a little less. She had made space for one person more. Every person dying brings you closer to your own death, so every death is basically your death. In every death one is dying and coming closer to the full stop. Before it happens, one has to become as much aware as possible.*

*If we trust life too much, we tend to become unconscious. If we start doubting life—this so-called life which always ends in death—then we become more aware. And in that awareness, a new sort of life starts; its doors open. The life which is deathless, the life which is eternal, the life which is beyond time.*

\* *The Passion for the Impossible, A Darshan Diary* by Bhagwan Shree Rajneesh; copyright 1978 by Rajneesh Foundation; published by Ma Yoga Laxmi, Rajneesh Foundation, 17 Koregaon Park, Poona 411-001, India; pp 222 - 225.

------------

This passage—one I have read many times—is a message of great personal significance, because only a few years later I find myself face to face with impending death. Death, if received with acceptance and awareness, can be a tremendous opportunity for growth. By going into it through meditation, I have seen into that new life beyond death and beyond time. But before it's time for me to face death, perhaps I should learn to dance with life.

[August 13, 1976, Poona, age 35] Receiving sannyas at darshan with Bhagwan

# 36
## Authentic Actor

*8/76, Age 35*

During the next several days I delight in my new identity, using every opportunity to allow the dance to come forth and dispel the deeply rooted seriousness. Henceforth life will be a celebration while the tension and tightness in my shoulders and chest begin to release their hold. As I go deeper into daily meditations, the recurring thoughts that continuously run through my head gradually cease.

After a week I request another darshan to ask Bhagwan how to live as a manager and householder back home. At the ashram I'm honest and authentic—open, free, spontaneous, relaxed, and gentle, but in the West such behavior would not be understood. The following exchange takes place at darshan, as recorded in *Dance your Way to God, A Darshan Diary:*

*Thursday, August 19, 1976*

*Bhagwan: Nartan, what about you?*

*Nartan (an American sannyasin): I feel so serene and floating Bhagwan, but I do have one question...it's about authenticity. I want to be authentic. And I'm not.*

*Bhagwan: That is what authenticity is.*

*Nartan: Everything I've done in my life has been absolutely successful. I've got a lot of money, I've got a good education, I'm good in sports, I've always been capable. But to be this way I've always had to say the things that were expected of me, to do the things that were expected of me. Now I don't want to do that anymore. If you asked me a question and I didn't know the answer, I would say what I thought you wanted to hear. Here I've been able to open...*

*Bhagwan: I know. You have opened. I have seen you opening.*

*Nartan: But I'm going back within two weeks. I'm president of a small company in Germany, and to be effective, I've got to be distant with people. I've got to be judgmental, decisive. I can't float and I can't love.*

*Bhagwan: It is not so difficult.*

*Nartan: So can I forget you and go back to that?*

*Bhagwan: No, no. There is no need to forget me. Remember me. Go there, and whatsoever you have been doing, continue to do; don't change it at all. The change has to be made in the attitude, not in the work. Up to now you were thinking that it was life. From now on think of it as acting; that's the only change. Go on saying the same things you were saying to people before; whatsoever they expect, go on saying. Do it even more nicely and beautifully because it is just acting. To be authentic does not mean that you have to be rude to people. To be authentic does not mean that you have to be ugly and rude in the marketplace. To be authentic simply means that you know what is acting and what is real...that you are not deceived by your acting, that's all.*

*So don't be deceived by your acting. Do it deliberately—don't do it unconsciously. Up to now you have been doing it unconsciously because you were thinking this is life. Now you know that this is not life.*

*So live in your inner world and for the outside.... For example, when you are talking to children, you talk in their language. It is not inauthentic. It is simply a consideration—that they are children and they will not understand any other language. If you go to a child, you take a toy to him as a gift. You don't take a very serious book to give him. You take a pictorial book that he can enjoy. It is a consideration.*

*When you are working in the world, you have to consider a thousand and one things. Nothing is wrong in that. Just be an actor and think of the world as a big drama. It is a very big stage where everybody is playing roles.*

*When you go to Germany and you start working and you smile when somebody comes—you receive him and you smile—do it deliberately, do it perfectly, because when one is doing it deliberately, one can do it more perfectly than ever. Really give him a good smile—as he never had before. When you are giving it and it is just a smile, why be miserly? And you know that it is not coming from the heart, but who is saying that it should come from the heart? All smiles are not needed from the heart. Knowing that it is just on the lips, make it as perfect as possible.*

*That person is not here to see your heart. The face is enough for him. So what is the point of putting your heart on the table before him? Do it deliberately, so that when you are putting your heart before somebody, you know that it is true, the authentic. It is no more part of the business world. You are not smiling as a commodity. And you will know— you have to know what is acting and what is real. When the real is needed, be real. When acting is needed, act. And there is no need to be confused, otherwise you will miss your whole life.*

*I am not here to mess up anybody's life. I am only here to help you to become more skillful. If you are a thief, I say do it with full awareness and consciousness. If your awareness changes it, I am not responsible for it. If by awareness you cannot remain a thief, it is for you to choose. Just choose awareness or choose your old way of sleep. But I am not here to say don't be a thief. Who am I? Why should I?*

*I am simply saying one thing—be aware. And when you become aware, many things which are really harmful will drop. And many things which are just politeness, mannerisms, which are not harmful at all...In fact they are very helpful. They function as a lubricating agent, otherwise you will be struggling with everybody and life will become just a constant war.*

*You have walked on somebody's toe and you say, 'Sorry.' You don't mean it—not even a single thought has crossed your mind of being sorry. You simply say, 'Sorry.' It is lubricating. He also knows that because he himself is doing the same. But where so many people are walking on each other's toes, a few mannerisms will be needed. You are not alone. And it is good to learn the mannerisms—but do it deliberately.*

*Act authentically—that's what I would like to say to you. When acting, act authentically, that's all. Good, Nartan.*

*\*Op. Cit., pp 345 - 348.*

-----------

This understanding strikes like a thunderbolt. I want to behave in a natural and honest way; however, to be successful and achieve goals, I do and say things that go against feelings. Now Bhagwan is giving me this simple insight. Bring awareness to what I do and recognize it's necessary to be inauthentic on occasion. Nothing is wrong with being inauthentic, which is often expected and accepted as being proper; to be otherwise creates unnecessary complications. One can be authentically inauthentic without thinking this is the way one really is. Much of this expected behavior is only a lubricant to make things go smoothly and avoid the waste of energy on unimportant concerns. What truly matters is not what one does, but the attitude and awareness one brings to the act. I can continue to behave like the "rock" but know that's not who I really am. I am the "dance" who, when helpful, retains the disguise of the "rock."

Seeing us as being asleep, Bhagwan tries to awaken us into recognizing we are enlightened beings. His techniques are the meditations and therapy groups, many of which are adaptations of Western ideas from the Human Potential Growth Movement. These techniques include catharting, witnessing, meditating, remembering, or just re-experiencing—practices useful for bringing to the surface deeply hidden feelings, repressions, and psychotic activity just below the level of awareness.

Therapists from around the world are here to lead or participate in groups such as Dehypnotherapy, Primal, Centering, Body Awareness, Rolfing, Rebalancing, Rebirthing, and more. Other offerings include

Eastern meditation-based techniques such as Vipassana, Kyo, Tantra, Zazen, and Prarthana. In addition, Bhagwan has created his own therapies with names like Tao, Enlightenment Intensive, Turning In, Awareness and Expression, and Tathata.

Because my previous experience with therapy groups is limited to a T-Group at Stanford that focused upon mannerisms in interpersonal relations, I'm unprepared for the deep psychology incorporated into my first therapy group here, Enlightenment Intensive. The therapist takes me back to childhood to relive never-completed experiences that linger in my subconscious. A deep sense of guilt arises because my untimely birth forced my father to drop out of college (temporarily) and my mother to forego her college education. I attribute my academic, athletic, and scouting success to a motivation to show I was worthy despite my disruptions to my parents' lives. As an undersized, red-haired, freckle-faced kid, I was subjected to teasing and derision that left me feeling helpless and inadequate. In slow, painful steps, through reliving such experiences, clarity gradually breaks through. I cathart. I cry. Anger erupts. Deep fears rise up. And I begin to understand many blockages in my life. But this therapy—in fact, this entire trip to Poona—is only a small step, the initiation of what will be a gradual process of getting in touch with things deep inside. Yes, things within have been stirred up. Now I must decide where to go from here.

These thoughts I express to Bhagwan, and the darshan transcription is published in *The Passion for the Impossible, A Darshan Diary.*

*\*Tuesday, August 24, 1976*

*Bhagwan: Nartan, do you have something to say?*

*Nartan: Well, I'm leaving tonight. I've been here two weeks, and I'm spinning. I'm going to digest this all—see if it works in the outside world.*

*The group (Enlightenment Intensive) was just terribly meaningful for me. I learned an awful lot of things about myself which have been rattling about inside and which I feel I got a little understanding for.*

*I do have one question. It deals with the concept of challenges. I've always spent my life seeking out challenges—dealing with them, usually mastering them, and going on to something else, another challenge.*

*I'm hearing two things from you. One is, that perhaps I'm just feeding my ego. On the other hand, in the past week you've been talking about life as a challenge, as a difficult challenge, and that we must really go into it. I do want to continue to seek out challenges. Can you help me to understand this?*

*Bhagwan: Both are the possibilities. One can just go on seeking challenges because it enhances the ego. Then the motive is wrong. What you are doing is right, but the reason you are doing it is wrong. If you simply love challenges and it is not in any way an effort to enhance the ego, then it is tremendously beautiful. Then whatsoever you are doing is right, and the motive is also right. Then you are one thousand per cent right. So just watch that—that's what I am saying.*

*Don't gather the ego. Go on finding new challenges, enjoy, but there is no need to collect the ego, to feed an ego, because if you are feeding an ego, then in fact you will not be able to enjoy the challenges; they become secondary. The purity is lost then; you are always hankering for the ego. You are not interested in challenges—you are interested in the ego. If the ego can be purchased at a cheaper cost, you would like to purchase it. If the ego is possible without the challenges, you will drop the challenges and you will choose the ego. Because it is impossible to become egoistic without challenges, you have to go into the challenges, but you are not enjoying them. Then you are missing the whole point of it. Otherwise it is tremendously beautiful.*

*Every moment there are new challenges. If we seek, we will find them. And it is thrilling to live continuously from challenge to challenge, from one peak to another. The higher you rise, the higher the peaks that become available, and you don't carry any burden of the ego. Then even if you fail in a challenge, you are not miserable. You are still happy that you accepted it. You are still happy that the opportunity was there. You are still happy that you went into it. If you succeed, there is no ego in it. You are simply thrilled, and you are ready to move ahead.*

*For a real lover of challenges, success and failure mean nothing. The whole value is in the challenge and the response, and the thrill that comes between crucial moments when on this side is death and on that side is life. The bridge is so narrow, just like a razor's edge. One false step and you fall into an infinite abyss. Then one lives at the peak of consciousness.*

*That's the beauty in mountaineering. Nothing is going to be achieved but the very thrill. That is the enjoyment in surfing; nothing is going to be achieved but the very thrill. That is the enjoyment when you go on driving your car faster and faster and faster. A moment comes when each moment is a risk...as if time stops, thinking stops. You are just going one hundred miles per hour. A slight this way and that (Bhagwan makes a movement with his hand, of a car veering to one side) and you are gone. Then you cannot afford to be sleepy. You are fully awake—every fiber of the body feels so beautiful in speed. But it has nothing to do with the ego. So enjoy.*

*The whole life is an adventure—it should be an adventure. But there is no need to gather the ego, because that becomes the burden. It won't allow you to go to very high peaks, because for the high peaks you have to leave all the burden behind, below you. You have to go almost naked without clothes. The higher the peak, the greater is the requirement to leave everything down below. You cannot carry much load—and the ego is the greatest load one can carry, and for no reason at all. It is as if you are carrying a mountain on your head. That crushes you. Life never crushes anybody—only the ego. And then when you succeed, you don't enjoy.*

*If an egoist succeeds, he never enjoys. If he fails, he fails very miserably, because the ego goes on goading. It says, 'What is this? You have to achieve more. You have to show more to the world. This is nothing.' The ego never allows you rest. It says, 'It's okay, but go higher, go ahead, do something bigger.' So when you achieve, it is not happy. If you fail, it is terribly unhappy. And an egoless person, when he succeeds, he's happy, he dances. When he fails, still he dances—because it is not a question of achievement or failure. It is a question of trying, it is a question of living in critical moments, in dangerous moments. It is the thrill that is valuable.*

*So there is nothing to be worried about. Just go on accepting challenges. And I am nothing but a challenge to you. I am creating something in you which will become your very life's challenge. And this mountain is such that you cannot exhaust it. By the time you reach the peak, you are no more, because the only way to reach this peak is to disappear. That's why I call religion the passion for the impossible. It is a passion for the impossible. The impossible happens—that too is true—but it happens only when you have disappeared.*

*So go into the world. Try whatsoever has happened to you. It will be deepened. Because this is my observation—that if something has really happened, then it goes on deepening by all life experiences. If it has not happened, then only it disappears. Good, Nartan.*

*Op. Cit., pp 46 - 51.

-------

Whenever Bhagwan answers a question, his response is intended only for that questioner. The question I ask, had it come from anyone else, would have evoked a different reply, so one can't read through the questions others have asked and expect to find an answer. Bhagwan's references to surfing and mountain climbing, two activities I enjoy immensely, are not coincidental. His last two words, "Good, Nartan," confirms these words, conveyed in a loving, non-judging way, are clearly meant for me.

When making my opening comment about wanting to try out what I had learned to "see if it works in the outside world," I suddenly regret this statement because by thinking practically, I am outer-world directed. But at the end of Bhagwan's comments, when he encourages me to "go into the world" and "try whatsoever has happened to you," a surge of joy rushes through me—joy that I will be going back to Germany and observing what will happen in my old world. Continuing to take on challenges, Bhagwan explains, is okay. Again, he makes the point that what matters is not what one does, but the attitude one brings to an activity. A greater sendoff I couldn't have asked for. *(A final gift, although I didn't know at the time, was that titles of both darshan diaries, "Dance your Way to God" and "Passion for the Impossible," were taken from the transcriptions of my two darshans.)*

My final words to Bhagwan are that I purchased 40 books and almost 100 taped discourses to keep contact with him. He smiles and says that I should create a meditation center in Hamburg. He gives the name of *Su Buddha* for the center which means "Well Aware." I laugh and ask if he's making me do something I don't want to do. He laughs also and says it's impossible to make anyone do anything he doesn't want. I leave in a state of happy confusion.

When I depart Poona later that evening, my heart is dancing, my head is dancing, my entire being is dancing. The rock is softening, beginning to crumble. In its place arises the dance. Authentic actor on the outside; creative dancer on the inside.

# 37
# Double Life

*8/76 - 9/77, Ages 35 - 36*

When I return to Hamburg charged with energy from the ashram, Barbara hardly recognizes me. I feel quiet and peaceful. Everything around me takes on heightened beauty and significance because now I see the world in a new light. As for Barbara, after listening to tapes of Bhagwan's discourses and reading his books while I was away, she also feels an attraction and is anxious to meet him. For the next week we enjoy our time together before I leave for New York to join my family.

When I meet Mary, Cyrena, and Liane in Quogue for a week's vacation, I'm amazed how much the girls have grown. They babble about all they have discovered during two months in America—television in English, hamburgers, corn-on-the-cob, ketchup, and peppermint ice cream. Unable to believe I really know about these things, they insist I try each to be sure. And they marvel that people everywhere speak English; in Hamburg only those few we know speak our language.

The girls, ages five and two, jump into all the fun activities I knew as a kid in this summer paradise where four generations of Schroeders have vacationed. I teach them to net little crabs that scurry under the yacht club pier. We have a rowing lesson which is tremendous fun, in spite of—or perhaps because of—being totally unsuccessful. When we launch a small pram for a sailing lesson, instead of looking up at the sail and tell-tales, the girls look into the water at the red and white jellyfish. "What happens if we fall in and get stung?" they worry.

One day we catch a horseshoe crab, and, despite my coaxing and reassurance, they refuse to touch it. Even when I hold it to my face and allow its slimy feelers and giant claws to explore my nose and ears, they remain unconvinced and keep a safe distance.

Any hesitation Cyrena and Liane have concerning the bay disappears when we go to the beach club. Although the breaking waves are two to three times taller than they are, they love to run and plunge into them. Only after being rolled by surging undercurrents do they become cautious.

After a typical day of sailing, fishing, crabbing, and swimming, we beeline to Al's, the village drugstore, to scarf vanilla fudge ice cream cones with chocolate topping—the same treat I enjoyed a generation earlier.

Although Mary has been to Quogue many times, she experiences it in a new way by observing how I introduce our daughters to its joys. She has never seen me so joyful, serene, overflowing with love, and relaxed. She is now consumed with an intense desire to go to Poona right away and considers breaking her teaching contract in Hamburg, but after weighing the logistic complications she decides against leaving so soon. Her yearning doesn't diminish during the school year, however, as she counts the days until she can go.

Following our vacation we return to Hamburg where our lives settle into a pleasant rhythm. Mornings I head off to my new job with Schlegel Engineering, and Mary takes the girls to school where Cyrena starts first grade and Liane returns to nursery school. Weekends we sail in Denmark until days shorten and then confine ourselves to activities closer to home.

On bicycles mounted with children's seats we search for trails to ride around Hamburg. One of two favorite trips is Clovensteen, an enormous forest preserve with a children's zoo, riding stables, and a rustic outdoor *gasthaus* where we load up on sweets at teatime. We discover new bike paths every visit, and each leads deeper into the pristine forest. Just as we think we're lost, we spy signs pointing the way back to the village.

The other favorite outing is to pedal down the steep hill behind our house to the boat landing on the Elbe River, then ferry across to *Altes Land*, a farming area of reclaimed fertile marshland that is the biggest fruit-producing region of North Europe. From there we bike to quaint villages—Stade, Buxtehude, Neuenfelde—where we load pears, peaches, apples, and cherries atop the girls in their seats. The best part of these trips is coming home to roast marshmallows in the fireplace. I often carry an empty suitcase to Rochester to replenish these white delicacies as well as pancake mix and maple syrup, which are not available in Germany. Any extra luggage space is likely to be crammed with dresses and shoes for Cyrena and Liane.

At Christmas I shut the plant for three weeks and take the family skiing at St. Anton in Austria. Because Cyrena is old enough to handle any slope with ease, we check Liane into daycare while we three explore the mountain. We celebrate Christmas Eve in this Tyrolean village by indulging in the time honored dinner of roast goose accompanied with Gluhwein followed by Lebkuchen and Sacher-Torte before stepping outdoors to watch the traditional fireworks display. Next day we return to Hamburg and one day later celebrate my 36th birthday.

This particularly cold winter is the only year locals remember the city's two lakes, *Binnenalster* and *Ausseralster*, freezing. After cleaning rust off the blades of ice skates we brought from the States, we join in the fun of ice skating in the heart of Hamburg.

We welcome 1977 with a quiet dinner at home before I'm off again to the States to report on the new company. Because meetings are likely to be confrontational due to massive ongoing losses, I need a few days to prepare a presentation for turning around the company and to brace myself for the storm likely to ensue. Presenting turnaround strategies will be a tough challenge because my proposal will be as distasteful to corporate staff as it will be later to the Germans. Years earlier I had presented an equally complicated plan for the first German company.

Despite resistance, the plan was approved and proved successful; I hope to get similar endorsement a second time.

At difficult times like this I find solace by the sea, so I take a few days of vacation and route the trip through the British Virgin Islands, my favorite cruising area, and sign on as crew on a 36-foot sloop sailing charter. Upon arrival in Rochester a week later, I'm rested and relaxed with copper-bronze skin—not a good look to negotiate with mid-winter, pale-white, corporate staffers.

With Schlegel Engineering in financial trouble, why did I take a ski vacation in Austria followed by a Caribbean sailing holiday? Feeling defensive, I explain: Because the manufacturing process requires three-shift operation seven days a week, the German plant cannot operate efficiently through the yearend holidays. German law requires that employees take five weeks of vacation; by closing three weeks in winter the company is down only two weeks in summer, peak season for the construction industry when installation crews must be at full strength. Because Americans typically get only two weeks of vacation, this explanation doesn't evoke much sympathy.

As anticipated, corporate colleagues receive my turnaround plan with protests and resistance. They want me to stick with many small contracts throughout Western Europe, whereas I propose seeking large projects anywhere in the world to utilize the advantage of our enormous sheets that are best suited to line large basins. For three days I face attacks from Chairman Dick Turner and several vice presidents but eventually win approval. Dick doesn't necessarily believe in the plan, but he believes in me and therefore gives his okay to proceed. He allows our operations additional autonomy by granting my request to make decisions locally that previously had to be referred to corporate. Dick makes his concerns clear, however, with a veiled threat that I'd better not be wrong. Recalling Bhagwan's guidance to be an authentic actor, I smile and assure him everything will be fine. Disturbed that the meetings were difficult and the corporate staff so adversarial, I realize that moving back to Rochester, as Dick had previously suggested, would be a mistake. Determined to make Schlegel Sheet a profitable business, I anticipate that afterward I will need to leave Schlegel.

In recognition for achieving success with the other German company, I receive a generous bonus of company stock plus options to purchase additional shares. Thanks to a company loan, I exercise the options thereby showing confidence in the turnaround plan. Next to the board chairman, I have become the largest employee shareholder. Now to buckle down and get this company moving!

Returning home, I learn that Barbara plans to join her sister Ehrengard for a two-week ski holiday in Austria. Because I have not seen much of Barbara since returning from India, with an unclear conscience I take a third vacation within six weeks and join them. We meet at Solden near where I had mountain climbed two summers ago.

In addition to the joy of seeing Barbara again, the first day on the slopes brings a wonderful surprise. When we get off the chairlift at the top of the mountain, I select an intermediate trail and push off. Pulling up a few minutes later to wait for her, I hear scraping in the snow as another skier immediately stops nearby. Looking back, I'm startled when I see it is Barbara. After exchanging a few words, I lead off with a series of tight parallel turns for double the distance. Stopping again and hearing another skier directly behind, this time I'm prepared to see Barbara's smiling face.

Next, I suggest an expert run and ask if she wants to lead. When she hesitates, I head straight down the fall line with her right behind. Glancing back without stopping, I see Barbara following my tracks and executing turns with the grace of a dancer. Now the mountain is ours, and for the rest of the day we ski every trail we can find. Clearly this ski area is not challenging enough, and in days that follow we explore others—Obergurgl, Leck, St. Christoph, St. Anton, and Zurs—all the while our relationship deepening.

After four days it's time to return to work and implement changes. Correcting attitudes is top priority because employees had been lulled into thinking the plastic sheet will soon inevitably become a commercial success. My predecessor, Heiner Hammer, had not told them about the precarious financial situation and bleak sales outlook; they had accepted the dream that Heiner created and have been awaiting the upturn.

Now it's time to make my move. To reduce costs, I slash staff from 60 to 35 and terminate all agency and distributor agreements. Next step is elimination of superfluous equipment and expenses including teleprinters, graphic transmission equipment, luxury phone systems, extra photocopy machines, and duplicate telex machines. Those employees who are left are in a daze and company morale sinks. I let them remain in this state a few days to ensure the previous feeling of easy success is dispelled. Then I inform the remaining core of engineers, machinists, technicians, and office staff that they will no longer be micromanaged and will have full authority to make their own decisions.

Next, I do something practically unheard of in a German company—I open the financial books for everyone to see. Almost every contract has lost money due to the need for constant repairs and modifications. Furthermore, the level of business is not close to covering costs. Customers are not happy, expenses are too high, and the order backlog is practically nil.

Calling a company meeting, I explain that we don't yet have a marketable product. We are pioneering (1) a new market for waste-basin liners, (2) a new product with plastic sheeting, (3) a new high-density polyethylene polymer, and (4) a new technology to produce and weld giant sheets. Many new companies have trouble overcoming only one of these four areas, but we're trying to perform them all at once. Dick Turner has given support for our future direction, and now it's up to us to build a successful business.

The American spirit of entrepreneurship is lacking in the German business world. The equivalent German word for entrepreneur, *Unternehmer*, actually has negative connotations. German employees typically prefer security and aren't comfortable dealing with risks—they'd rather work in a big, well-established company like Siemens or Volkswagen. Because such workers won't meet Schlegel's challenges, my speech should scare the employees away, but I'm pleasantly surprised that no one quits. Afterward, to show confidence in them, I give across-the-board seven percent salary increases.

The next phase of the turnaround is to close the offices that are spread in different parts of an old building in a deteriorating area of Hamburg. Communication among employees is difficult, something the previous manager used to his advantage by forcing all decisions to come through him. A simple solution is immediately at hand. Four years earlier, we constructed three floors in the new administration building for Schlegel GmbH, although only two floors are occupied. Finishing the interior of the third level allows us to move Schlegel Sheet operations into the same building. Not only do new offices offer a modern environment that eases communications, but they incur no rental expense. Vacating the old building and moving to this site heralds a new beginning.

Once the internal problems are straightened out, it's time to look outside. Many liner installations have failed, and clients are threatening to sue. Director Hammer created delays and avoided these responsibilities. After snows melt in early April, I dispatch installation crews to replace or repair earlier work. This undertaking isn't just to placate angry customers but also to train crews to avoid future technical problems. Moreover, it builds goodwill with former clients who now become favorable references. After clearing away these old problems, company morale improves significantly. When asked by potential clients about previous problems, the marketing staff can explain they have all been corrected.

One problem from the past, though, seems insurmountable. In the mountains of southern Iran, Schlegel Engineering had installed a liner for a water reservoir at the world's largest copper mine. The Sar Chesmeh facility is a prestigious development that the Shah of Iran has been following with personal interest. Because water is essential for processing copper ore, a pipeline had been built from Bandar Abbas on the Persian Gulf to deliver water more than 300 miles across the desert up to this reservoir. Owned by the Iranian Government, the mine is operated by U.S.-based Anaconda Copper Company with a French contractor and a British consulting firm overseeing this complex project.

From the beginning everything had gone wrong: Authorities at a port in Turkey impounded the ship carrying the Schlegel Sheet and welding equipment enroute from Hamburg to Iran; Iranian custom officials had delayed the crew's entry into the country; installation went badly;

coordination with interface organizations had not been well planned; and the sheet started to crack shortly after being installed. The situation had improved when our site engineer made repairs, but then luck turned against us again. When an earth slide occurred under the basin liner, the entire reservoir had failed presumably due to water leaking through the initial cracks in the sheet. Iranian officials want Schlegel to rebuild the reservoir including the earthworks, a multi-million-dollar expense. Heiner Hammer had visited the site and infuriated our partners by refusing to take responsibility.

The next step is up to me. I travel to Tehran to meet Mr. Tavakkoli, the government minister in charge of the project, and we become friendly when he chats about his years earning an engineering degree at University of Nebraska where he played varsity football. After establishing this agreeable relationship, I travel to Sar Chesmah and work my way through the cast of British, French, Iranian, and American nationals in an endless series of meetings. They are relieved that, compared to the obstinate, fulminating Hammer, I seem to be reasonable. Finally, we come to a solution whereby Schlegel will complete the job with a reasonable profit— my main objective. And the Iranians will save face—their main objective. Schlegel's field crews return to Iran later that summer and finish installation to everyone's satisfaction.

Back in Europe the market for lining waste basins is increasing rapidly because of well-publicized disasters related to ground water pollution from industrial waste. The Rhine, as well as most other rivers in Europe, has become an industrial cesspool, and court cases against polluters begin to multiply. After laboratory testing confirms our high-density polyethylene sheet is chemically resistant to virtually all industrial wastes, Schlegel Sheet becomes the top choice over all other lining materials.

Sales teams travel to Europe's largest chemical and industrial firms to offer design assistance for building waste basins as an alternative to releasing effluent into the environment. The strategy is successful, and contracts begin to come our way. One unexpected problem, however, is that many clients require anonymity, which prevents using them as references. As an example, we built the largest solid waste basin in Europe for the giant chemical firm, Bayer AG, in Leverkusen on the Rhine River where they had been dumping waste for decades. This project would be a great advertisement, but terms of the contract specify nothing is to be used for promotions or references. Bayer is concerned that if the world learns they have been producing so much waste, they might face claims for environmental damage.

As business grows, I open offices in France and England. After an accident at a chemical plant near Naples contaminates several square miles, we start developing business in Italy. Our sales people find interest in Schlegel Sheet wherever they go; however, markets are slow to develop. Everyone agrees waste basins are required and need to be lined with Schlegel Sheet, but private companies are reluctant to make a major investment with no return, and public agencies have no money. Until local municipalities pass legislation forcing polluters to clean up, or until enough political pressure makes government agencies invest in municipal and regional disposal basins, only a limited market exists.

As construction season continues, installation crews work on several smaller contracts, but there's not enough business to sustain operations and cover expenses. Because the American Schlegel Sheet company, which had been set up some years earlier in Rochester to market in North and South America, has had no success, Chairman Turner removes the president and gives me responsibility to run both companies. I suspect Turner has another motive—to entice me back to Rochester, as he has suggested several times during the past year. Because this organizational change requires a world view of area-sealing markets, for the next year I commute practically monthly between Rochester and Hamburg.

On the job I play the hard-driving manager and remain the actor, but at home I get in touch with how I really feel. Relaxed, comfortable, and at ease, I dote upon my daughters. At the end of May, Mary makes final plans for a three-week trip to Poona by arranging for a young Portuguese girl to take care of the girls during the day, leaving me to attend to them at night and on weekends. On the last day of school Mary finishes early and flies to India.

Three weeks pass quickly and just when we expect Mary to return, we receive a telegram saying she intends to stay another three weeks and will come home the middle of July. The attraction must be strong for her to stay away, and I'm glad she apparently has found something special. But the Portuguese au pair must return home, leaving me to care full time for Cyrena and Liane. Fortunately, neighbors offer to pick them up after school and stay with them until I come home in the evening.

Until now I have kept the children separate from Barbara, but with Mary away longer than expected, life might be simpler if I bring them together. Barbara agrees, so one Saturday afternoon I take the girls for a walk in nearby *Hirschpark* where they love to see the miniature deer and wander through the gardens. After a bit of romping, I suggest we rest on a park bench in a secluded area. Because a young woman is already sitting on the bench that's too small to accommodate the three of us, I suggest to Liane that she inquire if she could sit on the woman's lap. With no hesitation she asks, and that's how the girls meet Barbara. They are delighted she speaks English because they tend to be lazy about speaking German. Barbara enchants them with songs, stories, and acrobatics. As the afternoon wanes, Cyrena adds an unexpected touch to our plan by asking if Barbara can come for dinner, and everyone agrees this would be fun. At home the girls take Barbara by the hand and show her their rooms and their dolls while I grill steaks. The evening stretches into the late hours with everyone happy.

Next evening, we go to Barbara's apartment for dinner where we enjoy a repeat of the previous night's fun. When the girls insist the floor isn't too hard to sleep on, we spend the night. In no time Barbara becomes the temporary mother and the girls adore her. The following weekend I charter a boat in Denmark, and the girls eagerly show Barbara how much they know about sailing. Soon Barbara, who alternates morning and night shifts weekly at work, is spending all of her free time with us.

After Mary's telegram arrives later in July informing that she's again postponing her return, the four of us spend the rest of summer hiking, biking, sailing, and enjoying other fun adventures. Shortly before Mary is due to return, I receive a letter that brings a jolt. She's having a powerful experience in Poona and would have liked to stay on. However, she has a teaching contract and therefore plans to return in a week. Writing in glowing terms about experiences at the ashram, she is now a sannyasin and Bhagwan has given her the name *Deva Pashyo*, which means to *Encounter God*. It fits very well she writes.

Throughout her life Mary has thrown herself with intensity into everything she does. As a teacher she had set out with impassioned fervor that bordered on fanaticism to solve problems of disadvantaged Black and Hispanic children. When she learned to snow ski, she immediately went to a steep slope and practically pointed her skis straight downhill. Understanding her behavior, Bhagwan tells her to stop searching, striving, running, performing, and doing. He explains that God is inside her, and she need do nothing more than just encounter that which is within. Sensing this is the right direction, Mary writes that she has surrendered in a way that allows her to relax and let go of the tension that has for so long driven her life.

But here's the jolt in the letter: Mary describes a therapy session during which she learned she self-identified with her hair. People had always admired her hair, and she always took care of it in expectation that others would give her compliments. Because this fixation was blocking her from really seeing herself, she went to a local barber and for one rupee, about 12 cents, had her head shaved. Her decision did not arise from a sense of despair but rather from full emotional awareness. Afterward Mary felt a superficial layer had been stripped away allowing something authentic to emerge. She was thankful to do this within the loving and understanding structure of the ashram. But now that she's returning home, she asks that I explain this change to the girls, so they won't be shocked. When I tell them, they find it perfectly reasonable. After all, wanting to go bald is just another example of the crazy things their parents do!

The following weekend is the last one together with Barbara before Mary returns. Again, we charter in the Baltic and sail among the scattered islands east of Jutland. When we return Sunday evening, Mary has already arrived and is staying with neighbors until we can unlock the house. After taking Barbara home, we pick up Mary. What a wonderful surprise to see her aglow with love and serenity. Her radiance overwhelms us, and her hair has already begun to grow back. Considering women's hair styles are short this summer, the girls and I think she looks very mod. We stay up late listening to her insightful experiences. Happy to be home with the girls, Mary also explains that after another year of teaching, she plans to move permanently to Poona.

She and I soon have a talk, and I'm surprised when she asks for a separation. She has become aware that our marriage has no life and is dragging us both down. Although it offers security, comfort, and convenience, it lacks vitality and love. Furthermore, she's not interested in marriage counseling. She has lost interest in the activities we had enjoyed together—skiing, sailing, tennis, hiking, biking, and just fooling around, and our only real connection is the girls. Realizing we each have a pile of rocks to throw but doing so would only dissipate our energies and have unpleasant consequences for all, we work out during the nights that follow what we agree are reasonable terms. A few weeks later on a trip to Rochester I meet with an attorney who draws up a legal agreement.

Over the past year Barbara has seen wondrous changes in sannyasins who return to Hamburg from Poona and is amazed how I describe the gentleness and centeredness that has come over Mary. The loving way in which Mary and I handle our separation gives testimony to what can happen under the influence of Bhagwan.

In the fall Barbara and I leave for Poona. The installation crew recently completed repairs to the Sar Chesmah basin liner, and I want to inspect it before it is filled. Stopping at Tehran, I leave Barbara with friends from Germany while I go on to the site. The construction engineer is waiting, and we spend two days reviewing details of this trouble-plagued but finally completed project.

*(Although I could not see it at the time, bad luck continues to mar the outcome. Due to delays by another contractor, the government held back our payment and didn't issue the certificate of completion until the following spring. Then, just as it seemed we would receive final payment, rioting broke out which led to deposing the Shah who fled to Paris. The economy, including all work at Sar Chesmah, ground to a halt, and attempts to contact responsible authorities were to no avail. The ayatollahs, who suddenly were in charge, began eliminating all connections*

*to the West and executed many Iranians with whom we had worked. Sadly, this included Mr. Tavakkoli. Expatriates assigned to the project told horror stories about fleeing Iran as the revolution fomented and then exploded into full fury. It was painful for all of us in Hamburg and Rochester to watch as the project, along with the Iranian economy, fell into chaos.*

*Although the government never paid the final invoice, which included our profit, previous partial payments covered all expenses, allowing the firm to at least break even. Most importantly, Schlegel Engineering established an excellent image within the community of international consulting engineers and contractors, an image that would help secure large contracts a year later with Aramco in Saudi Arabia.)*

But just now, at the time of this site visit, everything seems rosy. We finished the project, and everyone is pleased. Schlegel Engineering has created a work of art high in these mountains—a job we are proud of in spite of formidable odds.

On this positive note I join Barbara in Tehran, and we fly the next day to Bombay.

# 38
# Love Play

*10/77 - 11/77, Age 36*

Descending onto the tarmac of Bombay's Santa Cruz Airport, Barbara and I are assaulted by humid, sickly sweet, putrid air. The noontime experience is similar to last year's except then I was lucky to have arrived in the cool of night.

Inside the terminal building the air isn't much better. Scrambling from one fan to the next, Barbara and I negotiate the health check, customs inspection, passport control, baggage claim, and currency exchange. While waiting, I notice fans are positioned toward the authorities and away from those in line. Thinking no one else notices, I reposition one fan to face directly toward us to welcoming cheers; immediately I learn the fans are not oriented haphazardly when several sub-officials rush up to reprimand me and reposition them. Aware that any protest could create further delays, I sheepishly step back into line. Reaching the head of the queue, however, I receive payback by being taken aside, supposedly for not having paperwork in order. The message is clear: The public be damned; we officials will take care of ourselves first.

Hot, sweaty, and tired, Barbara and I emerge from the international terminal intending to walk to the domestic terminal. The instant we step outdoors we pause and want to shrink back to avoid the onslaught of a double impact that hits without mercy. The horrid miasma of Bombay's stagnant swamp waters, open sewers, and rotting piles of organic matter, all enhanced by its ever-present, perspiring, overcrowded populace overwhelms. Overlaying these insufferable odors, the fragrance of sandalwood and other incense, used both as an offering to the deities and as a camouflage for the stench, has little mitigating effect. When we'd first deplaned, we hadn't noticed this stench because the lingering odor of jet fuel obliterated all else. Now we find ourselves almost wishing we could once again breathe those acrid, corrosive fumes to avoid the stink clogging our nostrils.

The second shock is an attack by a swarm of little boys eager to carry suitcases. Having learned on the previous visit the wrong way to handle this situation, now I'm ready. Most arriving passengers make the mistake of politely declining all offers. This response is interpreted by the would-be porters as a sign they must be more persistent and step up their sales pitch. Continuing to decline offers, visitors steadily raise their voices until they're practically raving in an attempt to escape the crowd that follows. To avoid this hassle, I give our bags to the first three boys who approach. Suddenly we are out of the market and no longer swarmed. Because the boys know tips depend upon their care with the suitcases, Barbara and I are assured the bags are secure as we stroll to the check-in counter at the domestic terminal for the flight to Poona.

Landing in Poona in late afternoon, we check into Blue Diamond Hotel, then amble over to the ashram. It's Monday, October 24th, and we'll stay only 12 days. I'm suddenly haunted with possibilities of what might happen during this period. I have made the first step in a new direction in my life—a direction that Bhagwan has shown me—one that feels right. What if Barbara finds the ashram experience abhorrent and rejects it? What if she isn't open and walks away? Wanting her to find something that touches deeply and brings her close to Bhagwan, I understand I must not interfere; she must proceed on her own. If I attempt to force something, I'll create a hindrance between her and this new world I have found. If she goes along just to please me, the experience will be hollow for both of us. I recall Bhagwan's advice to let go of expectations and simply accept whatever happens. If one remains open and drops preconceived notions, judgments, and prejudices, this surrender allows that person to become part of the flow and glow of life. As Barbara and I enter the Gateless Gate reception, I resolve to allow her whatever space she wants while I focus on my own feelings.

The visit this evening is brief. With the addition of more buildings, the ashram has grown in the past year, and the new Buddha Hall is four times larger. Running into sannyasins previously met, I welcome their greeting with exchanges of wordless hugs.

The next morning Barbara and I arrive at six o'clock for Dynamic Meditation—a meditation we had done many times in Hamburg. The one-hour, five-stage meditation, usually done blindfolded, involves deep breathing, catharsis, energy-loosening chanting and jumping, silence, and finally a celebratory dance. The air is pitch black when the meditation begins; when it ends, eyes open to the joy of a beautiful day in this semi-tropical paradise—a pleasant contrast to yesterday's arrival in Bombay.

After the meditation, we wander along garden paths to the canteen for a cup of chai. As the hour for discourse approaches, we settle down in Buddha Hall where it's a shock to see more than 2,000 sannyasins—more than double the number of last year—sitting silently. (Later I learn that sannyasins worldwide have also doubled, increasing from 60,000 to 130,000.)

When Bhagwan appears, I'm overcome by the same loving feeling as before. He glides gracefully up a few steps to his dais, gestures with the traditional Indian Namaste, sits, and after a momentary pause begins a 90-minute extemporaneous outpouring. This English series entitled "I Say Unto You" is about Jesus. Because Christianity is familiar to Westerners, I'm pleased for Barbara's sake. However, Bhagwan soon refutes this thought saying the spiritual tradition called Christianity has nothing to do with Jesus, and the message of Jesus has nothing to do with a tradition. Bhagwan creates a different picture from the one the Christian Church portrays. Rather than speak of a sad, suffering Jesus, Bhagwan focuses on the joy, celebration, and bliss that must have been his very essence.

Noting that the Bible mentions Jesus in only three periods of his life—birth, age 12, and three years of teaching from ages 30 to 33—Bhagwan talks about the period between ages 12 and 30 that Christian scriptures ignore, a period preserved in other ancient writings. He describes travels of Jesus and Thomas to ashrams and monasteries in the East, most notably to Nalanda in northern India, a spiritual center established 2,500 years ago at the time of Buddha and Mahavira, founder of the Jaina religion. Bhagwan supports his comments with references to writings and places that scholars have recorded. He also speaks of Jesus as an initiate at the Essene School of mysticism in Egypt, a connection confirmed by a number of historical Jewish scholars. In contrast to the Western Christian tradition, which suggests Jesus simply worked in his father's carpentry shop for 18 years before experiencing a sudden spiritual awakening, Bhagwan describes someone who was constantly on a spiritual quest. Other traditions describe Jesus' time at monasteries in Kashmir—called the Jewish Land of India, also known as the "Land of Milk and Honey"—experiences that Christian teachings never acknowledge.

My interest is not in this history but in Bhagwan's dual description of Jesus as a meditator who often went off alone into the wilderness as well as a social being who loved to eat, drink, and celebrate with friends—a man bearing no resemblance to the somber, mirthless Jesus I learned about as a boy. Barbara is equally enthralled, and, although Bhagwan tells us not to hang onto his words, we cling a little during this series.

From the onset Barbara is negative about life in the ashram, a usual reaction on a first visit, because it's difficult to understand what seem like peculiar goings-on. Nevertheless, I am not prepared for such a negative reaction and find it frustrating. Even if I were to try to explain what people are doing, what difference would it make considering the extent of her negativity? She judges everything by standards from her own background. But no one in the ashram is here to fulfill expectations of anyone else. People are here to work on their inner selves by getting in touch with something hidden deep within their psyches.

Barbara is bothered by the apparent lack of manners and by seemingly offensive behavior. People walk around as if in a daze. Spaced-out individuals sit silently in the gardens, staring up at trees or gazing straight ahead with unfocused expressions. When two people greet, Barbara is disturbed there is little or no verbal communication; rather there is often a prolonged hug followed by a silent parting as they continue separate ways. Sometimes one greets another only to receive a silent apparent rebuke. Seeing a tearful sannyasin, Barbara is surprised no one takes interest or seems to care about what is the matter. She sees others walking along laughing loudly for no apparent reason. None of these observations fits into her concept of how people should behave in a public setting. One should control oneself and respect civil courtesies. One should relate in a friendly manner. One should....

But this is the point she's missing. Most encounters in daily life beyond the bounds of the ashram adhere to superficial norms of so-called civilized behavior, and people play out expected roles that often run counter to inner feelings. When meeting strangers, we often pigeon-hole them by asking where they come from, what work they do, what family they have, etc. Bhagwan emphasizes the importance of staying in the moment and allowing feelings to flow forth; if one is crying inside, let tears come. No one should interfere by trying to console or commiserate in an effort to make the person happy. Similarly, if laughter is within, even with no apparent cause, let it flow forth—stay in touch with and freely express who you are and how you feel in any moment. There's nothing wrong with authentic expression, and one should respect whatever emotion another is feeling—no need to get involved. Because conventional rules of society teach us to restrain feelings of sorrow, joy, loneliness, love, or anger, we have lost the ability to be in contact with ourselves. In the ashram, people express rather than repress feelings—they flow with what's happening inside. Because Barbara is imposing expectations about how others ought to behave, she doesn't recognize the difficulties are her own.

Barbara's other problems occur in the meditations. Sitting silently with an empty mind is antithetical to the Western concept of "doing something" and is therefore hard to accept. Many techniques, designed to get energy moving and to open locked, dark recesses deep within, can be frightening. After several minutes in Humming Meditation, Barbara, frustrated and unable to see the point, bursts into tears. She's asked to leave the meditation hall so as not to disturb others but is encouraged to stay with her feelings and allow whatever comes up to happen. She leaves and misses the opportunity to discover what is going on within. Distraught, she would have left Poona right then if leaving were an option. But although she hates the meditations and is negative about what she perceives to be the stupid pretense of people around her, one thing keeps her from leaving—Bhagwan. His words each morning touch something deep within and make her realize there's something very valuable here.

For the next week Barbara participates in a limited way in the meditations, attends discourses, enjoys dance activities, and begins to talk with German sannyasins to understand these activities. During this period three things impress her. First, most sannyasins are college graduates, many with post-graduate degrees, and are therefore unlikely to become duped by a con artist. These are intelligent people who find something valuable, and she wants to learn more about them. Second, people don't talk much about where they come from, what work they do, or much of anything related to the past. They are here to be in the moment, and past is not relevant. Third, Bhagwan asks for nothing and makes no demands. He merely speaks about teachings of spiritual masters, philosophers, and other influential thinkers.

After a week, Barbara's negativism subsides and is replaced by confusion. Her eyes slowly open to what is going on. People aren't, as she had thought, just pretending; nor are they spaced out. They are very much in the here-and-now. Becoming more open and receptive, she sheds the blinders of preconceived notions and expectations. What she had at first thought was insensitive behavior toward one another, she now sees as sensitivity toward others and awareness about oneself.

The day Bhagwan speaks about what it means to be a sannyasin is a turning point. Not only the words he speaks, but also the feeling he awakens in her make an impact. First, he emphasizes that each sannyasin has his or her own relationship with him and him alone. We are not meant to establish relationships with each other or think of ourselves as bound into an inseparable community. Second, each person is different and has come to Bhagwan with a different experience. No one should try to relate to experiences of anyone else. Third, being a sannyasin means recognizing your uniqueness and not depending upon others for fulfillment. All that's needed is to relax and accept yourself as you are.

Many behaviors need to be dropped—greed, anger, jealousy, violence, possessiveness, judgment, domination, entitlement, comparison, competition, frustration—and they are summed up in the ego. Only by dropping the ego, which Bhagwan says is a false entity, can one hope to get in touch with one's inner core. Sannyas is a surrender of the unreal part, the ego, with all the conditionings and trappings that attend it. Then one can go deep in the journey into consciousness, which happens only through increased awareness; sannyas is the first step on this journey.

Coming out of discourse, Barbara is alight with a glow similar to what she observed in those she resented upon arrival. She schedules a darshan for three days later, and during the interval throws herself into meditations with full commitment. I also book darshan the same evening, but when time comes, am denied admittance because of a lingering odor "of the West" still in my hair. So, Barbara goes without me.

Two hours later she emerges from the gates of Lao Tzu House a different person. She moves in a blissful daze, and her eyes suggest something remarkable has occurred. Because this happens to almost everyone in the presence of this spiritual master, I am not alarmed. In this extraordinary place where the unusual happens frequently, I can relate to her experience. We hug as she allows tears of joy to pour forth. She is no longer Barbara. Bhagwan has given her the name *"Prem Vihar"* meaning *"Love Play,"* and his words fit perfectly—as they so often do for new sannyasins. Although she cannot remember his exact words, the meaning has penetrated deep and become part of her. She is Vihar, and other words that come with the name are less important. It isn't until three years later that the transcription of her darshan is published. The following excerpt is taken from *Only Losers Can Win in this Game, A Darshan Diary:*

*Bhagwan: Close your eyes.... Just be silent and listen to the sounds of the night. Just become the ears: be as if the whole body has become ears. Listen from every pore, every cell....*

*Barbara, a nurse from Germany, closes her eyes, her long thick hair falling over her face. Some baby birds cheep in the stillness. A tear wells up in her eye and begins the descent down her flushed cheek.*

*Bhagwan: This will be your name: Ma Prem Vihar, Prem means love, Vihar means play: love play. And let that become your very philosophy of life. Two things: be loving and be playful. If love becomes serious it brings misery. Life without love is not life at all. And that's what happens ordinarily: when people love they become so serious about it that the seriousness creates misery. They think the misery is because of love; then they start becoming afraid of love. They start withdrawing themselves from all love; they don't go on that path any more. They start existing lovelessly, because love brings misery, anxiety, anguish, sadness. So they avoid it. But then their life is a boredom, a sheer boredom, for no purpose at all. Without love, life is a boredom; with love, if it is serious, life becomes pathology, ill, unhealthy.*

*A healthy life needs two things: love and playfulness, A non-serious quality is needed for love. Love should be fun! Then there is great joy, and the joy goes on growing every day. Because it is just a play you don't take it seriously; it cannot create misery. So be loving but be loving non-seriously!*

*Copyright 1981 Rajneesh Foundation; published by Ma Yoga Laxmi, Rajneesh Foundation

17 Koregaon Park, Poona 411-001, India; p 478.

---------------

Shortly after we had met, Barbara told me that none of her earlier relations with men had lasted. She would feel herself getting tense when the situation became too serious; then, feeling cramped and curtailed, she would run from the relationship. This is what Bhagwan has been able to see and why he gives her a way to remove the block that prevents her from letting loose in love. He tells her to drop seriousness about a loving relationship and go into it with playfulness. The truth and relevance of his words are immediately obvious, and Barbara-cum-Vihar, feeling he has hit the target with these words, dissolves into tearful bliss. Not only has he seen the problem, but he has also given her a simple idea to eliminate it.

As darshan continues, Bhagwan asks if there is anything she wants to say. Barbara/Vihar replies that she has a question that concerns her work.

*Vihar: I am a nurse and part of my work is taking care of dead bodies. When people die it is not very nice; mostly they die very terribly. It is the smell and the dirt that really disgusts me. Then I become hard and I treat them like an object; it is like a dirty job. I try to avoid having to do it and let the others attend to it. I feel bad about it...feel guilty.*

*Bhagwan: Mm -mm. A few things to remember: first, once a person is dead, he is no more. It is just a dead body; it is dirt! You need not be worried about it; there is nobody left! So there is no need to feel guilty that you are not loving. How can you love a dead body? (chuckling) If you don't hate it, that's enough. A dead body is a dead body. Even the person himself has left it! (laughter) It was no more worth living in, so how can you....? You want to enter it and live there?! Mm? The person has left because it was rotten. Now the house is dilapidated; it is in a ruin and nobody lives there. It just has to be dissolved.*

*So nothing to be worried about! How can you be loving? Drop that idea! Be loving when a person is alive. Then even if he is in a dirty body, be loving...because he is not the body. Always be respectful to the person who is inside. Sometimes he is in an old body, an ill body, stinking, but he himself is not that. Take care of his body, be respectful towards it, but once he has left then it is just dirt—dust unto dust.*

*So clean the body, wash it. It is just a ritual really, mm? Now it is all meaningless. It has to be thrown back to the earth. We have to do a certain ritual: the bath, new clothes. In different countries it is done in different ways, but we are just trying to create a certain meaning about something that is absolutely meaningless; otherwise it will be too abrupt. Somebody has died and you suddenly throw him out. It will hurt you so we have to make the passage slowly, and make it as beautiful as possible. But basically it is all meaningless. The whole point is how to end it. So in one country you bury it, in another country you burn it, in another country, another way, but the whole question is disposal. The disposal has to be done in a certain way so it looks humane and polite, but the body is just empty.*

*So don't be worried about it and don't create any guilt about it. It is just natural. Good!*

* Ibid, pp 479 - 480.

-------------

Without using the word explicitly, Bhagwan again discusses non-seriousness. Vihar's concern about cleaning dead patients had something to do with maintaining a somber attitude. But Bhagwan tells her to drop all that. In one evening Vihar receives guidance on two fundamental issues of life—love and death.

For the next days we leave each other alone as she goes into the new space Bhagwan has created for her. She opens both to herself and to the whole of existence by simply accepting whatever comes her way.

With Vihar off on her own, I bring attention back to myself. Suddenly everything becomes a whirlwind. I look at relations with the two women in my life and confirm that the light has gone dim on Mary while a radiance of love shines on Vihar. The time is coming when I will have to stop dividing myself between these relationships. In addition, my work, although rewarding at the moment, is not the right long-term employment. A few days after Vihar's darshan, I pass the "smell test" and have another opportunity to sit before Bhagwan. I want to tell him the confusion from the fast train of events and the uncertainty about how I will have to force things to work out. But not sure which way to go, I'm at an impasse. The published transcription of my darshan follows:

*Saturday, October 29, 1977.*

*Nartan's only been here a few days and is leaving again soon.*

*Nartan: Things have been happening since I've been here*

*Bhagwan: They are happening!*

*Nartan: It's been very good, but I'm flowing too fast, things are changing too fast. I don't know if they're right.*

*Bhagwan: They are right! Just go with things. Don't be afraid and don't pull back, don't hold back. If they are going fast, you go fast.*

*Nartan: They've been going very fast and up till now I always forced things.*

*Bhagwan: Force is not right; you just go with it.*

*Nartan: It's always worked in the past.*

*Bhagwan: Yes, it can work but at a very great cost, and you have to pay for it later on. It works, otherwise why should people, ninety-nine percent of people do it? It is very rare to find a person who does things without force. We know only one way to do a thing and that is with force. But finally the force destroys us because we become fighters, warriors. We are no more lovers. Love happens only in a let-go, when you are floating with the stream and not fighting upstream.*

*In the world that fight is a must. The world is very competitive; you are not alone there. If you don't do things with force somebody else will. But in the inner world things happen without force because there is no competition; you are alone there. And once you have learned that things can happen without force....*

*Chinese have the right word for it, they call it 'wu-wei'; action without action. Things can happen without your doing; then they have a tremendous beauty. They don't tire you; they don't exhaust you, and you are not spent through them; you remain intact. Once you know that knack everything is possible. And you will learn it; it is coming by and by.*

*It will be hard in the beginning because you are trained in a particular way, and it is difficult: old habits die hard. The ego also feels good when you are doing something with force. When you allow things to happen the ego does not feel good. There is nothing for it, no support for it, no props for it. The ego starts dying from starvation.*

*Sometimes things do go fast, sometimes the river flows very fast. When you are just floating with the river you have to go with it; you cannot choose your pace. When the river is flowing fast you have to flow fast. When the river moves slowly you move slowly. You have to be with the river, you have to be in tune with it, but that will come. That will be a great day of celebration when it has come totally.*

\* *Ibid, pp 528 - 529.*

----------

The message is clear: Don't force the situation and don't resist it. Just allow it; whatever happens will be right. I am to go along with whatever engulfs me. *(Several years later I understand what he means about force working but only at a very great cost. The cost turns out to be my health; in the long run force didn't really work for me—or did it? The answer depends upon how I look at what has happened. Success and failure easily get jumbled together, and it's not always clear which is which. However, the message Bhagwan gives now is relevant. I am to flow with the cascade of events overtaking me.)*

There's a touch of irony in the way darshan continues. Bhagwan invites me to come back and next time stay a little longer to do some therapy groups. I explain I have already done two during this visit, and the dialog proceeds as follows:

*\*Nartan: ....I had a heavy trip this week. I was on the waiting list for Tao, and the person didn't show up so I came into the Tao Group. It was really an experience. In the afternoon session when the man showed up, I had to leave the Group. I've been hanging, feeling very heavy, all week.*

*Bhagwan says 'That's not good,' and tells Arup to make arrangements so that Nartan can join the next Tao Group....*

*Bhagwan: Do it, otherwise it will remain hanging. And it is a beautiful experience to go through.*

*Nartan: Did I just force my way into that?*

*Bhagwan: No, no, not at all...not at all. Mm? (laughter) Good, Nartan!"*

\* Ibid, p 530

-------------

But I know I had forced my way in. The Tao groups had been booked weeks earlier, and I would normally have no chance to get into one of them. But I set things up by telling Bhagwan about it, and this forces the situation that ultimately gets me into the group.

Bhagwan has assigned me three groups that tend to be Western-type encounter and cathartic therapies. Vihar's groups, by contrast, are Eastern-oriented with focus on meditation and silence. In the Tantra Yoga Group she develops headaches that the therapist says are forms of resistance, but because of my encouragement to stay with the group, she does. When the therapist gives her a deep massage that brings up problems with her mother, Vihar/Barbara screams them out. Afterward she feels more relaxed than she has for years.

In the five-day, residential Kyo Group, Barbara again resists because she wants to be with me rather than isolated with this group. But ultimately she surrenders and goes into it with an open mind. After a day she realizes the enjoyment of peace and quiet when withdrawn from the world and celebrates the solitude and bliss that follow deep meditations.

By now it's early November, and knowing the time has come to ask Bhagwan about Barbara's and my future together, we book a final darshan prior to a late-night departure. We wash thoroughly and put clothes in the sun to ensure no lingering odors. Bhagwan has become increasingly sensitive to smells and on several occasions experienced paroxysms of coughing when people with slight body or hair scents have gotten close. As a result, the sniffing controls are more stringent than ever, and if we don't get into darshan this evening, we won't have another chance. Upon arrival, we're relieved our bodies are certified as scentless and both of us are granted admission. Because others are not so lucky, darshan is small, which allows more time for private discussions with Bhagwan.

When Barbara/Vihar and I are called forward, I tremble with excitement and anticipation. Simply being near Bhagwan brings on this feeling, but it's more intense because of the question we intend to ask. Settled directly in front of Bhagwan, I say that Vihar and I love each other and want to ask if it is right to live together. Bhagwan knows about my marriage to Mary/Pashyo and about our two girls. After a moment's pause, he starts speaking and continues for about 10 minutes looking first at one and then the other of us. But as often happens, I become so absorbed by the loving energy it's impossible to recall in detail his words. (These comments, which would normally have appeared in *The Open Secret - a Darshan Diary*, were unfortunately not recorded.)

I do, however, remember his first five words, which sum up the message: "Live together, but remain separate." He says love means freedom, and when you love someone you allow that person freedom. Love has nothing to do with possessing or controlling; it has to do with allowing the other to be himself or herself. Just as two trees can't grow when they are tightly bound and live in each other's shadows and take rain from each other, so also, the two of us will be diminished if we become too close. We must stand apart in our own spaces and remember we are unique individuals. Barbara likewise remembers little that Bhagwan says, except that when speaking about not controlling each other, she recalls he was looking straight at me.

Bhagwan explains it's unfortunate that in the West we think of a couple as a "whole" made up of two 'halves', as in "better half" and "other half". Two individuals can meld together in deep beauty and harmony through their love, but it's impossible to lose the sense they are two. When they force themselves on each other and try to act as a single entity, this violates the dignity of each individual. Bhagwan must have seen how wary Barbara and I had been of past relationships in which we had lost a sense of who we are. He tells us to continue to open as he has seen us do the past days and continue to develop feelings and sensitivities. As each of us does this, we should allow the other to do likewise. Then he repeats, "Live together, but remain separate."

As we leave darshan that remarkable Saturday evening, November 5, 1977, I feel ecstatic. Things indeed are happening at a fast pace, and as Bhagwan encourages, I should float with it. With major changes coming, I'm not to force them, but simply wait until they happen.

Immediately after darshan, Barbara and I leave the ashram and travel by rickshaw to the taxi depot to arrange a four-hour drive to Bombay airport. We are oblivious to the rain, smells, and bouncing drive until arriving just past midnight in time to catch the flight to Frankfurt. Still absorbed in the lingering fragrance of this remarkable Indian who touches our lives with such beauty and love, we feel like open wounds—super-sensitive and dangerously exposed to contamination, yet unable to protect ourselves. Or perhaps we're more like delicate flowers in an open meadow unfolding in the light of a new sun. All we can do is turn toward the light, bend with the wind, and trust to existence that things will work out—as they so often do—for the best.

After a quick change of planes, we're soon in Hamburg where we go our separate ways.

[October 27, 1977, Poona] Barbara/Prem Vihar receiving sannyas

[November 5, 1977, Poona, age 36] Darshan: "Be together, but stay separate"

# 39
# New Beginnings

*11/77, Age 36*

When I return home from India in early November 1977, Mary is sensitive to my fragile state and warmed by my "Poona-glow" that returning sannyasins often emanate. She allows me time to readjust to home life and reenter the business world before discussing the signed separation agreement, which still seems reasonable to both of us.

Mary adds that because there's no point in continuing to live in the same house, she is willing to move out with the girls or let me be the one to leave. The anticipated moment has finally come, and Mary, not I, brings it up. I recall Bhagwan saying not to force anything but just let things happen. I arrange to move out the next weekend.

Why do we separate after 11 years together? I think the answer is found in a misunderstanding of the term, "I love you." What most people really mean to say is "I love us," which reflects how they feel together. What I had loved about Mary was the active lifestyle we shared for nine of those years. We skied, sailed, biked, hiked, camped, and traveled. But in recent years she lost interest in all these activities. Now we have little in common except love for our daughters.

As Mary draws away from activities we shared, she turns to painting and teaching, but they too don't hold her interest. She decides her calling is as a spiritual seeker and wants to devote herself to a meditative life. This quest started during her college years at Northwestern University and now resurfaces as her singular life goal. She wants to be with a living spiritual master, which means moving to Poona. Although I respect her new path, it isn't for me. I intend to continue an outward-focused life of travel, exploration, and discovery of the world's richness. With these differences between us, we foresee no basis for continuing the marriage.

On November 15, 1977, I pack my car with personal belongings together with a few pieces of furniture and drive away. I'm surprised how calm and unemotional this departure is, but Mary and I both know it's the right thing.

Barbara's name had come up a few times after Mary returned from Poona two months earlier. The girls had talked about the sailing and biking weekends and fun times at home, but Mary never inquired further. She likely didn't care because her mind was set on Poona. Now the time has come to tell her about the relationship.

I invite Mary to lunch and explain how Barbara and I feel about each other. The weeks Barbara and I spent together with the girls allowed them to develop their own relationships with her, making her practically part of their family. Cyrena and Liane, now 6 and 3, both love Barbara, and she loves them. I have moved in with her, and we are thankful to be together. Mary hugs me and says how happy she is for me.

As for herself, Mary wants only to lead a devotional life with the girls in Poona. On her initial visit she confirmed the ashram school is staffed by English-speaking teachers from the States, UK, Australia, New Zealand, and South Africa who all have teaching credentials from their respective countries. The ashram medical center is likewise run by Western-trained doctors who have privileges at several local hospitals. Ashram security is handled by Indian sannyasins who interact easily with the city's police force. All these considerations assure Mary that the girls will be safe and well cared for.

During the following months we adjust to the new arrangement. Once a week I return to the house, not as one who lives there, but rather as an invited guest, to make household repairs and sort out financial matters. Each weekend the girls visit Barbara and me, usually spending the night. When I still lived at home, the girls didn't see much of me because of business travels; consequently, they hardly notice my weekday absence. Coming to our apartment each weekend is an adventure they enjoy, and Mary is glad to have her peace for two days. Meanwhile Cyrena and Liane see as much of me as ever and feel they have two mothers.

Barbara and I go regularly to the Rajneesh Meditation Center in Hamburg to listen to Bhagwan's taped discourses and participate in the meditations. It is here that Mary-Pashyo and Barbara-Vihar meet. Eyes moisten as they look at each other and, while embracing, agree they want to be friends. Over the following weeks Barbara and I often join Mary and the girls either at their house or our apartment for dinner. Cyrena and Liane enjoy being together with three people they love.

Thus we settle into new beginnings. As Barbara's sannyas name, Prem Vihar, suggests, the themes are love and play. Everyone is open, direct, honest, and clear; and each of us now discovers the others in new ways. Things have happened fast as Bhagwan had said they would.

We know that our lives will cross many times in the future and that the love and trust established in these first weeks will smooth the path no matter what difficulties lie ahead.

*(Over the years I have often asked Liane and Cyrena how they felt about the divorce and if it changed their lives. Liane doesn't remember the divorce but can't recall any time that her mother, Barbara, and I weren't part of her life. Cyrena says she doesn't remember the divorce having an impact because thereafter we always stayed connected. She also recalls the fun trips between Hamburg, India, and the States, where she had regular visits with her grandparents.)*

# 40
# Parental Reflections

*11/77, Age 36*

Although I intend to visit my parents to explain the separation from Mary and my love for Barbara, I have an even more compelling reason. I want to share realizations gained in the Poona therapy groups about my relationship with them.

It is said that understanding early parental relationships can unlock the box holding resistances and fears that impede the free flow of one's life years later. Rather than looking inside this box, I, like most people, ignore it. But wanting to gain clarity, I dared to peek inside, opening the lid wider each time before becoming overwhelmed and slamming it shut. But by persisting I gained a feeling of freedom from these subconscious influences on my thinking and behavior.

Bhagwan explains, as do psychologists and therapists, that if anger, fear, or insecurity creates blind spots, one can uncover the causes by looking back into childhood. If these issues remain hidden, they fester and poison, but once brought into the light, they wither and die. In therapy groups at Poona, exploration of my childhood years helped clarify understandings about my parents' own upbringing that explain how they raised Wendy and me. Now I want to be with them to discuss these insights and also do something adult children seldom do with their parents: thank them for giving me the most wonderful childhood I could have imagined.

What insights did I have about Mom and Dad? The insights pertain to love—the open expression of love—or rather, the lack of such open expression. My parents had taken good care while raising Wendy and me. As far as they knew, that's what love was—providing three meals a day, tending to our daily needs, and seeing that no harm befell us. But there were no big, warm hugs to express love. Although often happily together, we never acknowledged the joy of togetherness. Our lives were organized with a no-nonsense attitude: Parents would bandage scraped knees, repair broken zippers, and pick up school supplies. Wendy and I felt well cared for, but that's different from feeling loved. When I queried others my age, they likewise admitted they never experienced open expressions of affection. This style of child-raising seems to have been typical of the post-Depression, WWII generation. My parents didn't intentionally withhold love. The way they raised their children reflected how their parents—and their parents before them—were raised.

When my father, George Weaver Schroeder, was born, his mother Annetta was 24 years old and his father Harry, 40. Because Harry was so much older, Dad never really knew his father, and relations between his parents, also burdened by an age gap, seemed to be more of convenience than of love. Harry had three children by a previous marriage. Needing someone to look after them, he likely chose Annetta to be a substitute mother to his children rather than a lover to him.

Also living in their large home in Flushing, New York, were Dad's maternal grandparents. Dad was raised in an enormous household that eventually totaled five children, two parents, two grandparents, and relatives who periodically dropped in and stayed a few months at a time. His young mother, whose responsibilities also included overseeing a live-in staff of four servants, had more than she could handle. With the household constantly abuzz, emphasis was not on celebration of life, but rather on logistics, simply getting things done. At age 14, Dad was sent to Choate Boarding School in Wallingford, Connecticut, returning for school holidays to Flushing and for summer vacations to Quogue, the family summer home. Relatives expressed little sensitivity, love, or feelings of any kind. Emotional reticence was the only model Dad knew when he had a family of his own.

Dad excelled in three areas typical for loners. First was sailing. Although he took along his sister (also named Annetta but nicknamed Tutu) as crew, he was basically alone with wind and sea. A superb skipper, he won more than a hundred sailing regattas; trophies were so numerous they had to be stashed away in attic closets because no display case could contain them all. In prep school Dad took up long-distance running—another activity often pursued by loners. He also excelled in academics, earning acceptance into the Class of 1941 at Princeton University.

At Princeton, Dad majored in engineering—a field focused on formulas and empiricism with minimal human contact. Throughout his 20-year management career with General Electric, he related to colleagues via the typical logic of the engineering sciences. Although admired as a creative engineer who was a pioneer in electronic cooking and awarded numerous patents for development of the microwave oven, he seldom became close to anyone.

In Louisville, when he made a midlife career change to the field of finance, his analytical approach helped promote him to head the largest bank trust department in the South. Once he began administering trusts, guardianships, estates, and client assets—exchanges involving extensive contact with clients and colleagues—Dad opened as a warm, people-oriented individual.

My mother also grew up in an atmosphere of limited emotional expression. Her mother, Patricia Stopford, was raised on a secluded manorial estate in Ireland. During WWI all her young beaus were drafted to fight on the Western Front in Europe. Lonesome without any social life, she placed an advertisement in a London newspaper seeking to correspond with a soldier. Alec Saxton, an Oxford-graduated Englishman, answered from the trenches in Belgium and the two began an active correspondence. They were young, lonely, and frightened, a common bond that nurtured their relationship. When a war injury returned my future grandfather to England on medical leave, he met and immediately proposed to the young lass who would become my grandmother. Alec returned to the battlefields of Flanders, but after the war he and Patricia married in England. Shortly thereafter my mother's older sister, Sheila, was born.

Enticed by a job with an American shipping company, the young family immigrated to New York where my mother, Natalie Moyra Saxton who went by Moyra, was born. However, the company went bankrupt necessitating the family to find another beginning in their new country. A job with Sperry Rand Corporation moved them to Indianapolis where Mom spent her childhood. Her parents picked a home in an upper-middle-class neighborhood, which added financial pressures to the difficult living situation of starting a new life in the midst of the depression.

Growing up in Indianapolis, Mom faced ostracism at school. Her home life was British, but her outside-of-home life was American. She was often picked on because the family was "foreign" and had modest finances. School lunch was one of her worst times. Unable to afford meals at school, Mom brought a sandwich that she would eat in secret after classes. One day several classmates discovered her hidden lunch and humiliated her by flinging it all over the playground. Mom told me this story often, and each time it grew more poignant as she recollected details.

When she tearfully told her parents, their explanation, intended to comfort her, only made the situation worse. Because her grandfather was the 5th Earl of Courtown, Ireland, the family was listed in *DeBretts Peerage*, the official English registry of noble families. *(Dad's family, as Mom learned after they were married, also had a notable lineage and was included in the New York Social Register, an index of America's high-society families.)* When Mom recounted these facts at school, classmates mocked her even more., and their taunting further alienated her. She, like Dad, grew up a loner.

Mom's feelings of inadequacy and rejection were heightened when it came time for college. Her older and younger sisters, Sheila and Doreen, attended Radcliffe, a top women's college in Cambridge, Massachusetts. The family later moved to Summit, New Jersey, where Mom, a senior at Kent Place prep school, was also accepted at Radcliffe. Everything changed abruptly that spring when she discovered she was pregnant. She attempted self-abortion—doing so by pounding her stomach with a brick—but to no avail. Because I was determined to make my way into the world, she scrapped college plans and backed into a hasty marriage. I was born four months later.

Even after circumstances improved in her life, Mom still felt bitter. Shelia's first marriage ended tragically when her husband was killed in the Second World War, and her second marriage ended in divorce. Her third was unhappy up to the day she succumbed to cancer. Doreen's husband was stricken with cancer a few years after they married, and for two decades until his death, he suffered. As her sisters' fortunes declined, Mom's, on the contrary, ascended; she could finally feel vindicated in a world that had caused anguish when she was young. But bitterness from childhood lingered.

Living in the shadow of achievers, Mom felt she had something to prove. After both sisters graduated from Radcliffe, they earned master's degrees and pursued careers. Dad excelled in nearly everything he touched—most notably sailing, engineering, and finance. Mom's mother was active in local politics, community government, and the League of Women Voters. Dad's mother—a pillar of eastern Long Island society, choir mistress at Quogue's Episcopal Church, and organizer of events at the community yacht, beach, and field clubs—was disapproving, mainly because Mom's pregnancy had forced her son to drop out of college (temporarily).

Were the jobs Mom held after Wendy and I were born a way to prove something? Or were they just an outlet for her energy? Whatever her motivation, Mom was active in each community where we lived. When Wendy and I started elementary school in Wauconda, Illinois, she launched a lunch program for grades K through five. After we relocated to Connecticut, she worked different jobs on the chicken farm where we lived. Once we settled in Kentucky, she served as director of the Louisville Children's Theater throughout my junior high and high school years. Subsequently, she joined the *Louisville Times* newspaper as an editor and writer. It's ironic that after being bullied by children of well-to-do families in Indianapolis, Mom, as society editor, mingled with the so-called Bourbon-Elite class of Louisville.

Mom and Dad stayed busy throughout the week. Immersed in his career, Dad had little time to join me in Boy Scout activities, camping, athletics, or just fooling around. Sailing and tennis were the only activities we engaged in together. Similarly, Mom had little free time for either Wendy or me. Apart from tennis, I recall few instances when she involved herself with my interests. But we were always together on vacations.

After I went to college and Wendy went out on her own as a nurse, Mom stopped working and focused her energies in new directions. First was volunteerism: She put in hours with Reading for the Blind, Meals on Wheels, United Way, Speed Art Museum, Kentucky Opera, Louisville Philharmonic, Louisville Ballet, and more. Second was her love for tennis and golf. She excelled at both and competed locally, regionally, and at the state level, winning championships along the way.

For several years she was the top woman golfer at Harmony Landing Country Club where she and Dad belonged for many years. Because it was a membership only for men, when Dad died Moyra was asked to leave (Southern tradition). She was so damn mad she looked for revenge. Although thereafter she could play only at the lesser public golf courses, not on the circuit of private clubs, she intensified her game. Her persistence paid off, and she won the local tournaments the next year, beating every woman from the Louisville Country Club, Harmony Landing Club, and Louisville's other private golf clubs. She then went to regionals and again beat all her old friends and went on to state where she was among the top finishers. Quite a lady!

As a child, the question for me was how to function in a world without spontaneous hugs and quiet gestures of love. My response was to seek to gain my parents' love by proving I was worthy. By accomplishing things that others thought important, I could earn recognition, and with that I imagined would come love. I pursued success, but achievement never brought the hoped-for result.

I was always at or near the top in tennis, scouting, sailing, academics, and leadership. But rather than enjoying my accomplishments, I was constantly assessing what my parents and others thought of me. I had their respect and admiration, but the warm expressions of love never materialized. New accomplishments only brought new frustration. As respect and admiration grew, so did distance from others.

No one can earn love or force it. Love just is, and it comes without any doing.

Although different from my approach, Wendy's was just as misguided. Because she wasn't feeling loved, she felt unworthy and unable to do anything about it. Whenever efforts failed, she accepted defeat as her fate and gave up. An average student, Wendy was devastated when Mom pointed out my outstanding school achievements. Moreover, Wendy never did well at tennis or sailing and was made to feel unworthy because of these shortcomings. Mom, perhaps intending to motivate her daughter, constantly criticized her. Had Wendy known that she was loved, the criticism could have been tolerable, but such was not the case.

Late in her teens Wendy unexpectedly began to bloom upon discovering three activities in which she could shine. Because these were areas separate from other family interests, she escaped comparison. In ballroom dancing Wendy found her first love and for years was a dance instructor in modern cotillion classes. Second, she had a beautiful voice and found immense joy as a member of the school's choral group and church choir. Third, she became an accomplished pianist. Furthermore, later in life, encouraged by her understanding, tennis-playing husband, Wendy became a proficient tennis player. Unfortunately, in spite of all this, Mom still found little ways to criticize Wendy.

Perhaps my observations reflect something Bhagwan once expressed: Children outgrow childhood, but parents seldom outgrow parenthood.

Thanks to Bhagwan's guidance and therapy sessions at the ashram, I gained insight into the reasons my parents never expressed love. Rather than anger toward Mom and Dad, I felt compassion. Why blame them? They had fulfilled the role of parents based upon the model of their own childhood experiences. In fact, they had been closer and warmer toward

Wendy and me than their parents had been toward them. Wendy and I were never sent to boarding school but enjoyed home life, vacations, and recreational activities as a family.

With this perspective, in the late autumn of 1977 I travel from Hamburg to Quogue, where my parents are vacationing, to tell them about the changes in my life. I also want to share my newfound clarity. I have no plan for how this will unfold. Rather than trying to control the situation, I intend to allow whatever will happen to happen.

The impending meeting has heightened drama because of something that occurred six weeks earlier when Mary wrote a letter to my parents explaining our separation. At that time she didn't know about Barbara, so her missive omitted a major part of the story. Immediately, I telephoned my parents and informed them Mary's letter was on the way but requested that they please not open it until I see them. They agreed to wait.

Summer beach communities assume a deserted character after the hordes of tourists depart in early September. Nature, as though restraining herself at the pleading of the chamber of commerce so tourists won't leave early, unleashes the pent-up winds, rains, and raw weather she has been holding back. When I arrive in Quogue on a stormy November morning, the ocean is a fury of foam clinging to the peaks of crashing waves that battle relentlessly to reshape the beach dunes. Unobstructed by moorings, buoys, shoal-water markers, and tethered boats that have been removed for the season, cold winds sweep across the bay. Downpours flush back to the sea the sands tracked by bare feet from the beaches into every corner of the village during the summer.

Strolling the desolate strands I had visited every year of my life, I sense the reborn elements of existence that we otherwise take to be unchanging. On one hand Quogue is the same every year. But this sameness always has a freshness, the way the blooming of spring flowers is forever new and yet is always a repetition. And so it is with me on this gray morning. Although major changes rearrange my life, I am still the same person waking up, eating breakfast, and following a day-to-day routine.

When evening shadows lengthen, I sit down to dinner with Mom and Dad at the same table I had known as a child. Four generations have gathered here: my blind great-grandfather in the tuxedo he wore every night; my grandfather, less formal in his suit and tie; my father, another notch down in sport coat, slacks, and tie; and then me in shorts and t-shirt with a jacket thrown over my shoulders to help assure my grandmother that her family hasn't totally declined. Apart from my parents, these people are now gone. Yet life seems unchanging here in Kirk Lea, so named because the home had been built in the field next to the village's Episcopal Church.

Dinner over, Dad draws from his coat pocket and hands me Mary's unopened letter. Relaxed, feeling close to both parents, I unravel the story. Except for a few questions they ask, I do most of the talking. After 11 years Mary and I, following a direction that's clear to us both, are separating with mutual sensitivity devoid of any emotional upheaval. We recognize it would be senseless for ourselves, as well as for Cyrena and Liane, to continue to be together. We each give thanks for the beautiful moments we shared. Most important, we agree our top priority is the well-being of the girls. They come first.

As they listen, my parents feel what I have to say at a deeper level. Naturally, they have concerns about the future, especially regarding the children; but they seem reassured by my calmness. Everything will work out fine if we all remain open and trust that life will take care of us.

When I finish explaining the separation, we open Mary's letter. Her account touches on the same points as mine. Her letter also indicates no anger, bitterness, or sadness. Rather, there is the same recognition that we need to go in different directions. It's heartwarming to see my parents' reaction to the situation. Without taking sides they accept our decision with understanding and affection for both Mary and me.

But that's only half the story. Now I tell Mom and Dad about Barbara. As I express my love for her, they share in my happiness. Earlier in Germany one scenario I discussed with Barbara was the possibility of bringing her to Quogue and hiding her outside the room until after I had told them about her. Then she'd come in, concluding the episode with a grand finale.

But my penchant for dramatic flair is a fantasy. I realize this foolish idea could backfire and destroy an intimacy I hoped to share with Mom and Dad. Besides, it could have been not only embarrassing, but a real tragedy if they reacted with a "Never-darken-our-door-again" or "Don't-you-have-any-sense-of-responsibility-to-the-children?" scene.

What about the other intention to share my new understanding about why they raised me as they did? It seems irrelevant now. As we end the evening, I go to each of them and for the first time give a long hug—a hug that says everything I want to communicate including thanks for the wonderful childhood they gave me.

These hugs are the closest I ever come with them to both giving and receiving total love.

# 41
# Crack – The First Sign

*11/77 - 11/78, Ages 36 - 37*

After explaining to Mom and Dad in Quogue about the new family dynamic, I head to Rochester for business meetings where I inform my boss and colleagues about changes in my life. (I had spoken with my German managers earlier about the matter.) Reactions ranged from sympathetic understanding to neutral acknowledgment. How easy it has been to explain these developments. I feel fortunate to deal with divorce now rather than in an earlier era when condemnation from co-workers could damage a career.

Back in Hamburg life settles into a pleasant routine living with Barbara in her one-room garden apartment. Even with my few pieces of furniture, we still have less than a dozen possessions. We sleep on a mattress on the floor flanked with orange crates that provide surfaces for books, wine glasses, and flower vases. On weekends Cyrena and Liane spread sleeping bags in a corner of the room.

When year-end holidays arrive, the girls and I spend Christmas Eve with Barbara in the German tradition and Christmas Day with Mary. Then Barbara and I drive to the French Alps village of Val Thorens, part of Trois Vallées, which is one of the world's largest ski areas. *(This becomes our annual ski getaway for the next two years.)* Two weeks of skiing, eating, and enjoying French culture culminate with celebrations for my 37th birthday a few days before greeting 1978.

Cold, stormy weather envelops northern Europe from December until April, but this year we find sun in February. Before heading to business conferences in the States, I include Barbara on a side trip to meet my parents for a one-week sailing charter at Eleuthera in The Bahamas.

Mom and Dad greet Barbara as if she's one of the family. The four of us enjoy a wonderful cruise aboard *Sea Away*, a 43-foot sloop, exploring the Exuma Islands. Each day we sail through clear, turquoise waters until sunset, then anchor in a protected cove to settle in for another night under the stars.

Following the cruise, Barbara flies home while I continue to Rochester. Now that I'm responsible for North America's area-sealing business, I expand travels beyond Rochester. Ironically, two projects are in Albuquerque and Louisville—both cities I think of as home. Off I go to Albuquerque to check the installation of Schlegel Sheet for the Public Service Company of New Mexico.

While there I call Mary's parents to give an update on her and the girls. But they cut me off. Beyond venting anger and bitterness about our divorce, they have no interest in communicating with me. Apparently, Mary had not told them about our separation in the same way I had explained to Mom and Dad. Her parents only know the cold facts without any background.

While in New Mexico I drive to Taos and discover that the ski area has developed from a small regional destination into an international ski resort. In the early 1960s everyone skiing in Taos—with the exception of an occasional Texan who accidentally drifted across the state line—was from New Mexico. On this sojourn I meet people from both coasts plus a few from Europe who have come to ski the acclaimed, waist-deep powder.

During this short holiday I reflect on the miracle of jet-age travel that began less than two decades earlier. One week prior to arriving in New Mexico, I had been sailing in The Bahamas; a week before that I was freezing in Northern Europe; and in just over a week I will travel one-third around the globe to return home. Nonetheless, when asked by strangers in the ski lodge where I'm from, I delight in saying I live in Albuquerque, thereby invoking a time warp to my earlier life there.

As the day approaches when Mary intends to move to Poona, we must decide how our lives will continue. Should I leave Schlegel and go with Barbara and the girls to Poona as well? Should the girls stay in Hamburg rather than face the uncertainties in India? Should Barbara and I move into the house when Mary moves out, or should I cancel the lease? Trying to analyze options, I become frustrated. Reflecting upon Bhagwan's advice to remain open to whatever comes, I wait for what happens.

When her teaching contract finishes, Mary plans to see her parents before setting out for Poona. Because they can't understand why she and I are still close and why she and Barbara have contact with each other, Mary wants to explain everything in a caring, loving way. She flies with the girls to New Mexico and clarifies with her parents that she, not I, initiated the divorce so she could devote herself to a spiritual path, and we had separated on friendly terms. Her parents' anger toward me now dissipates.

Back in Hamburg Barbara and I vacate her apartment and move into the house. Wanting to change the energy, we visit a paint store, buy wild colors of orange and yellow, and attack the bland, white walls. Soon the home takes on such a feeling of warmth that I don't recognize where I had lived for more than five years.

As late summer approaches we start dealing with logistics. Before the girls fly to India to join their mother, I want to see them for a vacation in Quogue. Mary agrees and flies with the girls to JFK. She continues to Bombay with the understanding that friends will bring Cyrena and Liane to India later on.

The girls and I continue to Quogue, where Barbara joins us a few days later. Although I feel like a tightrope walker balancing my job with family travels, everything works out, and we spend two weeks sharing wonderful remembrances from childhood summers—swimming in the ocean, sailing on Tiana Bay, catching fish and crabs at Shinnecock Yacht Club's dock, playing tennis, and bicycling everywhere.

In September we return to Hamburg for six weeks before friends will take Liane and Cyrena to India. Even though their remaining time in the West is short, I enroll the girls at the International School for the first half of the semester to give them an opportunity to reconnect with friends. During weekends we charter sail in the Baltic Sea, ferry across the Elbe, bike to buy fresh apples and smoked meats from local farms, make excursions around Hamburg, or just stay home and play favorite card and board games.

As time for their departure nears, I realize how bereft I will feel when my daughters disappear. Although Bhagwan had advised me not to manipulate situations, I plead guilty to trying to keep the girls in Hamburg. I suggest that if they want to stay, they are welcome. Finally, Liane, who misses her mom, decides to go to Poona while Cyrena, who has many friends in Hamburg, chooses to stay with us. I'm overjoyed with this solution. Although letting Liane go will be difficult, I know Mary would be dejected if neither child were to join her. A few weeks later we put Liane on a plane in Amsterdam with a friend to take her to her mother leaving Barbara, Cyrena, and me to settle in for another Hamburg winter.

Strategies at work that I implemented earlier in the year have paid off, and the firm has reached financial breakeven. We've cleaned up basin-lining problems from earlier installations and better understand the technical challenges that had caused failures in the past. New offices in England and France have brought in small contracts, and my reorganization of U.S. operations is yielding results. Strengthened marketing efforts throughout Europe have positioned Schlegel Sheet as the best lining material for containment of hazardous contaminants.

The time has come to implement the strategy I had fought for in Rochester, the one to which Chairman Turner had reluctantly agreed, the one upon which I am risking my job.

For the company to grow we need projects with extremely large waste basins. Recognizing that these projects are in the Middle East, we direct our marketing efforts to oil-producing countries where Kuwait, Abu Dhabi, Saudi Arabia, Iraq, Libya, and others have been industrializing their economies. Because these countries are located in fragile ecological zones where water supplies are more valuable for them than oil, it's essential to prevent industrial waste from percolating through desert sands into aquifers. These governments recognize their need for securely lined basins.

We soon learn a different type of business thinking. Contracts aren't to be won in Riyadh, Baghdad, Dhahran, Kuwait City, Tripoli, or Amman. Instead we must go to Houston, London, Paris, or Brussels because these Arab countries work through Western-based international consulting, construction, and engineering firms located in countries that 50 years earlier had been their colonial rulers. Therefore, our first step is establishing relationships with these companies.

We home in on a dozen construction projects requiring waste basins, sludge ponds, and evaporation pits but also learn that consulting engineers aren't the only ones who need to be sold. The typical customer—one of the oil-rich Arab governments—engages scores of consultants, contractors, and testing laboratory scientists who need to be convinced that Schlegel Sheet is the best—and also most economical—lining material. As contract negotiations continue, the clients send delegations of government ministers to hear presentations about our product. Because Schlegel's part in these mammoth projects is almost infinitesimal, our people often get the runaround as they try to promote Schlegel Sheet. But now that we're playing in the big-time, we expect this marginalized treatment.

We run into four unexpected stumbling blocks. First, our international marketing manager is Jewish and therefore restricted from visiting any Arab country. The solution is for me to assume his responsibilities when meeting people in these countries.

Second, arranging bribes and kickbacks—a normal practice in this part of the world—is both unethical and illegal for us as a subsidiary of an American company. To avoid this problem, a common practice is to engage agents and pay them a reasonable commission. What they do is their business, not ours, and is often key to getting things moving in the host country.

Third, Arab countries require that foreign firms work through in-country partners, with the intent of teaching them about Western business practices. To meet this requirement, on a trip to Dhahran I look up a Stanford Business School classmate, Khalid al-Turki. A member of the royal family with his own trading company, Khalid agrees to serve as our partner.

Fourth, because all contracts must be written in Arabic and comply with Sharia law, we engage an American law firm in the Middle East specializing in these matters.

In spring of 1978, these projects are developing satisfactorily, but one in particular has makings of a true bonanza. Sometime earlier after flying over his country, Saudi Arabia's King Khalid questioned why oil wells were flaring off natural gas, some as much as a million dollars' worth a day. Not receiving a satisfactory answer, he demanded that Aramco (Arabian American Oil Company) initiate a gas-recovery project, an initiative that would require a large number of multi-acre evaporation ponds.

We are up against competitors all considerably cheaper but quality-wise inferior to Schlegel Sheet. We make it to the final rounds of discussion. I travel several times to Saudi Arabia to meet with Aramco engineers and, with our engineering team, visit Aramco's U.S. headquarters in Houston to confer on final details of the proposal. During the following weeks, we receive a daily barrage of telexes and phone calls requesting additional information or amendments to our quote. As summer arrives, nerves are on edge because we have bet the company on this contract.

Finally, we receive the call. We are the successful bidder! No words can describe our relief and elation. With this order we can double the plant facilities and be guaranteed a steady delivery program for two years. Furthermore, we've positioned ourselves for almost unlimited business that could follow as the Saudis step up industrialization developments.

Our small operation suddenly becomes the most profitable division within Schlegel. I breathe an enormous sigh of relief. I had pursued a strategy about which many in Rochester—including Chairman Turner—had doubts, questioning the wisdom of pursuing huge international projects rather than confining ourselves to smaller local ones. However, this latter approach would never lead to rapid growth, nor would it unleash the full potential of Schlegel Sheet, which is better suited for enormous installations than for smaller projects that require much cutting, patching, and detail work.

*(It seemed like Schlegel Sheet had a great future. I made plans to open new plants in Ireland and, for North American markets, in Houston. Business boomed. No one, including me, could have anticipated that in the next year the entire business would fall apart.)*

It's now fall of 1978 and home life is great. Cyrena is doing well in school and has a full schedule of activities that keep her busy and happy. I enjoy new perspectives as I fill double roles of both father and, temporarily at least, mother. I even attend "Mothers" meetings at Cyrena's school.

Planning business trips for Friday or Monday, I often arrange for Barbara and Cyrena to come along on weekends. On a trip in October to Ireland, I take them to my maternal grandmother's birthplace in Courtown. Mary and I had visited here with Grummy several years before, and I want to tell Barbara and Cyrena about her childhood memories as the daughter of the Fifth Earl of Courtown. One story Grummy told was of the gardener guiding a horse-drawn mower across the lawn when suddenly the horse started to defecate. Not wanting to sully the earl's estate, the gardener grabbed off his hat and caught the droppings before they hit the ground.

I also share Grummy's story about the family burial plot enclosed within an iron fence originally located in woods behind the manor. Because a golf course had been built in recent years, the graveyard now sits in the middle of a fairway. Covered with waist-high weeds, the plot had been in disrepair with knocked-over tombstones encrusted with layers of grime. During our previous visit, Grummy set to work ripping out overgrowth, brushing off headstones, and tidying up the graves of her forebears. Golfers must have been shocked to see a 70-year-old woman rummaging around the graveyard.

After Grummy married my grandfather and moved to America, the next generation of her family continued to live on the estate. But when the great manor became too expensive to maintain, they gave this 17th-century relic to the Irish government, which subsequently had it demolished. Other homes the family once owned were sold and turned into hotels. Courtown is now a rundown, honky-tonk resort on the Irish Sea offering a weekend escape to the working class of Dublin.

The plight of Courtown reminds me of a business school case about failure of management to prepare for unpredictable changes. The family had not foreseen two social and economic upheavals—the potato famine in mid-1800s and the turbulent aftermath of World War I—and had failed in their primary responsibility to assure continuity of their businesses.

Grummy said that during the potato famine in the mid-1840s, her father created jobs by building a small harbor, and he also gave away his wealth to feed the people who worked his lands. Nevertheless, he lost everything. Why, I wonder, didn't he develop a fishing industry in the Irish Sea, which contains some of the world's most bounteous fish stocks? Did he experiment with other food crops to replace the potato? After World War I, why didn't community leaders work out solutions for the economy? Did they have a vision about the future? How a family with wealth and land holdings could be reduced to penury seems beyond comprehension. Yet here in Courtown before my eyes is a sobering reminder of how family fortunes can change.

During our travels I become aware of tension between Cyrena and Barbara. Cyrena uses every opportunity to command my attention. Jealous of time I spend with Barbara she tries to prevent us from being alone. Barbara resents intrusion of this seven-year-old into our life and grows tense over Cyrena's constant presence. I notice they get along better when I'm not around. I had been insensitive to this issue and now determine to avoid situations that bring up petty jealousies. In the same way that my forefathers had been blind to the deterioration under their noses, I had been oblivious to the problem I lived with every day.

On the next trip to the States I attend Mary's and my divorce hearing at Rochester's county courthouse. Mary had signed papers authorizing her lawyer to represent her. When our case comes up, the judge reviews the papers and then asks a series of questions:

Judge: "Where is your wife?"

Me: "She's in India."

Judge: "What's she doing there?"

Me: "She's living in a commune with a spiritual master."

The judge peers over his glasses in a disapproving manner and pauses. Suitably attired in a businessman's suit, I look respectable while my absent wife is, in the judge's eyes, scandalous. The grounds for divorce—officially I am divorcing Mary although it was she who asked for it—is a legal point called constructive abandonment. I never understood what it means, but our lawyers say it is a quick and easy way to obtain the divorce. Obviously sympathetic to me, the judge then asks, "Do you agree to the children remaining with the mother?" I answer an emphatic, "Yes," which surprises him. He glowers as if I'm committing my progeny to a life of ignominy, but he drops further questioning. Within minutes the case is finished. The divorce becomes final October 15, 1978.

In November I travel again to headquarters. Cyrena accompanies me, and after departing Rochester, we fly to Louisville for Thanksgiving with family and friends. One warm afternoon, I'm cutting firewood with my father when something happens that will have a tremendous impact on my life a year later. We had just cut down a large dead tree and were beginning to saw it into logs. Lifting a big limb to a better location for sawing, suddenly I hear...CRACK...like a rifle shot. A searing pain shoots up my back. Dazed, I drop the load and reel around, barely able to clutch another tree to prevent keeling over.

The pain is severe and unrelenting. With hesitating, tortuous steps I make my way with Dad's help back to the house. Once there, I lie down on the living-room floor and give Mom a quick lesson in shiatsu, a Japanese finger massage that can often relieve back pain. Although she does what she can, her efforts prove useless. I remain incapacitated.

Attributing the injury to a strained muscle that will heal with rest and time, I can barely move for several days. Even weeks after our return to Hamburg, the pains, although tolerable, persist.

# 42
# Bureaucratic Hassles

*12/78 - 2/79, Ages 37 - 38*

At the end of 1978 we close the plant for two weeks. Barbara, Cyrena, and I drive south to Val Thorens, the French resort where we skied the previous year. Although my back still hurts from the "crack" a month earlier in Louisville, I can ski without problems. Snow conditions are wonderful, and we celebrate my 38th birthday and New Year's Day with the French.

During this vacation Barbara and I discover a special reason to celebrate. Two months earlier we had decided we want to have a child, and she stopped taking the pill. Suspecting she might be pregnant, Barbara bought a diagnostic kit prior to leaving Hamburg. Before going to bed one evening, we set up the test, anxious about what we'll see the next day.

About 1:00 am I awake, grope for a flashlight, and creep into the bathroom where we had set the test kit on top of the medicine cabinet so it wouldn't get jarred. Pulling myself onto the sink, I balance precariously on knees and straighten up to see the test tube. I almost fall off the basin bringing the whole works with me. Turning the light beam directly onto the chemical solution and gazing closer, I see the most beautiful sight in the world—a dark, black ring suspended in the clear solution. I almost cry out for joy but decide to let Barbara discover for herself. I return noiselessly to bed and lie awake with excitement for quite a while.

About 5:00 am the covers rustle as Barbara makes her way to the bathroom. While I feign sleep, she turns on the light and climbs up on the sink. The next moment she comes running back in a tizzy. When I spring up, she knows I already know. We embrace.

We tell no one until returning to Germany where Barbara's doctor confirms our joy. Barbara's family is ecstatic, as are all our close friends. But when I call my parents, my father sharply retorts, "When are you going to get married?" Whatever understanding had opened with my parents six weeks earlier in Quogue suddenly seems gone. My parents now treat me with the same disapproval they received almost 40 years earlier upon revealing they were expecting me. Although hurt by condemnation from their parents, they judge us the same way. Barbara and I regret they don't share our joy.

Bringing a baby into the world in a foreign country creates bureaucratic problems as I learned previously with the births of Cyrena and Liane. Complying with government regulations is difficult because the needs of expatriate Americans don't conform to local laws. In such instances I look for a simplified approach that often bends the rules but remains in compliance with the law.

Obtaining birth certificates is only one of many problems. For example, consider my driver's license. In my entire life I took the road test only once for my first license in Kentucky at age 16. After moving to New Mexico following college, I kept the Kentucky license and renewed it by mail. After 10 years of renewals using different addresses—none of them in Kentucky—authorities caught on and refused my request. By then I was in Hawaii, but without a permanent home, I couldn't apply for a license; therefore, I used my office address as my residence. No one checked and I was issued a license—no driving test required. At that time Hawaii's licenses never expired. When I moved to Nevada, I used the same license. One day, however, I lost it and Hawaii refused to renew because I no longer lived there. I applied for a Nevada license, which I continued to use while living in California, Washington, DC, and New York.

Moving to Belgium, I automatically received a driver's license by showing my Nevada license. *(Heaven help me if I had needed to fill out a form in Flemish!)* Again, I'm in luck because Belgian licenses are non-expiring. This works well while in Belgium and for the first three years in Germany until I'm stopped for speeding and asked for both license and passport. Studying the documents, the police officer informs me that an American living in Germany can't use a Belgian license. I probably should have pulled out the Nevada license but didn't think fast enough!

After completing another administrative form without having to take a driving test, I am issued a German license, again non-expiring. Meanwhile Nevada continues reissuing my license despite my mailing requests from Germany and later from India. Now, whenever stopped for a traffic offense, I must decide quickly whether to produce the Belgian, German or Nevada credential. To avoid paying a fine, it's best not to use the license of the country where I currently reside. How I got all these licenses without once having a driving test after age 16 is a wonder.

Another government hassle concerns residency. To whom—or to what place—must I pay taxes? One year I earn income in California, Washington, DC, and New York. Each locale expects tax payments. Another year I have residences in Belgium, Australia, and Germany; in addition, the IRS and New York State demand a share. New York argues that because I work for Schlegel Corporation in Rochester, I have a state tax obligation; but I claim no liability because I'm not a resident and only pass through on business trips. To make a point, during one trip to Rochester I visit the local voter registration center to inquire about registering for the next election. The conversation goes something like this:

Me: "I'd like to register to vote."

They: "What is your address?"

Me: "I don't have one in New York."

They: "Then you can't vote here."

Me: "But I pay taxes to New York and the IRS."

They: "That's a different department over which we have no control."

Me: "But that's taxation without representation, and America fought a war many years ago to correct this injustice."

They: (after a long pause) "Then take it up with your elected representative."

Me: "But since I don't live in the States, I don't have one."

Bureaucratic issues that are easy for resident citizens to handle plague American ex-pats. I mull over the idea of creating a 51st state comprised only of expatriates. Such a place would have more people than four less-populated, geographic states. Whether living in Tokyo or in Tripoli, overseas Americans with no stateside address have the same problems dealing with both U.S. and foreign government agencies. However, without funds and time to pursue this 51st state idea, I lose interest.

Circumventing the system did, nevertheless, solve two more personal issues. When Cyrena and Liane were born, I went through red tape filling out forms to get U.S. birth certificates. At the time there was a legal question: Could children of overseas American parents qualify for American citizenship if they remained outside the U.S. for an extended period? For evidence that I maintained a stateside residence, I used Schlegel's Rochester company address. Because no one checked to confirm it was indeed a residence, American Consulates in Brussels and Hamburg issued birth certificates for Cyrena and Liane.

Another problem was getting divorced. Proceedings are handled by states, not the federal government, but Mary and I did not have a U.S. residence. We once again used Schlegel's Rochester address, risky because the authorities could have sent someone to validate our residence.

Now, during the cold, gray days of early 1979, I think about the looming bureaucratic hassle when Barbara's and my child is born. I want the baby to have a U.S. birth certificate and passport. Furthermore, Barbara and I want him or her to have "Schroeder" as a last name. But when I inquire at the U.S. Consulate, they say an offspring of an unwed alien has no claim to any rights as an American. The German authorities say a child of a German mother would be a German citizen and would have the mother's last name, not mine.

Barbara and I have nothing against getting married except for complications that we have, until now, chosen to avoid. Eligibility for American citizenship for a baby requires that proof of a marriage performed in Germany be furnished to the U.S. Consulate after being notarized in German, translated into English, and notarized again in English. Further thwarting this plan, marriage in Germany would require our birth certificates, which have long ago been lost, and obtaining replacements will result in delays. Marriage in America seems challenging because we have no U.S. residence and therefore no state has jurisdiction to marry us. It would be difficult to fabricate a stateside address, because Barbara's passport shows no U.S. entry stamps in more than 10 years except for one visit the previous year when we vacationed in Quogue.

Weighing the problems, we decide it will be easiest to get married in New York. If the company address in Rochester was sufficient for the divorce from Mary, it should be good enough to marry Barbara. I check possibilities of getting married by proxy so Barbara won't have to go to New York, but this is impossible. Making matters worse, we need a blood test, after which we must wait 10 days before the wedding.

We develop a plan to travel first to Rochester for the blood test, then to the Bahamas for a sailing honeymoon, followed by a return to Rochester to marry. Bringing Cyrena, we embark on this venture in mid-February, unaware that the biggest blizzard of the decade is swooping down from Canada. We beat the storm into Rochester by a few hours and spend the next few days stuck in snowdrifts while making rounds to get everything done.

First stop is the county court house for the marriage license. Asking for directions, we're told to go to the dog license bureau. Thinking we hadn't heard correctly, we ask again and receive the same answer. Sure enough, someone with a twisted sense of humor had combined the two offices. We plop down in the waiting room and chat with several dog owners who explain that, as a precaution against losing their pets in the coming storm, they're getting their licenses now. And what in the world, they ask, are we doing here in the middle of this storm trying to get a marriage license? Don't we know weather is better for that sort of thing in June?

Next stop is the county health department to have blood tests and start the 10-day waiting period. Afterward I have an appointment with a local doctor to follow-up on a medical exam I had earlier in Hamburg. The X-rays taken during last month's company physical showed lesions on the backside of my right ninth rib. Furthermore, the German doctor found two pea-sized lumps in lymph glands under each arm. After the Rochester doctor examines the X-rays, he too is concerned and suggests I stay in town another day for a bone scan. By now the snowstorm is unleashing its full fury and our outbound flight is canceled, providing an extra day to undergo the added test. Preliminary findings are not encouraging, but until final results are available, I ignore possible consequences.

The entire East Coast is now snowed in. With much of the population trying to travel south for mid-winter vacations, we give up hope of getting out any time soon. But two days later the storm abates, and we secure space on a previously sold out flight to Miami. Then we lose another two days because in Miami I receive an urgent message to join Dick Turner where he is vacationing on Amelia Island located off the coast in northern Florida. All flights are booked, but sensing this meeting could impact my career, I override my frugal instincts and charter a private aircraft for the 400-mile flight from Miami.

The meeting with Dick has both positive and negative implications. He is tremendously pleased with turnaround results in the area-sealing business and implies I can expect a handsome bonus at year-end. But he is adamant that I relocate to Rochester to join the corporate management team from which he plans to choose his successor. In addition, he wants to move Schlegel Sheet from Germany to America with me managing the entire operation.

I resist as before, but when Dick persists, I realize that refusal will cost my job. I propose a compromise wherein I will bring management of the business to the U.S. but situate it somewhere other than Rochester. I contend we need to be in a southern location to work outdoors all year round rather than trying to operate in storms like the one we are currently experiencing in Rochester. Once in America, I will be only an hour or so flying time to Rochester. Dick asks what timing I envision. "Two years," I reply, thinking this is as much as Dick's patience will allow. "I will need time to explore potential U.S. locations." *(Needless to say, I don't mention my aversion to Rochester where I am uncomfortable with the corporate staff and have no desire to reside.)*

When departing the next day, I perceive that Dick is pleased with what I have accomplished but uncomfortable with what I have proposed.

After I rejoin Barbara and Cyrena in Miami a few days later than planned, we fly to Nassau to meet my parents and a friend of Cyrena's from Louisville. The following day we board Windsong, a chartered 43-foot sloop, and our party of six sets off on Barbara's and my "honeymoon." This cruise has potential to be either a lot of fun or a disaster.

It turns out to be the latter because of my mother. She does not approve of Barbara's pregnancy, our lifestyle in Hamburg, Cyrena and Liane going to Poona, or Mary's move to India. In a roundabout manner she criticizes Barbara, who is in her fourth month, for being fat. She gives flattering attention to Cyrena's friend, thereby letting Cyrena know that if she wants this kind of devotion, she'd better lead a normal childhood in the U.S. A week of living in such close quarters with so many people makes my mother increasingly irritable. To maintain peace, it's best to appease, or better yet, avoid her. The cruise finally over, Cyrena, Barbara, and I are relieved.

Time now to return to Rochester for the party to introduce Barbara to my friends on the night before our wedding. By now the crowds that had escaped the northeast blizzard for the sunny south are returning home. In the confusion of sorting out air traffic, the airline cancels our reservations and there are no flights to Rochester in time for our party. After many attempts to find alternate flights, I give up and telephone everyone that the party is canceled.

Discouraged, I reflect on events over the past two weeks—blizzard blanketing the East Coast, problems getting the marriage license, anxiety about my medical results, flight delays, impromptu trip to visit Chairman Turner, my mother's hostility, cancellation of our wedding festivities, and now being stuck in Florida. Are these signs an indication we should not get married? For a moment I consider going directly home to Hamburg to rethink what to do. But when I see how happy the three of us are in spite of everything that has gone awry, I realize these tribulations are more of a cosmic joke than a deterrent. We're able to book a late-night flight to Rochester and arrive just after midnight just when the party would have broken up.

The next morning two friends from the office agree to be witnesses, and we drive to the justice of the peace. In a dark chamber of Rochester's courthouse, a humorless official performs the ceremony. He never cracks a smile—not even when I pay him with a banknote for 50 Deutsch Marks. The local newspaper carries an account of the marriage complete with the anecdote about the Deutsch Marks but unfortunately gets my name, name of the company, and name of my wife wrong.

Following the ceremony, I call my doctor and learn the medical results are inconclusive but I should assume everything is all right. With this reassurance *(which subsequently proves wrong)*, we board an evening flight to JFK and hold an impromptu wedding reception in Pan Am's Clipper Club Lounge. We spend our wedding night sitting up on a red-eye flight to London. In coach.

The final twist in the marriage saga is that when the certificate is posted from Rochester to Germany two weeks later, it gets lost in the mail. A copy of the marriage is sent, but German authorities refuse to accept it because they require the original. It isn't until the copy is notarized both by the U.S. Consulate and again in Germany that the authorities approve.

By this time we have stopped trying to figure out why everything is going wrong. What else can Barbara and I do except laugh at so many foul-ups? Could all these bureaucratic hassles be attributed to the fact that on this date, February 26, 1979, a total eclipse of the sun occurs? "Maybe," we chuckle, "the sun gods are just playing with us!"

# 43
# The River Flows Fast

*3/79 - 7/79, Age 38*

The past 18 months have been the most tumultuous of my life. Mary and I separated, and I settled with Barbara in her garden apartment. The sheet business, once Schlegel's biggest money-loser, became the company's most profitable division. Barbara met my parents on a wonderful charter sailing cruise in the Bahamas. Mary went to India and Liane joined her several months later. Barbara and I moved into my old home with Cyrena. At Thanksgiving I injured my back, and while skiing in France in December we learned that Barbara is pregnant. In January, following a charter sail out of Nassau with my parents, Barbara and I married in New York. Meanwhile, pressure from Chairman Turner to relocate to Rochester, which I refuse to do, means I likely will soon need to find a new job. Throughout these months the back pains persist.

During my previous visit to Poona in November 1977, Bhagwan had anticipated upheavals in my life and indicated I should just go with the flow, whether fast or slow.

*"Sometimes things do go fast, sometimes the river flows very fast. When you are just floating with the river you have to go with it; you cannot choose your pace. When the river is flowing fast you have to flow fast.*

385

*When the river moves slowly you move slowly. You have to be with the river...."*

Any one of these events would normally have shaken me to the core, but Bhagwan's advice to flow with the river of life has carried me through these recent ups and downs with composure.

Now I anticipate the river will slow for a while.

I am wrong.

When accountants in Rochester report that profits for the year have soared due to success of our division, Dick Turner gives me a huge stock bonus. Along with the increased value of the shares I already own, I might not need to find another job for quite a while.

Hamburg's gray skies grudgingly retreat as spring meekly creeps in to brighten days, and I turn thoughts toward sailing. Barbara and I want a getaway for just the two of us. It is April and with Barbara in the fifth month, this is the last possible time for a cruising adventure. Recalling the dream of sailing in Greece, I learn of a yacht-charter company in England that offers a two-week package in May on a 29-foot sloop for a flotilla cruise in the Ionian Sea.

Flotilla sailing gives charterers freedom to explore new destinations without worrying about unknown waters, local customs, breakdowns, and logistic hassles. A knowledgeable captain and crew—including a mechanic with replacement parts and a hostess familiar with the villages, language, and customs—lead the fleet in a pilot yacht. What could be better? I sign up.

A few weeks later Barbara and I leave Cyrena with my new mother-in-law in Bonn before flying to Rome for sightseeing. From Rome we travel by bus to Brindisi on Italy's east coast and catch an overnight ferry to the island of Corfu where we meet our fellow flotilla sailors, all English. Each party is assigned to one of a dozen 29-foot sloops. Besides minimizing the need to carry a variety of spare parts for emergency repairs, the advantage of cruising with identical boats is that they perform similarly so the fleet won't spread out too much during a day's sail.

Although relatively small, the boat is equipped with everything we need: comfortable double berth, convenient head, well-stocked galley, and spacious salon. In addition, because Barbara may not be able to get around easily, I can comfortably sail the sloop alone. Following a tour of Corfu in the afternoon and a getting-acquainted dinner in the evening, we overnight on board at the marina.

The next morning the captain briefs us on the weather and provides compass bearings to our destination 30 miles away. We motor from the harbor, hoist sails, and set out on a new adventure. The itinerary for the next 14 days takes us through the Ionian islands of Paxos and Anti Paxos, Levkas, Kefalonia, Ithaki, Meganisi, Skorpio, and others that figure prominently in Greek mythology. Well-thumbed copies of the *Iliad* and the *Odyssey* aboard each boat allow us to compare our adventures with those of Ulysses in ancient Greek times. Favored with westerly/northwesterly winds, we sail on a comfortable broad reach on these "wine-dark seas", as Homer describes them. Warm, sunny weather prevails, and Barbara and I savor each day as we explore the islands.

Toward the end of the cruise we prepare for a race with a course set around several islands. Although I thought I had outgrown the relentless drive to win, the urge to compete resurges. On race day, unable to move about safely, Barbara watches with amusement as I single-handedly cast off from the dock, rig sails, and head out to the racecourse. Although we have an excellent start and are first across the starting line, we're unable to match the speed of boats with three or four crew and fall back in the fleet.

Approaching the second island, I observe that boats ahead are stalled in the island's wind shadow. Sensing an opportunity, I alter course to sail wide of the island to catch a clear breeze. As the drifting sailors look on with dismay, I pass everyone, encircle the island, and maintain the lead to the finish line. Luck or skill? Perhaps a little of both.

Anchored in a small harbor later in the evening, I receive a second ego boost while dining in a waterfront *taverna*. The charter company on Corfu has forwarded a telegram sent from Rochester to Hamburg and on to me. Fearing bad news that might call me back to the office, I open it with trepidation. But a wave of delight washes over me as words jump off the page. Schlegel's Board of Directors has promoted me to company vice president.

This is what has come from the meeting with Turner on Amelia Island. With the large bonus plus this promotion, I am one of three top candidates to succeed him as president and chairman. Although elated, I also sense a not-so-subtle call to move to Rochester and become a team player. I know, however, I can't—or rather won't. Something inside me knows it's wrong. I'm not a team player and I don't like Rochester.

When the cruise ends, we return to Hamburg to await the birth of our child. One day in the office I receive a telephone call from a very excited Barbara who has just returned from a check-up with her obstetrician. She refers to our visit to Rome where we saw the statue of the she-wolf nursing the city's mythical founders, twins Romulus and Remus. Thereafter we had constantly joked about having twins, our own Romulus and Remus. Well, the joke is on us. Today's ultrasound showed two heads, four hands, four feet, and two beating hearts. Life is playing a little trick, and we love it.

Any experience gained from the single births of Cyrena and later Liane suddenly becomes irrelevant. Barbara and I immediately buy every book we can find about twins. Because twins often arrive early, we accelerate preparations in order to have everything ready by the end of July instead of late August.

Even before this date we become a full house. Because Mary and I had agreed that both girls would spend at least a month each year with me, Liane arrives at Amsterdam's Schiphol Airport from Bombay in May. Bronzed by the Indian sun, Liane bubbles with laughter while describing her seven months at the ashram. Soon after her arrival there last fall, she decided, without telling her mother, to become a sannyasin. She marched to the ashram office and asked for darshan with Bhagwan. Because this four-year-old was so clear and straightforward, the coordinators quickly arranged an appointment.

Bhagwan received her affectionately and gave a beautiful name, *Prem Rasila*, which means *Juice of Love*. Liane informs us that we are now to call her Rasila. As we talk with her in the airport, we see she is just that. She exudes vibrancy and love, touching both us and onlookers with her joy.

We spend the rest of the day at Holland's famed Keukenhof, the vast tulip gardens that attract visitors from around the world in spring when flowers are in full glory. These dazzling 80 acres of bloom feel like a celebration of our joyful reunion with Rasila.

I wanted Liane/Rasila to return at this time to finish the year at the Hamburg International School, which still has two months left—sufficient time to rejoin former classmates and get a feeling for school in the West. Each morning I have fun making sure both girls get dressed, fixing breakfasts, packing lunches, and driving them to school. Rasila participates in the school's spring activities—sports day, spring pageant, and field trips to the zoo and botanical gardens. Any concerns I had about her not fitting into life in Hamburg evaporate. Rasila's teacher reports that she is at or above expectations in all subjects except math. In non-academic areas, where I had been concerned that the divorce and move to India might have a negative impact, her teacher reports that Rasila is confident, self-assured, and mature for her age. Particularly significant, the teachers find her to be extremely sensitive and considerate of others.

I am also happy with Cyrena's development. Now eight years old, she initially shrank into a shell after the divorce, but her teachers report that over the year she has blossomed with confidence and is popular with her peers. The top reader in class, she performs above grade level in all subjects. I am thankful both girls have sailed through with relative ease what could have been a difficult and turbulent year.

Spring offers opportunities for weekend sailing charters in Denmark's archipelago in the Baltic Sea. Bike trips, excursions to the seashore, and hikes in the woods fill the rest of our free time. In early July I take the girls to London. From there Cyrena, chaperoned by a friend, flies to Poona. Then Rasila and I fly to Louisville where I leave her to get reacquainted with her grandparents. After a week of business in Rochester, I return to Hamburg to be with Barbara for the birth of our twins.

# 44
# Miracle of Birth

*7/79, Age 38*

I was born on a Friday and wonder if I chose this day so my father could have the weekend to be with his first child. Barbara's and my twins also arrive on a Friday, possibly so they could be sure their father wasn't off on a business trip.

Events begin on Thursday evening when Barbara's embryonic sac breaks. We call an ambulance and two attendants carry her from the upstairs bedroom down to the emergency vehicle that speeds off to *Altona Frauenklinik* (Altona Women's Clinic) with me following close behind in my car. Upon arrival Barbara is whisked to the delivery room and given an injection to stop contractions while the attending physician consults with her regular doctor.

After an uneventful night. I go to the office in the morning but return to the hospital about noon when contractions begin again. Only then do I realize how much history repeats itself. We're in the same hospital in the *same* delivery room with the *same* doctor who delivered Liane/Rasila four years earlier. (Although he's chubbier than I remember, I recognize him when he repeats the *same* jokes!)

Because the birth involves twins, extra equipment and staff are standing by. Barbara and I begin breathing exercises practiced at her childbirth classes. I have been present for the births of my daughters, but somehow this time I feel nervous and squeamish. What will I do if there are complications? How will I feel if I become the father of four daughters? Will I faint at the sight of blood? To avoid getting in the way, I leave the room when delivery begins and maintain a vigil through a crack in the door.

At 6:30 pm on July 27, the first head emerges. The birth is a struggle and when the baby's heart begins to fade, the doctor uses forceps to bring out the head followed by the body. Unable to breathe on its own, the baby is quickly placed in an incubator. It takes just five minutes to rush through all this, and at 6:35 the second baby enters the world without difficulty. I watch from a safe distance as people rush back and forth, carrying two bloody bundles from one machine to another. Someone mentions in passing they are two little boys, and with that news, released from the pent-up tension, I collapse into a hallway chair. Then brushing away tears of joy, I re-enter the delivery room, and Barbara and I hold each other for long, lovely moments.

*(Because the afterbirth is discarded, we didn't learn at the time whether there were one or two placentas, which would determine if the twins are identical or fraternal. Not until they are two years old do we learn the boys are identical.)*

Tense hours follow delivery. Unable to breathe on his own, the first little guy, Seton, is rushed to intensive care at the *Kinderkrankenhaus* (Children's Hospital) next door and hooked to an infant ventilator. When I see him an hour later, he has a breathing tube in his windpipe and a wild collection of tubes, drip lines, and probes connected to every part of his body. Concerned that his lungs aren't sufficiently developed to allow him to breathe, the doctors X-ray his chest. Although I wince at the thought of a dozen millirads blasting him so soon after birth, it's subsequently reassuring to know the lungs are fine.

Seton remains in this unit a few days and then returns to the baby ward—just about the time his brother, Belden, is rushed into intensive care.

Belden had been doing fine but suddenly turned yellow with jaundice, which suggests the liver isn't fully developed. After a few anxious days, danger passes. Seton Saxton and Belden Edward have arrived safely into the world.

With Barbara and the boys being cared for in the hospital, on Tuesday I depart for Rochester and at week's end join Rasila and my parents who are now in Quogue. After cramming as much sailing and beach activities as possible into our few days together there, Rasila and I fly to London. Here I pass her to a friend traveling to Poona, and the two board a flight to India.

Then I dash back to Hamburg to bring Barbara and the babies home. As a favor, the doctor has allowed her extra time in the hospital. The normal stay is five days but up to 10 for a caesarian delivery. The doctor is almost out of patience when I return to get Barbara nearly two weeks after her delivery.

Leaving the hospital, I carry a baby in each hand. Even though each infant weighs five pounds—hefty for twins—they're the tiniest creatures I've ever seen. Once home, we plop them into separate red and green trundle beds and organize a routine to keep them well fed and in fresh diapers.

I commemorate the day they were born with an overview of the world. I had photograph scenes of ordinary life in Hamburg and purchase all the daily newspapers to correlate their arrival with major events around the world. Now I organize the pictures and newspaper headlines into a scrapbook. Front page news includes floods in Houston, Jackie Kennedy Onassis' 50th birthday, and a hybrid lion born in Atlanta.

One item holds special significance. The United Nations has declared 1979 as "The Year of the Child," and Germany, which faces a declining birth rate, offers financial incentives for babies born this year.

Not only are Barbara and I being good citizens doing our part to increase the population—we are increasing our bank account with the receipt of double government stipends awarded for twins!

Friday 27 July 1979

2:00 am · Vihan tripped over telephone while walking to bathroom leaned over to pick up receiver - Water broke -

2:10 am · Called Ambulance

2:30 am · Arrived separately at hospital, contractions starte

2:45 am · PS was given coffee, V. was given exam by midw

3:00 am · Contractions coming at 5 min intervals, 45 s

3:35 am · Injection given intra-venously, contractions stopped

4:40 am · PS returned home

8:30 am · PS visited V on way to work.

2:15 pm · Hospital called PS. Halfway through

3:00 pm · PS arrived hospital, V had received "Peritoral" an was semi-doped.    6 cm

4:15 pm · 8 cm

5:30 pm · 9 cm, V had no feeling of contractions

6:30 pm · Birth of #1

6:35 pm · Birth of #2

[July 27, 1979, Hamburg, age 38] Timeline of births of Seton and Belden

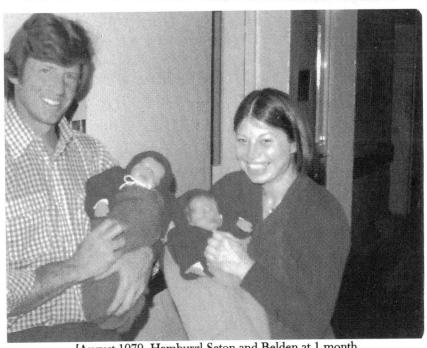

[August 1979, Hamburg] Seton and Belden at 1 month

# 45
# Fired

*7/79 - 12/79, Age 38*

After numerous business trips in recent months—several of which involved shuttling daughters between continents—I don't anticipate traveling any time soon. Suddenly, not one but four urgent business matters come up, and I must head to Puerto Rico, San Francisco, Denver, and Rochester. Feeling guilty for leaving Barbara alone to care for the boys, I reluctantly pack my bags.

A vice president from Rochester meets me in San Juan to check prospects for constructing a plant in Puerto Rico to produce Schlegel Sheet. The state's chamber of commerce director drives us to prospective building sites and offers incentives like minimal taxes, subsidized construction loans, low-cost labor, and free worker training programs. Months earlier I had determined Houston would be the best site, and the VP and I realize that Puerto Rico makes no sense. However, Chairman Turner had proposed it; therefore we have to go through the motions of checking it out. After a week we confirm what we already knew, but I have two more stops before returning to headquarters to report the findings.

Our Saudi agent, Khalid al-Turki wants me to visit him at his home in Marin overlooking San Francisco Bay before he returns to the Kingdom. I anticipate this visit could offer possibilities for a major business deal. But during two days with Khalid, his American wife, and their two children, conversation is limited to social talk and reminiscences about our days at Stanford. Upon realizing his purpose is to tempt me into considering employment with his company in the Middle East, I allude to how much I enjoy the job at Schlegel, and the subject never arises.

In Denver I check on a large project to line evaporation ponds for Denver Power Corporation. Our crew is a mix of Germans and Americans, which ensures that the installation benefits from experience of top personnel from both companies. All is going well.

Now I head to Rochester to report findings from Puerto Rico to our chief executive. Because Turner believes San Juan offers the best prospects for siting a new plant, convincing him otherwise is tough. First, I explain that because high-density polyethylene resin to extrude the liner is produced in Houston, importing raw material to San Juan would be expensive and risky. Second, because no markets for Schlegel Sheet exist in Puerto Rico, we would incur excessive costs shipping to mainland customers. I finally win the argument and Turner concedes the plant will be built in Houston. But once again I sense his irritation that I have not embraced his ideas—one more example of my contrarian approach. Although I held firm to what I believe is right, I return to Hamburg feeling shaken.

In late October I again leave Barbara for a lengthy trip, this time to the Middle East. Installation crews are finishing a major phase of the Saudi Arabia contract and I want to inspect the progress. Afterward I fly the short hop from Dhahran to Bombay and on to Poona to see Bhagwan and check on Cyrena and Rasila. *(My previous trips caused no difficulties for Barbara alone with the babies, and she encouraged me to go ahead to India. Although she never admits it, I think she prefers having me away, allowing time to devote herself exclusively to Seton and Belden.)*

On this third visit to the ashram, things are different. Rather than 2,000 visitors as before, the number has doubled. The ashram has built more facilities and rented eight nearby estates to accommodate these newcomers. Bhagwan gives morning discourses and evening darshans every day and responds to correspondence that inundates the ashram. To my eye he's as fresh as ever but also appears more fragile. His serenity touches me deeply.

I'm overjoyed to be back. Any concerns about Mary, Cyrena, and Rasila disappear the moment I see how happy they are. The girls attend the ashram school and are involved in music, dance, art, and other creative activities. With friends from all over the world, they receive wonderful exposure to different cultures and languages. As noted before, because Bhagwan insists that instructors be certified teachers in their home countries, the English-speaking staff is excellent.

Cyrena recently became a sannyasin, and in darshan Bhagwan gave her the prefix "Veet" to add to her name. "*Veet Cyrena*" means "*Beyond Control,*" and he encourages her to live this way. Mary and I think it's a perfect message. Cyrena tends to hold back in life, never moving into any situation until she feels in control. Bhagwan encourages her to stop imprisoning herself. He suggests that she fly, dance, sing, and flow into a more spontaneous life. When she becomes tense over something new, he explains, the name should remind her to let go of anxieties and open up.

At the ashram, I feel fragmented. Back home I live at a hectic pace, the days overflowing with busyness. My job continues to be exciting, and I enjoy the work; material things do bring some satisfaction, comfort, and pleasure, but this practical, logical life feels empty. Looking ahead, I see it will never fulfill me. After years of stifling feelings, I am learning to be in better touch with my heart. I have been living the prose of life but missing its poetry.

Bhagwan says that this disconnection occurs when growth begins. As one loses touch with the old world and gets glimmers of another way of being, one can feel fragmented and uprooted. Although the old is no longer tenable, nothing new has yet arrived to replace it.

I write a letter to Bhagwan regarding this dilemma and ask what groups I should engage in during this short visit. During other visits I participated in Western-type therapy groups designed to root out anger, fear, hostility, and whatever else creates blocks and anxiety. Now I expect

Bhagwan will send me to Eastern-type therapies that lead to meditation, letting go, floating, and becoming more open. I'm surprised when he suggests groups designed to get me in touch with the physical body: Reiki, Shiatsu, and Centering.

Wondering what he is trying to help me understand through these therapies, I sign up and soon experience several things about my body. I become aware of a dull, throbbing pain in the lower back, a pain that seems to have been there all along but now feels more pronounced. The location is exactly where I felt that sudden sharp pain months ago in Louisville while cutting firewood. Tuning in to this awareness, I become increasingly perplexed. Bhagwan has often urged love and care for the body because it is the temple for the soul. *(This guidance takes on a deeper meaning half a year later when I learn of my illness. Only then do I understand what Bhagwan had seen and how he had been preparing me with these groups.)*

Touched by the atmosphere of love in the ashram, I open up and relax. There is nowhere I want to be other than here enjoying this beautiful setting. I wonder: Should I send Schlegel a telegram quitting my job and bring Barbara and the boys to Poona? This time of reflection, however, reminds me how much I enjoy my work and the possibilities for the future that comes with the increasing value of Schlegel stock. If only I could combine life in the ashram with the world of work and live in a state of spiritual worldliness or worldly spirituality.

Rasila, now age five, decides she wants to be in Hamburg with her new brothers, and Mary approves. I telephone Barbara for her okay and am delighted when she agrees. A few days later Rasila and I fly home to Germany for a happy reunion with Barbara and our four-month-old sons.

In mid-November Barbara, Rasila, the boys and I fly to the States for a series of family events. First, we head to Quogue for the wedding of a cousin. Several days of festivities, reunions with my parents and relatives, and the usual hullabaloo precede the ceremony. Barbara and I smile as we think back to the crazy fun and delightful disasters that surrounded our marriage. We agree we much prefer our own nuptial—misadventures and all.

Rasila returns with Mom and Dad to Louisville while Barbara and the infants travel with me to Houston where I check on construction of the new factory. When I agreed to relocate to the States, I stipulated I would move near the Houston plant rather than to Rochester, an idea to which Chairman Turner reluctantly assented. For the next week, real estate agents lead Barbara and me through new homes around Houston. We try to muster enthusiasm for sunken baths, kitchens with built-in microwaves, and wall-to-wall stereo systems. Everything we see is neat, efficient, comfortable—even luxurious—but we can't imagine ourselves in these surroundings. Remembering how happy we were in the little one-room apartment with its meager furnishings, we feel the need to escape from what we're seeing here.

In this undecided state, we fly to Louisville for a traditional Thanksgiving with my parents and my sister's family. Then, taking Rasila with us, we fly to Rochester to report on the Houston plant before returning to Hamburg.

The weeks between Thanksgiving and Christmas are quiet for area-lining construction projects, and I devote this time to preparing plans and budgets for the coming year. I schedule a week-long conference in Hamburg at yearend to present these ideas to the entire area-sealing group, which includes staff from England, France, Germany, and the States.

A week before the conference, Dick sends a telex informing that he intends to join us. Although this seems strange, I continue to close out the year. The conference begins on a Monday, and I ask everyone to arrive by Sunday evening for a welcoming reception. Dick advises he will arrive Sunday afternoon along with another vice president who would benefit by attending. This is good news because the more people in headquarters who understand the business, the better.

Driving to the airport to pick up my boss on Sunday afternoon, I feel pleased with how well the business, as well as my personal life, is going. I'm looking forward to a skiing vacation right after the conference, and, although my back pain has worsened since returning from Poona, I feel fit and relaxed.

At baggage claim, Dick looks tense and tired. Under the best circumstances the flight from New York through London to Hamburg is wearying, and bad weather or delays can make the trip exhausting. But when Dick says he left New York early for two days in London, I don't understand his haggard look. At the Atlantic Hotel, I ask if he wants to rest before the reception. He instead requests me to come to his room. Over drinks, I begin discussing a large contract we recently won for a project in Iraq, but Turner quickly cuts me short.

"Peter, I think the time has come for us to part company from one another...."

# 46
# Good-Bye Schlegel

*12/79, Age 38*

Peeking out from under massive gray clouds, the setting sun lengthens shadows across Hamburg's skyline. The upper-floor window in the Atlantic Hotel looks out over the quiet waters of the *Binnenalster* and sparkling glints reflect from the city's seven famed towers.

Inside the hotel room I face Dick Turner, my boss for the past nine years. On this cold afternoon of the thereafter-to-be-memorable date of Sunday, December 16, 1979, I feel oddly detached from what is going on. Dick has just fired me. Yes, in spite of the fact that he has consistently given me top bonuses and recognition for outstanding performance, my boss just fired me. His words come as quite a shock, but surprisingly, I remain as calm as a spectator watching a movie or a passerby witnessing a distant scene.

Why, I ask myself, is Dick doing this? I mentally review my balance sheet with Schlegel where I've been president of five companies with superb results at each. I grew the Belgian subsidiary from a fledgling start-up into a solid, professionally managed company with markets throughout Western Europe, Eastern Europe, and Africa. In Australia I acquired two companies, increased profitability, doubled market share, revamped production, introduced new products, and planned a new Schlegel office in Singapore. At the first German company, I turned around a floundering subsidiary by replacing out-of-date products with updated manufacturing lines that opened new automotive, aircraft, and building markets throughout Europe. Within two years of taking over Schlegel Sheet companies in Germany and the U.S.—formerly the company's biggest money-losers—I redirected the businesses to become more efficient and turn income statements from red to black. I expanded Schlegel's customer base into the Middle East, grew the German operations, and initiated the building of plants in Ireland and Houston.

And what about the intangible pluses? I mentored others, six of whom had been promoted to managing directors of other Schlegel divisions. Having worked in all three business sectors—building products, automotive, and area sealing—I know the company's worldwide operations better than anyone else. As the only American manager who speaks several foreign languages and has traveled throughout Europe and Asia, I can communicate in business environments throughout the world.

Furthermore, my salary has been in the high six digits for five years, making me one of the best-paid employees. I know Dick recognizes my outstanding performance—confirmed when he said my bonus was the highest he had ever paid.

Granted, there have been minuses. I have a bulldog's reputation for getting things done my way. I haven't been the consummate team player, and I have come and gone independently, neglecting to inform headquarters of my schedule. Most important in Dick's eyes, I refused to move to Rochester or transfer management of Schlegel Sheet back to corporate headquarters. Although confident that my assets more than adequately offset liabilities, I have apparently overestimated that nebulous entry that drives accountants crazy—goodwill—or, in my case, I have underestimated the ill-will I've aroused in Dick.

Another reason I'm surprised, though, is the timing of this termination. Firing people immediately before Christmas is cruel because they can't get another job when companies are closed. All they can do is sit and stew. And Dick's odd timing is especially awkward right before Schlegel Sheet's worldwide employees gather to review operations and celebrate the year's spectacular results. As I stare into Dick's face, his eyes shift guiltily to the floor and then dart around the room to avert my gaze.

After a moment's silence I ask, "Dick, why are you doing this?"

Flustered, he looks at me and says, "Surely you're not surprised?"

He's astonished when I reply, "Yes. I am," which is true.

I have had an inkling for more than a year that I would separate from Schlegel, but never imagined it would occur like this. Suddenly, I understand. Bhagwan had told me not to force my way but instead to let things happen on their own. This is clearly the right time to leave Schlegel, and it's happening without my instigation. Because I succeeded in making Schlegel Sheet profitable, there's no higher position in the company without returning to Rochester, which I refuse to do. This is indeed the right time to leave.

Dick is clearly uncomfortable with our discussion and wants it to end. I wonder if my calmness makes him question whether he's making a mistake. He had probably considered removing me earlier but each time decided against it in view of my successes. Finally, I must have, in his estimation, gone over the edge. Whether true or not, Dick's mannerisms betray that he isn't sure of his decision. I now understand his haggardness when he deplaned at the airport—he was anxious about what he had decided to do.

Feeling sympathy for Dick, I tell him he should relax and stop worrying, because I have no problem with the situation.

"If that's how things are to be," I offer, "then fine."

Dick sinks back in his chair as I fill him in on the evening program. I suggest, and he agrees, that we say nothing about our conversation until the following day. This conference is important and I want it to get off to a good start this evening. Then I update him on activities of the firm along with urgent issues, and Dick agrees to pass matters to the vice president who will take over for a few weeks until a replacement is hired.

Next Dick pulls documents from his briefcase that outline specifics about my termination. The most important option: I have the choice either to sell my stock back to the company at the value to be determined after closing the current year or retain it. When I ask what he intends to do about a bonus, Dick replies he doesn't see why there should be any. I respond that although this is naturally up to him, withholding it would be unfair. Salary increases, I remind him, are given based upon the company's future expectations of performance, of which there are none, but a bonus recognizes past achievements, and I have surpassed goals set at the beginning of the year. *(A few months later Dick relents and gives me a $5,000 bonus, which is far smaller than I might ordinarily expect.)*

When Dick announces that Dan Fultz, vice president for human resources, has secretly accompanied him on this trip and is waiting in another hotel room, I leave to meet with him. After all, there is nothing more to discuss with Dick.

For the next hour Dan and I cover details. Because we have been friends for years, Dan feels awkward, but I assure him everything is all right and that we can get through the points without problems. The only decision left is whether to sell or retain my Schlegel stock. After telling Dan my first reaction is to hold onto it because its value presumably will continue to increase, he gives a quizzical look and, after a pause, talks as a friend.

"How much further do you think the stock will appreciate once you're out of the company?" he asks. "Consider carefully all the changes Dick will make in the area-sealing business when you won't be there to bring it back on track."

Prompted by his advice, I decide to liquidate the shares.

We drive to my office where Dan stands by while I clean out my desk; then we return to the hotel. To the surprise of Dick, Dan, and Jay Metzler, the vice president who will temporarily replace me, I join the three of them at the hotel bar for drinks. I see no reason to be excluded, and for the next hour we chat and joke as former colleagues before going to the evening reception to launch the conference.

Barbara is waiting up when I return home. While recounting the details I check inwardly for feelings of bitterness, anger, or resentment. I find none. Instead, I'm relieved, as if a burden has unexpectedly been lifted.

In the morning I pick up Dick and drive to the conference. We had agreed to announce my departure after my keynote address. As the group assembles, I scrutinize faces to see if news has leaked out, but apparently it hasn't.

I begin with a review of operations over the past several years. We had started with a small-volume business that was losing money but have now expanded operations many-fold, making us successful. I present facts and figures but save one detail for last. I explain we have had zero employee turnover for more than two years, and this continuity has been invaluable to our accomplishments. But now, I explain, there is to be a personnel change and a major one at that.

There's silence as every ear perks up. "I am leaving the company," I inform the group. Wanting to remove any speculation, I add, "Dick Turner has asked me to leave." To ensure there's no misunderstanding with German colleagues, I repeat this last portion in German.

Without waiting for any reaction or questions, I pick up my things and walk out of the room. Even though I will remain on the payroll another six months, this meeting concludes my career with Schlegel.

*(Afterward, I learned that the conference was the success I had hoped it would be. Subsequent developments, however, proved ruinous. Dick used the "divide and conquer" strategy by filling my position with three managing directors—one in Houston, one in Hamburg, and one in Rochester—and required all communications to flow through corporate headquarters. He transferred the business from Hamburg to Rochester, a change that brought the entire operation to a stop. Within six months, 11 of the 75 employees left the firm. No one in Rochester spoke German or visited Germany. No managers traveled to the Middle East, and the Saudi agent quit. Major projects in Iraq and Colorado lost money. Management curtailed production in Hamburg and scrapped plans for the plant in Ireland. The final blow came after one year when the new managing director in Hamburg quit followed by the chief financial officer.)*

In the days following my departure, I monitor reactions of both the "old Peter" and the "new Nartan." Peter focuses on two things—nursing an ego and achieving goals. Subsequent Schlegel events prove Peter right. The basin-liner business does not succeed in Europe once it's moved to Rochester. When the business doesn't run as well without me, the ego takes satisfaction. My achiever persona, however, is sad, because I had worked years to build a business that now is crumbling. Even though I'm no longer part of it, it is my legacy and I want it to succeed.

Meanwhile, Nartan reflects upon the teachings of Bhagwan. Using a mountain metaphor, Bhagwan said if one is happy or sad upon either attaining or not attaining the peak, the ego is present, and one has missed the moment. The moment is in the process, not the goal. If there is no ego, it doesn't matter whether or not one reaches the top.

Once I relate this insight to my work, I have an epiphany: Joy derived from my work should not depend upon the results. I'm overcome with gratitude for this understanding.

*(Schlegel continued on a downward spiral. Schlegel Sheet folded. In 1986 Dick Turner died of an aneurysm. In the absence of a strong management team in Rochester, the board voted to sell the company. In December 1988, an English firm, British Tire and Rubber, purchased Schlegel and immediately started stripping assets. It closed the German and Belgium businesses, terminated the employees, and sold the buildings and production equipment. The company was sold again in 1997 and in 2006 to companies that broke up the remaining divisions. English-based Amesbury Truth retained the Schlegel brand to market products worldwide to the window and door industries.)*

Looking back on that fateful December day, I'm grateful to Dan Fultz, who acted as a friend when he advised liquidating my stock. I sold the shares at their highest value before the company's downturn and dismemberment.

The timing for being let go *by* and for letting go *of* Schlegel could not have been better. Everything unfolded and flowed with no need for me to orchestrate these great changes.

Nartan is learning.

# 47
# Job Search

*12/79 - 1/80, Ages 38 - 39*

Severe back pains had made me miss work recently, so now that I'm free of the company I schedule a thorough medical examination in Hamburg. When X-rays show nothing unusual, the doctor treats me for sore muscles and sends me on my way. Because Barbara, Rasila (5 years), the twins (5 months), and I have no reason to linger in Hamburg, we advance the ski vacation in the French Alps a week.

Sunshine and new snow greet us at Val Thorens. Accommodations that we scouted out the previous year offer panoramic views of the mountains with the added attraction that the main chairlift is at our front door. We have nothing to do except enjoy two weeks of skiing. After a few days, however, searing pains streak up my back with any sudden move. Fearful that a fall could be serious, I ski with caution and stick to intermediate runs.

Two days after Christmas I celebrate my 39th birthday. As 1979 draws to a close, we have no idea where we will go, what we will do, or where we will be a year from now. With every option open, we greet 1980 with excitement and anxiety about unknown adventures ahead. The dark cloud is my back. The pain becomes so severe, we cut the vacation short and return to Hamburg.

The severance package with Schlegel provides unrestricted use of a national outplacement firm to assist in finding a new position. Not wanting another job quite yet, I nevertheless decide to pursue this opportunity. With the option of using any of the firm's outplacement offices, I choose Los Angeles to investigate prospects for relocating to California.

When my back feels better after a few days, Rasila and I fly to London to meet a sannyasin who accompanies her to Poona where she'll rejoin her mother and sister. I continue to Rochester to tend to two items. First, I consult with my doctor who makes another examination. He again finds nothing and suggests the problem is just strained muscles.

Second, selling the Schlegel stock is complicated because I had distributed shares to my family. This necessitates filling out stock powers, share certificates, promissory notes, agreements of sale, letters of instruction, and more paperwork.

Twenty years earlier in college I had set goals to reach at different ages. Attaining financial independence was the final goal to reach by age 40, and now, at age 39, it is about to happen. Assuming inflation doesn't get out of hand, the tiny piece of paper I'm soon to accept will remove money worries for years. Short of squandering the sum, Barbara and I should be able to live any way we chose. If it's invested wisely, I may never need to work again.

What an awesome moment when Schlegel's treasurer hands over the check! Although I exercise great restraint and manage to receive the check with dignified formality, I'm about to explode. It's hard not to scream with joy while solemnly shaking hands with Schlegel officers assembled for the occasion. (Dick Turner is noticeably absent.)

After exiting headquarters for the last time, I zoom straight to the bank to deposit the check to earn interest for that day. It's a struggle to keep a straight face at the cashier's window when presenting the 2 3/4" x 6" slip of wood pulp that opens such a wealth of possibilities. Afterward I proceed alone to a local restaurant avoiding the usual ones I used to frequent with business colleagues, because I want to be anonymous for this last visit in Rochester. Allowing myself to be the excited little boy I have squelched all day, I order a bottle of champagne to celebrate.

The outplacement office in Los Angeles is my final destination on the journey to explore job possibilities, but I detour along the way. First stop is Washington, D.C. One option is to work in government, and I have names of people at the Environmental Protection Agency who are involved with industrial waste basins. However, a few days traipsing in and out of drab offices in monotonous government buildings changes my outlook. Writing proposals as an administrator holds no appeal for an entrepreneur even if, as I am told, possible positions would be close to "real power," a reference to the President's office.

Next stop is Louisville for a weekend with Mom and Dad. I welcome the respite as conversations center mostly on family rather than on the turbulence in my life.

From Louisville it's off to Denver, the country's self-proclaimed energy capital, which only a year earlier was a candidate for the new Schlegel Sheet plant. Here I explore job options with small energy companies. The people running them are enthusiastic and entrepreneurial but undercapitalized, hoping for a lucky break to become leaders in the country's anticipated energy boom. Not wanting to be part of a herd of competitors, I check Denver off the list.

Next stop: San Francisco where I still know people at Stanford and in the business community. Job prospects with startups that offer equity stir excitement with hopes that an eventual IPO could make everyone a multimillionaire. Because I could launch another area-sealing company after the one-year, anti-competition agreement expires, I visit venture capital firms to explore prospects of raising seed money. Several respond positively—an indication that with a well-organized business plan, I could attract startup funds.

Next I drive down the peninsula to Stanford University to meet friends and professors from student days. I have vague notions about a job in a non-teaching position, and prospects appear bright in alumni relations, development, and fundraising. Sunny skies and balmy mid-January temperatures remind me why this part of California is an attractive place to live and raise a family.

From Stanford I fly to Los Angeles for a weeklong program with the outplacement consultants who assist in creating a new résumé, rehearsing job interview skills, lining up job references, and reviewing techniques to employ when seeking a new career. The job market looks good, including prospects to take over struggling companies, but I want to take time before making a decision. I have to acknowledge I've been kidding myself about pursuing any of these. What I really want to do is to go to Poona to join the ashram as soon as possible. We'll move out of the Hamburg house and head to India.

One problem remains: The back pain has become relentless. Barely able to carry a suitcase, I struggle through the airport and resolve to seek out a doctor in Hamburg. Although medical exams have so far turned up nothing, I know something is seriously wrong.

# 48
# Crisis

*1/80 - 2/80, Age 39*

After returning to Hamburg from the States, I see an orthopedist and a neurologist, but neither can determine what's wrong. Because I am now unable to walk and suffer just sitting or standing, the doctors check me into *Altona Krankenhaus* (Hospital) the following Monday, January 28, 1980, for a complete checkup. For two days while lying in bed, I undergo a thorough examination: blood, urine, X-rays, myelogram, and—because the German medical terms are beyond me—I'm not sure what else.

The third morning brings catastrophe. As I sit up in bed my back fails completely, and overwhelmed by pain, I collapse. My agonized cries send the nurses tearing out of the room to get a pain killer. A minute after receiving the injection, the medication takes effect. As the raw edge of the pain subsides, I ease my body into a tolerable position and dare not move for hours.

Feeling better in the evening, with assistance from orderlies, I again try to sit by inching up on one elbow to a semi-reclining position. With self-confidence, I push to a sitting position. Suddenly it happens again—a bright flash explodes in my head as searing pain wracks my body. My cries probably resound throughout the hospital. Unsure how to help, the orderlies stand frozen. I attempt to resume the tolerable position but to no avail. I sink a little lower, but still no relief. Losing coherence, I fall back howling in agony. Just as I hit the bed, a nurse gives an injection into my thigh. I grit my teeth waiting for the next minute to pass quickly. However, the pain remains intense. When I cry out for another injection, the nurses hesitate because they have administered the maximum prescribed dosage. Seeing my desperation, the head nurse breaks the rules and gives a second injection. I pass out.

*(Whenever I previously heard people with back problems complain, I politely listened, considering the issues to be on par with upset stomachs or severe headaches. I will never make that mistake again. I cannot imagine torment worse than experiencing every nerve turned into a channel of excruciating pain.)*

When I awaken 12 hours later, the neurosurgeon explains that although there's nothing wrong with my spinal cord, something has shown up in the tomographs of the vertebrae. He doesn't know exactly what is wrong, and the hospital has no orthopedic specialist. When I ask where I can go, he replies there's no place in Hamburg, but a specialist clinic in Muenster might....

I don't listen to what he says, because my mind is racing to work out a plan. If the largest city in Germany can't help, do I want to go to a smaller one? I piece together the situation. Although I am obviously having a major health problem, the doctors can't figure out what's going on. In business situations, I'd call an outside consultant who's an expert in the field. But who can I turn to now? Then I remember that my former father-in-law, Mary's father Dr. Lewis Overton, is one of the leading orthopedists in America.

I reach him by phone at a hospital in New Mexico. When I explain the situation, Lew offers to help, so I schedule a telephone appointment later that day for him to talk with my German doctor. When I ask the doctor here to call from my bedside, he's reluctant and proposes that his office is more convenient. Not wanting to insult him by saying I could help with English translation, I explain my firm will pay for the call only if it is from my bedside business phone. He agrees.

The doctors talk. The conversation begins in a professional manner with questions and answers flying back and forth. However, my doctor gets nervous. He asks why Lew is raising questions that are irrelevant.

After the conversation finishes and I'm alone, Lew tells me about other tests such as blood sedimentation, the doctors should have scheduled. As a specialist in neurology rather than orthopedics, my doctor hadn't addressed conditions outside his area of expertise. Now I understand why the German doctors are lost. Lew uncovered their oversight simply by asking about testing for abnormal protein in the blood, which they had not done because it was beyond their purview. This is the clincher that prompts my decision to get out of Germany as fast as possible and return to the States—no more tests in Hamburg and no dealing with experts from Muenster.

Lew confirms the wisdom of leaving Germany quickly, explaining that since WW II very few medical developments have come out of the country. Before the war Germany had been a leader, but now it is not the place to be for a medical complication.

I make another decision: When Barbara and I leave, we will not come back. The Hamburg era is over. Because of uncertainties in our life, I don't want to be tied to a house and possessions that would pull us back one day.

That evening at the hospital I share the events of the day with Barbara and explain why I want to pack up and go. She agrees. What I had decided after a lengthy analysis, she had long before concluded with simple intuition. She has been around hospitals and doctors enough to know my condition is complicated and Germany is not the place to deal with it. In her beautiful, quiet way Barbara tells me not to worry—she will handle whatever's necessary. She does so over the next three days.

When she visits at the end of the first, I ask what she did.

Barbara: "The first thing I did this morning was buy a watch."

Me: "Buy a watch? Buy a watch! What were you thinking?" I had expected her to say she went to the bank, ordered the packers, or sold the car.

Barbara patiently explains: "I have numerous things to do in the next days and many appointments. Furthermore, I have to keep track of when stores open and close, so what could be more logical than to buy a watch?"

I laugh. It's her show, and she does it her way. She spends the first day sorting everything out and most of it is "out." What is left she puts into three piles: one to take with us, one to be shipped to the States, and one to be sold. The second day she sells the car, cancels the house lease, shuts off utilities, and cleans out the kitchen. The third day she holds a yard sale and arranges for packers to ship belongings to Mom and Dad in Louisville. Finally, she arranges for disposal of the remaining trash. Throughout all this confusion she takes care of Belden and Seton, now seven months old, and visits me evenings.

Meanwhile, I arrange logistics over the phone. I decide to go to Louisville where I will have the support of my parents who line up a hospital bed and doctors to receive me. Then I contact airlines to book flights that can accommodate a stretcher. It hardly seems possible that everything can be done so quickly but many people pitch in to make it all work out.

From now on, Germany will be a memory.

I hope my pain will soon become a memory as well.

# 49
# Back Home

*2/80 - 5/80, Age 39*

How strange to say goodbye to Hamburg. For seven years I thrived as a corporate executive in this cosmopolitan city; now I'm an invalid without a home or job.

Early morning on February 17 an ambulance pulls away from *Altona Krankenhaus* with me uncomfortably strapped to a stretcher inside. Barbara and our seven-month-old twins follow in another car to the airport.

The next 24 hours are the strangest odyssey of my life. We transit six airports—Hamburg, Frankfurt, Brussels, New York, Atlanta and Louisville. At each layover I edge my fragile body off one stretcher onto another. Ambulances speed me across the runways to the next awaiting aircraft. Under the shadow of each new wing I shimmy onto another stretcher before being lifted by gantry to a service entry and welcomed aboard.

As a nurse, Barbara is permitted to inject morphine as needed. My slightest wrong movement evokes spasms of pain, and she administers a dose whenever my back seizes. Relief floods over me during the final move from an ambulance stretcher to a bed at Methodist Hospital in Louisville. I sink into a deep sleep.

I should have known the hospital routine wouldn't adjust for the six-hour time difference between Hamburg and Louisville. A scant few hours after my arrival, a cheery nurse bursts into the room with *"Guten Morgen, Herr Schroeder."* I do a double take. Has the journey been a dream? Am I still in Germany?

Seeing my groggy, puzzled look, the nurse—German by birth—reverts to English, explaining she's delighted to have a patient from her homeland. Once my nationality is clarified, we laugh and chitchat in German as she takes vital statistics. Meeting hospital staff throughout the morning, I feel jovial for the first time in weeks. The warmth and informality here contrast with the formal, no-nonsense attitudes at the German hospital.

I'm again taken aback when the doctor walks in with yet another greeting in flawless German, *"Guten Morgen, Herr Schroeder."* Another laugh, another clarification. Dr. Walter Badenhausen reassures me he left Germany as a child and received medical training in the States.

After exchanging pleasantries, Dr. Badenhausen outlines a fast-paced schedule of medical tests and exams. For two days I'm shuttled through examination rooms, each with machines that monitor my body with electrodes connected to banks of flickering lights. Once tests are finished, specialists take over: urologist, internist, hematologist, oncologist, neurologist, orthopedist, cardiologist, and a radiologist. Because there's no definite diagnosis, Dr. Badenhausen concludes that he, an orthopedic surgeon accompanied by a thoracic surgeon, has to "go in to determine the problem and patch up two vertebrae."

My operation is scheduled to take two hours. It requires four. Complications arise. Three pints of blood are unexpectedly needed. Dr. Badenhausen slices me open from the left thigh up and around to the middle of my back. Next, he cuts off the 11th floating left rib and carves it into strips to insert around the second lumbar vertebra replacing the three-quarters that had been eaten away. From the thigh, he collects bone scrapings to concoct a paste to pack into the reconstructed vertebra to hold the bits together until they fuse into a single unit. Due to unexpected complexities the surgeons decide not to repair another deteriorated vertebra; instead they sew me up and send me to the recovery room.

Two evenings later Barbara is with me when Dr. Badenhausen, ill at ease, enters my room. The Dr. Badenhausen of the week before was jovial and light-hearted but the man now at the foot of my bed is somber and matter-of-fact. Results of tissues sent to the pathology lab are not good. A strained silence. His complex explanation of the findings boils down to one hard fact: The diagnosis is multiple myeloma. It's a fatal form of bone marrow cancer. The silence in the room shouts at us.

I feel nothing. The doctor's words hang in the air, but I am a spectator to what is taking place. Dr. Badenhausen is talking about my body and telling me that shortly I will be leaving it. Yet I am as detached as if being told I will have my fingernails trimmed. Yes, something will happen to my body, but it won't touch that essence I know to be me. I am filled with a sense of inevitability.

Through the practice of meditation I understand I am not the body. I have caught a glimpse of the experience of death, learning to be the witness detached from a physical body. That's not to say I'm resigned to dying—not in the sense of giving up. Given the choice of life or death, naturally my preference is to live. But being detached and open, I am prepared to receive whatever is to come.

Similarly, six weeks earlier in Hamburg I felt no concern upon being fired. Now, it is a fact that I don't have much more time in this body. I find no anger, fear, or denial and have no plan to try to manipulate my way out. It all seems simple.

I feel tremendous love for Bhagwan who prepared me for this moment, and I'm thankful to be in a meditative state when it occurs. Barbara also responds with love and gentleness. Dr. B is surprised by our calmness. I have only one question, and he knows it without my asking.

"Six months," he speaks softly after another silence. "Some have made it almost two years, but your disease is too advanced."

He explains that in other operations similar to mine, he would simply sew up a patient with advanced myeloma. However, since I am unable to walk, he replaced one vertebra so I could be ambulatory for the time I have left. He hadn't touched the other deteriorating vertebra because it will stay intact for another six months, which is all that matters.

After he leaves, Barbara and I hold each other. Although we had sensed something like this was coming, neither had expressed it. Death is new for me, but not for Barbara. As an infant she had fled East Germany with her family to escape the onslaught of the Russians. In her distant recollection she recalls the bombings and fighting... the sudden death and destruction of war. Growing up as a refugee, she had learned the slow death that comes from hunger and deprivation. As a nurse she had tended patients who died. Now death has assumed a new form: rising up to take away her husband and the father of her children just when she arrives in a new country. But for the moment we have our love for each other—the only reality that touches us just now.

The next day I am again swept up in tests to determine how far the cancer has spread. Previous X-rays and a bone scan had found abnormalities in three ribs, and biopsies confirm cancer throughout these regions. New CT scans reveal that other vertebrae have been damaged by the myeloma. The final prognosis a week later is bleaker than originally estimated.

Multiple myeloma is treatable but considered incurable. A cancer in the bone marrow plasma cells, it falls within the medical jurisdiction of the hematologist. I am turned over to Dr. Manuel Grimaldi, a Spanish specialist who reassures that he, too, received his medical training in the U.S. Dr. Grimaldi outlines a two-phase program: chemotherapy to control cancer in the affected ribs and radiation to treat the damaged vertebrae. Chemo starts immediately, but radiotherapy is delayed three weeks to give the newly grafted bone time to fuse with the old vertebra. If treatment is started too soon, it will destroy the new bone; if delayed too long, the cancer will quickly progress.

After several weeks on my back it's time to learn to walk again. Physical therapists fit me with a back brace and warn me not to even think about being vertical without it. Now begins the program to reacquaint me with perpendicularity. A therapist straps me to a tilt-up table and cranks it upright. As I come past 45 degrees, blood rushes from my head, and I black out. Regaining consciousness, I practically gag as the therapist breaks ammonia capsules under my nose. Fortunately, improvement progresses rapidly. Within days I graduate from the tilt-up table and can take short walks.

When not in physical therapy, apart from losing myself to the amusements of television, I listen to tapes of Bhagwan's morning discourses and read books he has written. Other times I meditate. It's a gentle period, totally free of the *doing* mode of life. I'm living the classic Zen sutra, "Nothing to do, nowhere to go." The situation offers the opportunity to *be*, rather than to *do*.

I come to understand teachings of the ancient Tao master who, when asked what he did, replied, "When I eat, I eat; when I walk, I walk; when I sleep, I sleep; when I bathe, I bathe." Relearning to walk, I am totally present only to that moment. Previously I moved in a mindless, automatic way; now I am fully present. At first this awareness is prompted by fear of falling. Even after I get the hang of putting one foot in front of another, I recall what it means to be total in ordinary activities. While walking, I only walk.

Finally, I can take a shower, albeit still in my brace. Previously, showering had always been a hurried sideshow while making a plan or mulling over a problem. Now there are no extraneous thoughts. Gentle, warm drops create ecstatic sensations. I take soap in hand to a totally new experience. How many times have I missed the joy of these moments? And why?

Because I was the *doer*, which caused me to neglect the joy of *being*.

By the following week the shower becomes routine, but when I pull back from wandering thoughts, I again experience joy as before. The doer in me overlooks the pleasure of the moment; now I refuse to allow the robot to take over. I flow back into appreciation of the moment.

Every spring the dark, brown waters of the Ohio River course through the flood plains around Louisville as melting snow throughout the Ohio River Valley seeks its way to the sea. Strong currents sweep away logs, docks, loose boats, and houses that were foolishly built too close to water's edge. A mile back from the river's edge stands a 200-foot-high limestone bluff that marks an ancient riverbank created during the glacial ages. Perched safely atop this bluff, hidden in thick undergrowth, are stately homes with commanding views.

One of these houses—the setting for my two-month convalescence following discharge from the hospital—is my parents' home. Isolating me from the tumult of life is a low-lying, craftsman-style structure designed to meld with surrounding woods, and the downstairs living area becomes home for Barbara, the babies, and me. Large sliding glass doors afford views through spring vegetation to the river. During the day Barbara paints while I read and the boys amuse themselves with their toys.

Evenings we light a fire in the fossil-rock fireplace and welcome Mom and Dad downstairs for cocktails. Dad discusses his business and Mom reports local happenings. Belden and Seton roll in naked delight on the shag rugs as they experiment with new movements and sounds. I, too, discover new awareness. Having withdrawn from the world of doing, I tune in to mundane, but ever-so-significant, things around me. I note the babies' gurgles, Barbara's gracefulness, and winds dancing in the trees outside the window. All the little things glow with their own loveliness.

Finally, the new bone becomes strong enough to withstand radiation treatments. My mind begins to organize events to fit in with daily trips to the hospital—shopping, getting a haircut, visiting a friend. Suddenly life becomes a madhouse again and tension arises.

Then I recall Bhagwan talking about *Wu Wei*, the Taoist concept of action through inaction: Something happens, but there is no doer. The action comes on its own accord. Bhagwan cited the Zen expression, "Spring comes, and the grass grows by itself." I understand the message: drop plans and allow events to happen as they will.

The day radiation is to begin I bathe, eat, and walk fully attuned to each moment with no thoughts about what is to come. Barbara drives us to the hospital, a trip we will repeat every weekday for 25 days.

The first day, I get a tattoo.

I am told to strip and lie face down on a cold metal table beneath the cobalt machine. Technicians project beams of light upon my back and nudge me into position to align tumors with the collimated rays. While marking my back with felt-tipped pens, they joke about the difference between *topographic anatomy* and *anatomical topography*, which they conclude mean the same thing. After defining the perimeter of the area to be irradiated, they wait for the chief radiation oncologist to give approval. But Dr. Ben Birkhead has his own ideas, and the marking pens come out again. He finalizes a new pattern to include a peripheral segment outside the tumorous region. The critical question is how much periphery is prudent. Too large an area might damage the spinal cord. Too small a section might allow edges of the tumors to escape the beam.

I ask about dosage. From my days as a nuclear engineer at the Nevada Test Site, I know that one or two rads are cause for alarm. He laughs and says to recalculate the numbers: "You'll receive 5,000 rads: 200 rads each day for 25 days."

I recall Hiroshima where most of the 100,000 immediate survivors died within two or three years from myeloma and related cancers. "Five thousand rads within my skeleton?" I ask alarmed. "That's impossible!"

I glance nervously around the walls for diplomas to see where he received his medical training and am relieved the credentials are impeccable. Still, I can't believe these numbers.

Dr. Birkhead smiles as he flips through pages in a radiation textbook. "I'd like to give you more, but take a look at this," he says. A graph depicting radiation tolerance levels for the spinal column explains the probability of spinal damage as a function of dosage. Up to 5,000 rads the curve is flat with under a two percent risk, but above this level, the curve shoots sharply upward.

Considering this unnerving scenario, I suggest that we review the calculations, but Dr. Birkhead assures me it isn't necessary and the pattern is now final. However, he does warn, "Don't allow any more radiation to this part of your back, even if the cancer reoccurs. Once the present series is complete, you will have received the maximum allowable safe dosage."

Technicians tattoo the corners of the area to be radiated. Prick, prick, prick.... they imprint permanent ink spots and brand me for life. *(Years later as tattoos become popular with teenagers, I joke with my children that I had been in the vanguard of the trend!)*

Days later I see in a mirror that these permanent spots make the shape of the letter D—D for Doer. I feel like existence is reminding me—*Drop the Doer.* Just as radiation eliminates cancerous cells within the D-pattern, so I need to discard the compulsive doer within me. Playing further with this image, I note the *D* had been branded on my back; if I continue in my previous life's direction, I will be going backwards. But if I go forward, the *D* will be forgotten. Why had I suppressed this message for so many years?

Probably because the message is contrary to everything I had become. My upbringing instilled the idea that doers and movers get ahead, and getting ahead brings happiness. Wasn't this right? But although achievements make life comfortable, they do not nourish deeper needs. Some of my college classmates attained wealth and power, I note, but have found little happiness and peace.

I tolerate radiation well the first days but then suffer nausea, fatigue, and severe weakness. An irony surfaces when the treatment is finished. After 25 days of cobalt treatments, I observe reddish burns on my abdomen where radiation has passed through from my back. Looking in the mirror, I see *D* on my back and the mirror image on my stomach. My imagination wants to interpret this sign to live in the opposite way from the past, but I sense I've carried this symbolism far enough.

I recover quickly from the classic side effects of radiation therapy. After months confined in the brace, I'm ready to experiment with movement. With guidance from a physical therapist, I rediscover swimming.

After slipping cautiously into the pool, the water supports my weight and allows me freedom to move. I discard the body brace. What a joy to stroke arms and kick feet! The refreshing water flowing over my body comes as a new experience. I feel as ecstatic as a child first splashing in water. Every day I swim laps, each time becoming stronger.

As spring explodes with new growth, I too experience a resurgence of strength and energy. On short walks, I rejoice as forsythia buds burst into yellow splendor. With each unfolding of a daffodil, I too open to the beauties of life. By late April I can sit at the dining room table for meals and amble easily throughout the house.

Barbara and I never discuss the future. We aren't avoiding anything; rather, we trust that the future will take care of itself. By mid-May I have been out of the hospital two months, and it's time to move on. Mom and Dad have mixed emotions. They love having us and providing space for our family. They enjoy watching my recovery day by day but know we will be off on our travels before long.

Our destination is the ashram in Poona. An inexplicable force is drawing me to Bhagwan and his ashram where I intend to die.

We give grateful, heartfelt hugs to Mom and Dad and leave Louisville. A doer still lurks within but gets less attention as my life eases away from the old mode.

In a sense I have already died. The old life is gone—I am no longer a career executive and have no chance of returning to that life. Every morning I awake with awareness of my impending death but feel relaxed and calm. All medical possibilities are exhausted after receiving three traditional cancer treatments—surgery, radiation, and chemotherapy, crudely expressed as *cut*, *burn*, and *poison*. These treatments, the doctors say, will prolong life only for months...

... And there is nothing else I want to do. I have seen practically every part of the world, pursued successful careers in various fields, and attained financial independence. Four beautiful children light my life. Most importantly, I have loved and been loved.

The doing is over. What remains is simply to *be*—in full awareness—for however many (or few) days remain.

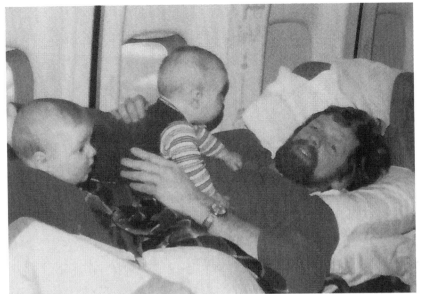

[February 17, 1980, age 39] 24-hour medical flight with six stopovers:
Hamburg/Frankfurt/Brussels/JFK/Atlanta/Louisville

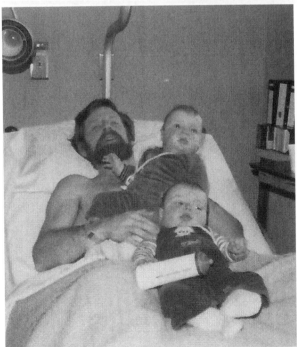

[February 26, 1980, Louisville Methodist Hospital] With Seton and Belden
moments before surgery

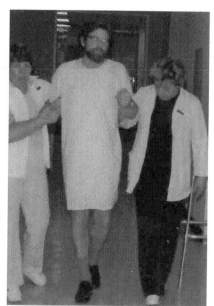

[March 1980, Louisville Methodist Hospital]
First time standing several weeks after surgery

[April 1980, Louisville]
Walking again, taller, thinner, rigid with back brace

# 50
# The Healers

*6/80 - 2/81, Ages 39 - 40*

How does one decide—assuming there is a choice—where to die?

My wish is to be with my family near Bhagwan. Finished with the outer world, I intend to spend my remaining days on a meditative, inward journey surrounded by those I love.

In late spring, Barbara, the boys—almost a year old already—and I travel to Poona. On the plane ride I reflect on how my life has collapsed in just half a year: I've been fired, moved out of Hamburg, searched coast to coast for a new job, been diagnosed with terminal cancer, and undergone surgery, chemotherapy, and radiation. Quite a lot in just six months!

Fortunately, I have financial security thanks to the sale of Schlegel stock and social security pensions from both the U.S. and Germany as well as payments from Schlegel's long-term care medical coverage. These pensions, which were triggered by the terminal diagnosis, stipulate that if I work, they will be rescinded. The trifecta—uncertain health, financial independence, and work restriction—radically alter my life. Although the former life has been ripped away, the transition to a new way of life is comparatively easy.

Seems strange to think that I'm making this trip to die. Before leaving the States, I had made final goodbyes to Mom and Dad as well as to friends and relatives. Now it's a matter of surrendering to whatever awaits.

Once back in Poona, Barbara and I quickly slip into the rhythm of ashram life. Bhagwan's 90-minute morning discourses alternate each month between English and Hindi. I engage in meditation retreats, therapy courses, bodywork, healing sessions, music groups, and other programs designed to help people become more spiritually aware. Mary works in the ashram, and the girls, now nine and six, attend school here seven days a week. For only $12 a day Barbara, the boys, and I rent a guest room the size of a small ballroom at the once-majestic Sundarban Hotel in Koregaon Park next to the ashram. Built during the British Raj, the hotel features ornate staircases, elaborate chandeliers, marble floors, and 12-foot ceilings. Within days we find a wonderful ayah (nanny), Mary Magdalena, who spends all day taking care of the boys. She loves pushing them in their pram around the city while enjoying the attention of ogling crowds in this country that idolizes twins.

Prem Chinmaya, a long-time ashram resident from the United States, dies the day after our arrival. We join the ashram community at the burning ghats beside the Mula-Mutha River for a sendoff amid celebration, music, and dancing. A couple of days later in discourse, I'm startled when Bhagwan talks about me in the morning discourse using my sannyas name *Nartan*. The discourse from June 14, 1980, was subsequently published in *Tao: The Golden Gate, Vol.1, chapter 4.*

*Just two days ago when Prem Chinmaya left his body, I received a question, "Bhagwan, even Prem Chinmaya's departure and the celebration were videotaped. Can't a sannyasin die in peace?"*

*But he was already dead! Now you can do whatsoever you want— videotape him, film him! Chinmaya must have been around laughing, enjoying.*

*And he died in utter peace, he died in absolute peace. And your videotape cannot disturb him. His cancer was not disturbing him, how can your videotape disturb him? He was in immense pain, but he remained a witness. He died a beautiful death. That's the way a sannyasin should die.*

*Now Nartan has come. Just yesterday he wrote a letter to me: 'I was fortunate to come and to see Chinmaya's departure and the celebration, because I am also suffering from cancer; the doctors have said I have only two years left. And I have come to be forever here.' Nartan was happy to see the way Chinmaya died and the way everybody celebrated his death.*

*"I teach you not only to celebrate life but death too, because death is the climax of life, the crescendo. If you have lived your life really, you will celebrate your death too. And he died so beautifully, in such deep surrender. Even Nartan was immensely happy to be present. Now his fear of death is gone. In fact, he is looking forward to it. (laughter)*

---------------

These words bring comfort. I do not fear my death, but Bhagwan's acknowledgment further reassures me.

Shortly after arriving in Poona, I meet two people who, in addition to Bhagwan, play a role in my healing. Balaji Tambe (BAL-a-gee TOM-bay) offers Ayurvedic treatments, meditation, yoga, and spiritual guidance. He's neither a doctor nor is he trained in medical science but has learned Ayurvedic medicine and is known as a Healer. I make an appointment and, together with a small group, take seats before this small, unassuming man sitting cross-legged on a bench in a one-room hut. There's no equipment or medical instruments, only a few chairs positioned so he can see each person. I take off my shoes, as requested, so he can view my feet. Balaji is said to be able to see illnesses within people's bodies, a power accepted in India but deemed improbable in Western allopathic medicine.

Nothing is said for minutes as his eyes wander up and down my body. Finally, I speak:

Me (gesturing to my chest): "The doctors in the West say I have...."

Balaji (interrupting): "Yes, I see. They probably call it cancer, but that's just a name and not what's going on. I see some things, but these are symptoms not the cause."

Me: "What do you see?"

Balaji: "The ribs and backbone, but you also have a lot of heat, which is not good. In any activity heat is a byproduct. When there's a lot of heat, it's bad for the body."

Following this short session that continues only a few more minutes, Balaji gives me two decoctions, *Ushirasava* and *Palashpushpasava*, to be mixed with teaspoons of hot water and tea respectively. He also hands me two bags of brown pellets to be taken, one with milk and the other with sugar.

Ayurveda is a 3,000-year-old Hindu holistic healing system. Medications are administered in pinches or teaspoonfuls together with a second substance—like milk, honey, sugar, water, or tea— that transports the medication to the organ where it is needed. Balaji explains that chemotherapy, which I have been taking, is like a machine gun firing throughout the body. In addition to killing cancer cells, it wreaks damage on organs and other parts of the body. Ayurvedic medications protect vulnerable areas, and he instructs me as to the dosages and time of day to take the substances he gives me. Then he asks that I make regular appointments to see him, which I do.

Our weekly sessions are often short and don't involve much talk. After examining my hands and feet, he gestures his approval and sometimes changes medications. After several weeks he says he is pleased with the progress.

Payment isn't necessary. Balaji explains that his spiritual master said he has a gift to heal people but should not profit from it. He charges one or two rupees for medications (less than U.S. $ 0.15) but gives his time freely. To pay bills, he runs a small electric supply shop while each week providing healing advice to dozens of people, many from the ashram.

Balaji puts me on a restricted diet and arranges nightly dinners according to his instructions at the Hotel Ritz, another once-elegant holdover from the British Raj. Balaji also introduces me to spiritual and meditative practices. For "color therapy," he confines me in a small room to watch an array of colors projected on a wall for two hours. In "dance therapy," I move my body to the rhythms of traditional Indian music performed by sitars and tablas. On other occasions, I stare at a blue light to open the third eye, said to be the gate that leads to higher consciousness.

Balaji often speaks about death and sends me to the burning ghats to watch cremations. In the West, death is usually kept from public view while in India it's part of daily life. When someone dies, family members carry the body throughout the village on a litter so everyone can join the procession to the river where celebrations and singing give a send-off to the soul as the body is burned.

Witnessing these cremations gives me a new perspective on death by taking away the secretiveness of how we dispose of a body in the West. Here there's nothing mournful but rather celebration because, unlike in the West, religions of the East embrace rebirth. Therefore, all those who die will be back soon. Because death is treated so openly, I soon get used to it being just a normal part of the human experience.

"There are three ways to think about death," Balaji says. "You can accept it, reject it, or ignore it. Everyone ignores it, but *you* can't. If you accept it, fine. If you reject it, we have time to help you embrace it. I am here to help you die if you choose, because a beautiful death is far better than leading an unfulfilling life."

When I protest that I don't particularly want to die, he says it's up to me. He explains the Hindu concept that whatever happens to individuals is their own creation. If someone attacks you, you have put out energy to make it happen.

"Do you know why you have created a suicide?" Balaji asks.

I stare in disbelief.

"Something in your subconscious wants this," he continues. "If we can shed light on it, we can understand and possibly change it."

I initially regard Balaji with suspicion. Trained as a scientist, I do not accept anything that does not pass the test of Baconian inductive reasoning; in other words, I doubt anything and everything until it has been proven.

When Balaji looks at—or should I say *into?*—each person, he talks about what he sees. He does not ask questions, nor does he ask anyone to speak. Afterward he offers bags of medication for purchase. However, I gradually begin to trust him for two reasons. First, I feel stronger and healthier. Second, others at the ashram confirm he has identified their problems just by looking at them.

Balaji experiments with different medications for me. One time he gives me flakes of gold, the purest of metals, but when he sees they have no effect because I can't absorb them, he discards this approach. He comments that I have strong, expanding, male yang energy that needs to be softened with an infusion of yin. Because the oceans and the moon are considered feminine forces, many yin infusions are derived from these sources. Pearls, for example, are often used in Ayurvedic concoctions, but need to be prepped so the body can absorb their beneficial effects. One mixture that seems to work for me is ash from pearls that have been ground, burned, and dried in moonlight.

The second person who continues my health treatment is Dr. R. L. Marathe (ma-rah-TAY), a hematologist and pathologist with his own clinic in Poona. In spite of protests from Louisville doctors, I left for India prior to completing the chemotherapy cycles. Because these treatments supposedly would give me only a few additional months to live, I prefer to spend time now in Poona and finish the chemo with Dr. Marathe. He agrees to treat me, probably his first American myeloma patient. Two days after arriving in India, blood tests indicate I'm in good health, and I begin four days of treatment with alkeran and prednisone tablets that I brought from the States.

Throughout summer I engage in therapies, group sessions, and daily meditations at the ashram. I initially continue to wear the back brace but soon feel strong enough to begin walking carefully without it. A week after arriving, free of this encumbrance for good, I'm participating fully in the life of the ashram. What a joy to feel unrestricted once again!

Westerners in India often develop stomach problems from bacterial infections, and babies are particularly vulnerable. One day Belden and Seton can't hold down food, won't drink, cry incessantly, and begin losing weight. We rush them to the local hospital, but the doctors have problems putting needles into their tiny veins to connect to bags of IV fluids with medication. In near panic Barbara and I start to book the next plane to London to take them for medical treatment, but a young Indian doctor tells us they won't last long enough for such a trip. He reassures us that with so many children in India, pediatricians here are the best. Reappearing half an hour later with a big smile, he informs us he has set up IV drips and the boys are on the road to recovery.

Problems are not over. Shortly after the boys return to our hotel room, Barbara develops jaundice. While attending to them in the hospital, one day she lunched at a nearby café—something people at the ashram warned us never to do. For two weeks Barbara is confined in isolation at the ashram medical center, leaving Magdalena and me to care for the boys with helpful friends.

One day Balaji tells me it's time to return to the States to see the Western doctors. I protest that my body feels fine. He responds it's not for the body but for my mind, which leaves me confused. But I agree because our three-month visas expire soon, and we need to leave the country for a required number of months before reapplying. Dr. Marathe administers two additional cycles of chemotherapy at six-week intervals in late July and again in early September prior to our departure.

Balaji calls me for a final session and explains that on our first visit he saw eight spots of cancer. Now he sees only three. I don't think about this again until my medical consultations in Louisville.

Mary and the girls also need to leave the country to renew visas. Mary and Rasila return to Mary's parents in Albuquerque. At the same time Barbara, Cyrena, the boys, and I book a bareboat flotilla sailing cruise in the Aegean Sea from a yacht charterer on the island of Rhodes.

The cruising itinerary takes us north to the Sea of Marmaris on Turkey's southwestern coast where we visit archaeological sites along the coastal villages. Locals fawn over us as the first Americans to arrive since U.S. military forces landed 35 years earlier. The highlight of the cruise is seeing the 2,500-year-old, rock-cut tombs of Dalyan. Stone carvers created ornate temple facades on the front of atriums with sculpted columns and decorated pediments leading to elaborate sepulchers in individual burial chambers. Comparing these burial customs with the public burning ghats in Poona and the private approach to treating the deceased in the West, I'm reminded how different societies handle death in different ways. When you come right down to it, post-death customs are basically just a disposal issue that we treat with ceremonies thinking this is respectful to the deceased.

After the cruise, we return to Louisville where Dr. Badenhausen comments how well I look. Before he sends me for X-rays, I remind him that previous images showed eight spots of cancer. "Now, I suspect you will find only three," I inform him.

After the films are developed, he shocks me by confirming there are indeed just three small tumors; he assumes that I had X-rays taken in India.

I hadn't.

Now I understand Balaji's parting words about the return to the U.S. being for my mind. With this confirmation, any doubts I had about Balaji immediately disappear.

While in Poona I had asked my father to purchase a new Volkswagen Vanagon camper, which will be our home as we pass the time before reapplying for India visas. Cyrena flies to Albuquerque to join her mother and sister while Barbara, the boys, and I set out on a three-month journey crisscrossing the American West. With the backseat removed, the toddlers, now just over one-year-old, have a perfect playpen full of toys, and a portable television with rabbit ears that picks up their favorite show, Sesame Street. *(This trip predates requirements for children to be restrained while driving, and, luckily, no mishaps occur along the way.)*

Name an attraction and we were likely there. National Parks, federal monuments, civil war battlefields, historical landmarks, theme parks, wildlife areas, Disneyland, and more. Some weeks we are on the road every day and other times settle for a week, usually on the coast or in the mountains when we chance upon a rental cottage at a scenic location. Otherwise, we seek out Holiday Inns because they usually have cribs and typically own their own restaurant or are not far from one. After Belden and Seton are asleep for the night, Barbara and I lock them in the room and slip away for a quiet dinner.

One night we have the shock of our lives. As we're ordering food, suddenly twin pajama-clad boys toddle into the dining room. They must have unlocked the door to their room, discovered the stairs, clamored down one flight to the ground floor, and found the corridor to the restaurant, before appearing proudly at our table. Shaken by the thought of what could have happened, from that time on Barbara and I adjust our routine to keep a closer eye on them.

While we've been touring in the Vanagon with the boys, Cyrena and Rasila have spent the months with their mother in Albuquerque. In late autumn we swing through the Southwest to pick up the girls in New Mexico on our way to Kentucky for Thanksgiving. Because I yearn for one final sailing cruise, they remain with Mom and Dad while Barbara, the twins, and I charter a bareboat sloop for a week's cruise in the British Virgin Islands.

Back in Louisville once more, we enjoy a family Christmas, memorable because it will likely be my last one. We then make what will presumably be final goodbyes, once again, with Mom and Dad before driving to Vermont for what will probably be my last week on skis. Our travels are fast-paced, but we want to cram in every possible adventure before my body weakens. Surprisingly, my health stays good.

Returning to Poona in February 1981 for the start of the English discourses, I anticipate picking up life as we had left it—daily discourses, therapy groups, meditations, chemo treatments with Dr. Marathe, and healing sessions with Balaji Tambe.

Instead, my life is thrown into turmoil.

[1980, Poona]
Balaji Tambe

[1980, Poona]
Burning ghats alongside Mula-Mutha River

[May 1980] Wearing back brace on a sailing charter in Denmark with Belden and
Seton

[September 1980, age 39] Sailing charter in Greece and Turkey without back brace

[December 1980] Sailing charter in British Virgin Islands, Seton (l), Belden (r)

It was the night after Christmas
And all through the house,
Only one creature stirred
And it wasn't a mouse.

She said to me softly
With a sort of a start
"I think the time's come
For us to depart."

She had her suitcase
And I had my hat,
We both really wondered
Where it was at.

We jumped in our car
With oh, such a clatter,
We worried that neighbors
Would ask, "What is the matter."

We left rather quietly,
Drove out of sight,
Without even saying
To anyone "Good night."

Belt Parkway to Whitestone
'Cross Long Island Sound
To New Rochelle Hospital
Fast as a hound.

Happy Birthday
poem to Peter
from George;
40th birthday
Dec 27, 1980

"At dawn the next day
The surprise that appeared
Was a red headed boy
who now has a beard.

Now four decades later
To Peter we say,
"Many happy returns
Of this very same day."

[December 1980, Louisville] Dad's 40th birthday poem

436

[January 1981, age 40] Skiing at Killington, Vermont with Barbara/Vihar

# 51
# A Twig in the River

*2/81 - 7/81, Age 40*

Aware that my health could start deteriorating anytime, I made every effort to spend the required five months away from India keeping as active as possible. Activities included: bareboat flotilla sailing cruise in Greece and Turkey; cancer check-up in Louisville; three months driving with family in our VW Vanagon camper coast-to-coast; Thanksgiving and Christmas with family in Louisville; another sailing cruise in the British Virgin Islands; skiing a week in Vermont; and visiting with friends all along the way.

Reapplying for visas brings a surprise. India is no longer issuing permits for travel to Poona because the thousands of followers of Bhagwan are overrunning the city. I dislike having plans disrupted, which is why controlling events and situations has always been important. Any surprise indicates control has been lost, and control is possible only by understanding the structure of a situation. In this case that means understanding the criteria that determine how visas are issued. Once I understand this problem, I am able to obtain family visas by stating we are tourists planning to travel throughout the north of the country in regions well away from Poona.

February 1981 finds us back at the ashram. Knowing how things work here, I anticipate having reasonable control over my life. My plan is to participate in one or two group therapies followed by counseling sessions and other programs that seem appropriate. I also anticipate resuming sessions with Balaji and Dr. Marathe.

But within a week after arrival, all my plans are blown to pieces. Bhagwan sends me a message asserting there is "no need to do any more groups, therapies, or classes." At the same time Dr. Marathe advises not to start the chemo cycle because an infection has shown up in my blood. Another kink arises: New visa regulations for Barbara and all other German citizens allow only a one-month stay whereas the rest of the family, as Americans, have three-month visas. When Balaji Tambe observes bloating in my body due to water retention, he prescribes two new Ayurvedic medications to protect the kidneys and prescribes a diet of fruits, nuts, vegetables, grains, and legumes. All plans and expectations have been ripped away.

In the midst of all this, I try to resolve administrative matters by mail with the German Finance Department, Internal Revenue Service, Diners Club credit card, First National Bank in Albuquerque, Price Waterhouse offices in Hamburg and New York, and my health-care provider in New York. Even after follow-up correspondence, I get no responses.

Nothing is going as planned. The structures and controls I had counted on to serve me have disappeared; there's nothing to do except float with what's happening.

Mornings I attend Bhagwan's discourses and throughout the day participate in the scheduled meditations, but this still leaves a lot of time on my hands. Then I recall an old interest that I decide to revive—writing. Having derived great pleasure as an editor/writer for my high school newspaper and later as a columnist for Stanford's business school periodical, I might have chosen journalism over engineering/physics as my career. I had kept this interest alive during the 10 years since graduate school by writing quarterly columns about classmate updates for the Stanford Graduate GSB magazine.

While pondering the question of what to write about, suddenly I have the inspiration to write this autobiography and dedicate it to my four kids. Expecting to die before too long, I realize my children will have few memories of me—and the boys, because they are so young, perhaps no conscious recollection at all. By writing my life story, I hope to connect my children to the father they will likely never really know.

After purchasing a Royal typewriter and writing supplies and setting up an office in our hotel room, I find myself devoting several hours each day to this revitalized interest. Everything that you, my patient reader, have read so far in this book is a result of weeks of writing that began in March 1981, in Poona. The writing is sporadic as I attempt to recall the timelines of earlier adventures—Let's see, did I first sail in Denmark in 1974 or was it 1975? It must have been 1974 because in 1975 we sailed in the Bahamas. While gazing out the window trying to piece together the details of my 40 years, it's soothing to look out on the hotel's manicured lawn surrounded by colorful flower beds—that is, it's soothing until the shock of seeing what the grounds staff is doing: Half a dozen laborers are down on their haunches cutting the blades of grass—with *scissors*.

In this manner the first weeks pass. When my blood test is once again normal, I resume chemotherapy. Balaji's new diet and medicines start to work, and soon I feel stronger than ever. Learning to listen to my body and feel how it responds to different foods and medications, I appreciate the steadying effects of this protocol.

But change is in the air. On March 24th, Bhagwan does not appear for morning discourse or darshan, and a spokesperson discloses he will remain in seclusion for several weeks because of an outbreak of chickenpox. This shouldn't be a problem, however, because English discourses aren't due to begin for three weeks, and I'm engrossed in my writing.

Two days later a German sannyasin woman, Pradip, dies of cancer in a local hospital. Sending her off with a celebration of music and singing at the burning ghats prompts thoughts of my own impending death. Birds, flowers, and trees are more alive than ever on this warm, sunny afternoon.

As we scatter her ashes in the river, I feel life and death have come together in harmony.

By the beginning of April, Bhagwan still has not appeared, the longest absence from his sannyasins in years. Deciding to get away from the ashram for a while, I head to Panchgani, a hill station two hours away, to take an art course. While painting landscapes around this village high in the Western Ghats, I welcome the opportunity to explore the countryside surrounding Poona.

During my absence Barbara participates in Turning In, a residential group that takes her deeper into meditation and gives insights into our relationship—a relationship she says that is not our first life together. When I return to Poona, Barbara and I have cosmology readings with Balaji who confirms that we had been together in another life, and our love now seems to "break loose and flow completely unbounded."

Bhagwan remains absent, and by now everyone is concerned. Late in April his caretaker announces that Bhagwan will begin a "New Phase" by communicating only in silence, which Bhagwan has said is the "deepest form of communication." Although he will be present at morning discourses (now called *satsang* meaning "*gathering together in the company of a spiritual master*"), he will not speak. For years he has prepared us for the day when he would no longer talk. Still a surprise, however, it is nothing compared to what is to come.

The world around me has changed. Nevertheless, I adapt to the new, coherent structure. On May 1st, Bhagwan reappears and inaugurates the new phase with the first morning satsang. Life assumes a different rhythm— mornings, sitting an hour and a half in Buddha Hall with Bhagwan while music plays; afternoons, watching a video of a discourse, writing my memoir, and participating in Kundalini Meditation—all interspersed with occasional shopping trips into the city to buy household supplies. Balaji is pleased with my progress, and because the blood test is now normal, Dr. Marathe starts chemo cycle No. 11. Things seem to be under control again.

But several new shocks await. Bhagwan's health problems become apparent. Often unsteady while walking into morning satsang, he sometimes grabs the back of his chair to avoid falling, and rumors fly that he will leave the ashram for medical treatment. Cyrena and Rasila come down with the flu and go to the hospital. Chemo treatment does not go well, and severe stomach cramps plague me. And while attempting to get her visa renewed, Barbara becomes entangled in an extortion scheme.

The beginning of the end is at hand. Bhagwan had announced in recent years that the ashram in Poona is too small, and one day he will leave for a new location. Suddenly it happens. On May 31st, Bhagwan and his closest sannyasins buy all the first-class seats on Pan Am's 747 flight from London to New York. Upon arrival he settles into an 11-acre estate known as Kip's Castle in central New Jersey's woodlands.

On June 1st, Balaji observes that I don't look healthy and, attributing the problems to chemotherapy, changes my medication. Next day my tongue starts stinging and I suffer bleeding hemorrhoids—symptoms of tension and anxiety. Detecting that I am stressed and my heat energy has increased considerably, Balaji prescribes stronger medication. Each morning I feel unsteady and sense a rushing in my body although I have stringently adhered to the recommended diet.

Balaji says I should not leave India in this condition but must remain until early July when his treatment and the arrival of the cooling monsoon rains, expected late June or early July, should put me back together again. The Yogi diet makes me more sensitive to hot and cold. With heat comes tension, unsteadiness, and a racing feeling; coolness brings calmness, steadiness, and relaxation. Any deviation in diet creates immediate effects the next morning.

With Bhagwan gone, Mary schedules a flight home with Cyrena and Rasila at the end of June. I book air tickets in July for Barbara, the boys, and me to Europe, but at the last minute Balaji again tells me not to go. Seeing that my health is worsening, he wants me to stay another month. We decide that Barbara and the boys will return to Germany as scheduled and I'll follow later.

All these losses and changes cause problems in my body. Balaji maintains it's not important that the ashram is closing and Bhagwan is gone. Here is an opportunity for me to examine my need for structure and control. He asserts that any sense of control is an illusion; instead of resisting the changes taking place, I need simply to watch.

So I watch and I allow and I flow. For four weeks living alone in a little rented room by the river, I appreciate everything that comes my way. People leave, the energy changes, parts of the ashram close down, and I accept it all. Expectations dissolve. I learn to feel more relaxed without structure for support.

During one of my sessions with Balaji I ask why he thinks I manifested the cancer as a suicide. The conversation goes something like this:

Me: "Why do you think I created the cancer as an attempt to commit suicide?"

Balaji: "We all are responsible for the life we lead and, even if it's not obvious, we create whatever happens to us. Earlier in life did you ever make plans for your future?"

Me, pausing as I reflect back to the timeline I made in college: "It was just a whimsical thought at the time, but I wanted to be a manager by age 24, run my own company by 30, manage a group of organizations by 35, and become financially independent by 40. And I reached each goal one or two years ahead of each deadline."

Balaji, after thinking for a moment: "By achieving all these goals, you subconsciously decided you had accomplished everything you wanted in life and concluded there was no point in remaining in this body. So you created the cancer."

He then explains that I have been living an achievement-oriented life based upon accomplishing, winning, competing, struggling, and fighting my way to attain these goals. Once I bring from my subconscious to my consciousness an understanding how I have defined my life, I have the possibility of re-defining myself in terms of loving, feeling, relaxing, cherishing, caring, and otherwise taking a softer, gentler approach to life.

"And then." He goes on, "You would have the choice whether to die or not."

Suddenly, I understand and it all rings true. If I can make this change in who I am, which has been the focus of my past four years with Bhagwan, I may be able to reverse the course of my cancer. I have gone up to the door of death, and maybe—just maybe—the door doesn't have to open quite yet. With this insight, I return to my room to meditate on this astounding possibility.

And then the monsoons arrive. Forceful currents of the Mula-Mutha River, now swollen above its banks, carry away the debris of Poona. Plants and trees along the shore are submerged, and no one could guess the river is shallow and gentle for most of the year. Above its rocky shores larger trees hold on—gulmohars, eucalyptus, mangos, papayas, and frangipanis bearing sweet-smelling blossoms. Gardens full of wild colors and fragrances grow rampant, thanks to the constant deluge.

Hidden among the verdant foliage, my room is screened on two sides, opening completely to the panorama and florabundance of this natural setting. Absorbed by this drama as I gaze out, my mind rests in peace and my heart is enraptured.

This fifth trip to Poona has lasted only five months, but many changes have swept me along like a twig in the turbulent river. The expectations, hopes, and plans when arriving have all been washed away. A frail essence remains, one that could be destroyed by the slightest force.

Before, there was resistance; now, there is yielding. Force has been replaced by gentleness. Where control and thinking dominated, now spontaneity and feeling take over.

All that's left is the absence of things that once filled me.

I question why I cling to structure and control, knowing now they are the antithesis of trust. Even when I think I control situations, I deceive myself. Existence will take care of every need I have without any effort on my part. Here is a growth opportunity that shows how the mind creates scenarios of control when left on its own. It's important to understand this compulsion in order to release it. Whatever happens will be beautiful and will be exactly what I need.

If a new ashram happens, great. If not, that's also good because there are many other places to invest my energy. Let me drop forever this compulsion to control. I never controlled anything, and there never was any structure. Only now do I understand. There is no need to resist or fight. Now is the time—always is the time—to float and trust.

At the end of July, I make final visits with Balaji Tambe and Dr. Marathe, both of whom have done as much as they can to restore my health, and they send me off with well wishes. The next day I fly from Poona to Bombay and board a late-night flight to Germany to join my family.

From there, we are off to the States to start a new life.

[Summer1981, Poona, age 40] Our room overlooking Mula-Mutha River with water buffalo grazing in background

# Epilogue

Spoiler Alert: I didn't die.

I didn't die 40 years ago in the timeframe the doctors had predicted. The last chapter brought me up to the age of 40. Since then I've been alive another 40 years as I recently celebrated my 80th birthday.

This epilogue serves as a catch-up beginning with the year following my family's departure from Poona. My dilemma at that time is this: I feel healthy—strong and full of energy with no sense of a debilitating illness; however, I'm near the limit of my doctors' prognosis, so I could be approaching the downward spiral in my health at any moment. How do I lead my life with two such conflicting realities?

Thinking there may have been progress in treating multiple myeloma, I regularly review the medical literature, but it's always the same: "...can be treated, but not cured."

Consequently, Barbara and I decide not to settle anywhere and not to make plans for the future. We load the Vanagon camper with necessities and set out with Belden and Seton, now two years old, to live for a year "on the road" until we gain clarity about what lies ahead.

Starting our journey in New England, we then drive north into Canada. As we move into autumn, we delight in the changing autumn colors for the following month as we travel west on Trans-Can #1 ending at Vancouver Island on the Pacific Ocean. From there we head south crossing the western United States into Mexico. After traveling down the Pacific Coast, we follow Mexico's southern borders with Guatemala and Belize eastward to the Yucatan Peninsula. Three months allows ample time to explore ancient temples, pyramids, fortifications, tombs, and cultural attractions before crossing back into the States at McAllen, Texas, and continuing on to the East Coast.

Sadly, Barbara's father had died while we were in Mexico, so we return to Germany to spend a few weeks consoling her mother in their family home in Bonn. Once back in the States, we enjoy a 20th Reunion weekend with my classmates at Princeton.

Bhagwan, meanwhile, has settled into the new commune, a 64,000-acre ranch in north-central Oregon, and commune organizers announce that the First Annual World Celebration will be held there in July. Suddenly, our direction becomes clear.

We arrive at *Rajneeshpuram* (Expression of Rajneesh, which refers to Bhagwan's surname) in early July exactly one year after departing the ashram in Poona. Spending that year on the road was wonderful. We shared fun adventures as a family while exploring three countries without the pressure of a time schedule or a rigid itinerary. But the best part? The best part is that despite the doctors' dire prognosis, I still feel fine. What had loomed before me as a final year with a difficult end turned out to be a great adventure instead, and now we're back with Bhagwan.

During the week-long celebration I reconnect with many friends I'd known in Poona and I feel Bhagwan's nourishing presence. Therefore, when the commune organizers extend an invitation to become a permanent resident at Rajneeshpuram, I accept. Because the commune is still under construction and not yet ready to accommodate children, Barbara and the twins move temporarily into a commune in Berkeley and visit me at the ranch on weekends. Later, when facilities have been further developed, they also move to the ranch. Working seven days a week, I'm assigned to the heavy equipment division where I operate bulldozers, dump trucks, high-lift loaders, tractor-scrapers, backhoes, compaction rollers, front end loaders, and, for most of the following two years, a huge excavator tasked with restoring the embankments of heavily eroded streams.

How does one know when a phase of one's life ends and it's time to move on? If the time has been happy, it will end with a sense of completion and a burst of good news. These signs have always told me when it's time for a change, so after spending a number of wonderful years in communes in two countries, Barbara and I know this period of our lives is complete. By the end of 1985, Barbara, the boys, and I leave the ranch and settle in Seattle not far from Mary, who had also recently moved there with Rasila and Cyrena.

Once the children are in school and we adjust to life as householders back in normal society, I ponder what to do with my remaining days. Returning to academia or the world of business isn't even a consideration because I have had my fill of both. And as much as I love skiing, sailing, scuba diving, and adventure travel, I reject what would feel like an indulgent lifestyle.

Then it dawns on me: I can combine these favorite activities with a sense of purpose by writing about them. After taking writing seminars and photography courses, I launch my career as a freelance, outdoor travel writer. I am on my way.

In the early years I write about local sailing regattas near my home in the Pacific Northwest, but when I branch out to cover more distant sailing events, I soon become buried in travel costs. Eventually, however, I learn how to arrange comped travel to cover my expenses with airlines, resort hotels, and recreational outfitters. This allows me to travel virtually anywhere in the world paying only out-of-pocket for tips and incidentals.

Over the years this approach has earned me trips to write about sailing events, both racing and charter cruising, in Australia, New Zealand, Japan, Croatia, South Africa, the Caribbean and Pacific island nations including Tahiti, Fiji, New Caledonia, Marshal Islands, Palau, and Tonga. I've also been able to arrange hosted travel to major ski resorts in the U.S. as well as to top ski destinations in Italy, Switzerland, France and Austria. To satisfy the demand by hard-core skiers seeking new adventures, magazines have sent me on assignments to lesser known ski areas in Turkey, Bulgaria, the Spanish Pyrenees, and New Zealand with future prospects in Kazakhstan, Serbia, Japan, Sweden (north of the Arctic Circle), and Andorra.

In recent years I've written and photographed an increasingly popular travel experience—European bike and barge trips. Participants fly into a major city to join their barge for a week's adventure along one of the many canals and rivers that crisscross the continent. Following each day's ride of 20 to 40 miles, cyclists meet up with the barge further along the river. The barge serves as home base with comfortable staterooms and private baths. A hostess and cook prepare breakfasts and dinners on board with lunches ordered at scenic villages along the way. My articles have described adventures along the Moselle, Saar, Main, Seine, and Danube Rivers, and I hope to discover many more.

This lifestyle combines two opposite dimensions. First, I travel out "there" to some exotic place to experience a unique adventure—sailing, skiing, biking, scuba diving, mountaineering, or whatever. I record everything I see and do in notebooks and countless photos. The schedule—which I love—is demanding and keeps me busy from early morning until late at night as I cram in as many experiences as possible.

Upon returning "home" loaded with notes and images that need to be filed, I enjoy a period of reflective peace and quiet as I compose the article for the assigning publication. The cycle takes me first to the "marketplace" and then back to "meditation" before it begins all over again.

Home life has always been meaningful and rewarding although circumstances change over the years. Mary had been a perfect partner supporting me in graduate school, agreeing to live in Europe while I managed Schlegel's overseas divisions, and being a wonderful mother to Cyrena and Rasila. She and I divorced because she had stopped doing the activities we had shared together for many years and wanted to pursue a spiritual life.

Barbara was likewise a perfect partner with her adventurous spirit and willingness to travel for months at a time in the Volkswagen camper with our infant twins. However, in the late 1990s, when the boys were in college, she wanted to settle down into her world of painting, so we separated. We bought her a house in New Mexico and she moved into the Santa Fe art community where she continues today pursuing her passion.

In 2003, while on a skiing press trip in Italy, I met Risa, a food, wine, and travel writer, who eight years later became my third wife. Ever since, we have traveled the world together dovetailing our writing assignments: I cover adventures while she focuses on food and wine.

My mother once quipped that I had two failed marriages; I pointed out, on the contrary, that I have had three perfect marriages; many people never even get one.

These past 40 years since my diagnosis with multiple myeloma have been full and rich. None of this could have happened without the onset of what was—and still today is—considered a terminal illness.

*How ironic that the most devastating medical prognosis imaginable could lead to, at least for me, a perfect second half of my life.*

*...And still the days and months and years roll on.*

I immensely enjoyed being this guy...

And I had a great time being this guy, too.

[December 27, 2020, Stevens Pass Ski Resort, Washington]
Celebrating my 80th birthday in grand style

# About the Author

As readers of this autobiography soon discover, Peter Schroeder has lived out both traditional and divergent lifestyles. Armed with degrees from Princeton (B.S.E.), University of New Mexico (M.S.E.), and Stanford (M.B.A.), he carved out successful careers in nuclear weapons testing and international business. Interspersed with his professional endeavors, he had stints of hopping freight trains across the country, hitchhiking around Europe, slacking as a surfer dude, impersonating a priest, living in four countries, receiving not one but two presidential deferments from the Viet Nam draft, living in ashrams in India and Oregon, and battling a fatal form of bone marrow cancer. In current times he can be found skiing, sailing, scuba diving, or pursuing other adventures at hotspots around the globe as an outdoor travel writer. When he's not on the road, he and his wife Risa divide their time between homes in Seattle, Washington, and Sonoma, California, where they tend to their Syrah vineyard and boutique winery.

Made in the USA
Middletown, DE
08 June 2021